Appalachia in the Making

Appalachia

EDITED BY

MARY BETH PUDUP

DWIGHT B. BILLINGS

ALTINA L. WALLER

in the Making

The Mountain South in the Nineteenth Century

The

University

of North

Carolina

Press

Chapel Hill

and London

The paper in this book meets the guidelines for permanence
and durability of the Committee on Production Guidelines for
Book Longevity of the Council on Library Resources.

Library of Congress Cataloging-in-Publication Data
Appalachia in the making: the mountain South in the
nineteenth century / edited by Mary Beth Pudup, Dwight B.
Billings, and Altina L. Waller.

   p. cm.

Includes bibliographical references and index.

ISBN-13: 978-0-8078-2229-6 (cl.: alk. paper)

ISBN-10: 0-8078-2229-9 (cl.: alk. paper)

ISBN-13: 978-8078-4534-9 (pbk.: alk. paper)

ISBN-10: 0-8078-4534-5 (pbk.: alk. paper)

   1. Appalachian Region, Southern—History. I. Pudup, Mary
Beth. II. Billings, Dwight B., 1948– . III. Waller, Altina L.
(Altina Laura), 1940–

F217.A65M69 1995   94-47135

975—dc20   CIP

cloth 05 04 03 02 01   5 4 3 2 1
paper 05 04 03 02 01   6 5 4 3 2

THIS BOOK WAS DIGITALLY PRINTED

CONTENTS

ACKNOWLEDGMENTS

Appalachia in the Making brings together fourteen original essays concerning various historical transformations during the nineteenth century in many of the region's distinctive locales. A collection of this nature owes its existence to the willingness of contributing authors to set aside momentarily their own fruitful individual projects in order to engage in a collective effort. First and foremost, therefore, the editors wish to thank the contributing authors for their spirit of collective enterprise. Not incidentally, the editors also thank the authors for their promptness in meeting deadlines and forbearance during unforeseen delays.

Appalachia in the Making was conceived at a recent annual meeting of the Appalachian Studies Association amid enthusiastic conversations among the editors about the unprecedented flowering of interdisciplinary scholarship about the region's past. The enthusiasm of the moment was tempered only by the rueful recognition that excellent scholarship about Appalachia rarely entered the thriving national debates over the nature and transformation of rural America. Put somewhat differently, the historical marginalization of Appalachia's economy, culture, and society seemed to be mirrored in its representations—or lack thereof—within national historical debates. Heady with the possibilities of a collection that would both showcase the new historical studies and bring Appalachia's historical experiences more forcefully into national discussion, the editors approached David Perry, acquisitions editor at the University of North Carolina Press, who was attending the conference that year. David immediately realized the possibilities of the collection. The editors owe a huge debt of gratitude to David Perry for his early and unstinting confidence in the project and his uncommon good humor.

The making of *Appalachia in the Making* involved a division of editorial labor among Dwight Billings, Mary Beth Pudup, and Altina Waller. All three editors were involved equally in conceptualizing the collection's focus, monitoring its ongoing progress, and determining its final shape. Each editor became responsible for working with several contributors on the completion and editing of successive chapter drafts. Collective editorial decisions were facilitated by the practice of all editors reading all the chapters at several different stages of manuscript review. Mary Beth Pudup assumed responsibility for managing the entire manuscript and acting as the principal correspondent with the University of North Carolina Press throughout the duration of the project.

The editors wish to extend their thanks to the manuscript reviewers for helpful comments on individual chapters. We also thank the reviewers for understanding the potential value of the collection and encouraging its publication. The editors issue a special thanks to John Inscoe, Kathleen Blee, and Alan Banks for their wise counsel over the course of the project. Pam Upton, assistant managing editor at the University of North Carolina Press, shepherded the manuscript from approval through publication with characteristic professional excellence.

Dwight Billings expresses gratitude to the University of Kentucky for an appointment as university research professor in 1993–94 that provided release from teaching for this and other research activities.

Mary Beth Pudup wishes to recognize the University of California Faculty Senate, Santa Cruz Division, for a series of small grants that funded conference calls, voluminous photocopying, and postage and express charges. Special thanks go to Ms. Melessa Hemler, College Eight faculty services supervisor, for her ever-cheerful assistance that occasionally went far beyond the call of duty.

Altina Waller wishes to thank SUNY-Plattsburgh for supporting conference calls, postage, and trips to the Appalachian Studies Conference. Much of the work was done while on a fellowship supported by the National Endowment for the Humanities for research and writing on Appalachian topics.

Appalachia in the Making

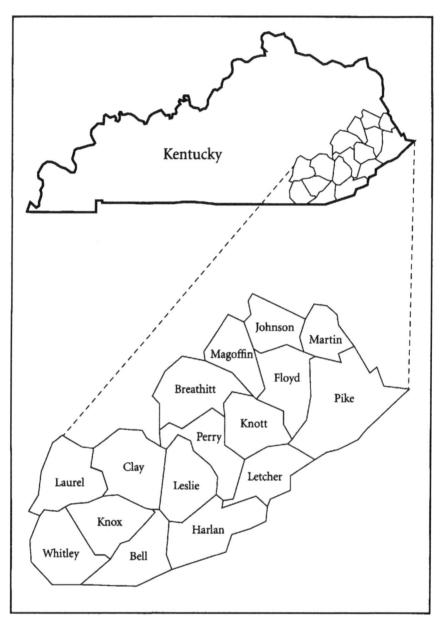

Map 1.1. Kentucky's Appalachian Counties. A map of Appalachia purporting to delineate the boundaries of the entire region would be at cross purposes with the arguments put forward in this volume, and therefore the editors make no apologies for its omission. Similarly, this map of Appalachian Kentucky, placed here for easy reference to the essays dealing with the subregion (especially Chapters 9, 10, 12, and 13), is not intended to perpetuate the conflation of the Kentucky mountain experience with that of the whole region.

INTRODUCTION   DWIGHT B. BILLINGS

MARY BETH PUDUP

ALTINA L. WALLER

Taking Exception
with Exceptionalism

The Emergence and
Transformation of
Historical Studies of
Appalachia

Appalachia first entered American consciousness as a distinct region and people in the decades immediately following the Civil War when popular writers such as Will Wallace Harney began to describe the "strange land and peculiar people" of the southern Appalachian mountains in the pages of popular periodicals such as *Lippincott's Magazine*, *Harper's*, and the *Atlantic Monthly*. Between 1870 and 1900 scores of articles, both fiction and nonfiction, were published that pictured ways of life in the highland South as vastly out of step, culturally and economically, with the progressive trends of industrializing and urbanizing nineteenth-century America. Such articles gave rise to a distinct genre of local color fiction that both exploited and tried to explain the strangeness of mountain life. In turn, the fiction and travelogues of popular writers such as Mary Noailles Murfree in Tennessee and James Lane Allen and John Fox, Jr., in Kentucky influenced more scholarly descriptions of the region that were written by early social scientists such as geographer Ellen Churchill Semple and sociologist George Vincent.[1] Effects of these early influences on thinking and writing about Appalachia are still felt today.[2]

By the end of this period William Goodell Frost, president of Berea College in Kentucky, had given the people of the southern mountains a name ("Appalachian Americans") and reconciled their presumptive backwardness to the social dynamism of fin de siècle America by focusing on the geographical, social, and economic isolation of the mountains. Mountain people, he said, were "our contemporary ancestors," a surviving remnant of the solid, white, pioneer culture that had first settled the eastern seaboard and contributed to the building of early American institutional life.[3] Frost's image of isolated mountaineers, articulated at this early date, provided a compelling trope, however misleading, that would prove highly serviceable for popular and scholarly accounts of Appalachia written throughout the next 100 years.

Frost portrayed the people of Appalachia as morally upright and therefore deserving the charitable and educational uplift efforts that institutions such as Berea College—with the help of northern philanthropy—were prepared to offer. But other popular accounts, especially those emphasizing such "peculiarities" of Appalachian life as moonshining and feuding, focused instead on apparently darker aspects of southern mountain culture, thereby initiating a pejorative tradition of writing about mountain people that still thrives in contemporary academic writing and popular culture.[4]

Henry D. Shapiro's intellectual history of the idea of Appalachia, *Appalachia on Our Mind: The Southern Mountains and Mountaineers in the American Consciousness, 1870–1920*, was the first important effort to set this tradition of writing about Appalachia in a historical perspective. Shapiro described how local color writers, advocates of the home missions and settlement house movements, folk song collectors, leaders of the handicrafts revival, and regional intellectuals such as John C. Campbell contributed to the "discovery," that is, the construction, of Appalachia as "a coherent region inhabited by an homogeneous population possessing a uniform culture"—a regional depiction more often than not benefiting the organizational goals and fund-raising efforts of its primary architects.[5] More importantly, however, by highlighting the discourses that constructed a "mythic system" about the Appalachian region and people, and by carefully effacing any of his own assertions about the "reality" of mountain life itself, Shapiro's postmodern study demonstrates that much of what is believed to be known about the life and people there is actually knowledge about a complex intertextual reality, "Appalachia."

The deconstruction of this social construct, which Shapiro calls the "myth of Appalachia," is one of the methodological premises of the fourteen original historical studies prepared for this volume. Each contribution illuminates important dimensions of early social life in diverse sections of the Appalachian mountains. But unlike a long tradition of Appalachian regional studies, none claims that the patterns described were necessarily unique to the highland South or general to the whole mountain region. The essays seek to place the study of Appalachia within the wider compass of comparative regional histories of the United States through which common themes of American history are nuanced by geographical difference.

The Growth of Appalachian Studies

As Shapiro has ably shown, contemporary assumptions that Appalachia is a coherent region occupied by a homogeneous people who share a unified culture have been influenced by traditions of writing about Appalachia traceable to early "documentary" accounts such as John C. Campbell's *The Southern Highlander and His Homeland* (1921), Horace Kephart's *Our Southern Highlanders* (1913, 1922), Samuel Tyndale Wilson's *The Southern Mountaineers* (1906, 1914), James Watt Raine's *The Land of the Saddle-bags* (1924), and Muriel Earley Sheppard's *Cabins in the Laurel* (1935). Although their descriptions of mountain life differ in important and interesting respects, together these works, when read uncritically, contribute to essentialist and universalist assumptions about Appalachia because they tend to treat diverse preindustrial localities in the southern mountains as if each were representative of a single, regionwide folk society, much like the villages of Mexico described later by Robert Redfield were made to represent peasant society as a whole.[6]

Early efforts to document and preserve preferred versions of the supposed folk culture of the southern mountains by enthusiasts of highland crafts and music, for instance, not only influenced and reshaped such practices but also contributed to highly selective interpretations of mountain life.[7] Thus, for example, when the English ethnomusicologist Cecil Sharp searched for traditional British ballads in 1917 and 1918 throughout supposedly isolated sections of the Appalachian mountains, he traveled from his base in Asheville, North Carolina, up and down the region bounded on the east by the Blue Ridge Mountains and on the west by the Cumberland Mountains.[8] One can only wonder what different impression of the cultural and ethnic diversity of the southern mountains his collecting might have conveyed had Sharp ventured into the central Appalachian coalfields of southern West Virginia, where half of the coal-mining workforce at the time were European immigrants and one-fourth were African Americans.[9] Instead, he contributed to the essentialistic image of a white Anglo-Saxon folk, frozen in time—"Yesterday's People" as Jack Weller would label them some fifty years later—who could still be found singing songs that had long since vanished from the British Isles they had left behind so many years ago.[10]

That knowledge of preindustrial Appalachia has more often than not been based solely on discursive knowledge of an intertextual reality (the myth of Appalachia) rather than historical knowledge of an actual place can be forcefully illustrated by the case of the great British historian Arnold Toynbee. His claim that the people of Appalachia had "relapsed into illiteracy and witchcraft" is one of the most pejorative and often quoted interpretations in the vast literature about Appalachia. For Toynbee, Appalachians were "no better than barbarians" who represented "the melancholy spectacle of a people who have acquired civilization and then lost it."[11] In answer to the sociologist James Brown's queries about the sources he had used to arrive at such a conclusion, Toynbee replied that although he had "been up into the mountains themselves once or twice," his was a "composite picture formed over the last twenty five years, as a result of a number of visits to a friend of mine living, not in the mountains, but within reach of them in East-Central Kentucky, together with two visits to Berea College." Toynbee added that he did "not believe that any of [his] knowledge of the mountain people [came] from books."[12]

The early treatment of preindustrial Appalachia as an isolated folk culture had at least two important scholarly consequences. On the one hand it contributed positively to a tradition of ethnographic studies of rural Appalachia that provide an indispensable viewpoint on social change in the mountains because of its close attention to the fabric of daily life, especially the family and community institutions of local society. Important ethnographic studies made by James Brown, Marion Pearsall, and John Stephenson in the 1940s, 1950s, and 1960s, respectively, have been complemented more recently by those of Allen Batteau, Carlene Bryant, Patricia Beaver, and Shaunna Scott, to name but a few.[13]

On the other hand, the construction of preindustrial Appalachia as a folk culture also had the negative effect of reinforcing the image of Appalachians as a "people without history," thus making the study of the region the proper professional domain of anthropology and ethnography rather than history. Thus in their classic, two-volume *History of Kentucky* published in 1922, William Connelley and E. M. Coulter concluded a 1,211-page survey of Kentucky history that almost never mentioned eastern Kentucky with a 14-page addendum on the "Cumberland Gap Region." This ethnographic sketch included a discussion of the "manners and customs of the people" there along with quotations from five traditional British ballads.[14]

Moreover, the disinclination to study the history of Appalachia was reinforced by ethnographers' frequent use of modernization theory as a narrative device. Thus attention was directed away from actual historical causes of regionwide social change and toward how local communities adapted to exogenous sources of change such as the "coming of the roads" and to the strains that were presumed to result inevitably from the social differentiation of formerly homogeneous rural communities.[15]

In the context of an important survey of Appalachian attitudes that was also influential in defining the boundaries of the region,[16] Thomas Ford codified the ethnographic tradition by identifying and operationalizing several cultural traits believed essential to Appalachia: "individualism and self-reliance," "traditionalism and fatalism," and "religious fundamentalism."[17] By comparing the attitudes of younger and older Appalachians and those of rural and urban Appalachians, Ford claimed to have demonstrated empirically the "passing of provincialism" throughout the mountain region, a finding that left intact the prevalent assumptions about what life in preindustrial Appalachia had been like.[18]

Renewed interest in the Appalachian region was stimulated in the 1960s by the publication of Michael Harrington's *The Other America* and by John F. Kennedy's widely televised campaign for the Democratic presidential nomination in West Virginia. Both events called attention to remarkably high levels of poverty in Appalachia, as did Kennedy's appointment of a presidential commission on Appalachia and the Johnson administration's subsequent War on Poverty that waged numerous and much-publicized battles in the mountains. Liberal American commentators and social scientists struggled to make sense of Appalachia's poverty in the context of apparent prosperity elsewhere in American society. From viewing Appalachia as a traditionalist subculture, it was but a short conceptual step to viewing Appalachia as a regionwide subculture of poverty.

The discursive link between Appalachia as folk culture and Appalachia as subculture of poverty was most clearly articulated in an introduction by the sociologist Rupert Vance to Jack Weller's widely read *Yesterday's People*: "Thus mountain isolation, which began as physical isolation enforced by rugged topography, became mental and cultural isolation, holding people in disadvantaged areas, resisting those changes that would bring them into contact with the outside world. The effect of conditions thus becomes a new cause of conditions, but the cause is now an attitude, not a mountain."[19]

Vance's cultural prescription for economic progress in Appalachia—his assertion that "to change the mountains [was] to change the mountain personality"—was matched by economic development theories that also assumed Appalachia's peculiar problems were the result of regional isolation.[20] Thus, changing the mountain personality *and* the economy meant opening both to the outside, in the latter instance by building highways to be "corridors" of development.[21] Once again, Appalachian history, read as an absence, was neglected.

Strategies of cultural modernization in the central Appalachian coalfields, initiated during the War on Poverty, especially among VISTA (Volunteers in Service to America) and the Appalachian Volunteers, took the form of sending young people into the mountain region to encourage civic participation and community betterment efforts, just as their youthful counterparts in the Peace Corps were doing in the Third World. As they became involved with indigenous struggles to win control of Office of Economic Opportunity programs, reform local politics, mobilize support for improved social services, and end the strip-mining of coal, however, Appalachian activists soon began to realize that the coalfield region's problems could be understood better in terms of economic exploitation and political domination than in terms of economic isolation, cultural traditionalism, and fatalism.[22]

The emerging political and economic knowledge of the youthful activists began to spill over into scholarly analysis of Appalachia, not least because many of the activists were college graduates who subsequently sought advanced academic degrees. In opposition to the received wisdom of mainstream modernization and development theories, these new Appalachian scholars borrowed insights from Third World dependency theorists as well as Robert Blauner's model of racial ghettos to develop a model of Appalachia as an internal colony.[23] In journals such as *People's Appalachia*, radical scholars called attention to the absentee ownership of Appalachia's land and mineral wealth that drained profits from the region.[24] Appalachia was poor, according to the internal colonialism model, because of the nature of its integration with—and not separation from—the American corporate economy. Further, advocates of the internal colonialism model showed how the denigration of Appalachian culture in modernization and culture-of-poverty theories went hand in hand with the exploitation of Appalachia's land, resources, and people as a form of legitimation.[25] Alternatively, they interpreted indigenous cultural patterns as forms of resistance to colonization.[26]

An early paradigmatic statement of the internal colonialism model was provided by Helen Lewis, who asked provocatively whether fatalism or the coal industry lay at the root of Appalachian poverty.[27] But it was Harry Caudill's widely read *Night Comes to the Cumberlands* that most forcefully advanced the internal colonialism model.[28] Although Caudill's brilliant work had contradictory effects—reopening the door to pejorative accounts of the long-term effects of welfare dependency, to attributions of fatalism and a self-sustaining culture of defeat, and even to genetic deficiencies—it nevertheless put Appalachian history and social and economic processes squarely at the center of attention for the first time.[29] By writing about the history of resource monopolization, railroads, and timbering; the building of coal towns; the boom and bust cycles that have endlessly plagued the coal industry; and the economic exploitation and political corruption in central Appalachia—all factors accounting for what he termed the "biography of a depressed area"—Caudill set the stage for the contributions of the younger generation of more academically inclined scholars and activists who came of age in the 1970s and 1980s.[30]

It is important to note that many members of this post-1960s generation of writers also participated in a broad-based and interdisciplinary Appalachian studies movement that had origins in both the academy and grass-roots organizations.[31] Appalachian studies courses and research centers were created on college campuses throughout the region during the 1970s and 1980s; the *Appalachian Journal: A Regional Studies Review* was initiated in 1973; and the Appalachian Studies Conference, now the Appalachian Studies Association, which attracts nearly 500 participants to its annual conferences, was established in 1978. Such developments gave a great impetus to the writing of Appalachian history. Furthermore, and probably for the first time, the discourse on Appalachia was produced as much inside as outside the region.[32]

The 1970s witnessed a torrid debate among Appalachian scholars over what theoretical model best captured Appalachia's experience with capitalism. As the title of one of the most influential books of that period, *Colonialism in Modern America*, suggests, notions of internal colonialism, initially associated with conditions in disenfranchised domestic ghetto communities and foreign regions like Northern Ireland, earned the greatest favor. The colonial model's wide appeal in Appalachian studies derived at least in part from renewed attention to absentee ownership of the region's land and other natural resources, not to mention of its production facilities.

Indeed, it is no exaggeration to claim scholarship inspired by the colonial model was the sine qua non of discrediting the culture-of-poverty thesis about Appalachia. In particular, the colonial model provided a coherent theoretical framework for two groundbreaking studies of the early 1980s. The first of these was John Gaventa's *Power and Powerlessness*. This study of eastern Kentucky, which is still widely read, asked the simple yet profound question of why exploited people do not rise up against the powers that be.

Central to the explanation were the peculiar kinds of domination exercised by institutions of absentee capital at the local community level.

The other key text was *Who Owns Appalachia?*, the report on a mammoth project that sought to document conclusively what was common but undocumented knowledge about the region: the preponderance of external ownership and control of local natural resources. *Who Owns Appalachia?* was also notable for carefully distinguishing among Appalachia's subregions by highlighting differences, for example, between areas of recreational second-home development in North Carolina and mineral ownership in West Virginia. Much of the emerging scholarship of the 1970s had favored eastern Kentucky and central Appalachia as a research focus. Consequently, theoretical discussion as well as written social history had all but ignored Appalachian subregions not dominated by the bituminous coal industry.[33] While knowledge about historical and contemporary Appalachian Kentucky and the coalfields fortunately deepened under this new scrutiny, the unfortunate tendency was for conditions there to be generalized to other subregions regardless of whether such generalizations were warranted.[34] Absentee ownership provided a focal point of common experience for much of Appalachia, but eventually factors such as the sectoral base of each subregion's economy (coal versus noncoal) as well as state boundaries became recognized as powerful lines of differentiation among historical experiences in Appalachian subregions.

The debate over political economy models also filled pages in the quarterly *Appalachian Journal*. A special double issue in 1983–84, edited by the short-lived Southern Mountain Research Collective and devoted to a "class analysis of Appalachia," bears a special relevance to the assessments collected here because of its explicit concern with "many historically and currently important internal struggles within Appalachia." In particular, the collective sought to position its class-analytic approach as the better alternative to the colonial model: "Especially unsatisfactory is the idea that the primary and formative social conflict in the Appalachian region is one between geographical regions (Appalachia vs. the United States or the 'outside') or between people who live in those different geographical regions."[35] In his study of the implications of the mining labor process and coal industry structure on underdevelopment in West Virginia, collective member Richard Simon was perhaps the most strenuous opponent of the colonial model. His subtle analysis of the economic underpinnings of social class relations in West Virginia provided a positive model of theoretically informed regional scholarship that did not reify "Appalachia."[36]

From the standpoint of history writing, however, the crowning accomplishment of this prodigiously creative period in Appalachian studies was undoubtedly Ronald Eller's *Miners, Millhands, and Mountaineers.* This definitive saga of Appalachian colonization and industrialization was published in 1982.[37] In looking back on this important work over a decade later, besides its monumental documentation of the broad outlines of regional industrialization, two aspects stand out. First, it presumes, as no single study would today, to be able to tell the story of the region as a unified whole, in a seamless narrative. Second, like Caudill's history before it, the thinness of its account of preindustrial Appalachia, prefigured in the earlier discourses of the Appalachian folk culture, reinforces the assumption that Appalachian history really only began with the history of industrialization when the region was "opened up" to the outside.

In his still trenchant examination of the "myth of Appalachia," Henry Shapiro complained that

> Even the debunkers, within and without the universities, who have risen to the occasion and challenged the accuracy of particular generalizations about the mountaineers in order to paint them in a more "realistic" light, have refused to ask the central question of their craft, about the reality of the phenomenon they seek to explicate. Instead, they have begun with the assumption that the mountaineers do in fact compose a distinct people with distinct and describable characteristics. They have argued from within a mythic system about the accuracy of mythology, and attacked the generalizations of folklore which are at once so vague and so potent as to defy examination or correction.[38]

What sets apart the essays in this collection from historical studies preceding them is both the effort to push the examination of mountain social life back further in time and the effort to deconstruct the concept of an essential and universalistic Appalachian past.[39] By placing the social history of preindustrial and industrializing mountain localities in a comparative context, these essays both challenge the long-standing assumption of Appalachian exceptionalism and, at the same time, deepen the recognition of the diversity of American regional social formations. Taken together, the goal of the essays is not to erase all difference and claim Appalachian history merely iterates that of every other place in the nation. Rather, the collective effort is aimed at mapping the points of similarity to and difference from the settlement and transformation experiences in other rural locales across the nation. In order to understand how the various contributors attempt to avoid the old assumption of Appalachia as a unified cultural entity, standing apart from the trajectory of American social and economic development, yet also attempt to preserve a recognition of American regional differences without essentializing them, it is helpful to place their essays in the context of recent developments in American social historiography and regional political economy.

Intersections with American Social History

Beginning in the late 1960s, "new" social historians began to challenge the assumption that individualism and capitalist competition had characterized American history from the earliest European settlements. Scholars first took on this task by reexamining the experience of colonial New England communities. Challenging traditional methods of studying the New England past through Puritan ideology, political leaders, and the merchant elite, new social historians insisted that only in-depth attention to the lives of ordinary people as discovered through local community, tax, and census records would reveal the genuine nature of those communities. The result was a body of work celebrating the culture of community in early New England—a culture that put cooperation before competition, stressed harmony rather than self-interest, and emphasized the willingness to sacrifice personal interests for the good of the community.[40] Only with the transition to capitalism, argued these historians, did New Englanders become "modernized" into competitive individuals. Thus the focus of the debate shifted to identifying just *when* the transition took place.

While the new social historians searched for communal values in the distant past of mainstream American history—that is, in colonial New England—social scientists and political activists found these values surviving and fully present in societies and cultures that they thought had not yet undergone a capitalist transition. In assuming that loss of community and cooperation could be blamed on the transition to capitalism, places and peoples that seemingly had been excluded from participation in capitalist development were held up as examples of the continued healthy existence of human values. Such societies and cultures, according to this hopeful view, could still be found among American Indians, in working-class urban neighborhoods, and, perhaps predictably given the above discussion of the myth of Appalachia, in the Appalachian mountains and other areas of the nonplantation South.[41] Where, in the early 1960s, liberal authors such as Michael Harrington and politicians such as John F. Kennedy had perceived only grinding poverty and abject hopelessness born of economic backwardness, radical historians of the 1970s discovered a vibrant folk culture embedded in cohesive humanitarian communities that were all the more remarkable because they had survived decades of exploitation and oppression. Parallels between the patterns of folk crafts, music, and cooperation in so-called traditional cultures such as those of Native Americans, African Americans, and immigrants are obvious and reflect the search for a cooperative model rather than any objective reality for these cultures.

Although these trends may be readily apparent in hindsight, when they were first introduced they turned the defining assumptions of American history on their heads. Areas of the United States that had been regarded as the most progressive, modern, and enlightened—the urban centers of the Northeast, Midwest, and West—were now judged as hopelessly lost to the inhumanity and commodification produced by capitalist modernization. Cultures and places conventionally regarded as marginal—Native Americans, immigrant communities, and Appalachia—were thought to have retained humanitarian, cooperative values and were considered fortunate to have escaped modernization. Indeed, the very term *modernization*, initially employed by economic historians to applaud the development of capitalist market relations around the world, was regarded by new social historians with suspicion and was frequently invoked to signify the destruction of human values in the service of market relations.

This underlying ideological agenda that defined the original "little community" studies of the new social history helps explain why Appalachia and even much of the South was initially neglected by these historians. The rural South was thought to have escaped modernization until well into the twentieth century and thus preserved a cooperative spirit despite poverty and racism. Social historians hoped to prove that the most urbanized, individualistic, competitive region—the Northeast—had in the past been communally conscious. Thus, Puritan communities, with their well-preserved records and their reputations for hypocritical religious piety underpinning an avaricious capitalistic mentality, seemed the obvious place to begin. The results included such innovative and influential works as Kenneth Lockridge's *A New England Town* (1978), Michael Zuckerman's *Peaceable Kingdoms* (1970), and Paul Boyer and Stephen Nissenbaum's *Salem Possessed* (1974), among many others.[42] These were solidly researched studies that shared the conclusion, now challenged by mainstream historians, that market capitalism impoverished social relationships within New England's families and communities.

Not until a decade after the initial appearance of the little community studies of New England did social historians become interested in the local history of communities in Appalachia. Until then, as described above, scholars and activists with anticapitalist sentiments who were also interested in Appalachia had devoted themselves to demonstrating that Appalachia *as a region* had been devastated by its relationship to the capitalist core in the Northeast. At that point colonial dependency theories, documenting the exploitation of Appalachian land, resources, and labor by timber and coal companies, seemed to suggest the most effective way of analyzing Appalachia's past. Yet scholars actually knew very little about the economy, social patterns, and historical development of preindustrial Appalachia at the level of local society. This lack of knowledge represented an implicit awareness that much was still to be done in understanding the history of the region and its relation to the broader picture of American history. When combined with the work of a second generation of new social and cultural historians, this recognition led to the emergence of little community and regional studies within Appalachia.

The first two such community studies published in 1988, Altina Waller's *Feud* and Durwood Dunn's *Cades Cove*, undercut the traditional assumption of Appalachian exceptionalism and demonstrated that historical records existed for a social science history of Appalachian communities that could supplement, if not supplant, existing folk and oral history.[43] Both studies reflected the continuing engagement of social historians with the question of community cooperation versus competitive market values, and both rekindled long-standing ethnographic interests in family and community while directly challenging assumptions about Appalachians as a people without history.[44] Describing different sections of the mountain region and different local economies, Waller argued for the persistence of traditional values despite internal community divisions over the invasion of capitalism in the Tug Valley section of the West Virginia and Kentucky mountains, while Dunn insisted on the prevalence of trade, a cash economy, and market values from the very beginning of settlement in eastern Tennessee.

Whether in New England or Appalachia, the new social history, clothed in the language of social theory and the methodology of quantification, appeared more objective than past histories based on elite sources and was certainly a useful corrective to past interpretations. Nonetheless, it was a romantic and hopeful view of the American past rooted in the countercultural beliefs of the 1960s that capitalism, competition, and individualism had corrupted an essentially cooperative American society. Not surprisingly, by the time the studies by Waller, Dunn, and others had appeared, a group of "market" historians had emerged in the mainstream of American history during the conservative Reagan era to challenge the premodern romanticism of the new social history. What bothered the challengers most was the assumption of social historians that there had existed some premodern or traditional mentality that operated differently from the capitalist mentality. The earliest Europeans, argued Winifred Rothenberg and others, were bent on individual profit making in a commercial economy, not on some utopian ideal of a cooperative society.[45] Echoing earlier scholars such as Louis Hartz, they insisted that America was "born capitalist."

The vitriolic nature and high visibility of this combat could not help effecting the renewed interest in Appalachian communities, and much research began to center around questions about the extent of isolation of Appalachian communities, the egalitarian versus hierarchical social structure, cooperation versus individual self-seeking and, perhaps most significantly, the question of a traditional versus a capitalist mentality. Thus in one of the earliest comparisons between Appalachian and New England community studies, Dwight Billings, Kathleen Blee, and Louis Swanson stressed the centrality of nonmarket, kinship-based forms of reciprocity in Appalachian subsistence farming communities but were criticized by Paul Salstrom for underemphasizing the entrepreneurial and speculative impulses that accompanied the settlement of the region.[46] Even more trenchantly, Gordon McKinney complained that overemphasis on the region's "moral economy" represented a "limited vision of the mountain past" that would potentially lead scholars to "ignore or repress such historical developments as the dispossession of Native Americans, African slavery, the exploitation of women, the misuse of the environment, elitist politics, rampant drug use, and reluctance to support education, all a palpable part of preindustrial life."[47]

The examination of Appalachia (as with other areas of the country) within the terms of this debate did perhaps obscure other important issues such as diversity within the region itself, the opposition of rural farming neighborhoods to urban centers, the existence of subcultures of African Americans and Native Americans, and the sometimes conflicting interests of women and men within families and communities. Fortunately for Appalachia's history, however, it had been a late arrival in the debate and thus escaped the near obsession with it that permeated New England history. Accepting Allan Kulikoff's suggestion that "a judicious synthesis" of the views of "market historians" and "social historians" more accurately "describes American reality than either of the two alone,"[48] historians of Appalachia have been able to move on to more fruitful lines of inquiry that emphasized the methods and insights of the new social historians in tandem with an emergent political economy approach.[49] This next stage of historical inquiry characterizes the essays in this volume.

If there is any one theme emerging from this set of essays, it is that nineteenth-century Appalachian regions and communities, when carefully scrutinized, resemble in fundamental ways regions and communities elsewhere in the United States. In fact, most of the authors find it necessary, within the body of their essays, to remind us that tenacious myths about Appalachia stand in the way of dispassionate historical inquiry and accurate comparison. John Finger contests myths about pioneer attitudes and relations with native Appalachians. Paul Salstrom tries to dispel the myth of the absence of entrepreneurialism in the settlement of Appalachia and the uniformity of its subsistence economy. John Inscoe traces the contradictory myths of African American presence and white Appalachian racial attitudes. Ralph Mann and Gordon McKinney explode the myths of geographical isolation and social homogeneity. John Alexander Williams and Wilma Dunaway take on economic egalitarianism. Alan Banks challenges the myth of class homogeneity. Altina Waller refutes the myth of a feud- and violence-prone culture. Only by studying Appalachian subregions as part of American history can we reconstruct the pathways that led to separate and unequal histories.

In short, these essays challenge the concept of Appalachian exceptionalism and suggest that careful study of economic, social, and cultural patterns in Appalachia reveal broad parallels to the development of other American regions and communities, thereby enriching the study of American history. At the same time, however, they question what were the economic, social, or political dynamics that resulted in Appalachia's economic impoverishment as well as the creation of these enduring myths.[50]

Enduring Contributions of Political Economy in Appalachian Studies

So long as Appalachian studies remained tied to region-as-folk-culture representations, scant attention was paid to the region's politics and economy as discrete domains of social life, let alone as repositories of social power and wellsprings of social change. This comfortable state of affairs, as we have seen, was first challenged during the 1970s and 1980s by the new generation of scholars and activists determined to refocus the contemporary debate over Appalachia's problems away from supposedly intrinsic cultural deficiencies and toward the keepers of the kingdom.

Now after more than a decade the debate over models—class analysis versus dependency theory, social history versus market history—has a perhaps quaint ring. But the contested issues of theory and method in Appalachia's political economy, as in historiography, resonated with wider debates then taking place over the nature of American society. As such, this honest and vigorous conversation attracted an even larger and more geographically diverse set of scholars into Appalachian studies to pursue what David Whisnant has called "second level Appalachian history."[51] In many respects this newer generation of scholarship pursues the many research frontiers opened by early political economy critiques discussed above.

Chief among those frontiers is the study of the economy and society within Appalachia's subregions during the nineteenth-century preindustrial era. Despite their many points of difference, the critiques of twentieth-century capitalism in Appalachia shared a common starting point in a largely unexamined conception of the region's preindustrial history. Social and economic history during the nineteenth century was associated with a traditional mountain subculture. This historical entity was largely undifferentiated and undefined except through its opposition to the capitalist development that supplanted it. A much eulogized, benevolent traditional mountain subculture drew a sharp contrast with capitalism's economic and social upheavals. The uncritical acceptance of this vision of preindustrial Appalachia had the effect of polarizing the region's economic history between a dimly yet romantically perceived domestic production system in the nineteenth century and natural-resource based industrial development in the twentieth century.

More recently, scholars have eschewed the stark polarization between the nineteenth and twentieth centuries in order to examine crucial long-term aspects of Appalachia's economic and social history. In this volume, for example, Salstrom and Dunaway show how subregions of Appalachia's earliest settlement and development were variously conditioned by their incorporation as peripheral regions in the capitalist world system, resulting in degrees of land speculation, inequality, slaveholding, and tenancy that profoundly challenge the romantic vision of the Appalachian past before industrialization. From the vantage point of Marxism rather than world systems theory, Banks examines how the necessary preconditions for capitalist industrialization including a wage labor market and capitalized landownership were achieved in eastern Kentucky long before Mr. Peabody's coal train actually began to haul away the region's timber and mineral resources. Billings and Blee examine how long-term trends in eastern Kentucky farming and population growth limited indigenous capital formation, while Pudup documents the enduring process and pattern of rural settlement that were only incompletely displaced by the capitalist transformation at the turn of the century. Anglin shows the importance of gender relations in regional development processes, and Lewis documents the impact of timber extraction on the rural social relations of agriculture in West Virginia.

As the collected essays demonstrate, scholars have begun to examine the continuing impact of preindustrial legacies in order to understand how historical conditions have influenced the various paths that Appalachian subregions have followed to capitalist industrialization. One key aspect is the relationship between early domestic production systems and their ability to support local industrial capital formation. Another emergent concern, closely related to the nature of the region's preindustrial economies, is the social origins of local Appalachian elites.

Developing a long-term conception of Appalachia's economic history has required new attention to how practices such as general farming and home manufacturing operated as basic sectors in generating economic surplus. Questions surrounding the extent and distribution of surplus production frustrate efforts to conceptualize neatly Appalachia's various farm economies as exclusively commercial or subsistence oriented. The formerly prevailing view held mountain farming a repository of folk culture practices rather than the basis of a preindustrial economy. The discovery of Appalachia's preindustrial economy has revealed long-forgotten and previously unimaginable commercial activity and greater than once-believed degrees of social differentiation.

The contributions included here pick up the lively debate that has issued from these discoveries. Evidence of land speculation, surplus production and exchange, farm tenancy, and the like seem to support contentions by scholars such as Robert Mitchell that commercial relations had thoroughly penetrated Appalachia's mountain fastness early and thence determined the region's subsequent development.[52] Other evidence about apparently widespread subsistence-level production and lackluster capital accumulation support a somewhat different appraisal of the mountain farm economy, one which, as Mary Beth Pudup argues, allows the presence of commercialization but does not assign it the dominant and deepening tendency.[53]

As the discussion of community-level history made clear, the subsistence versus commercial production debate in Appalachia is a subset of a larger national debate over American origins requiring a judicious synthesis of opposing views. The debate has had the salutary effect of stimulating research about nineteenth-century regional conditions. But the debate as it has taken place in Appalachia is somewhat false, owing to the fact that it confuses critically different levels of historical experience and historical analysis. Evidence of commercial relations at the local level would seem to undermine an interpretation that subsistence characterized wider regional economic dynamics. But individual household productions and consumptions cannot be added up by simple arithmetic to yield the characteristics of a regional economy. Put somewhat differently, regional economic dynamics bear a complex relationship to individual household production and exchange decisions.

By understanding how different levels of historical analysis are involved in the commercial versus subsistence orientation debate in Appalachian history, it is possible to move forward beyond a frustrated search for universalist statements to characterize both the region as a whole and individual rural households within it. Commercial production and exchange were both common at the local level owing to the participation of many individual households. At the regional level, however, many subregions of Appalachia lagged far behind other American regions in the depth and dynamism of their commercial development. The essays collected here, by providing in-depth local analysis of different subregions, will help yield more meaningful understanding of the macroregion called Appalachia.

Another emergent concern, closely related to the nature of the region's preindustrial economies, has been the social origins of Appalachia's local elites. Virtually everywhere in the writings on internal colonialism, elites were assigned vital roles in facilitating the new capitalist regime. They were seen as a central component of the "infrastructure of dependency" and as co-conspirators with absentee colonizers.[54] This commonly held view is captured in the oft-quoted passage from Eugene Conti's study of Kentucky elites that "throughout the nineteenth and early twentieth centuries, the uplands' relationship to the broader American economy and polity was mediated by an indigenous elite. This local elite pursued essentially a modernizing role, diffusing change from the American metropolis to Appalachian hollers."[55] In short, elites were the chief local beneficiaries of capitalist development, as exemplified in Appalachia's most famous indigenous robber baron, John C. C. Mayo.[56]

But from where in the traditional mountain subculture did these elites arise? Undifferentiated conceptions of the preindustrial era in Appalachia make the answer anything but obvious. Furthermore, the issues at stake extend far beyond identifying the social origins of local elites in Appalachia to general questions of historical processes shaping the region from within and without. Absentee capital investment, industrialization, and rural transformation did not spring full-blown on a pristine countryside but instead took place within long-settled rural social formations. The very existence of elites presupposes rural populations that were internally stratified, which, in turn, presupposes historical processes responsible for social differentiation. What were these processes? Was the population stratified at the outset during the settlement process, as Wilma Dunaway suggests in her chapter, and if so, what long-term effects can be traced from the settlement era? What was the nature of property ownership and property relations? How did farming and other domestic productions contribute to social differentiation?

Burgeoning new scholarship has been addressing such questions. Waller's study of the fabled Hatfield and McCoy feud, for example, portrayed this ostensibly kinship-based struggle in terms of intraclass conflicts within a fractured indigenous elite. Pudup linked social differentiation to land-ownership, longevity, and control over political officeholding in south-eastern Kentucky, and Billings and Blee demonstrated that rural communities there were no less unequal than settlements elsewhere in the rural North or South.[57] John Alexander Williams traced the emergence of West Virginia's modern capitalist class from its roots in the quest for statehood by Old Dominion elites. John Inscoe's study of slavery in western North Carolina, along with Gordon McKinney's earlier analysis of mountain republicanism there, are important reminders that in certain subregions of Appalachia, slave ownership was a key element in elite privilege.[58]

The essays comprising this book make common cause with the emerging scholarship on Appalachia's economy and society during the preindustrial era. Together this new body of work builds upon earlier research inspired by political economy by locating preindustrial Appalachia within the same wide ambits of theoretical discourse governing comparative historical scholarship of rural societies throughout the world. Refusing the "world we have lost" romanticism about a traditional mountain subculture as well as assumptions about a unified historical experience, the essays are distinguished by their careful attention to the often subtle nuances of geography and often stark realities of social structure. Separately and as a collection they contribute a wealth of new knowledge about the social and economic history of this era based on prodigious research using information sources previously untapped in studies of the region. The essays raise as many questions as they attempt to answer and will thereby stimulate future scholarship and debate about the history of Appalachia's fabled hills and hollers.

Notes

1. See Mary Noailles Murfree [Charles Egbert Craddock, pseud.], *In the Tennessee Mountains* (Boston: Houghton Mifflin, 1884); James Lane Allen, *The Blue-Grass Region of Kentucky and Other Kentucky Articles* (New York: Harper and Brothers, 1892); and the numerous novels of John Fox, Jr., esp. *The Trail of the Lonesome Pine* (New York: Charles Scribner, 1908).

2. E. C. Semple, "The Anglo-Saxons of the Kentucky Mountains: A Study in Anthropogeography," reprinted in *Bulletin of the American Geographical Society* 42 (August 1910): 561–94; G. Vincent, "A Retarded Frontier," *American Sociological Review* 4 (1898): 1–20.

3. See W. G. Frost, "Appalachian America," *Woman's Home Companion*, September 1896, pp. 3–4, 21, and "Our Contemporary Ancestors in the Southern Mountains," *Atlantic Monthly*, March 1899, pp. 311–19.

4. For an early critique of academic writing, see S. Fisher, "Folk Culture or Folk Tale: Prevailing Assumptions about the Appalachian Personality," in *An Appalachian Symposium: Essays in Honor of Cratis D. Williams*, ed. J. W. Williamson (Boone, N.C.: Appalachian State University Press, 1977), pp. 14–25. For a recent discussion of mass media stereotypes, see J. Speer, "From Stereotype to Regional Hype: Strategies for Changing Media Portrayals of Appalachia," *Journal of the Appalachian Studies Association* 5 (1993): 12–19.

5. H. Shapiro, *Appalachia on Our Mind: The Southern Mountains and Mountaineers in the American Consciousness, 1870–1920* (Chapel Hill: University of North Carolina Press, 1978), p. ix.

6. See R. Redfield, *The Little Community* (Chicago: University of Chicago Press, 1955). Among early writers, however, John C. Campbell stood out for recognizing the diversity of social patterns in Appalachia and for pointing out to readers that "conditions in the Southern Appalachian region are little known and the people have suffered much from unqualified generalization" (J. Campbell, *The Southern Highlander and His Homeland* [Lexington: University Press of Kentucky, 1969], p. 131).

7. D. Whisnant, *All That Is Native and Fine: The Politics of Culture in an American Region* (Chapel Hill: University of North Carolina Press, 1983).

8. Sharp's travels in Appalachia and his interpretations of mountain music and culture are discussed in M. Karpeles, *Cecil Sharp: His Life and Work* (London: Routledge and Kegan Paul, 1967), pp. 141–71.

9. H. Gillenwater, "Mining Settlements in Southern West Virginia," in *West Virginia and Appalachia*, ed. H. Adkins, S. Ewing, and C. Zimolzak (Dubuque, Iowa: Kendall-Hunt, 1977), pp. 132–58.

10. J. E. Weller, *Yesterday's People* (Lexington: University Press of Kentucky, 1969).

11. A. Toynbee, *A Study of History* (New York: Oxford University Press, 1947), p. 149.

12. Toynbee admitted to Brown that this was a "rather slight acquaintance on which to give any account of [Appalachian mountain people] and their life." See J. Brown, "An Appalachian Footnote to Toynbee's *A Study of History*," *Appalachian Journal* 6 (Autumn 1978): 31.

13. J. S. Brown, *Beech Creek: The Social Organization of an Isolated Kentucky Mountain Neighborhood* (1950; reprint, Berea, Ky.: Berea College Press, 1988), portions of which are republished in *Mountain Families in Transition*, ed. H. Schwarzweller, J. Brown, and J. Mangalam (University Park: Pennsylvania State University Press, 1971); M. Pearsall, *Little Smokey Ridge* (Birmingham: University of Alabama Press, 1959); J. B. Stephenson, *Shiloh: A Mountain Community* (Lexington: University Press of Kentucky, 1968). See also A. Batteau, "Mosbys and Broomsedge: The

Semantics of Class in an Appalachian Kinship System," *American Ethnologist* 9, no. 3 (1982): 445–66; P. D. Beaver, *Rural Community in the Appalachian South* (Lexington: University Press of Kentucky, 1986); F. C. Bryant, *We're All Kin: A Cultural Study of a Mountain Neighborhood* (Knoxville: University of Tennessee Press, 1981); and S. L. Scott, *Two Sides to Everything: The Cultural Construction of Class in Harlan County, Kentucky* (Albany: State University of New York Press, 1995).

14. W. E. Connelley and E. M. Coulter, *History of Kentucky* (Chicago: American Historical Society, 1922), 2:1197–1211.

15. In an article that attempts to show how historical insights may nonetheless be recovered from ethnographic studies where standard sources of historical information are unreliable, fragmented, or nonexistent, K. Blee and D. Billings (quoting Thomas Bender) write, "Modernization theory logically deduces patterns of social change in rural Appalachia from presumed requisites of 'modernity,' which are conceptualized 'independent[ly] of time, place, or context: independent[ly], in short, of history.'" See Billings and Blee, "Reconstructing Daily Life in the Past: An Hermeneutical Approach to Ethnographic Data," *Sociological Quarterly* 27, no. 4 (1986): 443–62.

16. Ford and his associates modified John C. Campbell's influential definition of the region as 256 highland counties by excluding those in Maryland and South Carolina for a total of 189 counties. The official federal designation of Appalachia by the Appalachian Regional Commission includes not only highland counties in Maryland and South Carolina but also those in New York and Mississippi as well for a total of 397 counties. For an excellent discussion of regional definitions of Appalachia, see K. B. Raitz and R. Ulack, *Appalachia, a Regional Geography: Land, People, and Development* (Boulder, Colo.: Westview Press, 1984), pp. 9–35.

17. See T. Ford, "The Passing of Provincialism," in *The Southern Appalachian Region: A Survey*, ed. T. Ford (Lexington: University Press of Kentucky, 1967), pp. 9–34.

18. For an early critique of the Ford survey and an empirical demonstration that the attitudes that Ford associated with Appalachia were not distinct to the region but were more appropriately thought of as southern and rural, see D. Billings, "Culture and Poverty in Appalachia: A Theoretical Discussion and Empirical Analysis," *Social Forces* 53 (December 1974): 315–23.

19. R. Vance, "An Introductory Note," in Weller, *Yesterday's People*, p. vii. Among the numerous culture-of-poverty approaches to Appalachia during the 1960s, see, esp., R. Ball, "A Poverty Case: The Analgesic Subculture of the Southern Appalachians," *American Sociological Review* 33 (1968): 885–95. For a recent application of culture-of-poverty theory, see D. Cattell-Gordon, "The Appalachian Inheritance: A Culturally Transmitted Traumatic Stress Syndrome?," *Journal of Progressive Human Services* 1, no. 1 (1990): 41–57, and its critique by K. Tice and D. Billings, "Appalachian Culture and Resistance," *Journal of Progressive Human Services* 2, no. 2 (1991): 1–18.

20. Vance, "Introductory Note," p. ix.

21. This economic development literature is reviewed critically in D. Walls, "Central Appalachia: A Peripheral Region within an Advanced Capitalist Society," *Journal of Sociology and Social Welfare* 4, no. 2 (1976): 232–47.

22. The examination of the social history of the War on Poverty in Appalachia has barely begun, but see John Glen, "The War on Poverty in Appalachia: A Preliminary

Report," *Register of the Kentucky Historical Society* 87 (1989): 40–57. On the Appalachian Regional Commission, see M. Bradshaw, *Regions and Regionalism in the United States* (Jackson: University Press of Mississippi, 1988), and D. Whisnant, *Modernizing the Mountaineer* (New York: Burt Franklin, 1980).

23. R. Blauner, "Internal Colonialism and the Ghetto Revolt," *Social Problems* 16, no. 4 (1969): 393–408.

24. See R. Diehl, "Appalachian Energy Elite: A Wing of Imperialism?," *People's Appalachia* 1 (March 1970): 5–7; also E. Malizia, "Economic Imperialism: An Interpretation of Appalachian Underdevelopment," *Appalachian Journal* 1 (Spring 1973): 130–37. This line of empirical research culminated in a vast, six-state, eighty-county survey by the Appalachian Land Ownership Task Force, *Who Owns Appalachia?: Landownership and Its Impact* (Lexington: University Press of Kentucky, 1983).

25. See articles collected in H. Lewis, L. Johnson, and D. Askins, *Colonialism in Modern America: The Appalachian Case* (Boone, N.C.: Appalachian Consortium Press, 1978).

26. H. Lewis, S. Kobak, and L. Johnson, "Family, Religion, and Colonialism in Central Appalachia: Or, Bury My Rifle at Big Stone Gap," in Lewis et al., *Colonialism in Modern America*, pp. 131–56.

27. H. Lewis, "Fatalism or the Coal Industry?," *Mountain Life and Work* 46, no. 11 (1970): 4–15.

28. Critical analysis of Appalachia's economy and society was not invented during the 1960s but was built upon important earlier studies such as the United States Department of Agriculture's *Economic and Social Problems and Conditions of the Southern Appalachians* (Miscellaneous Publication no. 205, Washington, D.C.: Government Printing Office, 1935). Embracing the mountainous portions of nine states with the explicit goal of portraying widely contrasting conditions among Appalachian subregions, the study was conducted to serve as a planning document for depression-era relief efforts and, in retrospect, appears more attuned to local conditions than the later efforts of the Appalachian Regional Commission.

29. H. Caudill, *Night Comes to the Cumberlands: A Biography of a Depressed Area* (Boston: Little, Brown, 1962). Also compare Caudill's deeply pessimistic *A Darkness at Dawn: Appalachian Kentucky and the Future* (Lexington: University Press of Kentucky, 1976).

30. In addition to published works such as Whisnant, *Modernizing the Mountaineer*, much of this body of scholarship consisted of widely read dissertations, including Douglas Arnett, "Eastern Kentucky: The Politics of Dependency and Underdevelopment" (Duke University, 1978); Alan Banks, "Labor and the Development of Industrial Capitalism in Eastern Kentucky, 1870–1930" (McMasters University, 1980); Eugene Conti, "Mountain Metamorphosis: Culture and Development in East Kentucky" (Duke University, 1979); Richard Mark Simon, "The Development of Underdevelopment: The Coal Industry and Its Effects on the West Virginia Economy, 1880–1930" (University of Pittsburgh, 1978); Neil Tudiver, "Why Aid Doesn't Work" (University of Michigan, 1973); David S. Walls, "Central Appalachia in Advanced Capitalism: Its Coal Industry Structure and Coal Operator Associations" (University of Kentucky, 1978); and John C. Wells, Jr., "Poverty amidst Riches: Why People Are Poor in Appalachia" (Rutgers University, 1977).

31. For an overview of the origin and recent development of organized Appalachian studies, see A. Banks, D. Billings, and K. Tice, "Appalachian Studies, Resistance, and Postmodernism," in *Fighting Back in Appalachia: Traditions of Resistance and Change*, ed. S. Fisher (Philadelphia: Temple University Press, 1993), pp. 283–301.

32. The broad contours of this academic discourse are well represented by two special issues of the *Appalachian Journal*, S. Fisher, J. Williamson, and J. Lewis (eds.), "A Guide to Appalachian Studies," *Appalachian Journal* 5 (Autumn 1977): 1–192; and T. McGowan (ed.), "Assessing Appalachian Studies," *Appalachian Journal* 9 (Winter–Spring 1982): 1–242. Both issues include useful bibliographies as well.

33. A notable exception was Gordon McKinney's important political history *Southern Mountain Republicans, 1865–1900: Politics and the Appalachian Community* (Chapel Hill: University of North Carolina Press, 1978), which focused especially on the Appalachian sections of the Carolinas.

34. For an otherwise insightful work that essentializes Appalachian regionalism as a response to the coal industry, see A. Markusen, *Regions: The Economics and Politics of Territory* (Totowa, N.J.: Rowman and Littlefield, 1987).

35. This special issue, vol. 11, nos. 1–2, entitled "Essays in Political Economy: Towards a Class Analysis of Appalachia," was edited by the Southern Mountain Research Collective comprised of Alan Banks, Steve Fisher, Jim Foster, and Doug Gamble. Quotes are from the introduction, p. 19.

36. Social historians who examined class relations within the mountains rather than the history of their "colonization" also produced nuanced works that avoided the reification of Appalachia, such as D. Corbin, *Life, Work, and Rebellion in the Coal Fields: The Southern West Virginia Miners, 1880–1922* (Urbana: University of Illinois Press, 1981), and J. Hevener, *Which Side Are You On? The Harlan Coal Miners, 1931–1939* (Urbana: University of Illinois Press, 1978).

37. R. Eller, *Miners, Millhands, and Mountaineers: Industrialization of the Appalachian South, 1880–1930* (Knoxville: University of Tennessee Press, 1982).

38. Shapiro, *Appalachia on Our Mind*, p. 264.

39. The effort to avoid universalizing and essentializing interpretations of Appalachian experience that parallels the contributions in the present volume characterizes several recent studies of race and gender differences during both early industrialization and more recent labor struggles. See, for example, R. Lewis, *Black Coal Miners in America: Race, Class, and Community Conflict, 1780–1980* (Lexington: University Press of Kentucky, 1987); J. Trotter, Jr., *Coal, Class, and Color: Blacks in Southern West Virginia, 1915–1932* (Urbana: University of Illinois Press, 1990); M. Anglin, " 'A Lost and Dying World': Women's Labor in the Mica Industry of Southern Appalachia" (Ph.D. diss., New School for Social Research, 1990); S. W. Maggard, "Eastern Kentucky Women on Strike: A Study of Gender, Class, and Political Action in the 1970s" (Ph.D. diss., University of Kentucky, 1988). For other contributions to the preindustrial history of Appalachia, see R. D. Mitchell, ed., *Appalachian Frontiers: Settlement, Society, and Development in the Preindustrial Era* (Lexington: University Press of Kentucky, 1990).

40. See, esp., C. Clark, "Household Economy, Market Exchange, and the Rise of Capitalism in the Connecticut Valley, 1800–1860," *Journal of Social History* 13, no. 2

(Winter 1979): 169–90; J. A. Henretta, "Families and Farms: *Mentalite* in Prein-dustrial America," *William and Mary Quarterly*, 3rd ser., 35 (January 1978): 3–32; and M. Merrill, "Cash Is Good to Eat: Self-Sufficiency and Exchange in the Rural Economy in the United States," *Radical History Review* 3 (Winter 1977): 42–71.

41. Among the most influential studies was S. Hahn, *The Roots of Southern Populism: Yeoman Farmers and the Transformation of the Georgia Upcountry, 1850–1890* (New York: Oxford University Press, 1983), which examined the capitalist transformation of the Georgia piedmont during the last decades of the nineteenth century. Also see S. Hahn, "The Unmaking of the Southern Yeomanry," in *The Countryside in the Age of Capitalist Transformation: Essays in the Social History of Rural America*, ed. S. Hahn and J. Prude (Chapel Hill: University of North Carolina Press, 1985), pp. 179–203, as well as other contributions in the same collection.

42. For citations and an excellent critical overview of this literature, see A. Kuli-koff, "The Transition to Capitalism in Rural America," *William and Mary Quarterly*, 3rd ser., 46 (January 1989): 120–45.

43. A. Waller, *Feud: Hatfields, McCoys, and Social Change in Appalachia, 1860–1900* (Chapel Hill: University of North Carolina Press, 1988); D. Dunn, *Cades Cove: The Life and Death of a Southern Appalachian Community, 1818–1937* (Knoxville: University of Tennessee Press, 1988).

44. For historical research on family patterns, see T. Arcury and J. Porter, "House-hold Composition in Appalachian Kentucky in 1900," *Journal of Family History* 10 (1983): 183–95; T. Arcury, "Household Composition and Early Industrial Transfor-mation: Eastern Kentucky, 1880 to 1910," *Journal of the Appalachian Studies Associa-tion* 2 (1990): 47–68; D. Billings and K. Blee, "Family Strategies in a Subsistence Economy: Beech Creek, Kentucky, 1850–1942," *Sociological Perspectives* 33, no. 1 (1990): 63–88.

45. W. B. Rothenberg, "The Market and Massachusetts Farmers, 1750–1855," *Jour-nal of Economic History* 41 (1981): 283–314.

46. D. Billings, K. Blee, and L. Swanson, "Culture, Family, and Community in Preindustrial Appalachia," *Appalachian Journal* 13 (Winter 1986): 154–70. Salstrom's extensive critique and the authors' reply were published as letters to the editor in *Appalachian Journal* 13 (Summer 1986): 340–52.

47. G. McKinney, "Preindustrial Jackson County and Economic Development," *Journal of the Appalachian Studies Association* 2 (1990): 1–10.

48. Kulikoff, "Transition to Capitalism," p. 128.

49. Important recent examples include C. Baker, "East Tennessee within the World Economy, 1790–1850: Precapitalist Isolation or Peripheral Capitalism?," pa-per presented at the Appalachian Studies Conference, 1992, Western Carolina Uni-versity, Cullowhee, N.C.; H. T. Blethen and C. Wood, "The Antebellum Iron Indus-try in Western North Carolina," *Journal of the Appalachian Studies Association* 4 (1992): 79–87; M. Crawford, "The Farm Economy, the Market Economy, and Ante-bellum Social Relations in a Southern Mountain Community: Ashe County, North Carolina, 1850–1860," paper presented at the meeting of the Southern Historical Association, 1991, Fort Worth, Tex.; D. Hsiung, " 'Community' in Antebellum Ap-palachia: Upper East Tennessee, 1830–1860," paper presented at the meeting of the Appalachian Studies Association, March 1993, East Tennessee State University,

Johnson City; R. Mann, "Mountains, Land, and Kin Networks: Burkes Garden, Virginia, in the 1840s and 1850s," *Journal of Southern History* 58 (1992): 411–34; R. Weise, "Selling Mineral Rights in Floyd County, Kentucky," paper presented at the meeting of the Appalachian Studies Association, March 1993, East Tennessee State University, Johnson City; R. T. McKenzie, *One South or Many?: Plantation Belt and Upcountry in Civil War Era Tennessee* (New York: Cambridge University Press, 1995); and B. Rasmussen, *Absentee Landowning and Exploitation in West Virginia, 1760–1920* (Lexington: University Press of Kentucky, 1994); K. W. Noe, *Southwest Virginia's Railroad: Modernization and the Sectional Crisis* (Urbana: University of Illinois Press, 1994).

50. For a recent overview of poverty in Appalachian subregions, see D. Billings and A. Tickamyer, "Uneven Development in Appalachia," in *Forgotten Places: Uneven Development in Rural America*, ed. T. Lyson and W. Falk (Lawrence: University of Kansas Press, 1993), pp. 7–29.

51. D. Whisnant, "Second Level Appalachian History," *Appalachian Journal* 9 (Winter–Spring 1982): 115–23.

52. R. D. Mitchell, *Commercialism and Frontier: Perspectives on the Early Shenandoah Valley* (Charlottesville: University Press of Virginia, 1977); also see contributions in Mitchell, *Appalachian Frontiers.*

53. M. B. Pudup, "The Limits of Subsistence: Agriculture and Industry in Central Appalachia," *Agricultural History* 64 (1990): 61–89.

54. See, esp., Arnett, "Eastern Kentucky."

55. E. A. Conti, "The Cultural Role of Local Elites in the Kentucky Mountains: A Retrospective Analysis," *Appalachian Journal* 7 (Fall–Winter 1979–80): 51–68.

56. Although it erroneously depicts Mayo's career as "strange" and exceptional, see H. Caudill, *Theirs Be the Power: The Moguls of Eastern Kentucky* (Urbana: University of Illinois Press, 1983).

57. M. B. Pudup, "The Boundaries of Class in Preindustrial Appalachia," *Journal of Historical Geography* 15 (1989): 139–62; D. B. Billings and K. Blee, "Appalachian Inequality in the Nineteenth Century: The Case of Beech Creek, Kentucky," *Journal of the Appalachian Studies Association* 4 (1992): 113–23.

58. J. A. Williams, *West Virginia and the Captains of Industry* (Morgantown: West Virginia University Library, 1976); J. Inscoe, *Mountain Masters: Slavery and the Sectional Crisis in Western North Carolina* (Knoxville: University of Tennessee Press, 1989); McKinney, *Southern Mountain Republicans.*

Cherokee Accommodation and Persistence in the Southern Appalachians

Cherokee Indians have lived in the southern Appalachians longer than any other people, and for them the nineteenth century represents an especially important transition. Those 100 years opened with a remarkable "civilization" program, continued in the next generation with deportation of the tribal majority, witnessed efforts by the remnant Indians to retain both their lands and their culture, and concluded with a growing accommodation to the dominant white culture and a changing economy. Throughout these experiences the Cherokees displayed a remarkable ability to adapt—indeed, to incorporate necessary changes into their society—amid a cultural continuity and self-identification separating them from whites and blacks. Their presence and cultural persistence made the southern Appalachians a truly triracial society.[1]

Although Cherokee military resistance to white expansion had ended less than a decade before, by 1800 the approximately 16,000 tribal members were already adjusting to the dictates of the federal government.[2] A new civilization program was in effect that encouraged (even coerced) tribes to adopt white economic, social, cultural, and religious models. The Indian was to become a white person with red skin. Government agents and missionaries sponsored by various religious denominations labored to convince Indians that to survive in an expanding America it was necessary to become a Jeffersonian yeoman, to forsake the tribal identity.[3]

Though the civilization program had only limited success among most tribes, reformers delighted in chronicling Cherokee progress toward the normative standards of white society. Changing gender roles were one manifestation of this. Cherokee females, like middle-class white women, were encouraged to conform to a "Cult of True Womanhood" that reduced their earlier, more varied roles and exalted them as homemakers and keepers of the family hearth. They no longer had primary responsibility for agriculture and instead spent more time practicing domestic arts like spinning and weaving. Female participation in tribal politics, common in earlier days, dwindled while traditional matrilineal and matrilocal features blurred as Cherokees moved toward a patrilineal society shaped by acculturated males. These new circumstances imposed limitations and new expectations on men as well as women. Cherokee males could no longer take to the warpath, practice blood revenge, or even hunt as often as before, and the more civilized of them increasingly labored in the fields like white yeomen.[4]

Cherokee domiciles and patterns of landholding also changed. By the 1820s most tribal members no longer lived in well-defined villages but as nuclear families scattered along creek and river valleys in log cabins very much like those of nearby whites.[5] Their agriculture was mostly at the subsistence level. In contrast, Cherokee elites, consisting of acculturated mixed-bloods and a few full-bloods, lived in large frame or stone homes comparable to those of their most prosperous white neighbors. Their dual role as Cherokees and planters offered an obvious advantage, for the tribe allowed members to occupy and cultivate as much tribal land as they wished without the irksome necessity of purchasing it. Like their white counterparts, these elites relied on black slaves to produce cotton and corn for a growing regional market. By 1835 tribal members owned more than 1,500 slaves, with a disproportionate number belonging to elites.[6] Many Indians, elites and commoners alike, also raised livestock, and cattle drives from tribal lands to regional towns like Knoxville were not uncommon.[7]

Cherokee leaders appreciated at least the secular aspects of schools operated by various Protestant denominations, but many Indians of all ranks staunchly opposed white religious indoctrination. Methodist and Baptist missionary-teachers concentrated their efforts in the mountainous parts of North Carolina and Georgia, while other denominations chiefly ministered to the more economically advanced and acculturated Indians of Georgia and southeastern Tennessee. By the 1830s there was a growing number of converts, partly because some Christian practices correlated nicely with traditional Cherokee religious rites.[8]

Many Cherokees readily acknowledged the utility of reading and writing English, while others viewed such instruction as a form of cultural imperialism that threatened traditional society. After years of labor Sequoyah, a mixed-blood conservative, completed a Cherokee syllabary in 1821 that enabled many in the tribe to read and write in their own language. By 1828 there was even a tribal newspaper, the *Cherokee Phoenix*, published in both English and Cherokee. In an effort to turn this literacy to their own advantage, white missionaries soon published Christian texts in the syllabary. Even though the number of Cherokees who could read in their own language was still well below 20 percent in 1835, more than half of all households had a member who could read either Cherokee or English.[9]

The early nineteenth century also witnessed a growing trend toward centralized political authority within the tribe, culminating in 1827 with adoption of a written constitution for the Cherokee Nation; this document was modeled on that of the United States and several southern states. The principal chief, whose powers were analogous to those of a president, was John Ross, only one-eighth Cherokee in blood and the descendant of a Scottish trader.[10] Legislative and judicial bodies (and a series of tribal laws) also reflected the influence of white America.

Impressive as these changes were, they hardly defined Cherokee society of the early nineteenth century and must be viewed with caution. The missionaries and other whites on whose accounts we chiefly rely were enthusiastic about tribal "progress" and generally ignored or downplayed a continuing traditionalism. As late as 1835 females still headed at least one-third of all Cherokee households, and many no doubt continued traditional functions like "farming, supervising an extended household, caring for children and kinsmen, and perhaps even exercising some power in local councils."[11] Throughout the Cherokee Nation people practiced a cultural syncretism that blended familiar ways of life with the new.[12] Within the white-introduced institution of livestock raising, for example, Cherokee patterns varied widely depending on location and the persistence of traditional gender roles. Along the Tennessee River, mixed-blood male elites developed a planter/rancher form of herding derived from Spanish, British, and Creek influences that was "oriented toward extensive, commercial production of beef cattle."[13] This kind of herding incorporated certain features of the earlier hunting tradition—like intimate knowledge of the terrain and comparative freedom to roam—and thus "acted as a transition to a market-based economy."[14]

In contrast, ordinary Cherokees living in more mountainous areas adopted the upland South pattern of subsistence farming-herding. Here, in areas such as western North Carolina, females easily incorporated ownership of livestock into their traditional roles as owners of the family home and fields.[15] Here, "the look of the land was more traditional, and the farmstead was still to a large extent a woman's domain."[16] Women, in fact, subtly resisted changes in their status as primary agricultural providers, and the continuing mythic story of Selu, the corn-mother, reinforced this role.[17] Basketry, the most prevalent Cherokee craft, also remained a female domain and featured familiar materials, patterns, dyes, and techniques of weaving.[18]

The circumscribed nature of Cherokee change is apparent in other ways as well. In the mountain districts the inroads of Christianity were not so pronounced, despite the efforts of Baptist missionary Evan Jones.[19] Clan identification and prohibitions against marriage within the clan continued, along with traditional ceremonies and contests like stickball. Even though these remote areas were part of the Cherokee Nation's legislative districts, it is not clear to what extent ordinary Indians living there paid attention to tribal politics. Even among the more civilized areas of the Cherokee Nation, the transition from the autonomous village structure to a centralized government was in part simply an adoption of an Anglo-American institutional structure as a means of preserving tribal autonomy against the demands of white-dominated state and federal governments. As William G. McLoughlin and Walter H. Conser, Jr., observe, "What was taken by contemporary white observers as 'civilization' was simply the acquisition of sufficient skills for economic survival and for political self-government—part of a conscious strategy to resist removal and maintain autonomy."[20]

The whites who came closest to understanding that Cherokee "progress" was a means of preserving tribal autonomy were the political leaders of southern states such as Georgia. Governor George R. Gilmer and others correctly perceived that Cherokee assertion of nationhood was a challenge to Georgia's own sovereignty and that state's future expansion. Local whites were also at least partially correct when they argued that the Cherokee Nation was primarily the creation of wealthy, acculturated Indians who wished to preserve their economic position at the expense of more traditional Cherokees. The economic disparity between Cherokee political leaders and the rest of tribal society, and the periodic resistance of traditionalists to these changes suggest as much.[21] Thus Cherokee civilization of the early nineteenth century must be seen as a multifaceted phenomenon incorporating progress and traditionalism at the same time and existing in different degrees in different areas of the Cherokee Nation.

Whatever the extent of acculturation among Cherokees, many white southerners found their continued presence an intolerable obstacle to state expansion. By the 1820s, despite numerous land cessions and the voluntary removal of a sizable tribal minority, the Cherokee Nation still retained a block of thousands of square miles in western North Carolina, southeastern Tennessee, northern Georgia, and northeastern Alabama. Tribal claims to nationhood, moreover, exacerbated white animosity by challenging growing southern notions of state sovereignty. By the time of Andrew Jackson's election in 1828, citizens of Georgia were clamoring for removal of the Creeks and Cherokees from the bounds of that state. Before long the state simply ignored federal treaties by appropriating and reorganizing Cherokee lands as counties, distributing those lands in lotteries, and rejecting all authority claimed by the Cherokee Nation. Other southern states, though less forceful, also advocated Indian removal. The general assembly of North Carolina, for example, ignored recent changes in Cherokee society and informed Congress that "the red men are not under the restraints of morality, nor the influence of religion; and they are always disagreeable and dangerous neighbors to a civilized people."[22] With passage of a removal bill in 1830, Congress was committed to the negotiation of new treaties whereby tribes would exchange their eastern homelands for new homes west of the Mississippi River.[23]

Principal Chief John Ross and other Cherokee leaders used all their political wiles in trying to block removal, and they enlisted considerable popular and congressional support, but all to no avail. Federal agents played upon growing divisions among the Cherokees themselves and in December 1835 "negotiated" the fraudulent Treaty of New Echota with a small minority of tribal leaders.[24] Despite Ross's attempts to prevent its ratification, the United States Senate approved the treaty in May 1836. Within two years some 16,000 members of the Cherokee Nation would have to vacate their homeland and move to present-day Oklahoma. Still the tribal majority refused to move. In the spring of 1838 federal troops and state militia systematically scoured the nation, rounded up peaceable Cherokees by the thousands, and incarcerated them in makeshift stockades to await deportation. Despite Gen. Winfield Scott's orders that removal be carried out with all humanity and respect for the Indians, abuses inevitably occurred. Cherokees died in droves, both in stockades and on the trek westward over the Trail of Tears.[25]

The tragedy of removal has received so much scholarly and popular attention that many whites assume Cherokee habitation in the southern Appalachians ended in 1838. But approximately 1,400 Indians remained as scattered isolates, the majority residing in western North Carolina, where after the Civil War they and their descendants would coalesce into the Eastern Band of Cherokees and receive federal recognition as a distinct tribe. Like many other tribes, the Eastern Band has a creation myth explaining its origins—in this case its seemingly providential escape from deportation. The central figure in this story is Tsali, an aging Cherokee whose wife was supposedly abused by federal troops during the removal roundup. Enraged, Tsali killed two soldiers and escaped with his family into the mountains. General Scott was determined to avenge this act but appreciated the difficulty of finding the fugitives in such rugged terrain. So, the story goes, he worked out a deal. In exchange for apprehending Tsali and his family, the other fugitive Cherokees could stay in their beloved homeland. When informed of this, Tsali decided to avoid the ignominy of having his own people track him down and surrendered to face certain execution. His sacrifice, then, enabled many fellow North Carolina Cherokees to remain.

The facts concerning Tsali differ somewhat from the hagiography, but the real import of this story is on the symbolic and mythic level. Tsali is a readily understandable and wholly legitimate symbol of the Cherokees' attachment to their homeland.[26] As hagiography and creation myth the tale is unique only in that it has become embodied in "Unto These Hills," an enormously popular outdoor pageant staged every summer in the town of Cherokee, North Carolina. Since its debut in 1950 it has attracted some 5 million paying customers.

One of the disadvantages—or virtues—of creation myths is that they reduce complex causality to simple faith and certitude, but the true story of the North Carolina Cherokees is somewhat more difficult to unravel. In 1839 about 700 Cherokees lived around Quallatown (near present-day Cherokee) in the mountainous western part of the state. Some of these people were related to fifty-one individuals who had taken advantage of treaties in 1817 and 1819 to separate from the Cherokee Nation and live on private reservations outside the tribal domain. By the time of removal most of these "citizen" Indians clustered near Quallatown under the leadership of Yonaguska (Drowning Bear), their head man or chief.[27] According to Gregory Dowd, Yonaguska was one of the few successful Indian nativists of the period. Unlike Tecumseh and other famous warrior-nativists, Yonaguska led a nonviolent resistance to removal and white domination; like Handsome Lake among the Senecas of New York, he was able, with the assistance of a few sympathetic whites, to fashion a limited Cherokee autonomy within an increasingly powerful Anglo-American context. Like Handsome Lake, he escaped the degradation of alcohol by falling into a deathlike trance and awakening a changed man, describing his visit to the spirit land and preaching a message of guidance to his people: avoid alcohol and Christian missionaries and never forsake the Cherokee homeland.[28]

Though their precise legal status was unclear, Yonaguska's Quallatown Indians claimed to be citizens of the state of North Carolina and therefore entitled to remain; they also pointed to a clause in the Treaty of New Echota that allowed certain "qualified" Cherokees to stay. Defending their interests was William Holland Thomas, a white merchant and adopted son of Yonaguska. Fluent in Cherokee and well versed in the law, Thomas worked assiduously to convince state and federal authorities of the right of these Indians to remain.[29] For many years he would be an effective broker between the two races. That his adoptive kinsmen were inoffensive, living on marginal lands, and a convenient source of labor for neighboring whites also worked to their advantage. Thus a variety of factors protected the original Quallatown inhabitants from the army's roundup in 1838, and General Scott was careful to distinguish between them and the Cherokee majority subject to removal. When he attempted to persuade them it was in their best interests to join the emigrants anyway, Yonaguska replied that if they moved to Indian country, the whites would soon want their new lands, too. It was best for his people to remain.[30]

Unlike these longtime residents, many Cherokees living in Quallatown in 1839 were recent refugees from the Cherokee Nation. Some had certificates of qualification to remain and had openly moved to Quallatown, but others lacked such documentation and had simply hidden in the mountains until the army left in November 1838. Col. William S. Foster, commander of the departing troops, in effect admitted his lack of complete success by encouraging the remaining fugitives to join their brothers in Quallatown. As far as the economy-minded War Department was concerned, its role in removal had ended.[31]

Besides the 700 people at Quallatown, another 400 or so North Carolina Cherokees lived in scattered clusters along the Hiwassee, Valley, and Cheoah Rivers, mostly in present-day Cherokee and Graham Counties.[32] Like their brethren in Quallatown, the Cheoah people (today's Snowbird Community) were almost entirely full-bloods and among the least acculturated of all Cherokees. The Indians living along the Valley and Hiwassee Rivers were more heterogeneous, ranging from staunch, full-blood traditionalists to highly acculturated mixed-bloods and Cherokees by marriage.

Perhaps another 300 or more Cherokees lived in nearby areas of Georgia, Alabama, and Tennessee. These included a number of mixed-bloods and whites who had married into the tribe. They often owned their own land, sometimes kept a few slaves, and in general were much more acculturated than their North Carolina kinsmen.[33] A few could be counted among the Cherokee aristocracy. In December 1838 the State of Georgia even granted full rights of citizenship to twenty-two of these families, which "shared a mixed ancestry, affluence, and educational level common to the Cherokee elite."[34] But many other southern Appalachian residents of lesser status remained silent about their Indian ancestry and quietly "passed" for whites. Not until the twentieth century would their descendants proudly proclaim their mixed heritage.

The most pressing need of the North Carolina Cherokees was to secure an adequate land base, and here William Thomas proved invaluable. As early as 1836 he began purchasing thousands of acres of mountain land for the Quallatown people, using his own funds as well as small amounts from the Indians themselves. Later he performed the same service for the Cheoah Cherokees. The Indians would repay him from funds owed them by the United States under the 1835 treaty and that Thomas himself intended to collect as their attorney. Despite what some scholars have claimed, Indians could legally own property (indeed, a few did), but Thomas kept almost all of these properties in his own name—both as collateral for the funds he had spent and as a supposed safeguard against the Indians being dispossessed. When Yonaguska died in 1839, Thomas became de facto chief of the Quallatown Cherokees. He also had frequent contact with those at Cheoah, but other whites and mixed-bloods competed with him for influence among the Indians living along the Valley and Hiwassee Rivers.[35]

The Cherokees had elected to remain in North Carolina in an effort to preserve a society that in many respects was traditional and, in the eyes of whites, nonprogressive. Citizenship would presumably allow them to live as they pleased. North Carolina, however, refused to recognize them as citizens or even to affirm explicitly their right to remain; on the other hand, it did not bother to deny their claims, either. So in an effort to persuade the state to confirm their rights, the Cherokees found it expedient to emphasize their acculturation and civilization rather than their traditionalism. William Thomas, their mentor and broker with white society, devised this strategy and followed it consistently, especially while serving as a prominent state politician from the late 1840s to the Civil War. The Indians willingly followed him and his plan for a full generation.[36]

Thomas portrayed the Indians as Jeffersonian yeomen, model citizens of

North Carolina living in bucolic and self-sufficient splendor. In 1845 he said that all 781 residents of Quallatown were agriculturalists, including a number of skilled artisans who made plows, gunstocks, and barrels for whites and Indians alike. The Quallatown people were hardworking, healthy, and, in stark contrast to the degradation of many other Indians by alcohol, thriving under a temperance society created by the late Yonaguska. According to Thomas there was not a single drunkard at Quallatown and only about eight individuals who ever used alcohol of any kind—helping to explain why there had not been a murder or even a simple assault among residents in recent years.[37]

Many people believed Christianizing the Cherokees was a necessary corollary for civilizing them, and the diligent Thomas nudged his kinsmen toward piety by importing Cherokee bibles and hymnals from the West (about one-fifth of the Quallatown population could read and write Cherokee). White preachers occasionally visited, and the Methodist Episcopal Church established a mission there. Soon there were several native preachers as well, one of whom impressed Whig journalist Charles Lanman when he visited in 1848. Lanman attended a service with about 150 mostly female worshipers and found their conduct "as circumspect and solemn as I have ever witnessed in any New England religious assembly.... Their form of worship was according to the Methodist custom, but in their singing there was a wild and plaintive sweetness which was very impressive." The preacher, "in dwelling upon the marvellous love of the Saviour, and the great wickedness of the world," was "affected to tears, and when he concluded there was hardly a dry eye in the house."[38]

Such pious decorum could be misleading, however, for the Cherokees creatively blended the more satisfying aspects of Christianity with traditional beliefs and rituals. Like rural white southerners, they could be "absolutely fiends" in their emotions and gesticulations at camp meetings and revivals. Another example of their religious syncretism was the way a man such as Enola (Black Fox) could be a shaman one day, invoking traditional incantations, and a hellfire preacher the next. The Cherokees, at least, saw no inconsistency in this. After the Civil War they increasingly preferred the loosely structured Baptist denomination because it was the primary religious affiliation of neighboring whites, it offered maximum congregational freedom, and its baptism by immersion resembled traditional "going to the water" purification rituals.[39]

The Indians across the state line in the Ducktown Basin of Polk County, Tennessee, provide another example of this cultural syncretism. During removal they had all either emigrated to the West or joined the North

Carolina Cherokees at Quallatown, Cheoah, or Valley River. By the early 1850s, however, twelve Cherokee households (numbering thirty-four people) were back in the basin; all had at least one member who had lived there before removal. They operated small subsistence farms, worked as day laborers for nearby whites, or cut cordwood for the furnaces at the Ducktown copper mines. In 1851 five of them joined a predominantly white Baptist church and, "despite the language barrier and some cultural miscommunications," they and most of the other native-speaking Cherokees enjoyed its fellowship for some forty years. "One man was ordained to minister to his fellow Cherokees and another represented the church at several association meetings." Despite increasing interaction with whites, "marriage customs, matrilineal residence patterns, and native language use continued" well after the Civil War.[40]

In North Carolina as well as in Tennessee, Cherokee relations with their neighbors were generally good, and Thomas, leaving nothing to chance, frequently enlisted white support of his adoptive kinsmen. In 1842, almost certainly at his instigation, a number of residents testified to the general assembly that the Quallatown Indians were temperate, industrious, and following the road to civilization. No doubt part of this testimonial was due to the Cherokees' availability for menial labor and the fact that Thomas made certain they would never presume too much in the way of social intercourse. Indeed, the seeming amity hardly obscured the fact that some local whites were condescending toward the Indians and did not view them as permanent neighbors. One man claimed that "the best understanding exists" between the two races but that a treaty to "provide for the removal of the Cherokees West in a friendly way at some future day as they may desire to go, after the old & infirm are no more, would give Satisfaction Generally."[41]

One complicating factor in Indian-white relations was the number of Cherokees returning to North Carolina from Oklahoma. In 1843 a special legislative committee expressed fear that western North Carolina would become a haven not only for those with a legal right to remain but for the "refuse" of the Cherokee Nation. In the opinion of the committee, "The mixing of these people with our white population must have a demoralizing influence which ought to be resisted by all the means within our power." It supported a new Indian removal, but the state senate tabled its report; clearly North Carolina did not view removal as a pressing issue.[42] Just as clearly, the Cherokees were not going to leave voluntarily. A federal attempt between 1841 and 1844 to persuade them to emigrate failed dismally, the victim of passive Cherokee resistance, the machinations of William Thomas, and the government's own penuriousness. Another attempt in the mid-1850s also collapsed.[43]

To buttress their claims of citizenship, the North Carolina Cherokees dutifully paid property taxes, worked on public roads, and assumed other civic responsibilities. They were careful, however, not to offend whites by demanding some of the normal perquisites of citizenship such as voting, serving in the militia, or sitting on juries. They well understood that they ranked below whites in the social hierarchy of the southern Appalachians and simply wished to live in their homeland as unobtrusively as possible. They staked out a middle ground between whites and blacks in that triracial society. The growing racial paranoia among whites following Nat Turner's 1831 slave uprising helped produce an ambivalence toward Indians: "Their place in southern race relations was undefined. The Lumbees of southeastern North Carolina might be treated as blacks (or near blacks) because of their uncertain ancestry, but the Cherokees were defiantly, unquestionably, *Indians*. What should be done with them? Perhaps it was best not to define their status too precisely but to leave it ambiguous."[44]

In general, Cherokees looked with disfavor on blacks and refused to associate with them, perhaps because they feared being classified by whites as "colored" or mulattoes. In 1859 one local council attempting to regularize Cherokee marriages specifically prohibited intermarriage with blacks.[45] Despite such obstacles, Indians did sometimes intermingle, cohabit, and even intermarry with free blacks and slaves. In fact, one of William Thomas's slaves acted as a kind of magistrate and performed several marriages between his people and the Cherokees. Census takers from the Indian Office expressed bafflement about whether to include the offspring of such liaisons on the Cherokee rolls; the Indians themselves, in accordance with their matrilineal traditions, usually recognized only those whose mother was of Cherokee blood.[46]

By the time of the Civil War, Cherokee society in North Carolina was a blend of traditional and white-influenced life. Cherokees resided as nuclear families in log cabins and practiced an agriculture much like that of their poorer white neighbors. Each family cultivated a few acres of corn and vegetables, kept a small orchard of apple and peach trees, and allowed livestock to roam freely in the mountains. Hunting and fishing added variety to their diet, and in 1844 alone the Quallatown Indians killed 540 deer, 78 bears, 18 wolves, and 2 panthers. (It appears, however, that hunting steadily declined in importance through the rest of the century.) For other necessities the Indians bartered corn, animal hides, ginseng, or their labor.[47]

Though Thomas avidly espoused Cherokee acculturation, he inadvertently—and of necessity—promoted traditionalism. By purchasing large blocks of marginal land as a restored homeland for the Indians, he forced them to cluster more closely together, to live as tribal communities apart from their white neighbors. To ensure good order and a degree of autonomy he also divided the Quallatown Indians into three communities named for Cherokee clans: Bird Town, Wolf Town and Paint Town. Later there would be two more—Big Cove and Yellow Hill (present-day Cherokee). In the early years residents met in council houses and deliberated over matters of mutual concern. Their chiefs had considerable influence but no coercive authority; in matters concerning relations with whites, they usually deferred to Thomas. The traditional "harmony ethic"—the striving for consensus—continued, and one white who attended such a meeting was dumbfounded that 300 to 400 Indians could deliberate without argument.[48] Before the Civil War there was little of the factionalism found among the more acculturated Cherokee Nation in the West.

Many other facets of life reveal the Cherokees' cultural conservatism. In Quallatown and Cheoah only a few people could speak English, and many could not even read the Cherokee syllabary. Education consisted of occasional visits by itinerant pedagogues employed by Thomas or, more commonly, one Indian informally instructing another in the syllabary. Economic cooperation continued in the form of the *gadugi*, an institution defined as "a group of men who join together to form a company, with rules and officers, for continued economic and social reciprocity." An outgrowth of early communal activities, the *gadugi* coexisted and overlapped with the council government of Wolf Town (and perhaps some other communities) and was involved in such things as clearing fields, constructing buildings, making loans, and burying the dead. It would continue to evolve through the nineteenth and twentieth centuries.[49]

Other reminders of the Cherokee past abounded. Clan affiliation continued, as did traditional ceremonies and rituals like the Green Corn Dance, which marked the beginning of the Cherokee new year and coincided with the ripening of crops. Despite Thomas's attempts to regularize Cherokee marriages, husbands and wives easily united and drifted apart without formal vows. An Indian wedding "in the white fashion" was unusual enough to appear in Thomas's diary.[50] Conjurors still invoked ancient incantations, and one young man, Swimmer, was learning traditional lore at the knees of his elders and recording it in the Cherokee syllabary. To that extent, at least, literacy in Cherokee was as much a conservator of traditionalism as a step toward white civilization. By the end of the nineteenth century Swimmer would be a famous shaman whose notebooks represented a treasure trove for anthropologists.[51]

Perhaps the most dramatic manifestation of traditional Cherokee life was the ballplay or stickball, a contest that had been widespread in aboriginal America and that was much like today's lacrosse. For the Cherokees and other southeastern tribes the ballplay had tremendous import, serving as a means of resolving disagreements among towns and occasioning great ceremonialism. For spectators it was a dress-up affair for socializing and gambling. The contest itself was so rough and violent that Cherokees referred to it as the "little brother of war." Charles Lanman witnessed one contest in the 1840s and said "it often seemed as if the players would break every bone in their bodies as they threw each other in the air, or dragged each other over the ground. . . . The exercise was of a character that would kill the majority of white men."[52] Whites of all social classes joined the Indians as eager spectators, giving the shrewd William Thomas an opportunity to do some politicking.

Cherokee basketry offers another perspective on tribal adaptability within a traditional context. Women continued to practice this ancient craft, but it is possible some men also participated. Stripped of most of its sacred overtones, basket making increasingly became a source of income for some families as they catered to local white markets in Tennessee and North Carolina. Rivercane was still the most common material, but Indians were beginning to emulate white basketmakers by using white oak splits and adding handles and lids. African American and Choctaw Indian influences also may have been present. Otherwise the craft featured traditional dyes, doubleweave techniques, and designs that varied according to area of residence and "clan, family, or community traditions."[53] The craft continued to evolve so that by the end of the century readily available commercial dyes were used more often than natural pigments. Through their basketry, Cherokee women were both conservators of tribal tradition and bridges to white stylistic and market preferences.[54]

For the Cherokees, as for many whites in western North Carolina, the Civil War was a disaster. William Thomas became a staunch secessionist and as commander of his own military unit, the Thomas Legion of Indians and Highlanders, at one time or another mustered most of the able-bodied Cherokee males into Confederate service.[55] During the early part of the war they were stationed in East Tennessee on guard duty or pursuing bushwhackers and deserters. By late 1863 the federal takeover of Knoxville had driven the legion back into western North Carolina, where whites and

Indians alike suffered unprecedented privation. Thomas lamented that some of his Indian troops and their families were "in a starving condition"; women and children were even reduced to gnawing on the bark of trees or eating weeds to survive. A few Cherokees moved into nearby areas of Georgia and South Carolina, where conditions were not so desperate.[56]

Even amid such trying circumstances, Cherokee troops received high praise from Thomas and other Confederate officers for their devotion to duty. Their one lapse from exemplary service occurred when a few warriors, enraged by the death of an Indian officer, scalped several dead and wounded Yankee soldiers. Predictably, Unionists resorted to an old, demeaning stereotype by portraying them as bloodthirsty and "long-haired, greasy-looking savages who could not even speak a word of English, or understand a plea for mercy."[57] Andrew Johnson, the staunch Unionist from Tennessee, delivered an address in New York City in which he overdramatized the plight of southern Unionists by saying, "Women are now insulted, children murdered, fathers and sons chased and hunted in the woods by red Indians, who cut off their ears and show them as trophies."[58]

Not all Cherokees supported the Confederacy. At least one switched to the Union side because he was married to a slave, while others became discontented with the South for less specific reasons. Some, living near the Valley and Hiwassee Rivers where there was less loyalty to Thomas, had been pro-Union from the outset. In the Ducktown Basin of East Tennessee, local Indians mainly sided with the Union, "although a few soldiers fought on both sides."[59] Perhaps as many as thirty Cherokees served with the Third North Carolina Mounted Infantry Volunteers, a Union outfit, and participated in a bold raid from Tennessee deep into North Carolina in June 1864. Such Indians sometimes referred to Confederate Cherokees as Anighisgi, a people in tribal lore who were mortal enemies. After the war the prosouthern majority retaliated by vilifying or even murdering the former Unionists.[60] The old days of harmony and consensus were gone forever.

The afflictions besetting the Cherokees at the end of the war were almost biblical in scope: fields in ruin; landholdings in jeopardy; a smallpox epidemic that claimed about 125 lives; inadequate nutrition, housing, and education; an increasing resort to alcohol; and the disappearance of a consensual society. Factionalism was now rampant, in part because of the divisiveness of war but mostly because of William Thomas's decline. Now past sixty years of age and discredited for having led the Indians into a losing war, Thomas faced mounting financial distress and recurring mental illness. Prominent and not-so-prominent mixed-bloods eagerly competed to fill this vacuum of leadership and led rival delegations of supplicants to Raleigh and Washington seeking help.[61]

The State of North Carolina could offer little assistance, but in 1866 for the first time it explicitly affirmed the Cherokees' right to remain—no doubt partly as a reward for their loyalty in the late war.[62] Left unsaid, however, was whether the Indians were citizens. The United States government was more supportive. In July 1868, after considering the problems attending a voluntary move by the North Carolina Indians to Oklahoma, Congress finally recognized them as a distinct tribe (soon to be called the Eastern Band of Cherokee Indians).[63] The Bureau of Indian Affairs within the Department of Interior would supervise their affairs and, the Indians hoped, provide vital assistance. The Cherokees were ecstatic because government recognition and guardianship confirmed their distinctive place in southern Appalachia.

In December 1868, without authorization from the Indian bureau, supporters of George Bushyhead, a mixed-blood, held an impromptu council at Cheoah and drew up a rudimentary constitution. Under its provisions Bushyhead was elected council chairman and was therefore entitled to call himself principal chief. In 1870 the Cheoah council replaced Bushyhead with another man, only to confront a rival faction at Quallatown that drafted its own constitution and elected Flying Squirrel, a full-blood, as chief. For the next few years the two groups vied with each other for legitimacy, but when Lloyd R. Welch succeeded Flying Squirrel in 1875, the Quallatown Indians gained ascendancy. Though its leaders were predominantly mixed-bloods, they shrewdly attended to the concerns of the full-blood majority.[64]

Meanwhile William Thomas's financial problems posed a major threat to the tribe. Heavily in debt, he held most of their lands in his own name—in part, ironically, to safeguard them. When his major creditor seized those properties in 1869, some dispirited Indians left to join their kinsmen in Oklahoma. Fortunately, amid lengthy and complex legal proceedings, the United States government helped the Eastern Band piece together a reservation. The largest tract, consisting of the Quallatown settlements, was called Qualla Boundary. The reservation also included numerous outlying tracts encompassing today's Snowbird Community in Graham County and the Indians of Cherokee County. By 1900 the reservation contained roughly 96,000 acres—about 78,000 acres on the Qualla Boundary and 18,000 in outlying tracts.[65]

Despite assuming guardianship over the Eastern Band in 1868, the federal

Map 1.1. Approximate Landholdings of the Eastern Band of Cherokee Indians, 1900

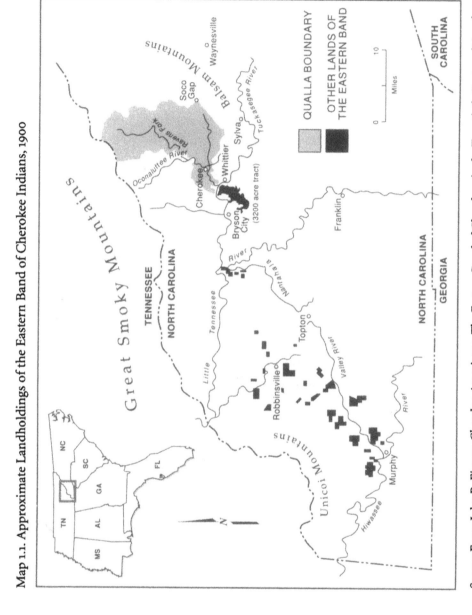

Source: From John R. Finger, *Cherokee Americans: The Eastern Band of Cherokees in the Twentieth Century* (Lincoln: University of Nebraska Press, 1991); reprinted by permission of the publishers.

government exercised a mixed or concurrent jurisdiction with the State of North Carolina. This was partly because the courts had never determined the exact legal status of the Cherokees. Were they, for example, citizens? In many respects the state treated them as such by collecting their taxes, trying them in state courts, and allowing them to vote (it apparently had gerrymandered Swain and Jackson Counties to reduce their political influence). In 1889 it also asserted its authority by establishing the Eastern Band as a state corporation and later amended and extended this act to create a new system of tribal government. In 1897, however, a federal circuit court undermined state authority by declaring that members of the Eastern Band were noncitizen wards of the federal government. North Carolina used this decision to justify denying the vote to Cherokees, but otherwise it continued to claim joint jurisdiction until a series of court decisions after World War II upheld the supremacy and plenary nature of federal jurisdiction.[66]

Systematic Cherokee education began in 1876, when William McCarthy, the first resident federal agent, established four day schools on Qualla Boundary and a boarding school at Cheoah. But McCarthy faced a multitude of problems in educating the Indians, especially the poverty of his students: "Scarcely any have shoes, and many of both sexes are nearly naked," he noted.[67] When McCarthy could not produce immediate results, the government quickly closed the schools and instead sent promising Cherokee students to board at nearby "academies" and "colleges" that were little more than glorified grammar schools. Some of these institutions were desperate for warm bodies and actually bid for the opportunity to educate Indians. The president of Weaverville College, for example, promised to board, educate, and clothe up to twelve Cherokees for ten months at $150 each; he emphasized, however, that this did not include costs of medical attention or burial.[68]

It appears that Cherokee students generally behaved themselves and made about as much progress as other pupils. Males had a mixed curriculum of academic, agricultural, and mechanical instruction, while female students spent most of their time sewing and learning other domestic skills. Convincing Cherokee parents to allow their children to go away for such education was often difficult, and some of the students themselves were so unhappy in those strange surroundings that they ran away. Most, according to one agent, were eventually "captured." On one occasion a drunken Cherokee father appeared at an academy and withdrew his child over the protests of the teachers and principal—having resorted to liquor, perhaps, to overcome a traditional Cherokee reluctance to give offense, especially to whites.[69]

Because the government recognized the desirability of reestablishing reservation schools, it agreed in 1881 to a ten-year contract with the Quakers to provide an educational program on Qualla Boundary. Quakers had long been interested in Indian education and since the Civil War had become a powerful force in advocating reform of Indian policy. Contracting with Christian denominations, moreover, was common at that time because the Indian bureau lacked its own comprehensive educational program. The Quakers operated a large boarding school for boys and girls in present-day Cherokee until 1892, when the federal government reassumed educational responsibility.[70]

Despite the best efforts of government agents and Quaker teachers, only a minority of Cherokee children attended school in the late nineteenth century. Most were still native speakers who at best learned English as a second language. Some who did attend eventually matriculated at out-of-state schools such as Hampton Institute in Virginia or Carlisle Institute in Pennsylvania, where about 132 Eastern Cherokees studied between 1879 and 1914. Federally sponsored education was clearly superior to that available to neighboring white and black children, yet the Cherokees, like other Indians, often found it of little value on a reservation where there were no jobs; some returnees from Carlisle and Hampton drifted into alcohol abuse.[71]

Cherokee agriculture offered little hope for economic advancement and in certain respects even declined in the late nineteenth century. Only about 10 to 15 percent of the rugged, forested reservation was suited to farming, and a significant part of that was pasturage. According to knowledgeable visitors, the agriculture of both poor whites and Indians was hidebound and primitive, constrained by ignorance, environment, and inadequate financial resources. Cherokees typically planted with a hoe or cut a few shallow furrows with an oxen-drawn, bull-tongue plow. Like many of their white neighbors, they still fenced just a few acres of crops and allowed their livestock (nearly all of inferior quality) to roam freely through forests and mountain meadows. Whites and Indians alike seldom pruned or otherwise took care of their apple and peach trees. Other problems included soil exhaustion, periodic insect infestations, and erosion caused by cultivation of slopes of thirty-five degrees or more. Efforts to encourage better agriculture through instruction at the boarding school and its demonstration farm were largely unsuccessful. Cherokee farming remained at best a subsistence occupation, supplemented by informal barter exchanges and occasional wage labor.[72]

By the 1880s the "Cherokee" population in the southern Appalachians had shifted and become more heterogeneous. Since the Civil War, several hundred Indians had taken advantage of federal assistance and moved to Oklahoma. By 1884, according to a special census, 2,956 Cherokees remained east of the Mississippi—1,881 in North Carolina, 738 in Georgia, 213 in Tennessee, and 71 in Alabama.[73] Many of the individuals listed had only a trace of Cherokee blood, and probably less than 1,300 qualified as members of the Eastern Band. Within the band itself, residence patterns had changed dramatically in the previous fifteen years, as many families moved from outlying areas to Qualla Boundary; by 1880 boundary residents outnumbered those of Graham, Cherokee, and Macon Counties by more than two to one. Some of these families included husbands or wives with little or no Indian blood.[74] The growing population on Qualla Boundary obviously increased pressure on the limited land base, prompting more cultivation of the steep slopes and, according to some recollections, the draining of previously unused bottom lands by acculturated and "white Indians."[75]

The increasing intermarriage and cohabitation of Indians with whites and blacks both on and off the reservation heightened confusion over who was a "real" Cherokee. There was also the dawning realization that being listed as Cherokee offered obvious advantages in any future division or dissolution of the Eastern Band's assets. That possibility loomed ever more likely when Congress passed the General Allotment Act in 1887, giving the president discretionary authority to divide tribal reservations into individual allotments. Most white reformers believed a swift transition to private property would help Indians become more "American." After incorporation of the Eastern Band in 1889, its members were divided on the issue of allotment, but they certainly did not wish outsiders to share in any division of tribal property; that was one reason the band required a person to have at least one-sixteenth Cherokee blood for enrollment as a member. The band struggled to maintain that standard, but in the 1920s the federal government unilaterally enrolled many individuals with less Indian blood. Cherokee opposition to their inclusion helped prevent allotment, and to this day the reservation remains under federal trusteeship.[76]

Complicating the matter of tribal membership was the changing economy of the southern Appalachians. After the 1880s capitalists increasingly invested enormous sums of money in exploiting the mineral and timber resources of the region.[77] Most of the Cherokee lands were heavily forested, and timber trespass by whites and Indians alike was the most common crime on the reservation, especially in outlying parcels in Graham and Cherokee Counties. Throughout the 1890s the tribal council negotiated sales of timber reserves (for prices that seemed ridiculously low to some observers), then deposited the revenues in an Asheville bank for periodic distribution to members of the band. That was another reason whites clamored to be enrolled. The advent of the southern lumber industry also enabled Cherokees to find ready employment in nearby logging camps and mills, and by 1900 this growing emphasis on wage labor had brought about a significant decline in the number of cultivated acres on the reservation.[78] During the next two decades newly constructed passenger and logging railroads helped bring the Qualla Boundary Cherokees into daily contact with the outside world. Despite periodic downturns, the lumber industry would dominate the tribal economy until the late 1920s.

Considering such changes, it is hardly surprising that the ethnologist James Mooney, writing in 1900, attached so much symbolic import to the recent death of Swimmer, the famous keeper of tribal lore: "Peace to his ashes and sorrow for his going, for with him perished half the tradition of a people."[79] The Cherokees, Mooney believed, were rapidly acculturating and moving into the modern era. But this assessment was premature and required qualification. The 1,379 members of the Eastern Band listed in the federal census that year still retained significant attributes of cultural nationalism: their own language, a body of myths and legends defining their history, their own lands, and, in varying degrees, certain shared assumptions and traits. Most important was their tenacious desire to remain Cherokee, an internal self-identification that has proved decisive in the twentieth century. This pride has been enhanced by that of many other Americans who now, after generations of embarrassed silence, eagerly proclaim their Cherokee heritage.

Notes

1. Appalachian blacks of the period have received significantly less attention than whites or Indians. Two recent accounts touching upon the topic are John C. Inscoe, *Mountain Masters: Slavery and the Sectional Crisis in Western North Carolina* (Knoxville: University of Tennessee Press, 1989), and Wilma A. Dunaway, "Southern Appalachia's People without History: The Role of Unfree Laborers in the Region's Antebellum Economy," paper presented at the annual meeting of the Social Science History Association, November 1989, Washington, D.C.

2. Russell Thornton, *The Cherokees: A Population History* (Lincoln: University of Nebraska Press, 1990), p. 43.

3. Studies on the Cherokee move toward civilization include Henry Thompson Malone, *Cherokees of the Old South: A People in Transition* (Athens: University of Georgia Press, 1956); and William G. McLoughlin, *Cherokee Renascence in the New Republic* (Princeton: Princeton University Press, 1986).

4. Theda Perdue, "Southeastern Indians and the Cult of True Womanhood," in *The Web of Southern Social Relations: Women, Family, and Education*, ed. Walter J.

Frazer, Jr., R. Saunders, and Jon R. Wakelyn (Athens: University of Georgia Press, 1985), pp. 35–52, and "Cherokee Women and the Trail of Tears," *Journal of Women's History* 1 (1989): 14–30.

5. Douglas C. Wilms, "Cherokee Land Use in Georgia, 1800–1838" (Ph.D. diss., University of Georgia, 1974), and "Cherokee Land Use in Georgia before Removal," in *Cherokee Removal: Before and After*, ed. William L. Anderson (Athens: University of Georgia Press, 1991), pp. 1–28. There were significant variations in these homesite patterns, however. See Richard Pillsbury, "The Europeanization of the Cherokee Settlement Landscape Prior to Removal: A Georgia Case Study," *Geoscience and Man* 22 (1983): 59–69.

6. William G. McLoughlin and Walter H. Conser, Jr., "The Cherokees in Transition: A Statistical Analysis of the Federal Cherokee Census of 1835," *Journal of American History* 64 (December 1977): 695–97.

7. McLoughlin, *Cherokee Renascence*, p. 64; Wilms, "Cherokee Land Use in Georgia before Removal," pp. 9, 22–23; Brad Alan Bays, "The Historical Geography of Cattle Herding among the Cherokee Indians, 1761–1861" (M.A. thesis, University of Tennessee, 1991).

8. On this missionary work, see William G. McLoughlin, *Cherokees and Missionaries, 1789–1839* (New Haven: Yale University Press, 1984), and *Champions of the Cherokees: Evan and John B. Jones* (Princeton: Princeton University Press, 1990).

9. McLoughlin and Conser, "Cherokees in Transition," pp. 688–92.

10. For Ross's career, see Gary E. Moulton, *John Ross, Cherokee Chief* (Athens: University of Georgia Press, 1978).

11. Perdue, "Southeastern Indians and the Cult of True Womanhood," p. 46.

12. Mary Young, "The Cherokee Nation: Mirror of the Republic," *American Quarterly* 33 (Winter 1981): 502–24; Thomas Hatley, "Cherokee Women Farmers Hold Their Ground," in *Appalachian Frontiers: Settlement, Society, and Development in the Preindustrial Era*, ed. Robert D. Mitchell (Lexington: University Press of Kentucky, 1991), pp. 37–51.

13. Bays, "Historical Geography of Cattle Herding," p. 86. The multicultural origins of southeastern cattle herding are discussed in Terry G. Jordan, *North American Cattle-Ranching Frontiers: Origins, Diffusion, and Differentiation* (Albuquerque: University of New Mexico Press, 1993).

14. Bays, "Historical Geography of Cattle Herding," p. 103.

15. Ibid., pp. 88–89, 112; Perdue, "Southeastern Indians and the Cult of True Womanhood," p. 46; Hatley, "Cherokee Women Farmers Hold Their Ground," p. 49.

16. Hatley, "Cherokee Women Farmers Hold Their Ground," p. 49.

17. Versions of the Selu story appear in James Mooney, *Myths of the Cherokee*, Nineteenth Annual Report of the Bureau of American Ethnology (Washington, D.C.: Government Printing Office, 1900), pp. 242–49.

18. Sarah Hitch Hill, "Cherokee Patterns: Interweaving Women and Baskets in History" (Ph.D. diss., Emory University, 1991), pp. 135–38; see also Betty J. Duggan and Brett H. Riggs, "Cherokee Basketry: An Evolving Tradition," in *Studies in Cherokee Basketry*, by Betty J. Duggan and Brett H. Riggs (Knoxville: Frank H. McClung Museum, 1991), pp. 23–46.

19. McLoughlin, *Champions of the Cherokees*.

20. McLoughlin and Conser, "Cherokees in Transition," p. 702.

21. Theda Perdue, "The Conflict Within: Cherokees and Removal," in Anderson, *Cherokee Removal*, pp. 55–74. Perdue also emphasizes the clash between Cherokee elites and an emerging tribal middle class.

22. *American State Papers*, 38 vols. (Washington, D.C., 1832–61), *Public Lands*, 5:394.

23. A standard account of these developments is Ronald N. Satz, *American Indian Policy in the Jacksonian Era* (Lincoln: University of Nebraska Press, 1975).

24. Grace Steele Woodward, *The Cherokees* (Norman: University of Oklahoma Press, 1963), pp. 171–91. A sympathetic view of the "treaty party" of Cherokees is Thurman Wilkins, *Cherokee Tragedy: The Story of the Ridge Family and the Decimation of a People*, rev. ed. (Norman: University of Oklahoma Press, 1986).

25. Still a standard reference is Grant Foreman, *Indian Removal: The Emigration of the Five Civilized Tribes of Indians*, rev. ed. (Norman: University of Oklahoma Press, 1986). For additional bibliography on the topic, see Howard L. Meredith, *Cherokee Removal: An Historiographic Report* (Oklahoma City: Oklahoma Educational Television Authority, 1978); William L. Anderson, "Bibliographic Essay," in Anderson, *Cherokee Removal*, pp. 145–47. For the complex and controversial matter of Cherokee mortality during removal, see three works by Russell Thornton: "The Demography of the Trail of Tears Period: A New Estimate of Cherokee Population Losses," in Anderson, *Cherokee Removal*, p. 85; "Cherokee Population Losses during the Trail of Tears: A New Perspective and a New Estimate," *Ethnohistory* 31 (1984): 289–300; *The Cherokees*, pp. 73–76.

26. Detailed discussion of the Tsali episode is in John R. Finger, *The Eastern Band of Cherokees, 1819–1900* (Knoxville: University of Tennessee Press, 1984), pp. 21–28, and "The Saga of Tsali: Legend Versus Reality," *North Carolina Historical Review* 56 (1979): 1–18.

27. Information on the reserves is in Brett H. Riggs, *An Historical and Archaeological Reconnaissance of Citizen Cherokee Reservations in Macon, Swain, and Jackson Counties, North Carolina* (Knoxville: Department of Anthropology, University of Tennessee, 1988). For the 1840 Quallatown figures, see "Present state of civilization among the Cherokee Indians of Qualla Town," accompanying letter of William H. Thomas to William Wilkins, 3 March 1845, RG 75, M-234, 89:542–43, National Archives (herinafter cited as NA).

28. Gregory Evans Dowd, *A Spirited Resistance: The North American Struggle for Unity, 1745–1815* (Baltimore: Johns Hopkins University Press, 1992), pp. 195–96.

29. Thomas's career is discussed in Finger, *Eastern Band of Cherokees*, and in E. Stanly Godbold, Jr., and Mattie U. Russell, *Confederate Colonel and Cherokee Chief: The Life of William Holland Thomas* (Knoxville: University of Tennessee Press, 1990).

30. George E. Frizzell, "The Legal Status of the Eastern Band of Cherokee Indians" (M.A. thesis, Western Carolina University, 1981), pp. 15–17; Finger, *Eastern Band of Cherokees*, pp. 18, 20–21.

31. Foster to Gen. Winfield Scott, 24 November 1838 (enclosure "C" of File S-568-1838), RG 94, NA; petition dated 18 November 1838 (enclosure "D," ibid.);

proclamation, 24 November 1838 (enclosure "E," ibid.); depositions of Joseph Welch, Euchella, Edward Delozier, Jonas Jenkins, Joel Sawyer, and John Chambers, Records of the Fourth Board of Cherokee Commissioners, RG 75, NA.

32. The figures of William H. Thomas indicate there were at least 1,087 North Carolina Cherokees in 1840 ("Census of the North Carolina Cherokees, 1840," William H. Thomas Papers, Duke University, Durham, N.C.). Compare with "Supplementary Report of Cherokee Indians Remaining in N.C., 1835–1840," compiled by Thomas (microfilm at Museum of the Cherokee Indian, Cherokee, N.C.).

33. Many letters in RG 75, M-234, NA, confirm the presence of such Cherokees in states adjoining North Carolina.

34. Sharon P. Flanagan, "The Georgia Cherokees Who Remained: Race, Status, and Property in the Chattahoochee Community," *Georgia Historical Quarterly* 73 (Fall 1989): 585–86.

35. Finger, *Eastern Band of Cherokees*, chaps. 2–3; Richard W. Iobst, "William Holland Thomas and the Cherokee Claims," in *The Cherokee Indian Nation: A Troubled History*, ed. Duane H. King (Knoxville: University of Tennessee Press, 1979), pp. 181–201.

36. John R. Finger, "The North Carolina Cherokees, 1838–1866: Traditionalism, Progressivism, and the Affirmation of State Citizenship," *Journal of Cherokee Studies* 5 (Spring 1980): 17–29.

37. "Present State of Civilization among the Cherokee Indians of Qualla Town," accompanying letter of William H. Thomas to William Wilkins, 3 March 1845, RG 75, M-234, 89:542–43, NA; Charles Lanman, *Letters from the Alleghany Mountains* (New York: Putnam, 1849), pp. 107–8.

38. Lanman, *Letters from the Alleghany Mountains*, p. 96.

39. Finger, "North Carolina Cherokees," p. 20; Finger, *Eastern Band of Cherokees*, p. 64; Catherine L. Albanese, "Exploring Regional Religion: A Case Study of the Eastern Cherokee," *History of Religions* 23 (May 1984): 358.

40. Personal communication from Betty J. Duggan, doctoral candidate in anthropology, University of Tennessee, Knoxville.

41. J. Kerner to William A. Graham, 31 May 1842 (quote), in *The Papers of William Alexander Graham*, 6 vols., ed. J. G. de Roulhac Hamilton and Max R. Williams (Raleigh, N.C.: State Department of Archives and History, 1957–76), 2:319; memorial from citizens of Haywood County, Legislative Papers 583, "Cherokee Indians and Cherokee Lands" folder, North Carolina Division of Archives and History, Raleigh (hereinafter cited as NCDAH); petition of citizens of Macon and Haywood County, 17 August 1842, 29th Cong., 1st sess., *Senate Document 408* (Serial 477, Washington, D.C., 1846), pp. 21–22.

42. "Report of Joint Select Committee upon Indian Removals" and "Resolution in Relation to the Removal of the Cherokee Indians," 25 January 1843, Legislative Papers 583, "Cherokee Indians and Cherokee Lands" folder, NCDAH.

43. Finger, *Eastern Band of Cherokees*, pp. 31–40; John R. Finger, "The Abortive Second Cherokee Removal, 1841–1844," *Journal of Southern History* 47 (1981): 207–26.

44. Finger, *Eastern Band of Cherokees*, p. 50.

45. Anna G. Kilpatrick and Jack F. Kilpatrick, "Chronicles of Wolftown: Social

Documents of the North Carolina Cherokees, 1850–1862," Bureau of American Ethnology *Bulletin* 196 (Washington, D.C., 1966), p. 59.

46. Hiram Price to Joseph G. Hester, 30 December 1881, RG 75, M-1059, 3:78, NA; affidavits and other materials, ibid., 3:69–84, NA; N. J. Smith to Hiram Price, 13 December 1882, RG 75, Letters Received, NA; Finger, *Eastern Band of Cherokees*, pp. 50, 68, 143; Walter L. Williams, "Patterns in the History of the Remaining Southeastern Indians, 1840–1875," in *Southeastern Indians since the Removal Era*, ed. Walter L. Williams (Athens: University of Georgia Press, 1979), pp. 194, 198.

47. Finger, *Eastern Band of Cherokees*, chap. 4.

48. Felix Asley to William Holland Thomas, 29 April 1845, William Holland Thomas Collection, Western Carolina University, Cullowhee, N.C.

49. Raymond D. Fogelson and Paul Kutsche, "Cherokee Economic Cooperatives: The Gadugi," in "Symposium on Cherokee and Iroquois Culture," ed. William N. Fenton and John Gulick, Bureau of American Ethnology *Bulletin* 180 (Washington, D.C., 1961), pp. 87, 96–97; Kilpatrick and Kilpatrick, "Chronicles of Wolftown."

50. Thomas Diary, 23 September 1848, Thomas Collection.

51. Swimmer's impact is most apparent in Mooney, *Myths of the Cherokee*, and James Mooney, *Sacred Formulas of the Cherokee*, Seventh Annual Report of the Bureau of American Ethnology (Washington, D.C.: Government Printing Office, 1891). For an overview of conjuring, see Raymond D. Fogelson, "A Study of the Conjuror in Cherokee Society" (M.A. thesis, University of Pennsylvania, 1958).

52. Lanman, *Letters from the Alleghany Mountains*, p. 103. See also James Mooney, "The Cherokee Ball Play," *American Anthropologist*, o.s., 3 (1890): 105–32; Raymond D. Fogelson, "The Cherokee Ball Game: A Study in Southeastern Ethnology" (Ph.D. diss., University of Pennsylvania, 1962).

53. Hill, "Cherokee Patterns," pp. 210–15 (quote on p. 215).

54. Ibid., chap. 5.

55. Cherokee participation in the war is discussed in Finger, *Eastern Band of Cherokees*, chap. 5; and Vernon H. Crow, *Storm in the Mountains: Thomas' Confederate Legion of Cherokee Indians and Mountaineers* (Cherokee, N.C.: Museum of the Cherokee Indian, 1982).

56. William Thomas to Governor and Council of South Carolina, 28 February 1864, in *The War of Rebellion: A Compilation of the Official Records of the Union and Confederate Armies*, 128 vols. (Washington, D.C.: Government Printing Office, 1880–1901), ser. 1, vol. 53, supp., pp. 313–14; Thomas to Major-General Breckenridge, 27 April 1864, Thomas Papers; Margaret Love to Governor Vance, 10 May 1864, Governor Vance Papers, NCDAH.

57. Robert A. Crawford to Governor Andrew Johnson, 11 June 1863, Andrew Johnson Papers, Library of Congress.

58. *New York Times*, 15 March 1863, p. 8.

59. Personal communication from Betty Duggan, doctoral candidate in anthropology, University of Tennessee, Knoxville.

60. Finger, *Eastern Band of Cherokees*, pp. 96–97, 102.

61. Ibid., chap. 6.

62. *Public Laws of the State of North Carolina Passed by the General Assembly at the Session of 1866* (Raleigh: William E. Pell, 1866), pp. 120.

63. *U.S. Statutes at Large* 15 (1869): 228.

64. Detailed discussion of this factionalism is in Finger, *Eastern Band of Cherokees*, chap. 6.

65. Ibid., pp. 110–11, 118–25, 171–72; John R. Finger, *Cherokee Americans: The Eastern Band of Cherokees in the Twentieth Century* (Lincoln: University of Nebraska Press, 1991), p. 1. Today the Eastern Band's reservation has a little over 56,000 acres.

66. The Cherokee legal status is discussed in detail in Finger, *Eastern Band of Cherokees*; Finger, *Cherokee Americans*; Frizzell, "Legal Status of the Eastern Band"; George E. Frizzell, "The Politics of Cherokee Citizenship, 1898–1930," *North Carolina Historical Review* 61 (1984): 205–30; Ben Oshel Bridgers, "An Historical Analysis of the Legal Status of the North Carolina Cherokees," *North Carolina Law Review* 58 (August 1980): 1075–1131.

67. McCarthy to Commissioner of Indian Affairs J. Q. Smith, 21 January 1876, RG 75, M-234, 110:375, NA.

68. A. J. McAlpine to R. B. Vance, 9 December 1879, RG 75, M-234, 112:902–4, NA.

69. October 1880 report of A. J. McAlpine, RG 75, M-234, 112:347, NA.

70. Finger, *Eastern Band of Cherokees*, chaps. 7–8; Sharlotte Neely Williams, "The Role of Formal Education among the Eastern Cherokee Indians, 1880–1971" (M.A. thesis, University of North Carolina, 1971); Sharlotte Neely, "The Quaker Era of Cherokee Indian Education, 1880–1892," *Appalachian Journal* 2 (Summer 1975): 314–22; Joan Greene, "Federal Policies in the Schools of the Eastern Cherokees, 1892–1932" (M.A. thesis, Western Carolina University, 1986).

71. Finger, *Cherokee Americans*, pp. 28–29. As late as 1917 Agent James Henderson asked one Cherokee at Carlisle, "Do you realize that you have a better opportunity to make something of yourself than any poor white boy on or near the Cherokee Reservation?" (Henderson to Roger Mumblehead, 22 December 1915, RG 75, Box 16, Cherokee Agency, Federal Records Center, East Point, Ga.).

72. Finger, *Eastern Band of Cherokees*, pp. 127–28; Finger, *Cherokee Americans*, pp. 7–8, 18–20.

73. Joseph G. Hester Roll, 1884, RG 75, NA.

74. Finger, *Eastern Band of Cherokees*, p. 140.

75. Robert K. Thomas, "Culture History of the Eastern Cherokee," unpublished paper for the Cross-Cultural Laboratory of the Institute for Research in Social Sciences, University of North Carolina, Chapel Hill, May 1958, p. 15.

76. This and related matters are discussed in Finger, *Cherokee Americans*, chap. 3.

77. For an analysis of these changes, see Ronald D. Eller, *Miners, Millhands, and Mountaineers: Industrialization of the Appalachian South, 1880–1930* (Knoxville: University of Tennessee Press, 1982).

78. Finger, *Eastern Band of Cherokees*, pp. 169–74; Finger, *Cherokee Americans*, pp. 11, 17–19, 21–22.

79. Mooney, *Myths of the Cherokee*, p. 237.

Speculators and Settler Capitalists

Unthinking the Mythology about Appalachian Landholding, 1790–1860

Displacement of Native Americans

The British Proclamation Line of 1763 marked the watershed of the Appalachian Mountains as the limits for European American colonization of North America.[1] Areas west of the line were reserved as Indian hunting grounds, and families who had "inadvertently seated themselves upon any lands . . . reserved to the Indians" were ordered "to remove themselves from such settlements." Tidewater planters, however, had been engaged in speculation in lands beyond this line since the 1740s. Consequently, permanent settlements had already been established too far west along the Virginia frontier. Needless to say, speculators were not deterred by the constraints of the Proclamation Line. For example, George Washington admonished his planter associates that they should not neglect the opportunity "of hunting out good lands, and in some measure marking and distinguishing them . . . (in order to keep others from settling them)."[2]

In southern Appalachia, European American resettlement could not advance until several Native American groups had been displaced. By the early 1700s the Tuscaroras, the Senedos, the Toteros, and the Shawnees had been pushed westward by colonial encroachments. However, the largest indigenous Appalachian populations were the Cherokees, who claimed almost all the region's lands, and a few Creeks who resided in present-day northern Alabama.[3]

Virginia, North Carolina, and Georgia titled indigenous lands to speculators and to war veterans long before cessions had been negotiated with resident peoples. Worse, land companies organized their own treaty meetings in order to secure illegal acquisitions. In the face of royal edicts against private claims on Indian lands, the Transylvania Company arranged the lease-purchase of 20 million acres of Cherokee lands located in present-day Kentucky, Tennessee, and North Carolina. After the heads of the Loyal and Greenbrier Companies were appointed as boundary commissioners at the 1770 treaty of Lochaber, the new line was run far enough west to clear 800,000 acres of western Virginia lands for resale and resettlement. The Ohio Company of Virginia even attempted to weaken Cherokee control over their lands by extending "them Credit for [goods] in the Companies Store."[4]

As a result of such maneuvering, bloody land disputes between the Indians and the white encroachers continued along the southern Appalachian frontier until after the Revolutionary War. Between 1763 and 1773 settlers engrossed 4,545,908 acres from the indigenous peoples. By the end of the Revolutionary War, Cherokee territory had been diminished by nearly 60 percent. Between 1800 and 1819 the Cherokees "ceded" an additional 3 million acres of their hunting grounds and their settled areas, leaving only a small enclave of Cherokee and Creek villages in southeastern Tennessee, western North Carolina, northern Georgia, and northern Alabama. Federal legitimation of state control over local Indians, intense racism, planter pressures for fresh cotton lands, and the discovery of gold in Indian territory culminated in the forced removals of the remaining Cherokees and Creeks from southern Appalachia between 1832 and 1838.[5]

No Public Domain in Southern Appalachia

Southern Appalachia was never a unified frontier; in reality, the region was resettled in four major historical stages. Before the 1763 Proclamation Line had been mandated, repopulation was well under way in western Maryland, the Valley of Virginia, northwestern South Carolina, and West Virginia's eastern and Ohio River edges. In a second phase, upper eastern Tennessee, northwestern North Carolina, and the area around Madison County, Kentucky, were repeopled between 1770 and 1789. In the flurry of postrevolutionary expansion, emigrants flowed into eastern Kentucky, the Cumberland

Plateau of middle Tennessee, southwestern North Carolina, and central West Virginia. The final era of resettlement did not occur until the later 1830s— after the forced removal from southern Appalachia of the remaining Native Americans.[6]

Except for northern Alabama, southern Appalachia's lands were redistributed long before federal land policy had been formulated. Consequently, westward movement into the Appalachian frontiers involved private acquisition of the state-controlled holdings of Virginia, North Carolina, Georgia, and South Carolina. Moreover, the federal laws designed to establish the rights of small homesteaders and squatters came too late to benefit Appalachia's poorer landless emigrants, for the Midwest was the first frontier to feel the impact of nationally regulated land policies and homestead provisions.

By the mid-1700s a few of the wealthiest Tidewater planters and British court favorites had expropriated much of the Valley of Virginia and western Maryland. By the 1730s Blue Ridge Virginia and present-day West Virginia had been carved into large estates.[7] The Ohio Company absorbed a large slice of the remaining frontier by negotiating a Crown grant for 500,000 West Virginia acres. The Greenbrier Company and the Loyal Company engrossed more than 300,000 acres in eastern West Virginia and southwestern Virginia. During the 1740s Tidewater merchant capitalists gained control of four-fifths of the surveyed lands in western Maryland. Practically every wealthy Maryland Tidewater planter or merchant speculated in that state's Appalachian lands. In western North Carolina a few Virginia Tidewater planter families, the Loyal Company, and the Henderson Company engrossed much of the northern sector.[8]

Absentee Engrossment on the Southern Appalachian Frontier

By the turn of the nineteenth century, northeastern merchant capitalists, land companies, and southern planters had amassed a whopping majority of all southern Appalachian lands. During the frontier years absentee landholders owned three-quarters of the region's total acreage, as Table 2.1 demonstrates. In Virginia and West Virginia little acreage was left for residents. After 1790 distant speculators gobbled up more than 90 percent of the lands when the Virginia assembly began to sell its frontier areas at very cheap prices.

In 1793 the Virginia treasury was peddling Appalachian lands for an average of two cents per acre. The effect of selling at below-market valuations was to stimulate distant brokerage-house trading in Virginia treasury

Table 2.1. Absentee Engrossment of Southern Appalachian Lands, 1790–1810

| Appalachian Counties | Acres Owned | | | |
| | Residents | | Absentees | |
	No.	%	No.	%
Kentucky	56,855.5	.438	72,961.0	.562
Maryland	169,795.9	.671	83,410.0	.329
North Carolina	237,914.5	.571	178,676.0	.429
South Carolina	48,824.5	.480	52,852.0	.520
Tennessee	120,368.3	.311	266,201.0	.689
Virginia	328,994.5	.107	2,757,465.3	.893
West Virginia	324,388.5	.067	4,525,153.0	.933
Region	12,526,649.8	.241	39,451,150.2	.759

Note: N = 8,162. Derived from analysis of manuscript county tax lists; for sources and methodological detail, see Dunaway, "Incorporation," tab. A.1 and appendix. No county tax lists or deeds are accessible for Alabama or Georgia. At the 95 percent confidence interval, these samples are large enough to obtain estimates of percentages that are within ± <3 percentage points of actual population values.

warrants. After Virginia opened her western lands for sale in 1792, the state sold 2,590,059 acres to just fourteen speculators. Within less than five years Virginia's flooding of northeastern markets with these cheap warrants had thrown her Appalachian lands "into the hands of a few individuals."[9]

By examining land grants made in this era, it is possible to assess the extent to which acreage was falling into the hands of settlers. In three West Virginia counties the absentee landholders were predominantly speculators from other states—with fewer than a quarter of the grantees being West Virginians who resided outside the county in which the lands were situated. It is likely that investors were already gambling on amassing mineral lands. The greatest level of distant speculation and the largest grants occurred in the mountainous county (Randolph), where more than nine-tenths of the lands were allocated to absentees and each speculator averaged 21,980 acres. Four-fifths of the ridge-valley county (Hampshire) parcels accrued to non-residents who averaged 706 acres each. The least distant trading was directed toward the hill-plateau county (Monongalia), but nonresidents still monopolized more than two-thirds of the granted parcels and averaged 2,405 acres each.[10]

Because the region's most intense speculation occurred in the frontiers that had been shaped by the land policies of Virginia, eastern Kentucky also experienced high levels of engrossment. It is likely that absentee ownership of eastern Kentucky lands was even higher than the 56 percent reflected in Table 2.1, for many local courthouse officials colluded with distant speculators to have their tax records "disappear." One gubernatorial assessment points out that the major weakness of the state's nineteenth-century tax system was that "much land of non-residents [was] not listed." By the end of the 1700s one-quarter of the entire area of Kentucky had been claimed by twenty-one land barons. By late 1794 northeastern land mongers were pouring into Kentucky to speculate in Virginia military and treasury warrants, often obtained through distant brokerage houses. Since nearly four-fifths of eastern Kentucky's land claims were made by absentee speculators, it is likely that three-quarters or more of eastern Kentucky's frontier lands were held by absentees.[11]

In 1783 North Carolina threw open its own western sector and the lands of Tennessee for purchase at very cheap prices. Shortly, North Carolina land jobbers began a speculative rampage that resulted in the disposal of 4 million acres within seven months. In Tennessee merchant capitalists, land companies, and distant planters amassed more than two-thirds of the Appalachian lands (see Table 2.1). The John Gray Blount Land Company (owned by an eastern North Carolina planter–shipping magnate) effected a virtual monopoly in the acquisition of state land warrants, netting 1,184,460 acres in western North Carolina and Tennessee that were marketed in the Northeast and in Europe. In 1795 the Blounts owned almost the entire land area of present-day Hawkins County in eastern Tennessee. Obviously the Blounts had expectations of financial windfalls on the expanding frontier. Perhaps their most elaborate scheme was the proposed joint development with a New York capitalist of a 150-mile-square city adjoining Knoxville; lots for the new city of Palmyra were to be sold only in Europe.[12]

Soon after the Revolutionary War a few absentee speculators—predominantly North Carolina planter-merchants or state officials and eastern capitalists—monopolized all the available lands in western North Carolina. Kept by a Philadelphia capitalist during his travels through western North Carolina, a 1795 business journal provides unique insights into the techniques utilized by absentee investors to engross the southern mountains. The "spirit of specewlation" was pandemic in North Carolina's small towns and courthouses where each "confab on the Business" pointed the outsider to land trades with nearly every new acquaintance. In less than three wintry weeks John Brown "Procured near five hundred thousand Acrs" in Buncombe, Burke, and Wilkes Counties. State assemblymen and county surveyors were bribed to manage paperwork favorably and to delay fees, but "keep it secret." The state treasurer even forewarned him to hasten his filings in order to circumvent the stricter regulations to be enacted by an impending new law. When other tactics did not produce quick results, Brown even tried to convince a Buncombe County official to "sell his place as surveyor" to a more cooperative crony.[13]

The earliest grants in 1787 were to North Carolina planter-officials David-son and Moore for several thousand acres in Buncombe, Burke, and Ruther-ford Counties, including all the best agricultural lands along the Swannanoa River. In the early 1790s John Gray Blount acquired 496,640 acres, encompassing half the land area of Madison, Yancey, and Buncombe Counties. Forty absentee speculators engrossed the entire land area of present-day McDowell County. Eastern mineral speculators William Cathcart and George Latimer agglomerated 332,780 acres, incorporating all of Mitchell and Avery Counties and most of Jackson County. In addition North Carolina planter families and state officials—such as the Alexanders, the Sharpes, the Davidsons, Robert Henry, Waightstill Avery, Lambert Clayton, and Ephraim George—invested their own money and that of eastern backers in huge tracts of Appalachian land. David Allison absorbed 250,240 acres, embracing most of Haywood County and about half of Buncombe County. Philadelphia merchant capitalist Tench Coxe accumulated thousands of acres east and west of the Blue Ridge. Holdimon and Eschlemon amassed 200,960 acres, comprising two-thirds of present-day Jackson, Swain, and Macon Counties.[14]

These engrossers paid only fifty shillings to one pound per 100 acres for western North Carolina holdings. Subsequently they resurveyed their plats into smaller parcels, advertised in eastern cities, and sold farms at considerable profit. Due to the insider monopolizing techniques of such capitalists, it is likely that much more than the 43 percent of western North Carolina territory reflected in Table 2.1 remained in the hands of absentee holders in the early 1800s. Nonstate investors are probably underrepresented in these early tax lists because of their evasive and illegal tactics. In order to sidestep the North Carolina law requiring land claimants to be state residents, speculative claims were registered in the names of local agents. For example, Philadelphia capitalist John Brown paid several locals to make entries in their own names for more than 1,133,000 acres.[15]

Similarly, absentee speculators amassed more than half the acreage of northwestern South Carolina (see Table 2.1). By examining the early deeds of this area, we can get a unique glimpse into how frontier land transfers were transacted. To measure the extent to which land was being acquired by local people, I categorized all 374 land transactions that occurred between 1789 and 1792. Less than one-half (174) of the deeds were made between resident buyers and sellers; however, 200 (53.5 percent) of the deeds were made to absentees. In nearly one-third of the transactions, residents made deeds to absentees, and another one-fifth of the land sales were paper trading between distant buyers and sellers. Only four of the deeds represented estate settlements, and all of these transferred the land to nonresidents, not to local family heirs. Two of the deeds resulted from public auctions of land to settle unpaid debts or taxes, a favored technique by which frontier speculators amassed holdings cheaply. In sharp contrast only twenty-two (5.9 percent) of the sales were transactions in which absentee sellers turned over lands to actual settlers. In short, distant trading occurred routinely, acreage was filtering down very slowly to resident farmers, and there was little evidence that local family members were inheriting land.[16]

In contrast, less distant trading occurred in western Maryland than in any of the other southern Appalachian zones. Investors were less attracted to speculate there because Maryland's quitrents, prices, and taxes were higher than those in Virginia or Pennsylvania. Moreover, Maryland Tidewater planters monopolized the Appalachian lands, squeezing out-of-state speculators out of the market.[17]

Much of the explanation for western Maryland's lower levels of engrossment lies in the land regulations enacted there. Four key redistribution policies set Maryland apart from the other southern Appalachian states. In contrast to Virginia and North Carolina where wealthier officers could appropriate a military bounty of up to 10,000 acres, Maryland awarded officers only 100 acres. Registration of land records and taxation were decentralized into Maryland counties beginning in 1671, making absentee tax avoidance more difficult. In addition Maryland had passed eighteenth-century legislation to reserve parcels to parties who would cultivate it, a land policy that was not duplicated by any other southern Appalachian state. Finally, as early as 1718 Maryland legislated positions for nine public surveyors for each county, an unprecedented maneuver that averted the quagmire of duplicated claims that plagued the rest of the region.[18]

Capitalists Involved in Appalachian Speculation

Table 2.2 permits an even closer pinpointing of the types of profiteers who invested in the westward expansion of southern Appalachia. Absentee planters and merchant capitalists owned most of the lands in southern Appalachia, except in western Maryland. Even though small investors made up a majority of the total number of absentee holders, they owned only a very small portion of the total land area. Distant trading was facilitated by brokerage houses in Richmond, Philadelphia, Washington, D.C., New York, and Boston, where military land warrants were bought for resale and margin trading. Brokerage houses traded in scrip or warrants (claims for acreage) and shares (in land companies' stocks). The most wealthy capitalists, such as Robert Morris of the North American Land Company, engaged in the practice of dodging, by which the speculator sold lands in Europe before acreage or warrants were actually purchased on Appalachian frontiers.[19]

Land companies were active in every section of the region, but northeastern merchants were particularly oriented toward Virginia, West Virginia, and Tennessee, where nearly three-fourths of the total absentee acreage was under their control (see Table 2.2). Regionally based merchants and planters made up another powerful market segment for trading in Appalachian lands. Wealthier elites in adjacent counties of the same state accumulated sizable holdings through public auctions, inheritance, speculative trading in rental properties, and the operation of absentee-owned plantations.[20]

Early nineteenth-century trading in southern Appalachian lands evolved into an interlocking, systematic network in which distant speculators utilized several levels of petty capitalists to acquire, market, defend, and lease their frontier investments. Financiers relied on land jobbers to manage their extensive holdings. Men like Daniel Boone for the Transylvania Company or Uria Brown of Baltimore were hired on commission to mark off frontier tracts, supervise surveys, pay taxes, deal with courthouse officials or local attorneys, effect tenancy agreements, and vend agricultural produce collected in rents. Jobbers "set out [to the frontier] on the business of speculating on military land warrants."[21]

In dealing with the adverse claims of small West Virginia homesteaders in the early 1800s, Uria Brown demonstrated the crucial role played by the land jobbers in protecting the interests of distant engrossers against settlers and squatters who lacked political connections and legal sophistication. Following the advice of another jobber (an agent for holdings extending from the Mississippi River to western Pennsylvania), Brown determined to "Appear solid & firm & presist in Establishing the rights of Lands" claimed by his client, a Baltimore capitalist, "as the Tuffest skin shall hold out the Longest; & surveys on surveys is there nee Deep and deeper."[22]

Three other types of professionals were also essential to the land speculation process. Local attorneys often contracted with parties holding military warrants to "carry the claim into grant," the legal fee being one-half the land. In addition lawyers settled adverse claims and managed the lands of absentee heirs. Some of these frontier lawyers, such as O. P. Temple of

Table 2.2. Speculators in Southern Appalachian Lands, 1790–1810

	Average Absentee Holding (acres)	Merchant Capitalists		Distant Planter Capitalists	
		Acres	%	Acres	%
Kentucky	1,463	17,031.0	.244	5,934.0	.081
Maryland	153	23,444.0	.281	6,971.0	.083
North Carolina	730	42,553.5	.238	96,294.3	.539
South Carolina	359	18,545.5	.351	13,129.2	.248
Tennessee	1,626	187,594.0	.705	30,800.0	.116
Virginia	3,237	2,211,000.5	.802	33,095.0	.012
West Virginia	5,485	3,087,025.0	.682	1,187,626.5	.262

Note: N = 8,162. Derived from analysis of manuscript county tax lists; for sources and methodological detail, see Dunaway, "Incorporation," tab. A.1 and appendix. No county tax lists or deeds are accessible for Alabama or Georgia. At the 95 percent confidence interval, these samples are large enough to obtain estimates of percentages that are within ±<3 percentage points of actual population values. Sixty-one local history

eastern Tennessee, David Goff of Randolph County, West Virginia, or Lewis Maxwell of Weston, West Virginia, amassed their own estates by utilizing "insider" information about clients' claims to acquire their own choice holdings. For instance, Maxwell allowed the taxes on a client's lands to become delinquent; then he bought them at public auction. He responded to a complaint from this client by countering, "I cannot act as agent for you to pay taxes on the land you claim. The same land was sold to me . . . and I have a deed for it. I have paid the taxes thereon and have tenants now in possession of the land."[23]

Surveyors, such as George Washington or William Calk, reconnoitered newly opened frontiers. By laying off large tracts into smaller farm parcels that ran "to the top of them mountains," such entrepreneurs made Appalachian holdings more profitable to sellers who could commingle cultivable acreage with steep woodlands. Seeing no conflict with their public duties, county surveyors routinely offered their services to large landholders. For instance, the public surveyor for Lewis County, West Virginia, advertised his services to one absentee land baron, assuring him that he made "a business of hunting up land and surveying it on commission for men liveing at a distance."[24]

Such courthouse officials sought to make their own fortunes by engaging in land ventures. Distant speculators employed local discoverers, often petty

Adjacent Area Merchants and Planters		Small Investors and Heirs		Total Absentee
Acres	%	Acres	%	Acres
42,828.0	.587	6,396.0	.088	72,961
47,351.0	.568	5,644.0	.068	83,410
38,340.0	.215	1,488.3	.008	178,676
21,177.3	.401	000.0	.000	52,852
29,770.0	.112	18,037.0	.067	266,201
508,531.2	.184	4,838.3	.002	2,757,465
206,250.0	.046	44,251.5	.010	4,525,153

sources, census lists, and genealogical sources were utilized to identify absentee land-holders.

[a] Includes northeastern capitalists and land companies.
[b] Planters residing in other states.
[c] Planters and merchants residing in non-Appalachian counties of the same state.

bureaucrats, to select and survey lands purchased by means of military warrants. John May, for instance, amassed a vast empire in eastern Kentucky lands while serving as court clerk of Jefferson County. When land jobber Uria Brown complained about the large bill for delinquent taxes on an absentee parcel of 50,000 acres, the court clerk of Harrison County, West Virginia, offered "for $150.00 . . . to get a Law passed by the Legislature of Virginia to strike off all the taxes." In the case of Alexander Quarrier, public corruption was even more aggressively proffered. While Kanawha County tax assessor, Quarrier served absentee engrossers by arranging for their delinquent taxes to "disappear" from public records. For example, he wrote to land baron Eugene Levassor that "the Sheriff is always in my debt . . . but recollect his list of delinquent lands are every year returned to me, and it is my duty to certify copies of these delinquents to the auditors at Richmond; of course your lands are not on this list. And the best evidence that the taxes are paid is that they are not returned delinquent. And I beg you to be assured that so long as I live your interests here shall suffer in nothing that I can avert."[25]

Land speculation was the fervor of the times, and even small local farmers and middling planters engaged in the marketing of this seemingly endless commodity. Frontier landholders with surplus acres frequently sold, traded, or rented acreage. The resident elite, such as Thomas Jefferson

(Albermarle, Virginia), Albert Gallatin (Monongalia, West Virginia), or William Lenoir (Caldwell, North Carolina), accumulated thousands of the region's acres. However, the wealthiest Appalachians also engaged in long-distance land speculation, investing their accumulated dollars outside the region.[26]

Many local merchants and planters acted as the county agents for distant capitalists. Land barons, such as Eugene Levassor, followed the practice of selecting "an agent in each county where the land lies." These petty capitalists handled sales and collected rents for one-third commission, plus expenses. Even wage laborers engaged in land speculation. Tenants were employed to move to the frontier to "seat" large holdings and prepare the land for occupancy by a later purchaser. Without settling on the land, outlyers made minor improvements on the speculator's holdings to meet legal requirements. Some local people were even hired by land jobbers to "destroy the Corners of Unseated Lands" to enlarge the boundaries of newly surveyed claims.[27]

Speculation and Landlessness on the Appalachian Frontier

Through their land-engrossing strategies, distant merchant capitalists, absentee planters, and local elites choreographed—rather clumsily—the advancing resettlement of southern Appalachia. Eager for wealth accumulation, Tidewater planters and northeastern merchants systematically engaged in profit-oriented tactics that bypassed small homesteaders or kept prices out of their reach. By 1810 the repopulation of Virginia's frontier areas was lagging behind that of the rest of the region. Even though emigration began there fifty years later, North Carolina, Tennessee, and South Carolina were repopulated at a faster pace than were the Virginia-controlled frontiers. West Virginia was re-inhabited much more slowly than western Maryland, even though there was little topographical difference between the two areas and even though emigration into Maryland began a decade later. The principal reason that West Virginia had not been more fully resettled by the 1780s "[wa]s that the greater part if not all the good Lands, on the main river, [we]re in the hands of persons who d[id] not incline to reside thereon themselves, and possibly h[e]ld them too high for others."[28]

There can be little doubt that the morass of overlapping titles and official collusion with absentee engrossers slowed repopulation of southern Appalachian frontiers. In an 1816 report Kentucky's auditor lamented that the state had mistakenly sold thousands of acres belonging to resident smallholders, even after they had faithfully paid taxes upon their purchases from out-of-state sellers. Kentucky's land titling was so haphazard that absentees sold lands to residents without transferring deeds, then the state confiscated such lands when the out-of-state seller failed to pay taxes.[29] An early nine-teenth-century land jobber prophesied the two-century-long litigation that would ensue from hastily drawn boundaries and multiple titling. Uria Brown wrote in his 1816 journal that Ohio speculators "would purchase no Lands in Virginia at any price: for the Titles of Land there was worse than the Titles in Kentucky." Moreover, he predicted, "the titles in Kentucky w[ill] be Disputed for a Centry to Come yet, when it [i]s an old Settled Country."[30]

Throughout the region, speculators held large tracts of land off the market for as long as thirty years, waiting for prices to rise. George Washington's tactics were typical. To one inquiry about his Kanawha County holdings, he replied, "I am not inclined to part with any of these Lands, as an induce-ment to settle the rest. My mind is so well satisfied of the superior value of them to most others, that there remains no doubt on it of my obtaining my own terms, as the country populates and the situation and local advantages of them unfold."[31] When land was marketed, it was often too expensive for homesteaders.[32] As a result most of southern Appalachia's best agricultural lands were inaccessible to small farmers. Consequently the region was re-peopled more slowly than Ohio, "where lands [could] be bought in small tracts for farms, by real settlers, at a reasonable rate, whereas the Virginia lands belonging mostly to wealthy and great landholders [were] held at four or five times the Ohio price."[33]

Resettlement was further deterred by land speculators who held large warrants for western lands until their value increased. This practice had the most direct impact on emigrants to eastern Kentucky. A 1785 traveler re-ported seeing 721 ordinary homesteaders in a thirty-mile stretch of the Wilderness Road; however, very few of such poorer landseekers achieved their dream. "And when arrivd at this Heaven in idea," he queried, "what do they find? a goodly land I will allow but to them forbidden Land."[34] Actually Kentucky redistributed very little land to people who lived on and cultivated the soil. Rather than legislate the transfer of acreage to small homesteaders in the early 1800s, Kentucky's policymakers favored land grants to "monop-olizing capitalists" for "the purpose of speculation" and to promote indus-try.[35] As a result less than one-third of Kentucky's frontier titles were held by actual inhabitants. In Floyd, Laurel, Pulaski, and Whitley Counties there were no settlement entries among the early grants.[36] Despite legislation restricting Green River claims to squatters who had already resided there one year, Kentucky even sold more than three-fourths of that land to absentee speculators.[37]

Capitalistic speculation not only deterred resettlement of southern Appalachia but also stimulated the further concentration of land into the control of settler-elites. In the face of two layers of land engrossment, poorer Appalachians stood little chance of competing for farms or town lots. On the one hand, absentee owners controlled a sizable majority of the region's lands. On the other hand, local planters, professionals, and merchants—such as Virginia's Thomas Jefferson, Kentucky's Peyton Skipwith, and Tennessee's John Sevier or William Blount—also speculated and amassed sizable holdings.[38] As a result southern Appalachia's frontier lands were very inequitably distributed. The commodification of land was so extensive that the soil was monopolized by the privileged local elites as the basis for sustaining their social and economic status within a highly polarized economic structure. The wealthiest quartile of households engrossed more than four-fifths of the region's resident-held acres.[39] In western Maryland and western North Carolina the top quartile engrossed two-thirds of the resident-held acreage. One-quarter of the eastern Tennessee and eastern Kentucky families monopolized more than three-quarters of all acres titled to residents. Nine-tenths of the resident-owned acreage of Appalachian Virginia and West Virginia was held by only one-quarter of the households. At the most extreme the top 15 percent of Appalachian South Carolina households owned all the resident acreage. Moreover, the "engrossing of the better lands by the great planters . . . had a part in pushing the poore and less efficient producers back from the rivers onto the ridges and westward away from navigable rivers."[40] In Frederick County, Virginia, for instance, the largest plantations and towns were situated in the eastern Shenandoah Valley; smaller holdings were more often located in the western part of the county, toward the mountains and foothills.[41]

By the end of the 1790s absentee speculators controlled a majority of southern Appalachia's lands; however, most of the emigrants flowing into the region were poor. Contrary to our historical mythology, there was little prospect for a poor family to acquire land in southern Appalachia. There was no free land, and none of the state land laws conceded rights to "trespassers having no color of title." Consequently many early squatters were pushed off their improved land by those holding grants or military warrants.[42] For instance, when the Transylvania Company arrived to lay off a new town in eastern Kentucky, they displaced such a group of squatters. "About fifty men, most of them young persons without families" were "determined to live in the country," after they had emigrated from Pennsylvania. The trespassers "had got possession some time before" the company arrived, and they had proceeded to make improvements. However, Transylvania officials scoffed that such poor transients lacked the means "to hold land."[43]

Settlers were even charged for acreage to which they had been granted "preemption" rights, and squatters were liable for damages to absentee holdings, under legislation such as Kentucky's Occupying Claimant's Law. Consequently land remained inaccessible to the poor, for every Appalachian state sold its public holdings. Moreover, a landless family needed at least $1,000 to set up a forty-acre farm on the frontier.[44] As a result the region's average and poor populace—those most dependent upon the soil for survival—owned very little land. In fact, three-quarters of the Appalachian families owned less than 16 percent of the resident-held acreage.[45] Even though the extent of landownership varied slightly from one Appalachian zone to another, at least two-fifths of settler households in every geographical sector were landless. For southern Appalachia as a whole, nearly three-fifths of resident households owned no land.[46]

Land Speculation on the Last Indian Frontiers

By 1815 only the Cherokee and Creek territories of southern Appalachia remained closed to resettlement. During his travels through eastern Tennessee, a French aristocrat observed that whites had encamped illegally, waiting like vultures for the inevitable demise of the Cherokee Nation. Along the Tennessee River, he observed, "the region's lushness ha[d] attracted several colonists, who settled here despite the proximity of uncontested Cherokee territory."[47] The Cherokees complained repeatedly to the Indian agent about encroachers near their settlements. Even when federal troops removed them, the intruders "returned as thick as crows that are scattered from their food by a person passing on the road, but as soon as he is passed they return again."[48] In northern Alabama encroachers trespassed on Creek territory, as well. "All along the river [colonists] owned herds of cattle which they kept in the range on the Indian side of it."[49]

After additional Indian cessions and the forced removal of the region's remaining Native Americans between 1815 and 1835, southern Appalachia's final frontiers opened in western North Carolina, southeastern Tennessee, northern Georgia, and northern Alabama. State redistribution of these acres was even more inequitable than had been late eighteenth-century land dispersion. In a last-ditch move to expel all Cherokees from within their borders, each of the states enacted legislation denying landownership to

Native Americans. Even individual Cherokees, who had been granted small parcels and citizenship by the United States, lost their lands in state sales or were pressured to relinquish title to them. In Tennessee newly acquired Cherokee lands were sold in parcels of 160 to 640 acres, at $2 to $7 per acre. North Carolina surveyed only those lands worth more than 50 cents per acre, auctioning acreage mostly in 640-acre tracts, ranging in price from $4 per acre for first-quality to 50 cents per acre for worst quality.[50]

By structuring parcel requirements and prices so that only inferior acreage was within the reach of poorer settlers, state land policies favored large speculators. In addition absentee buyers circumvented residency requirements by hiring local attorneys or jobbers to act as their agents. Typical of the engrossment that ensued was the agglomeration of thousands of acres through the ninety-six Peet (New Orleans) and Gilbert (New York City) grants in Cherokee, Clay, and Graham Counties.[51]

Neither North Carolina nor Tennessee granted preemption rights to poorer settlers. Not until after 1823 did Tennessee acknowledge squatters' needs by allowing them to purchase for a six-month period their occupied parcels at $1.50 per acre—a higher price than the 12.5 cents per acre offered to later nonresidents. Not until thirty years later did North Carolina legislate preemption rights. Beginning in 1850 the state made available to such families previously unsurveyed areas that "were not considered worth twenty cents per acre." In addition to charging them 20 cents per acre, North Carolina required these squatters to pay their own titling costs, even though the state had publicly surveyed earlier grants.[52]

It is enlightening to examine the redistribution of Cherokee lands in Georgia, the only Appalachian state to offer free land. Any resident family head, widow, orphan, or veteran was eligible to receive a gold lot or 150 acres, plus 50 acres per family member or slave. In reality Georgia was not very successful at redistributing these lands to actual settlers. Moreover, Georgia declared squatters on Indian lands ineligible for the lottery. Despite state requirements that grantees live on the awarded parcels for at least five years, nearly half the land was held by absentees, two years after the lottery. In spite of Georgia's "free" acreage policy, 16 percent of the households held all the land, while the majority of Habersham County families remained landless.[53]

Speculation in the Public Domain

After 1819 southern Appalachia's federal public land opened in northern Alabama. The Huntsville Land Office was overtly corrupt under the supervision of speculator John Coffee. Coffee's official clique advertised their willingness to "give any information to people wishing to purchase to an advantage." For "a liberal per centum," the land office staff offered to "do business on commission, and receive in pay either a part of the land purchased; or money." In return for his collusion and protection, the clerks paid Coffee half their bribes from selling information, locating tracts, or purchasing lands for engrossers.[54] The public land office reflected the interests of wealthy planters who represented a sizable proportion of the speculators in northern Alabama. A Winchester, Tennessee, lawyer could sit on his porch along the turnpike and watch emigrants "flocking from every quarter of the adjacent territories. A large quantity of the travellers [we]re from old Virginia some of them having a hundred slaves in family."[55]

In addition to activity by the Yazoo Companies and the North American Land Company, numerous small combines of public officials, southern planters, and eastern backers engrossed the public domain. Using insider information from Coffee's clerks, syndicates organized to eliminate competition at public sales. By sending scouts out along the roads into Huntsville, these companies persuaded new emigrants to join their ranks or lose all hope of buying land. At the auctions, the companies operated as cartels to prevent prices from rising above desired levels and to squeeze out contenders for the best river tracts.[56]

In addition the combines solicited "hush money" from squatters who had already made improvements on acreage, promising that company speculators would not bid against them when their tracts were auctioned. When these monopolies outbid them at the sales, homesteaders were forced to pay higher than the appraised value to retain their improved parcels. Because there was keen rivalry for river and valley tracts, poorer settlers were pushed off such lands. Using insider information and bribes to the combines, planters and company-employed shills bid prices above the level squatters could afford. Subsequently the rush for northern Alabama lands generated an intense class struggle, as squatters organized their own schemes to resist the speculators. Teams of settlers rode through the countryside, marking prices on sections that had already been improved. "Those marks they took care to have considerably above the real value of the land. The company purchasers and other men of capital who went to explore the country previous to these sales finding such immense value set upon lands as they supposed, returned home and did not attend the sales."[57]

As a consequence of monopolistic tactics and official fraud, northern Alabama lands were overwhelmingly engrossed by absentee speculators and wealthy settler elites. Because public lands were redistributed in 160-acre parcels at $2 per acre, two-thirds of the settler households were priced out of the market and remained landless. Planters were so successful in monopolizing the best agricultural tracts that poorer settlers were driven into the least cultivable sections of northern Alabama. Once squatters were pushed off improved valley holdings, they sought and resettled tracts not desired by the speculators. Most of the public land entries lay along creeks or streams where the population density was twelve to thirteen people per square mile. Consequently the poorer squatters resorted to the hillier and more mountainous lands where there were only two persons per square mile in 1820.[58]

Continued Speculation and 1860 Landownership Patterns

Land speculation continued well into the mid-nineteenth century, with the active participation of local elites. Throughout the region, absentee owners or their heirs withheld from the market large tracts of land that had been acquired during the late eighteenth century. Such engrossers were always waiting for prices to rise or for future exploitation of minerals or timber. For example, European investors, such as those associated with Eugene Levassor, were just beginning to sell their Kentucky and West Virginia holdings in the 1820s. New York land baron John Greig did not dispose of 23,108 acres of prime Monongalia County farms until three decades after the start of resettlement. James Swan and Albert Gallatin retained control over their West Virginia holdings into the 1830s. In addition investors still collected rents on lots obtained when the frontiers opened, and Appalachian towns were heavily engrossed by absentee speculators.[59]

Well after the frontier years, wealthier planters of eastern Virginia and Bluegrass Kentucky invested part of their profits in nearby Appalachian holdings. Beginning in the mid-1800s local elites also bought up Appalachian mineral lands for distant capitalists. For example, O. P. Temple of Knoxville represented eastern interests in the Ducktown, Tennessee, copper mines, and he helped a Philadelphia firm to acquire Campbell County mineral lands. Johnson N. Camden, John W. Marshall, and Henry O. Middleton often utilized Philadelphia and New York backing to purchase West Virginia mineral holdings.[60]

Local merchants, lawyers, or public officials continued the frontier practice of serving as agents to lease acreage, invest in mineral holdings, or market timber for absentee owners. For instance, William McCoy and John Rogers managed rental properties in nine West Virginia counties for distant investors.[61] Facing the threat of passage of the Homestead Act in the 1850s, local land agents advised engrossers to move quickly to dispose of their Appalachian holdings before emigrants were attracted to cheaper opportunities in the Far West. Lewis Maxwell warned several of his clients that the homestead bill had not passed Congress "but will likely do so in a year or two, if so such land must fall in value. I believe that lands in this section of Country will sell higher the present and next year than at any time thereafter for the next ten years."[62]

Because they could not "sell profitably" to southern Appalachia's landless families, land speculators advertised their holdings in Europe to attract foreign immigrants. In 1845, for example, Cincinnati merchant Louis Chitti advertised in Europe 200,000 acres of Levassor's holdings in Lewis, Doddridge, and Gilmer Counties for the establishment of new immigrant "colonies in Western Virginia."[63] As a direct result of such long-term investment strategies, land was out of the reach of at least half of southern Appalachia's settler families. With so many large tracts of the region's lands concentrated into the hands of absentee speculators and local elites, acreage was neither cheap nor easily acquired. Consequently nearly half the region's households remained landless in 1860.[64]

Conclusion

Half a century before the decolonization of North America from the British Empire, southern planters and eastern capitalists expropriated vast territories of southern Appalachia from the Native American groups who lived and hunted there. In the economic and cultural collision that followed, new settlers displaced the Tuscaroras, the Shawnees, the Senedos, and the Toteros and forcibly expropriated the ancestral lands of the Cherokee Nation. Once the frontiers had been depopulated of their indigenous inhabitants, speculator and settler capitalism expanded into the region.

An interlocking network of distant brokerage houses, planters, merchants, corrupt local officials, and resident petty capitalists structured the redistribution of land on the Appalachian frontiers. By 1810 three-quarters of the region's acreage was absentee owned, and distant speculators laid out towns, sold or leased farms to settlers, and engrossed areas believed to offer wealth in minerals. Because of the concentration of land into the hands of a few absentee speculators and local elites, resettlement of the region was deterred. There was no such thing as free land or squatters' rights on the southern Appalachian frontiers; yet a majority of the emigrants to the region after the Revolutionary War were too poor to afford the prices set by speculators. Consequently land provided the economic basis for the structuring of a polarized Appalachian society in which the wealthy gentry amassed a majority of the acreage while more than half the settler households remained landless.

Notes

Funding for this research has been provided by the Woodrow Wilson National Fellowship Foundation and by an Appalachian Studies Fellowship from Berea College.

1. To permit the broadest analysis of the region's diversity, I have utilized the boundaries for southern Appalachia that are described in John C. Campbell, *The Southern Highlander and His Homeland* (New York: Russell Sage Foundation, 1921).

2. First quote is from 1763 proclamation in Charles J. Kappler, *Indian Affairs: Laws and Treaties* (Washington, D.C.: Government Printing Office, 1903–29), 4:1172. Second quote is from Worthington C. Ford, ed., *The Writings of George Washington* (New York: Putnam, 1889), 2:220. See also Phyllis R. Abbott, "The Development and Operation of an American Land System to 1800" (Ph.D. diss., University of Wisconsin, 1959); B. A. Hinsdale, "The Western Land Policy of the British Government from 1763 to 1775," *Ohio Archaeological and Historical Publications* 1 (1887): 207–29; Delf Norona, ed., "Joshua Fry's Report on the Back Settlements of Virginia (May 8, 1751)," *Virginia Magazine of History and Biography* 46 (1948): 22–41.

3. The Tuscaroras were pushed inland from coastal areas in several historical stages. In one era they settled in Amherst, Nelson, and Bedford Counties in Virginia. Shawnee villages had existed in western Maryland; western North Carolina; Frederick County, Virginia; and parts of West Virginia. The Senedos and the Toteros were seminomadic peoples who had lived along the riverbanks in the Blue Ridge foothills. See Louis Evans, *General Map of the Middle British Colonies and of the Country of the Confederate Indians*, 2nd ed. (Philadelphia: H. C. Carey, 1755); *Archives of Maryland*, vol. 23 (1884); Margaret T. Peters, *A Guidebook to Virginia's Historical Markers* (Charlottesville: University Press of Virginia, 1985); William G. Lord, *Blue Ridge Parkway Guide* (Washington, D.C.: Eastern Acorn Press, 1990), 1:139.9, 2:383.5. The histories of these Native American nations are detailed in numerous other sources and, for that reason, will not be repeated here. See, for example, R. S. Cotterill, *The Southern Indians: The Story of the Civilized Tribes before Removal* (Norman: University of Oklahoma Press, 1954); Louis DeVorsey, *The Indian Boundary in the Southern Colonies, 1763–1775* (Chapel Hill: University of North Carolina Press, 1961).

4. DeVorsey, *Indian Boundary*; Philip M. Hamer, *Tennessee: A History, 1673–1932* (New York: American Historical Society, 1933), 1:241; Archibald Henderson, "A Prerevolutionary Revolt in the Old Southwest," *Mississippi Valley Historical Review* 17 (1930): 198–204; Shaw Livermore, *Early American Land Companies: Their Influence on Corporate Development* (New York: Octagon Books, 1968), pp. 74–82, 90–97; Marshall Harris, *Origin of the Land Tenure System in the United States* (Ames: Iowa State College Press, 1953), 301–2. Short quote is from Lois Mulkearn, ed., *George*

Mercer Papers Relating to the Ohio Company of Virginia (Pittsburgh: University of Pittsburgh Press, 1954), p. 144.

5. Lewis C. Gray, *History of Agriculture in the Southern United States to 1860* (Gloucester: Peter Smith, 1958), 1:123; William L. Anderson, ed., *Cherokee Removal: Before and After* (Athens: University of Georgia Press, 1991), pp. vii–viii; Charles C. Royce, *Cherokee Nation of Indians* (Washington, D.C.: Bureau of American Ethnology, 1884). Numerous studies detail these removals; see, for example, Grant Foreman, *Indian Removal: The Emigration of the Five Civilized Tribes of Indians* (Norman: University of Oklahoma Press, 1953).

6. For information on resettlement phases, see Gray, *History of Agriculture*, 1:119–26.

7. The largest of these estates included Ross and Bryan Grant (100,000 acres); Borden Grant (925,000 acres); Roanoke Grant (100,000 acres); Beverly Manor (118,491 acres); Patton Grant (120,000 acres); Carter Grants (100,000+ acres); Greenway Court and Leeds Manor of Lord Fairfax (100,000+ acres); Van Meter and Kercheval Grants (40,000 acres); McKay and Heyd Grant (100,000 acres); Peyton Randolph (400,000 acres); Bernard Moore (100,000 acres); Hiscock and Griffin (100,000 acres); and Thomas Lewis (100,000 acres). For greater detail, see Charles E. Kemper, "The Settlement of the Valley," *Virginia Historical Magazine* 30 (1922): 169–82; *Kegley's Virginia Frontier, 1740–1783* (Roanoke: Southwestern Virginia Historical Society, 1938), p. 245; Robert D. Mitchell, *Commercialism and Frontier: Perspectives on the Early Shenandoah Valley* (Charlottesville: University Press of Virginia, 1977), p. 65; William D. Bennett, "Early Settlement on the New River System," *North Carolina Genealogical Society Journal* 10 (1984): 2–23; Warren R. Hofstra, "Land Policy and Settlement in the Northern Shenandoah Valley," in *Appalachian Frontiers: Settlement, Society, and Development in the Preindustrial Era*, ed. Robert D. Mitchell (Lexington: University Press of Kentucky, 1991), pp. 109–10.

8. Harris, *Land Tenure System*, pp. 299–300; Livermore, *Land Companies*, pp. 74–82; Paula H. Anderson-Green, "The New River Frontier Settlement on the Virginia–North Carolina Border, 1760–1820," *Virginia Magazine of History and Biography* 86 (1978): 416–18; Thomas P. Abernethy, *Western Lands and the American Revolution* (New York: Appleton-Century, 1937), p. 5; Elizabeth A. Kessel, "Germans on the Maryland Frontier: A Social History of Frederick County, Maryland, 1730–1800" (Ph.D. diss., Rice University, 1981), p. 95; Clarence P. Gould, "The Land System in Maryland, 1634–1820," *Johns Hopkins University Studies in Historical and Political Science* 31 (1913): 86–87; Bennett, "Early Settlement," 22. For example, Daniel Dulaney acquired 16,550 acres, which he surveyed into 100- to 300-acre parcels for sale or lease to German emigrants; see Aubrey C. Land, "A Land Speculator in the Opening of Western Maryland," *Maryland Historical Magazine* 48 (1953): 191–203.

9. Lee Soltow, "Land Speculation in West Virginia in the Early Federal Period: Randolph County as a Specific Case," *West Virginia History* 44 (1983): 111; Gaillard Hunt, ed., *The Writings of James Madison* (New York: Putnam, 1901), pp. 15–17; Henry P. Scalf, *Kentucky's Last Frontier* (Prestonburg, Ky.: n.p., 1966), pp. 469–70; *Annals of Congress*, 4th Cong., 1st sess., p. 340.

10. Derived from analysis of all land grants made before 1810 in the West Virginia counties of Randolph, Monongalia, and Hampshire, listed in *Sims Index: Land*

Grants of West Virginia (Charleston, W.Va.: State Auditor's Office, 1952). Residents were identified by utilizing an alphabetized statewide listing. For sources and statistical detail, see Wilma A. Dunaway, "The Incorporation of Southern Appalachia into the Capitalist World-Economy, 1700–1860" (Ph.D. diss., University of Tennessee, 1994), tab. 3.2.

11. After 1797 Kentucky's nonresident lands were recorded with the state auditor, and taxes were paid directly to the state treasury. Consequently, absentee landholders do not appear on county tax lists after 1796. See Nollie O. Taff, *History of State Revenue and Taxation in Kentucky* (Nashville: George Peabody College, 1931), pp. 17–18. The names of several well-known resident large landholders (e.g., the Clays) do not appear at all in county tax lists, or their names appear in some years but not others. It is likely that county tax assessors extended this exclusionary treatment to wealthy absentees as well. Short quote is from governor's message in Kentucky *House Journal,* 1869, p. 5. See Paul W. Gates, "Tenants of the Log Cabin," *Mississippi Valley Historical Review* 49 (1962): 5; Frederika J. Teute, "Land, Liberty, and Labor in the Post-revolutionary Era: Kentucky as the Promised Land" (Ph.D. diss., Johns Hopkins University, 1988), pp. 234–36.

12. John was the brother of William Blount, delegate to the Constitutional Convention and first governor of the Territory South of the River Ohio; see Alice B. Keith, "Three North Carolina Blount Brothers in Business and Politics, 1783–1812" (Ph.D. diss., University of North Carolina, 1940), pp. 108–10, 278–90, 296–98.

13. A. R. Newsome, ed., "John Brown's Journal of Travel in Western North Carolina in 1795," *North Carolina Historical Review* 11 (1934): 284–313; quotes from pp. 285, 295, 298–99, 303, 313.

14. Ray A. Billington, *Westward Expansion: A History of the American Frontier* (New York: Macmillan, 1967), p. 203. The Earl of Granville held the only colonial grant that encompassed parts of western North Carolina, including much of Randolph, Buncombe, and Haywood Counties to the Tennessee state line. Granville had located a land office at Edenton and sold parcels through agents. After the Revolutionary War, this grant was declared forfeit by the Supreme Court, and the lands were largely redistributed. References are to present-day county boundaries in western North Carolina. Information on grants was aggregated from George H. Smathers, *The History of Land Titles in Western North Carolina* (Asheville, N.C.: Miller Printing, 1938); Jason B. Deyton, "The Toe River Valley to 1865," *North Carolina Historical Review* 24 (1947): 423–66; William D. Bennett, "Josiah Brandon's Burke County, North Carolina, 1777–1800," *North Carolina Genealogical Society Journal* 7 (1981): 9; Ora Blackmun, *Western North Carolina: Its Mountains and Its People to 1880* (Boone, N.C.: Appalachian Consortium Press, 1977), 1:164–65.

15. Newsome, "John Brown's Journal," pp. 284–313.

16. Derived from analysis of all deeds registered in the 1789–92 Pendleton District deed books. Occupation and residency of buyers and sellers were usually specified; in addition, residency was also checked against the 1790 census. Estate or debt settlements and public auctions were distinguished from other transfers. For sources and statistical detail, see Dunaway, "Incorporation," tab. 3.3.

17. In the 1780s Maryland lands were selling at an average price of £5 (more than $20) per acre. See Harris, *Land Tenure System,* p. 247; Gould, "Land System," pp. 62–63.

18. Lee Soltow, "Land Inequality on the Frontier: The Distribution of Land in East Tennessee at the Beginning of the Nineteenth Century," *Social Science History* 5 (1981): 282, 290 n. For North Carolina and Tennessee military bounties, see *Laws or Laws Relative to Lands and Intestate Estates* (Knoxville: Roulstone and Wilson, 1800), pp. 35–40. In Virginia the land office and taxation were centralized at Richmond; see Harris, *Land Tenure System*, pp. 249, 334–52. In 1782 Kentucky squatters petitioned the Virginia assembly to require grantees to cultivate and improve the land; see James R. Robertson, *Petitions of the Early Inhabitants of Kentucky to the General Assembly of Virginia, 1769 to 1792* (Louisville, Ky.: Filson Club, 1914), pp. 66–68. However, Virginia never legislated any requirement more than nominal evidence of seating (e.g., constructing a makeshift cabin or use of the land by tenants).

19. Sixty-one sources were utilized to categorize absentee holders, including several genealogical and census listings and the following sources: W. S. Laidley, "Large Land Owners," *West Virginia Historical Magazine* 3 (1903): 243; Abernethy, *Western Lands*, p. 228; Scalf, *Kentucky's Last Frontier*, pp. 181–82; Robert D. Arbuckle, "John Nicholson, 1757–1800: A Case Study of an Early American Land Speculator, Financier, and Entrepreneur" (Ph.D. diss., Pennsylvania State University, 1972), pp. 482–83; Livermore, *Land Companies*; Bennett, "Early Settlement," p. 22; Soltow, "Land Speculation." Military land warrants encouraged land engrossment because of the manner in which these bounties were awarded. The acreage was staggered to reflect the status of the soldier so that the wealthiest officers acquired the largest grants of 2,000 acres and more; see Harris, *Land Tenure System*, pp. 255–67. For information about brokerage houses, see Robert P. Swierenga, "The Western Land Business: The Story of Easley and Willingham, Speculators," *Business History* 41 (1967): 1–20. There was extensive brokerage trading in military warrants because most soldiers sold their land bounties; see *American State Papers*, 38 vols. (Washington, D.C., 1832–61), *Public Lands*, 7:333–76. For the practice of dodging, see A. M. Sakolski, *The Great American Land Bubble: The Amazing Story of Land-Grabbing, Speculations, and Booms from Colonial Days to the Present Time* (New York: Harper and Row, 1932) pp. 36, 42, 52–53.

20. Southern Appalachian lands were owned by some of the country's wealthiest land barons, including Henry Banks, Coldwell and Vansweller, Francis and William Deakins, Jonathan DeWitt, Standish Ford, Michael Gratz, Hollingsworth and Pentecost, Robert Morris, Wilson Nicholas, James Swann, William Tilton, and Alexander Walcott (aggregated from 1790–1810 county tax lists). The Louisa Company and the Yazoo Companies were syndicates of merchant and planter capitalists; see Livermore, *Land Companies*.

21. Quote is from 1787 letter in William Calk Papers, University of Kentucky Library, Lexington, Ky. See jobber ads for military warrants in *Kentucky Gazette*, 21 April 1792.

22. Brown has left a detailed journal of his early 1800s jobbing for Baltimore capitalists in western Maryland and West Virginia. Quote is from "Uria Brown's Journal of 1816," *Maryland Historical Magazine* 10–11 (1915–16): 346. Similar midwestern land jobbers were found by Paul W. Gates, "The Role of the Land Speculator in Western Development," *Pennsylvania Magazine of History* 66 (1942): 314–33.

23. Neal O. Hammon, "Land Acquisition on the Kentucky Frontier," *Register of*

the Kentucky Historical Society 78 (1980): 315; Teute, "Land, Liberty, and Labor," p. 226; many letters in O. P. Temple Papers, University of Tennessee, Knoxville, Tenn., and in David Goff Papers, West Virginia University, Morgantown, W.Va. The quote is from a letter dated 28 July 1850 in Lewis Maxwell Papers, West Virginia University, Morgantown, W.Va.

24. As a public surveyor Washington mapped much of the Virginia and West Virginia area where he amassed an estate of 29,754 acres; see John C. Fitzpatrick, ed., *The Writings of George Washington from the Original Manuscript Sources, 1745–1799* (Washington, D.C.: Government Printing Office, 1939), 37:295–302. Calk laid off the town of Boonsborough, thereby acquiring prime town lots and linkages to locate prime river lands nearby; see entries dated April 1775 in "William Calk, His Journal," in Calk Papers. Quote is from a letter dated 2 January 1854 from a prospective buyer who complained about this surveying method, in the Eugene Levassor Papers, West Virginia University, Morgantown, W.Va.; second quote is from a letter dated 18 January 1840, also in Levassor Papers.

25. Sakolski, *Land Bubble*, 32; Teute, "Land, Liberty, and Labor," 225. Short quote is from "Uria Brown's Journal," pp. 365–66. Brown subsequently hired the clerk "as Agent over these several tracts of lands." Long quote is from Quarrier letter dated 17 July 1855, Levassor Papers.

26. Information about landholdings of Jefferson and Gallatin aggregated from 1800 county tax lists for Albermarle and Monongalia, Virginia. Maps and plats of Gallatin's lands found in the Felix G. Hansford Papers, West Virginia University, Morgantown, W.Va. For information about Lenoir, see Bennett, "Early Settlement," p. 22. The following are typical examples of the investment practices of the region's wealthy elite: Elisha Hall (Frederick, Va.) developed a syndicate of Philadelphia and Virginia investors who speculated in Blue Grass Kentucky lands; see Hammon, "Land Acquisition." James Lewis (Albermarle, Va.) invested in Alabama and Mississippi lands; see Gordon T. Chappell, "Some Patterns of Land Speculation in the Old Southwest," *Journal of Southern History* 15 (1949): 467. John Sevier and William Blount (eastern Tennessee) chartered a company to speculate in Alabama lands around Muscle Shoals; see A. P. Whitaker, "The Muscle Shoals Speculation, 1783–1789," *Mississippi Valley Historical Review* 13 (1927): 365–86.

27. First quote is from a letter dated 18 November 1854, Levassor Papers. See 29 July 1808 Agreement, McCoy Family Papers, West Virginia University, Morgantown, W.Va. In the mid-1800s, West Virginia merchants Samuel Tolbert (Lewis County) and John Rogers (Monongalia County) acted as agents for out-of-state landowners; see Talbott-Tolbert Family Papers and John Rogers Papers, West Virginia University, Morgantown, W.Va. See also Hammon, "Land Acquisition," pp. 310, 308; Reuben G. Thwaites, *Travels West of the Alleghanies* (Cleveland: Arthur H. Clark, 1904), 3:278. Second quote is from "Uria Brown's Journal," p. 363.

28. Fitzpatrick, *Writings of Washington*, 28:393.

29. "Report from the State Auditor's Office," 28 December 1816, Kentucky Land Office Records: Nonresident Land Owners, 1792–1843, obtained from the Family History Center, Church of Jesus Christ of the Latter Day Saints, Salt Lake City, Utah.

30. "Uria Brown's Journal," pp. 153–54.

31. Fitzpatrick, *Writings of Washington*, 28:436–37.

32. In 1730 Virginia grantees resold valley lands for six times the purchase price; see Thomas P. Abernethy, *Three Virginia Frontiers* (Gloucester: Peter Smith, 1962), p. 55. In 1793 western Maryland agricultural lands within fifteen miles of town were selling for $16 to $24 per acre; see Harry Toulmin, *The Western Country in 1793: Reports on Kentucky and Virginia* (1794; reprint, San Marino, Calif.: Castle Press, 1948), p. 54. In Tennessee lands sold for $2 per acre until the 1820s, with much higher prices for river lands. Only the worst mountain acreage sold cheaply at 12.5 cents per acre; see Henry D. Whitney, ed., *The Land Laws of Tennessee* (Chattanooga: J. J. Deardorr and Sons, 1891), pp. 58–61.

33. The Virginia lands described in the quote lay in Virginia, West Virginia, and Kentucky. See Edward St. Abdy, *Residence and Tour in the United States of America* (London: John Murray, 1835), 3:89.

34. "Memorandum of M. Austin's Journey from the Lead Mines in the County of Wythe in the State of Virginia to the Lead Mines in the Province of Louisiana, 1796–1797," *American Historical Review* 5 (1899–1900): 525–26.

35. "Governor's Message," *Kentucky Senate Journal*, 1828.

36. Derived from analysis of all 1787–1800 Appalachian land grants in eastern Kentucky. For sources and statistical details, see Dunaway, "Incorporation," tab. 3.6.

37. Frank W. Porter, "From Backcountry to County: The Delayed Settlement of Western Maryland," *Maryland Historical Magazine* 70 (1975): 338; G. Hulbert Smith, ed., "A Letter from Kentucky, 1785," *Mississippi Valley Historical Review* 19 (1932): 93. A similar pattern emerged in West Virginia, where postrevolutionary settlers owned less than 13 percent of the total acreage in three counties; see Abernethy, *Western Lands*. Only 33.5 percent of all land grants in Kentucky were settler and preemption claims; see Neal O. Hammon, "Settlers, Land Jobbers, and Outlyers: A Quantitative Analysis of Land Acquisition on the Kentucky Frontier," *Register of the Kentucky Historical Society* 84 (1986): 250, 259.

38. For examples of local planters who invested in Appalachian lands, see Peyton Skipwith Papers (1796–98), Filson Club, Louisville, Ky.; Edwin M. Betts, ed., *Thomas Jefferson's Farm Book* (Princeton: Princeton University Press, 1953); "Journal of John Sevier," *Tennessee Historical Magazine* 5, 6 (1919–20): 156–94, 232–64, 18–68.

39. Derived from analysis of manuscript county tax lists; $n = 9{,}223$. For sources and statistical details, see Dunaway, "Incorporation," tabs. A.1, 3.7.

40. Avery O. Craven, "Soil Exhaustion as a Factor in the Agricultural History of Virginia and Maryland, 1606–1860," *University of Illinois Studies in the Social Sciences* 13 (1926): 62.

41. Analysis of unpublished 1809 map of Frederick and Jefferson Counties, Virginia, at Library of Congress. See also Hofstra, "Northern Shenandoah," p. 124.

42. Entry dated 15–16 December 1773 in *Executive Journals*, 6:552–54.

43. "Extracts from the Journal of Col. Richard Henderson, 1775," in *A Documentary History of American Industrial Society*, ed. J. R. Commons (Cleveland: Arthur H. Clark, 1910), 2:225–26.

44. For example, the Loyal Company charged £3 per 100 acres for lands to which southwestern Virginia squatters had already been granted preemption; see Abernethy, *Western Lands*, pp. 90, 218. For other information about treatment of squatters,

see Gates, "Tenants," pp. 11–14; Teute, "Land, Liberty, and Labor," p. 153. Even poor relief carried a price tag. For example, North Carolina and Virginia enacted poor relief, empowering surveyors to lay off tracts of waste lands for destitute residents. Still, payment was due from the poor within two and a half years; see Smathers, *Land Titles*, p. 68; Harris, *Land Tenure System*, p. 246. See also Clarence C. Danhof, "Farm Making Costs and the Safety Valve," *Journal of Political Economy* 49 (1941): 317–59.

45. Derived from analysis of manuscript county tax lists; $n = 9,223$. For sources and statistical details, see Dunaway, "Incorporation," tabs. A.1, 3.7.

46. Derived from analysis of manuscript county tax lists; $n = 9,223$. For sources and statistical detail, see ibid., tabs. A.1, 3.8.

47. Stephen Becker, trans., *Louis-Phillipe, King of France: Diary of My Travels in America, 1796–99* (New York: Delacorte, 1977), pp. 66, 99.

48. The manuscript records of the Cherokee Indian Agency in Tennessee (1801–35) indicate the extent of illegal settlement on indigenous lands. For example, see letters or reports dated 17 June, 26 August, 17 November 1803; 22 February, 25 March 1805; 12 January, 20 February 1807; 22, 23 April, 23 May 1809; 6 September 1810; 1, 10 February, 2 March, 1 June, 12 September 1813; 18 February 1815; 7 July 1819. Quote is from Turtle-at-Home to Meigs, 1 October 1809.

49. "Autobiography of Gideon Lincecum," *Mississippi Valley Historical Review* 8 (1910): 448.

50. Smathers, *Land Titles*, pp. 82–85; Hamer, *Tennessee*, 1:255.

51. These lands were purchased from Peet and Gilbert in the early 1900s (see Smathers, *Land Titles*, p. 96) by the Champion Paper Company, around which there has been much present-day controversy over environmental degradation.

52. Hamer, *Tennessee*, 1:261; Chapter 25, Public Laws of 1850–51, *Code of 1883 of North Carolina*, 2:101–5.

53. Analysis of 1820 and 1830 deeds and census manuscripts. For sources and statistical details, see Dunaway, "Incorporation," tab. 3.9.

54. Chappell, "Some Patterns," pp. 467–68; quote is from *Huntsville Republican*, 21 January 1818.

55. Letter from James Campbell to Elizabeth Campbell, 18 November 1818, in Campbell Papers, Duke University Library, Durham, N.C.

56. Chappell, "Some Patterns," p. 472; Livermore, *Land Companies*, pp. 146–62; Whitaker, "Muscle Shoals Speculation"; *American State Papers, Public Lands*, 7:548–49.

57. *American State Papers, Public Lands*, 5:376–81. Such prime lands sold for $4 to $13.25 per acre; see Malcolm J. Rohrbough, *The Land Office Business: The Settlement and Administration of American Public Lands, 1789–1837* (New York: Oxford University Press, 1968), pp. 110–11. Quote is from a letter dated 8 January 1819 in Campbell Papers.

58. George Powell, "A Description and History of Blount County," *Alabama Historical Quarterly* 27 (1965): 112–13; John M. Allman, "Yeoman Regions in the Antebellum Deep South: Settlement and Economy in Northern Alabama, 1815–1860" (Ph.D. diss., University of Maryland, 1979), p. 139.

59. Neil A. McNall, "John Greig, Land Agent and Speculator," *Business History*

Review 33 (1959): 527–29; Levassor Papers; George W. Summers, "James Swan's Western Lands," *West Virginia Review* 12 (1934–35): 13–15; Henry M. Dater, "Albert Gallatin—Land Speculator," *Mississippi Valley Historical Review* 26 (1938): 21–38. Absentee engrossment of town lots evident from analysis of manuscript county tax lists.

60. For planter investments, see Barbour Account Book (1803–22), Barbour Family Papers, University of Virginia Library, Charlottesville, Va.; Warrick Miller Papers (1816–42), Filson Club; Means-Seaton Papers (1818–39) and Wickliffe-Preston Papers (1800–1840), University of Kentucky, Lexington, Ky. For mineral investments, see letters dated 29 September 1856 and 14 February 1859 in Temple Papers; many letters and agreements after 1830 in Johnson Newlon Camden Papers, John Williamson Marshall Papers, and Henry O. Middleton Correspondence, West Virginia University, Morgantown, W.Va.

61. O. P. Temple of eastern Tennessee and Lewis Maxwell and David Goff in West Virginia were land agents for absentee landholders; see Temple Papers; Maxwell Papers; Goff Papers. There are many lease agreements and letters in McCoy Papers and Rogers Papers.

62. Letter on Virginia Senate Chamber stationery dated 24 March 1853 in Maxwell Papers.

63. Copy of emigrant prospectus and plat maps, Levassor Papers. Also see earlier discussion of the marketing tactics of the John Gray Blount Land Company dealing in Tennessee and North Carolina lands.

64. Derived from analysis of a systematic sample of 3,056 households drawn from the 1860 Census of Population manuscripts. For sources and statistical details, see Dunaway, "Incorporation," tabs. A.4, 3.10.

Newer Appalachia
as One of America's
Last Frontiers

Historians have recently shattered the myth of a homogeneous Appalachia and are now investigating the nature and origins of the differences within the mountain region. I argue that southern Appalachia's internal economic differences can best be understood through the economic histories of what I call the region's three economic subregions. In this chapter I examine these subregions one by one, but not neglecting their relations with one another and with economic developments outside the region. At first it may sound implausible that economic developments have profoundly differed in three distinct Appalachian subregions. Could conditions have actually differed so much in different parts of the region as to explain the major economic differences now found? Isn't the region all hills?

Here the informed reader will answer that the region contains several different types of hills. If, for instance, you board an airplane in Roanoke, Virginia, and fly roughly northwest, you will fly over numerous wide and farm-filled valleys that are separated from one another by wooded ridges about 1,000 to 1,500 feet high. But then you will reach a wooded ridge that fails to descend into any valley. Geographers have called this "a mountain with one side, extending from Tennessee to Pennsylvania." They consider it "one of the most clearly marked plateau fronts to be found anywhere, . . . known for hundreds of miles as the Allegheny Front, a steep incline with an ascent of 1000 or 1500 feet from the east."[1] As you continue flying northwest beyond that front, you will see no more wide valleys for hundreds of miles. You will be crossing the Appalachian Plateau—an ancient tableland that eons of erosion have dissected into thousands of narrow hollows that twist and turn in all directions.

This Appalachian Plateau was the last great frontier in the eastern United States—a vast subregion of Appalachia where, less than 100 years ago, people were still venturing out with guns and dogs to hunt not only game animals but their own livestock.[2] Eventually, to the west, this immense dissected plateau merges into the rolling prairies of central Tennessee, central Kentucky, and central Ohio.

The plateau contrasts not only with the wide and fertile valleys that border it to the southeast—particularly with the Great Appalachian Valley in which Roanoke sits—but it contrasts also with the Blue Ridge country of North Carolina and Georgia. That Blue Ridge country is different both from the wide valleys and from the dissected plateau that rises northwest beyond the valleys.

Today the Appalachian Regional Commission (ARC) parcels Appalachia into three subregions that it labels northern, central, and southern.[3] The ARC places most of the Appalachian Plateau in its central subregion; nonetheless, much of the plateau lies in the ARC's northern subregion, and some of it falls into the ARC's southern subregion. This division presumably fits the ARC's public policy purposes, but it does not correlate with topography as well as the division that I have constructed, a division based on the historical sequence of Appalachia's settlement. The region's settlement sequence was prompted primarily by topography, by the lay of the land. As Frederick Jackson Turner once generalized, early American settlers poured "their pioneer plastic life into geographic moulds."[4]

My attempt to explain the region's economic heterogeneity will start with the topographical differences within the region. Beyond their direct effects, however, the topographical distinctions also led to a sequence of settlement that then took on a dynamic of its own. Thus, not all of the economic differences between the three subregions that I call older, intermediate, and newer Appalachia (see Map 3.1) resulted directly from their topographical differences. What shaped many of the differences more immediately was that the frontier closed at three different times in the three subregions. The

Map 3.1. Stages of the Appalachian Frontier

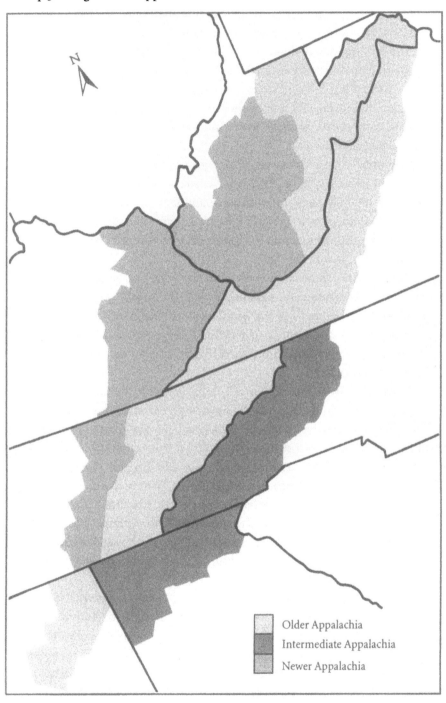

Source: From Paul Salstrom, *Appalachia's Path to Dependency* (Lexington: University Press of Kentucky, 1994); reprinted by permission of the publishers.

subregions became well settled and lost their frontier fluidity during three different eras of America's overall history.

Older Appalachia's frontiers closed between the 1770s and the 1830s. Intermediate Appalachia's frontiers were closing from the 1830s through the 1870s. Much of newer Appalachia still displayed frontier characteristics at the end of the nineteenth century. These were three very different eras in America's past, characterized by different conditions. In this chapter I will discuss certain demographic and technological differences between these three eras, but I will concentrate primarily on monetary differences. Changes in American monetary conditions over the long sequence of southern Appalachia's frontier closings became as crucial as demographic and technological changes in shaping the economic differences that we see today within the region.

Older Appalachia

Older Appalachia is so called because it was the first of southern Appalachia's three subregions to become well-settled by whites. It includes the Great Appalachian Valley, underlain by crop-nurturing limestone and running from Winchester, Virginia, in a southwesterly direction more than 600 miles to the Sand Mountain country of northeastern Alabama. This older subregion also includes numerous smaller valleys that are likewise limestone bedded and that run parallel to the spacious northeast-southwest trough of the great valley. Starting near Winchester in the Shenandoah Valley, frontier development worked its way southwestward through this large subregion from roughly the 1720s until the 1830s.

At first the technology and the larger economy of that early era made profitable here the gathering of ginseng and the use of guns and traps to collect pelts. As ginseng and wild animals thinned, considerable investment was made in farmland.[5] Many early settlers reaped profits not only from actual farmland but also from potential farmland that could be acquired at low cost and then could be held "for a rise." Considerable investment also went into exchangeable farm products, particularly into livestock, which was an investment that supplied its own transportation to markets.

In the 1780s a French visitor to the American backcountry wrote that "when you see the Shenandoah you think you are still in Pennsylvania."[6] Regarding this early era Gregory H. Nobles says that "the eighteenth-century southern backcountry became a kind of Pennsylvania writ large."[7] This characterizes the frontier era of the Great Appalachian Valley and the rest of older Appalachia. In early rural Pennsylvania, James T. Lemon tells us, "every man's goal was to hold property. Small holders had to look after themselves and their families." Pennsylvania's early rural settlers, says Lemon, were thrown "onto their own resources, so that land was staked out on a first come, first served basis. Everyone was forced to act individualistically, thus reinforcing the view that land was a commodity for exchange. . . . Most saw the land speculator, the pristine entrepreneur, as the paradigm."[8]

Another study of early Pennsylvania, this one specifically of far southwestern Pennsylvania during the 1770–1800 era, examines the settlement process as a sequence. Its findings, like Lemon's, resemble what Appalachian scholars are now discovering about the sequence of early settlement farther south. In southwestern Pennsylvania during the 1790s, we are told, the landowning elite as yet

> had neither the power nor the continuity to keep out new members. The area was too new; too many opportunities still existed. Nevertheless, the fluidity of the early years of settlement was passing. It existed as it had originally, only in the border townships. In the river townships, fewer people could now purchase very large estates, and the remaining great landowners were better able to dominate. Class lines, insofar as landownership defined them, were hardening; opportunity to own large tracts was declining. In these older areas, few lands remained to be claimed. The pressure of population—due both to births and to newcomers—forced land subdivision. Other things were also beginning to compete with land as the major indicator of wealth. The fact that three of the new major landowners of the 1790s were local, industrial enterprises indicates where much of the new opportunity lay and what the future had in store.[9]

The author adds that "the greatest opportunities were open only to those who had the wealth and resources to take advantage of them" and that "by 1796, those natural processes that sort out and stratify people, that create a class structure in any society, had already left their imprint on the frontier society of western Pennsylvania."[10]

Let us not quibble about whether those processes that sort out and stratify people are or are not natural. The point is that frontiers can be considered the beginning of an economic cycle. Much of what was exchanged in frontier areas was simply potential. Relative to their investment, sellers of potential received the exchange system's highest rewards—for sellers of potential could profit without producing anything. Natural resources, including tracts of land, were often exchangeable simply for their potential future uses. Nothing could have expanded exchanges more efficiently.[11]

Small wonder that, as James T. Lemon says, most early rural Pennsylvanians "saw the land speculator, the pristine entrepreneur, as the paradigm."

Recent case studies of the frontier era in specific parts of older Appalachia are discovering that these areas buzzed with entrepreneurial initiatives. The very earliest settlers admittedly experienced rigors in meeting their basic needs, but, following those initial hardships, abundant land allowed agriculture to emphasize livestock raising, and relatively little effort often sufficed to guarantee everyone's subsistence, leaving people with time to seek income beyond their actual needs. What Tench Coxe declared in 1794 about the New England and mid-Atlantic states applied all the more in older Appalachia. Coxe said that a "union of manufactures and farming is found to be convenient on the grazing and grass farms, where parts of almost every day, and a great part of every year, can be spared from the business of the farm, and employed in some mechanical, handycraft, or manufacturing business."[12] (In early Appalachia, however, most of the grazing occurred in the woods rather than on "grass farms.")

During the early settlement of older Appalachia, large potential profits inspired a rapid expansion of exchanges through speculative activity. In several areas pioneers found salt deposits from which they reaped great profits. The older subregion's largest salt bonanza turned up in far southwestern Virginia's Smyth and Washington Counties. Commercial development began there in 1782 and sprouted a long-distance salt trade up and down the great valley. Close at hand, an iron-making industry was spawned to supply kettles for boiling down the brine to produce dry salt.[13]

One part of older Appalachia where iron making flourished on a grand scale (by the standards of that early day) was the Upper Monongahela Valley of today's north-central West Virginia. Topographically plateau country, its limestone-based soils and its early settlement put it in older Appalachia. The elements needed for iron making were plentiful there, and the total cost of making pig iron ran only about $15 a ton. As the nineteenth century began, that area's iron makers could sell all the iron they could make for about $100 a ton.[14] Such profits soon prompted expansion and competition. By 1818—despite no change in iron-making methods—the price of Monongahela iron had fallen to only $58 a ton.[15] Throughout the early nineteenth century much of the iron (including the nails) that was marketed in the Ohio Valley and the Lower Mississippi Valley came from the Upper Monongahela Valley. But by the mid-1840s this iron industry had declined, and in the mid-1850s came a coup d'grace to its competitive position as large shipments of Upper Michigan iron ore began reaching iron makers in Cleveland, Buffalo, and Pittsburgh by water. Then the Upper

Monongahela area not only lost its iron-export markets, but it became an iron importer. Its locally made iron could no longer compete even in its local markets.[16]

Little money circulated through the hands of iron makers there. The area's leading iron maker advertised in 1804 that he would exchange his bar iron not only for cash but also for "wheat, rye, corn, beef, pork, tallow, beeswax, country linen, [and] flax and hemp, at a generous price."[17] A few miles north across the state line in Pennsylvania's Fayette County—so an early local historian relates—"an old furnace man told me that he once conducted business continuously for three years and saw during that time only ten dollars in money."[18]

Similarly, in the 1780s and 1790s in the Valley of East Tennessee, the extensive ledger of a merchant located in what is now Hawkins County reveals that only 7 to 19 percent of his credit entries (his receipt entries) included any cash payment. Most of his customers paid him in skins, furs, iron, cattle, horses, or salt—all of which were standard barter items.[19] Thus there too, and probably throughout almost all of early Appalachia, barter was more pervasive than cash purchases. By contrast, at Winchester, Virginia (which was the major entrepôt of the overall region), cash did change hands in a high proportion of market transactions by the 1790s at the latest.[20]

Most early settlers sought or at least welcomed not only the gains that they could achieve as producers but also purely speculative gains. As time passed, however, and as profit margins narrowed, the problem of assuring their own subsistence often loomed increasingly large in their calculations. As frontier conditions waned, increasing difficulties in assuring economic security demanded attention. For their economic security, settlers desired what they called a "competency"—by which they meant enough land and other resources to provide a household with a comfortable living.[21] Few households tried, however, to produce everything that they needed. Despite the scarcity of money, most households practiced intense exchange relations with other households and with merchants. They used moneyless exchanges not only to acquire the non-home-produced components of their subsistence but also to garner profits for themselves. Utilizing known prices, they established rough monies-of-account with each other, and on that basis they built up their own localized economic networks, exchanging favors with one another in a spirit of voluntary reciprocity. Although their resultant "subsistence-barter-and-borrow systems" bypassed contracts of exchange, and although such systems left the timing of each favor to mutual convenience, their systems nonetheless prompted them to deliver goods and services in a spirit of voluntary exchange rather than with any attitude of obligation. Charity aside, and except within families and households, almost every delivery of goods or services throughout Appalachia's history has been part of some exchange.[22] The workings of those exchanges have often eluded the analytic assumptions of outside observers, but the fact of their existence is obvious because (with the exception again of family obligations and of charity) able-bodied people who failed to reciprocate favors almost invariably ceased to receive any.[23]

Since older Appalachia was the first Appalachian subregion that was well settled, and since it was settled while vast spaces elsewhere in the United States still remained unsettled—by whites anyway—this older subregion was well populated several decades before its people began experiencing much difficulty in moving elsewhere. Ease of outmigration during its formative frontier years (and for decades afterward) allowed older Appalachia's rate of population growth to decrease substantially while Appalachia's other two subregions still remained sparsely populated and fast-growing frontiers. Except for the Civil War decade of the 1860s, newer Appalachia's decennial population growth never fell below 24 percent until the 1920s. In intermediate Appalachia, meanwhile, population growth never rose above 24 percent in any decade after the 1870s. As for older Appalachia, there the population growth rates rose above 24 percent during only three of the decades after the 1790s. (See Table 3.1.) Among older Appalachia's primary population outlets, incidentally, were intermediate and newer Appalachia.[24]

Thus, easy outmigration continued from older Appalachia well after its frontiers closed and its population growth slowed. In consequence, most of its farm households managed to maintain relatively large farms despite their farms' generally high soil fertility. Therefore, no subsistence crisis—no "Malthusian crisis"—ever threatened this older subregion. Its first settled locality, the Shenandoah Valley, saw frontier conditions already ending by 1776. Those frontier conditions had included rapid population growth, large potential profits per investment, and abundant resources that, besides providing direct sustenance and profit, also prompted a rapid expansion of economic exchanges.[25]

At the older subregion's southwestern extremity in the Sand Mountain country of northeastern Alabama such frontier conditions continued into the 1830s—as likewise they did in numerous remote crannies of this large and diverse older subregion, such as in southwestern Virginia's Burkes Garden.[26] But it is significant that even two decades later, in the 1850s, the surplus population of this older subregion could still find attractive migration outlets—including not only Appalachia's other two subregions but also newly opening sections of the fertile Midwest.[27]

Table 3.1. Percentage of Population Growth in Appalachia's Subregions, 1790s–1940s

Decade	Older Appalachia	Intermediate Appalachia	Newer Appalachia
1790s	57.7	58.5	482.6
1800s	21.1	39.0	78.7
1810s	23.6	28.4	108.4
1820s	30.1	65.0	58.0
1830s	13.0	60.0	39.0
1840s	27.4	64.0	62.3
1850s	13.2	30.5	48.6
1860s	6.8	9.6	17.7
1870s	34.1	34.7	46.2
1880s	20.1	22.3	32.7
1890s	19.2	16.1	24.2
1900s	15.0	6.4	32.8
1910s	12.4	7.1	26.5
1920s	11.7	17.5	19.7
1930s	10.7	16.7	17.4
1940s	13.8	8.8	4.1

Sources: U.S. censuses of population, 1790–1950.
Note: Early figures are often approximate due to slight boundary variations.

Intermediate Appalachia

To the south and east of older Appalachia, intermediate Appalachia encompassed the mountains and valleys of North Carolina and Georgia. In North Carolina the major valleys stood at significantly higher elevations than older Appalachia's major valleys, and until the 1830s much of this Carolina and Georgia high country was reserved for Cherokees. Thus this subregion attracted relatively few white settlers until the Great Appalachian Valley to its northwest had grown thickly populated.

Tyler Blethen and Curtis Wood have traced the career of a Scotch-Irish immigrant, James Patton, who spent many years traveling between Philadelphia and western North Carolina. Starting in 1789 Patton carried northern merchandise to the mountains of North Carolina and, on his return north, drove livestock to the cities of Baltimore, Philadelphia, and, later, Washington, D.C. In Patton's early years little money could be found in western North Carolina, but livestock was already being exported. Besides driving hundreds of cattle north, Patton also brought furs, beeswax, feathers, snake root, and ginseng out of the mountains. By 1793, after only three round trips, Patton had multiplied his capital from $200 to $2,800, and he had bought land in North Carolina and settled his family there. By 1795 he owned a string of stores in western North Carolina villages.[28]

During the frontier era that the intermediate subregion experienced, the first major sources of profit were furs, ginseng, livestock, and farmland. Later, gold mining became a major source of profit and drove the expansion of exchanges. In 1830 mining employed 25,000 people in North Carolina and ranked second only to farming among North Carolina occupations. Meanwhile, a new gold rush was getting under way in the mountains of northern Georgia.[29]

Those North Carolina and Georgia gold rushes constituted a form of hunting and gathering, however. No major value-added activities arose in intermediate Appalachia until a spate of small iron-making operations appeared in the 1840s and 1850s.[30] In the late 1820s iron had fetched five cents a pound, but after small bloomery forges began multiplying in the 1840s, the price stood at only four cents a pound.[31]

Almost by definition a frontier has to be a place where larger gains are available than the gains that are available in the areas from which it can easily be reached. John C. Inscoe shows that, in 1850, when the number of sheep per person in western North Carolina was 82 percent higher than the number of sheep per person in the rest of North Carolina, the area's population was shooting upward—rising 40.3 percent during the 1840s. Not just sheep were plentiful at that time in western North Carolina. The total number of cattle per person was 50 percent higher, the number of milk cows per person was 41 percent higher, and the number of hogs per person was 12 percent higher than in the rest of North Carolina.

Just ten years later in 1860, however, the number of sheep per capita in the mountain area had fallen to only 66 percent more than the number per capita in the rest of North Carolina. In cattle, the mountains' per capita figure was down to only 23 percent more, in milk cows down to merely 22 percent more, and in hogs per capita still only 13 percent more than the number per capita elsewhere in the state. Significantly those less dramatic advantages in western North Carolina's livestock per person were accompanied by less population growth—only 27.0 percent during the previous ten years (the 1850s) compared with the 40.3 percent rise that had occurred in the 1840s.[32]

The gradual movement of the frontier westward toward the High Smokies can be traced by the size of livestock holdings. In the Asheville vicinity about 1810, nineteen wills and inventories reveal, on average, a holding of twenty-two hogs per household. Cattle averaged only eight per household (and these were not large cattle), but three holdings listed more than twenty cattle. Only half of the lists included sheep, and their average numbers were fewer than the average cattle holding. Husbandry was not practiced to the exclusion of cultivation, however, since sixteen of the nineteen lists include plows. By far the largest crop was corn (maize), with oats, wheat, and barley following, in that order.

In the farthest western reaches of North Carolina, in Cherokee County, however, the holdings per household were still larger than those as late as 1850. Cherokee County had not been opened to white settlement until 1838, and as of 1850 its average farm held twenty-seven hogs, fourteen cattle, and eleven sheep[33]—significantly more than the average 1810 holdings based on the surviving inventories near Asheville.

In the intermediate subregion as a whole, including northern Georgia as well as western North Carolina, frontier conditions generally ended during the 1830s to 1870s. Nonetheless, timber exploitation would later rekindle frontierlike conditions when rail lines were built into remote recesses of the Smokies.[34]

Newer Appalachia

On the other side of the Great Appalachian Valley, to its northwest beyond the Allegheny Front, lay the dissected plateau country that is variously called the Cumberland, Allegheny, or simply the Appalachian Plateau. Here, frontier conditions continued longest. As the last of Appalachia's three subregions to be well settled, this plateau is called newer Appalachia. It constituted the last extensive frontier in the eastern United States. Not until the 1880s did its frontier conditions show signs of ending, and some of it remained wilderness into the twentieth century. Thus this last-settled subregion was still partly frontier during the rapid industrialization that began here in the late nineteenth century—a circumstance which entailed tumultuous consequences that attracted the entire nation's attention and that were linked to "Appalachian" images featured in the nation's new mass-circulation newspapers.

If we compare population growth rates, we find older Appalachia showing virtual demographic stability by the 1830s. (See Table 3.1.) Intermediate Appalachia did not display demographic stability until the 1880s or 1890s, and newer Appalachia continued growing by large decennial leaps until the 1920s. Dwight Billings and Kathleen Blee note that "fertility rates in Appalachia were higher than in any other major region of the United States in the nineteenth century. Rates remained exceptionally high but declined somewhat in the twentieth century; they remained highest in East Kentucky."[35] (Besides encompassing eastern Kentucky, newer Appalachia also includes southwestern West Virginia and east-central Tennessee, plateau areas that likewise carried high population growth well into the twentieth century.)

Understanding an economy requires understanding the perspectives of all its major participants. By the time newer Appalachia's frontier conditions were ending in the 1880s, few attractive new frontier areas remained in the rest of the United States—that is, few that many mountain farm families found attractive. From the 1830s onward the Ozarks had received a flow of Appalachia's young men and women, but by 1880 the Ozarks were more thickly settled than Appalachia. By then the average Ozark farm size was down to 121 acres, almost 50 acres less than the average Appalachian farm.[36] Even the rest of the trans-Mississippi West—beyond the Ozarks' comfortably Appalachian culture—offered mere pickings by the 1880s for newcomers who (like most Appalachian farm families) could bring little money to a new location.

One reason why major industrialization then began in plateau Appalachia was the increasing demand for lumber and coal in the nation's markets. Another compelling reason was the willingness of many Appalachian people to work for low wages. Their other earlier options had offered more autonomy and had been more attractive, but now those options were fast losing their viability. For thousands of plateau people the 1880s inaugurated a shift away from full self-employment toward working at least partly as the wage-earning employees of other people. The plateau's frontier opportunities were ending, and no new frontier beckoned. Purely speculative or gathered gains no longer abounded, and most economic assets now required increased amounts of initial investment before they could acquire exchange value.

Looking closer at what was occurring, we can differentiate four forms in which self-employed people made investments that yielded income. Some people were investing their land ("land" meaning all natural resources), some were investing productive goods (also called capital goods), some were investing money, and some were investing their labor. During each of the successive frontier eras enacted in Appalachia's subregions, most people made investments primarily in the form of their labor. Because most of older Appalachia's postfrontier farm families managed to maintain relatively large and productive farms, they could continue investing their labor. But many of newer Appalachia's farm families, still replete with children

Table 3.2. Average Farm Size (acres), 1850s–1940s

Decade	Older Appalachia	Intermediate Appalachia	Newer Appalachia
1850s	280.0	303.3	350.4
1870s	226.0	182.4	228.9
1880s	165.9	145.0	172.7
1890s	145.3	124.9	129.8
1900s	114.0	101.1	101.4
1910s	100.6	91.5	90.0
1920s	97.4	80.2	88.8
1930s	88.8	74.2	80.5
1940s	78.3	67.6	64.2

Sources: U.S. censuses of agriculture, 1850–1940.
Note: The 1860 census figures seem incorrect and are omitted here.

and lacking any attractive population outlet, could not manage to keep their farms large enough to supply a comfortable livelihood by merely investing labor. One reason is that their subregion was far more rugged than older Appalachia, but it is also crucial that it was settled later. In the late nineteenth and early twentieth centuries many of newer Appalachia's farm families had to quit investing at least some of their labor in order to begin exchanging it. They began exchanging some of their labor for wages instead of continuing to invest all of it in their own land (or in land that they had use of) to garner their own profits. Because they needed the extra income that wage work offered, they were willing to work cheaply to get it.

Had any inviting new frontiers remained by the time newer Appalachia's frontiers finally closed, far less of a turn toward wage labor would have occurred there. The majority of Appalachia's miners probably always preferred farming to mining.[37] But since no inviting frontiers remained, the newer subregion's average farm size continued rapidly shrinking until the turn of the century, whereas the average farm size in the older and intermediate subregions had already started leveling off by the 1880s. Between 1850 and 1890 the average farm size in the older subregion fell only 48.1 percent, a decrease of less than half. In the intermediate subregion the fall was by 58.8 percent. In the newer subregion, however, those forty years saw average farm size fall 63 percent—a decrease of almost two-thirds. (See Tables 3.2 and 3.3.)

Outmigration from the other two subregions was also stymied in the late nineteenth century.[38] But by then demographic growth had drastically

Table 3.3. Percentage of Shrinkage in Average Farm Size, 1870s–1930s

Decade	Older Appalachia	Intermediate Appalachia	Newer Appalachia
1870s	26.6	20.5	24.6
1880s	12.4	13.9	24.8
1890s	21.5	18.9	21.9
1900s	11.8	9.5	11.2
1910s	3.2	12.3	1.3
1920s	8.8	7.5	9.3
1930s	11.8	8.9	20.2

Sources: U.S. censuses of agriculture, 1870–1940.

slowed in those subregions (see Table 3.1), which saved most of their farms from shrinking very fast and saved most of their people from any need to work for paltry wages.

Meanwhile—and not only in Appalachia but throughout most of the United States—the 1870s and 1880s were offering Americans a declining prospect for attaining good returns from labor investments in low-capitalized farming. Subsequent decades would offer a prospect still worse. The Civil War Congresses had limited the value of both the land and the farm products of everyone who was already farming by dispensing free homesteads and by donating millions of acres to railroads, which busily laid tracks across dry plains that should never have been plowed, but were.[39] The 1870s saw total United States farm output jump by 53 percent, more than double the country's population growth during that decade.[40] The value of farm products fell, lowering profits from what farm families in all parts of the country would otherwise have gained and thereby also lowering, in economic jargon, the "opportunity cost" that Appalachian people paid by staying in place.

Before the Civil War, in 1861, a single day's farm labor in southeastern Iowa had bought five bushels of corn or forty pounds of pork.[41] When labor had been valued that highly, people with only their labor to sell—or to invest—had been able to accumulate other assets, such as land. After the 1870s, however, migrants who left Appalachia could no longer expect to find such high purchasing-power wages available elsewhere.

Meanwhile the postbellum land giveaways west of the Mississippi River, in tandem with the building of railroads, were also drastically reducing the ability of Appalachian farmers (and particularly of plateau farmers) to participate in supplying the agricultural markets of even their own region.

Thanks to farm mechanization in the Midwest and to railroads reaching from the Midwest to Appalachia, midwestern producers began supplying many Appalachian food markets more cheaply and reliably than Appalachia's own producers could supply them.[42] In one major exception to this market takeover, farmers in Virginia's section of the Great Appalachian Valley were able to supply grains and meat to neighboring cities as cheaply as those products could be supplied from the Midwest.[43] Elsewhere in Appalachia, however, farming grew more oriented toward meeting only subsistence needs, and this subsistence farming continued to make high labor demands because it provided no money with which to participate in the farm-mechanization revolution that was heightening productivity per farmer elsewhere in the United States. As the nineteenth century ended and the twentieth century began, tens of thousands of Appalachia's farm households were largely abandoning farming as an investment—as an enterprise—and were reducing their farm output to little beyond their own home provisions and a few neighborhood exchange items.

This transition was particularly acute in the subregion where attractive farmland had grown scarcest, in newer Appalachia. There, by 1890, a large segment of the farm population was starting to supplement its subsistence farming with wage earnings, especially with wage earnings from coal mining but also from timber and railroad jobs.

The sequence of settlement does not, of course, explain why rich seams of bituminous coal underlay the plateau, but the plateau's late settlement does help to explain why so much of its coal was mined. Coal extraction came to dominate newer Appalachia's economy not only "because it was there" but also because a subsistence crisis began to threaten this subregion, motivating many of its people to work for wages so low that numerous coal operators were attracted to the plateau from perfectly good coalfields elsewhere in the United States.[44]

Spurred by their subsistence needs, the plateau's miner-farmers worked cheaply. From 1897 to 1926, for example, the average West Virginia coal miner received, at most, only 80 percent as much in wages as the average coal miner elsewhere in the nation.[45] This occurred despite the average West Virginia coal miner working substantially more days.[46] The disparity was rooted in West Virginia's relatively worse subsistence situation, prompting West Virginia coal miners to accept lower wages than coal miners elsewhere were willing to accept. West Virginia's relative status continued worsening for decades. In 1889 the average wage of West Virginia coal miners per ton of coal was 83.1 percent of what coal miners were receiving per ton in the rest of the United States. Twenty years later, in 1909, West Virginia coal miners were accepting a mere 72.7 percent as much per ton as coal miners were receiving in the rest of the United States. They were accepting the nation's lowest coal-mining wage per ton. West Virginia's other coal-mining costs roughly equaled the national average, but its low wages made its total average cost of production the nation's lowest per ton.[47] With this profit-stimulus for its coal operators and this attraction for coal operators and investors to relocate in West Virginia from elsewhere—or at least to send investment money there—that state's share of the nation's total coal output rose from 9.96 percent in 1900 to 26.19 percent by 1930, which brings to mind an insight enunciated by Richard Wilkinson, that a "population's increasingly exploitable situation . . . provides the basis for the growth of capitalist institutions."[48]

Labor's relative cheapness in West Virginia also apparently affected that state's mine fatality rate. As of fiscal 1907 (July 1906 through June 1907) West Virginia miners were being killed on the job at the rate of 356 a year, which equaled 7.34 mine deaths per 1,000 miners per year, over three times the average fatality rate in the rest of the country's coal mines. In presenting this fact West Virginia's chief mine inspector commented that "our State has a high tonnage for each person employed, but a low tonnage for each life lost. It would appear that a large tonnage is gained at the expense of life."[49]

In this context of low wages despite high labor demands per worker, plentiful children provided short-term benefits to mining families in West Virginia and in the rest of newer Appalachia. In the short run, families often gained more by combining mining with farming than they could gain from either enterprise separately. Writing from southern West Virginia's Kanawha County in 1896 an organizer for the United Mine Workers reported that, in coal towns there, "every available spot of ground seems to have received attention from the plow or spade, the houses resemble the homes of the market gardener. . . . This explains their comparatively comfortable position. They raise all the vegetables they require and this assures them that the wolf shall be kept from the door."[50] Historian David Alan Corbin quotes one early twentieth-century miner as saying, "We needed a garden. We didn't always have enough [money] for food even when I was working." In southern West Virginia's Logan County a miner with ten children said, "The only way we could feed all of them on my pay was to raise a garden." A miner with six children said, "If we didn't raise hogs, corn and potatoes, we didn't eat." Another miner said, "We grew everything so we had to buy very little from [the company store]."[51] In southern West Virginia's Raleigh

County the Children's Bureau of the U.S. Labor Department found in 1923 that over 70 percent of miners' families raised crops and some form of livestock.[52]

Corbin mentions that "generally the job of caring for the family garden fell upon the miner's sons not yet old enough to work in the mines and his wife and daughters."[53] Mining families thus gained benefits from the subsistence work of their children, and large families continued common even after the plateau subregion began yielding its coal. Near the height of the plateau's coal age, in 1920, the average mother married to a miner in the United States had given birth to more children than the average mother married to a man practicing any other major occupation, including farming.[54]

Many coal operators saw that their profits could be raised thanks to the subsistence agriculture carried on by mining families. Operators often encouraged large gardens by providing free fencing and plowing and by offering seeds and fertilizer at cost. Such programs had begun by 1910 and continued into the 1930s. Many operators awarded annual prizes (some from large companies ranging as high as $600) for the best garden grown by a miner's family.[55]

By the 1920s, newer Appalachia had lived for several decades under the shadow of a threatening subsistence crisis that only income from the nation's coal markets was holding at bay. At the same time, to perpetuate that coal-mining income, miners and their families had to continue subsidizing the plateau's coal industry by simultaneously practicing a subsistence agriculture whose labor demands were worsening the subregion's long-term Malthusian threat by rewarding human reproduction. Plateau families' dual-employment work strategy thus tended to benefit them only in the short term. In the long run their strategy helped to impoverish both themselves and their environment while subsidizing coal companies and other industries that paid less than family-supporting wages.

The Role of Money

To explain the sequence of Appalachia's settlement and the economic results of its transition from frontier conditions to postfrontier conditions, we must remember three things. First, Appalachia was settled by stages. Second, as technology changed over time and as the larger national economy in which Appalachia participated was changing as well, a changing spectrum of Appalachia's resources attracted prime exchangeability. Third, a system of economic exchanges was already well established in colonial British

America before the Appalachian region received even its first white settlers in the 1720s.

In early Appalachia, as James T. Lemon says of early Pennsylvania, "every man's goal was to own property." Smallholders participated as well as large-holders because "small holders had to look after themselves and their families."[56]

James T. Lemon's description of early Pennsylvania could double as a rough description of each section of Appalachia during each section's frontier era. If we wish to understand frontiers, we must visualize them as "fronts." They were cutting edges of an inherently expansionary exchange system.[57] How that system worked was simple. It valued goods and services in accord with their exchangeability, and it expressed its values in prices. Prices in turn were produced by money changing hands. Although most frontiers experienced money scarcity, the early settlers nonetheless used prices in their exchanges, deriving those prices from quotations that reached them directly or indirectly from city markets where large amounts of money did change hands.[58]

By the time southern Appalachia's settlement began in the 1720s, much of British America's money supply consisted of paper money. In England the creation of paper money to augment specie had exploded during the 1690s and the early 1700s to finance simultaneous war and colonial expansion.[59] England's American colonies were soon issuing paper money as well.

Thus removed were restraints that previously had kept the money supply in approximate balance with the total value of other assets such as land, labor, and productive goods (e.g., tools and machines). Now, as the supply of paper "sterling" kept increasing, inflation stayed limited because sterling-mediated exchange relations were rapidly expanding as well. The spread of English-penetrated frontiers kept increasing the stock of land, labor, productive goods, and commodities that were available for exchanges mediated by the growing supply of English (and colonial) money. English (and other European) money supplies carried Eurocentric exchange relations to the ends of the earth, entangling many of the assets of non-Europeans in Europe-based values.[60] Among other results, this triggered frontier wars and inspired what John Brewer calls "an ideology of aggressive commercial expansion."[61]

Meanwhile, since paper money had to promise its own redemption on demand, its creation had to be matched by the creation of new debt that was owed to whoever had issued the money and promised to redeem it. Paper money, along with stocks and other paper securities, thus gradually created a colossal hierarchy of debt. One consequence was that age-old goals such as family security and reproduction came to depend on entrepreneurial exertion and investment by at least some proportion of the economy's participants.[62] Almost everyone's income, in other words, came to depend on a steadily growing percentage of society's overall income being composed of profit. When profit was not forthcoming (such as during depressions), then debts could not be paid and family security in turn was also threatened.

Thus nothing is mysterious, or even cultural, about what has intensified the search for profits during the past 300 years. The age-old predilection to accumulate wealth and join the elite continued to help drive the search for profits, but what greatly intensified that search was the skyrocketing level of debt. Appalachia's first white settlers were self-employed, but they were also in debt. They needed enough profits not just to maintain their livelihood but also to pay their debts. Because self-employment still pervaded Appalachia in that early era, the search for profit was correspondingly pervasive. In early Appalachia, as in early Pennsylvania, "every man's goal was to own property." Smallholders participated—this bears repeating—because "small holders had to look after themselves and their families."[63] If we wish to find family security and economic reproduction that required no major profit income, we will have to look back beyond Appalachia's settlement to America's very earliest colonial era, and also of course to the Old World before its expansion of paper money.[64]

Does the making of profit require exploitation? Perhaps, but so long as natural resources remained plenteous, it was not necessary that *people* be greatly exploited. Indeed, the people who settled early British America, and particularly those who settled older Appalachia, thereby made themselves hard to exploit.

When thousands of rent-racked flax and linen producers evacuated tiny leaseholds in Northern Ireland and came to America, and when many of them then migrated southwestward down the bountiful Great Appalachian Valley, exchange relations flourished among them. Merchants' ledgerbooks document that. Many of those exchange relations also depended on credit— such as on advances of merchandise that outside wholesalers provided to local storekeepers. Thus, seeds of capitalism were present from the very beginnings of Appalachia's settlement. But full-blown capitalism such as we know today is a distortion of balanced exchange relations in which money is dominant and the exchange positions of labor, of land, and of producer goods are subordinated to the position of money. During the early era when older Appalachia was first being settled, the people who were directly investing their labor, land, and producer goods could still hold their own against that era's money investors. But their position kept worsening.

When the Founding Fathers met in 1787 and devised a political balance between legislative, executive, and judicial branches of government, they created a prototype that could then usefully have been extended to the field of economic exchanges, but that did not occur. The political balance devised in 1787 inspired no economic provisions to maintain a balance between the exchange values of the nation's labor, land, productive goods, and money. United States society grew increasingly dominated by people who created and controlled money.

A rough economic balance nonetheless continued between the nation's regions, however, partly because paper money could equally be created everywhere—in all of the nation's regions and in small towns as well as in large cities. Although real wealth and control gravitated toward monied people and thereby accented class divisions, nonetheless the money interests of each region retained relative autonomy vis-à-vis the money interests of other regions. Not until the Civil War was favoritism conferred between the money interests of the various U.S. regions. Meanwhile, prior to the Civil War, Appalachia's initial frontiers were being settled and were "closing." As each of those earlier Appalachian frontiers in its turn closed, financial interests held growing power in local exchange relations, but the financial interests that did so were often local.[65]

During the Civil War, Congress enacted a far-reaching triumph for money's large-scale creators at the expense of its small-scale creators. Between 1863 and 1865 a series of congressional acts created a national banking system and, in addition, ended the ability of state-chartered banks to create banknotes, monopolizing that right in the hands of nationally chartered banks. National charters were restricted to institutions capitalized at $50,000 or more. Such institutions were concentrated in the oldest regions of the United States, where money and other assets had been accumulating longest. In newer regions a far larger proportion of wealth consisted of land and other natural resources, assets that the national banks were not authorized to accept as collateral for loans—that is, as mortgages. The Civil War legislation also required that banknotes be backed over 110 percent by money already extant and on deposit with the U.S. Treasury. Robert P. Sharkey says of the national banking system that "human ingenuity would have had difficulty contriving a more perfect engine for class and sectional exploitation: creditors finally obtaining the upper hand as opposed to debtors, and the developed East holding the whip over the undeveloped West and South. This tipping of the class and sectional balance of power was, in my opinion, *the momentous change*" of the 1850–73 period.[66] Jonathan Hughes finds that, after the Civil War, local and regional money interests rapidly grew subordinated to nationwide money interests. "By the end of the 1870's," he says, "there existed a giant American financial system, virtually a national market for money."[67] Only after this momentous change did Appalachia's last frontiers finally close in the newer subregion, the plateau subregion.

In surveying the overall course of Appalachia's economic history, we see its least-balanced exchanges eventuating mainly after the end of the region's 1770s–1880s century of successive frontier closings. We see also those least-balanced exchanges occurring primarily in the newer subregion, the last of the three subregions to lose its frontiers. We also see those least-balanced exchanges transpiring after a drastic Civil War-born disenfranchisement of the nation's local and regional money interests in favor of nationwide money interests.

Culturally, Appalachia often appeared internally homogeneous. Economically, however, no such Appalachian homogeneity existed. But neither can the economic differences just outlined between Appalachia's three subregions be explained solely by internal factors; it is necessary to take into account what was occurring elsewhere in the United States, for while Appalachia's successive frontiers were closing, the economic gains that the region's ordinary people would have been able to achieve elsewhere were simultaneously narrowing. That increasingly magnified the significance of what they had already amassed—especially (early) in the form of land engrossment and (later) in the form of financial wealth.

Appalachia was settled and it passed from frontier to postfrontier conditions within a British America and a United States that was thronged with commercial exchanges throughout the whole sequence. The sequence started in the fertile valleys of older Appalachia when conditions allowed most families to practice self-employment and to achieve considerable economic autonomy. A century and a half later, Appalachia's settlement sequence finally ended in the agriculturally fragile hills and hollows of newer Appalachia. By then the United States was more rife than ever with exchanges, but also by then the opportunities for self-employment and for economic autonomy had drastically shrunk, the exchange positions of labor, land, and productive goods had grown dominated by money, and Civil War legislation had subordinated Appalachia's own money interests to outside money interests.

Notes

The author wishes to thank the West Virginia Humanities Council and the Appalachian Fellowships of Berea College for grants that supported his research. In addition, he appreciates helpful comments on earlier drafts from Donald R. Adams, Jr., Jonathan Prude, and Randolph A. Roth.

1. J. Russell Smith and M. Ogden Phillips, *North America* (New York: Harcourt, Brace, 1942), pp. 253, 245.

2. The livestock hunted by its owners consisted mainly of hogs. For examples, see P. H. Butler, "Reminiscences," *Hickory and Lady Slippers* 4, book 2 (1979): 66–67; reprinted from the *Widen* (W.Va.) *News*, January 1936–December 1938.

3. The ARC's subregions are mapped in Ralph R. Widner, "Appalachian Development after 25 Years: An Assessment," *Economic Development Quarterly* 4 (1990): 294.

4. Frederick Jackson Turner, *The Significance of Sections in American History* (New York: Henry Holt, 1932; reprint, New York: Peter Smith, 1950), p. 38.

5. The thinning of both wild animals and ginseng followed the older, intermediate, newer sequence. On early ginseng depletion in part of older Appalachia, see Otis K. Rice, *The Allegheny Frontier: West Virginia Beginnings, 1730–1830* (Lexington: University Press of Kentucky, 1970), pp. 165–66. On later ginseng depletion in parts of newer Appalachia, see John Davison Sutton, *History of Braxton County and Central West Virginia* (Sutton, W.Va.: Privately printed, 1919), pp. 207–9, 211–14; Edwin Albert Cubby, "The Transformation of the Tug and Guyandot Valleys: Economic Development and Social Change in West Virginia, 1888–1921" (Ph.D. diss., Syracuse University, 1962), pp. 127–31. As for pelts, major pelt shipments from parts of older Appalachia were ending by the 1820s. Their scarcity in north-central [West] Virginia by the 1830s is mentioned in Reardon S. Cuppett, "Harrison Hagens and His Times" (M.A. thesis, West Virginia University, 1933), chap. 2, p. 4. The 1822 prices for pelts in Preston County, [West] Virginia, are also provided there. From parts of newer Appalachia, however, major pelt shipments continued for another half-century, into the 1870s. See Charles Henry Ambler, *West Virginia: The Mountain State* (New York: Prentice-Hall, 1940), p. 453.

6. Jacques Pierre Brissot, quoted in Warren R. Hofstra and Robert D. Mitchell, "Town and Country in Backcountry Virginia: Winchester and the Shenandoah Valley, 1730–1800," *Journal of Southern History* 59 (1993): 621 n. 8.

7. Gregory H. Nobles, "Breaking into the Backcountry: New Approaches to the Early American Frontier, 1750–1800," *William and Mary Quarterly*, 3rd ser., 46 (October 1989): 651.

8. James T. Lemon, "The Weakness of Place and Community in Early Pennsylvania," in *Early Settlement and Development in North America*, ed. James B. Gibson (Toronto: University of Toronto Press, 1978), pp. 197, 201–2.

9. R. Eugene Harper, *The Transformation of Western Pennsylvania, 1770–1800* (Pittsburgh: University of Pittsburgh Press, 1991), p. 47.

10. Ibid., pp. 139, 140. Harper's claim here that "natural processes" sort out and stratify people may grate on some readers. But on this point, see Richard Bendix, *Max Weber: An Intellectual Portrait* (Berkeley: University of California Press, 1977), pp. 259–60.

11. It would be interesting to know what proportion of the money supply of the early United States was backed by the collateral of resources that as yet yielded no return except through speculation on their potential.

12. Tench Coxe, *A View of the United States* (Philadelphia: William Hall, Wrigley & Berriman, 1794), p. 442; quoted in Timothy T. H. Breen, "Back to Sweat and Toil: Suggestions for the Study of Agricultural Work in Early America," *Pennsylvania History* 49 (1982): 250.

13. Ella Lonn, *Salt as a Factor in the Confederacy* (New York: Walter Neale, 1933), pp. 25–28; John Allais Jakle, "Salt and the Initial Settlement of the Ohio Valley" (Ph.D. diss., Indiana University, 1967), pp. 257–59. Likewise, in the first-settled part of newer Appalachia—which was western Virginia's Kanawha Valley—salt making was a major industry by 1810. See John E. Stealey III, *The Antebellum Kanawha Salt Business and Western Markets* (Lexington: University Press of Kentucky, 1993).

14. Samuel T. Wiley, *History of Monongalia County, West Virginia* (Kingwood, W.Va.: Preston Pub. Co., 1883), p. 256. Just north across the state line in Pennsylvania's Fayette County a 1794 "reduced" cash price for cast iron was advertised as £35 ($93.33). Sarah Heald, ed., *Fayette County, Pennsylvania: An Inventory of Historic Engineering and Industrial Sites* (Washington, D.C.: National Park Service, 1990), p. 41.

15. Greenville Iron Furnace, Preston County, [West] Virginia, Ledger, 1818.

16. James R. Moreland, *The Early Cheat Mountain Iron Works* (Morgantown, W.Va.: Monongalia Historical Society, 1992), chaps. 7, 9, 10, 13, 15, 22.

17. Advertisement by Samuel Jackson, 17 May 1804; quoted in Wiley, *History of Monongalia County*, p. 682.

18. Franklin Ellis, *History of Fayette County, Pennsylvania*, 2 vols. (Philadelphia: L. H. Everts, 1882), 1:509. More generally, see Arthur Cecil Bining, "The Iron Plantations of Early Pennsylvania," *Pennsylvania Magazine of History and Biography* 57 (1933): 122–25.

19. Ledger "B," kept 1782–94 by the merchant Thomas Amis in present-day Hawkins County, Tenn.; cited in Lucy K. Gump, "Half Pints to Horse Shoes: Meeting the Needs of a Growing Eighteenth-Century Appalachian Frontier," paper presented at the meeting of the Appalachian Studies Association, March 1993, East Tennessee State University, Johnson City, p. 3, as revised May 1993.

20. Hofstra and Mitchell, "Town and Country in Backcountry Virginia," pp. 638–41, 645.

21. Daniel Vickers, "Competency and Competition: Economic Culture in Early America," *William and Mary Quarterly*, 3rd ser., 47 (January 1990): 3–4, 13–29.

22. An in-depth analysis of exchange networks in Wayne County, W.Va., is provided by John Lozier and Ronald Althouse, "Social Reinforcement of Behavior toward Elders in an Appalachian Mountain Settlement," *Gerontologist* 14 (1974): 69–80. Today's revival of such nonmonetized exchanges is examined in Edgar Cahn and Jonathan Rowe, *Time Dollars* (Emmaus, Pa.: Rodale Press, 1992), with historical comparisons on pp. 15–28, 63–64, 71.

23. For numerous examples, see Ralph Mann, "Mountains, Land, and Kin Networks: Burkes Garden, Virginia, in the 1840s and 1850s," *Journal of Southern History* 58 (1992): 411–34. Theoretical discussion of these localized exchange systems appears in Paul Salstrom, "Subsistence-Barter-and-Borrow Systems: An Approach to West Virginia's Economic History," *West Virginia History* 51 (1992): 45–53. Both of these essays also discuss how bartering in Appalachia interacted with the larger

exchange system of the United States. A similar low-money exchange pattern has been discovered by frontier studies throughout the United States.

24. Ronald D. Eller, *Miners, Millhands, and Mountaineers: Industrialization of the Appalachian South, 1880–1930* (Knoxville: University of Tennessee Press, 1982), p. 126.

25. Robert D. Mitchell, *Commercialism and Frontier: Perspectives on the Early Shenandoah Valley* (Charlottesville: University Press of Virginia, 1977), pp. 37–39, 96–100.

26. On the settlement of Burkes Garden, see Mann's outstanding study, "Mountains, Land, and Kin Networks," esp. pp. 414–15.

27. For example, ibid., p. 426, describes people moving in the 1850s from Burkes Garden in southwestern Virginia to seek better opportunities in southern Wisconsin.

28. H. Tyler Blethen and Curtis W. Wood, Jr., "A Trader on the Western Carolina Frontier," in *Appalachian Frontiers: Settlement, Society, and Development in the Preindustrial Era*, ed. Robert D. Mitchell (Lexington: University Press of Kentucky, 1991), pp. 157–60.

29. John R. Crawford, "Private Money, Public Money: The Gold of North Carolina," paper presented at the meeting of the Appalachian Studies Association, March 1990, Helen, Ga., p. 3; David Williams, " 'Such Excitement You Never Saw': Gold Mining in Nineteenth-Century Georgia," *Georgia Historical Quarterly* 76 (Fall 1992): 695–707.

30. H. Tyler Blethen and Curtis W. Wood, Jr., "The Antebellum Iron Industry in Western North Carolina," *Journal of the Appalachian Studies Association* 4 (1992): 81, 84; U.S. Bureau of the Census, *Census of 1840, Compendium* (Washington, D.C.: Government Printing Office, 1841), pp. 174, 198.

31. Some of this price fall probably derived from currency deflation. See U.S. Bureau of the Census, *Historical Statistics of the United States: Colonial Times to 1970*, bicentennial ed. (Washington, D.C.: Government Printing Office, 1975), pt. 1, p. 211 (tab.).

32. Calculated from the U.S. Census for those years and from John C. Inscoe, *Mountain Masters: Slavery and the Sectional Crisis in Western North Carolina* (Knoxville: University of Tennessee Press, 1989), pp. 16–17 (tab.). Inscoe's figures exclude Alexander County from his mountain section (p. 26, map), but my figures include Alexander County.

33. H. Tyler Blethen and Curtis W. Wood, Jr., "Scotch-Irish Society in Southwestern Carolina, 1780–1840," unpublished paper, n.d., pp. 16–17.

34. The dating of lumbering in the Smokies is summarized in Florence Cope Bush, *Dorie: Woman of the Mountains* (Sevierville, Tenn.: Nandel, 1988), pp. 76–77, 84.

35. Dwight B. Billings and Kathleen M. Blee, "Family Strategies in a Subsistence Economy: Beech Creek, Kentucky, 1850–1942," *Sociological Perspectives* 33, no. 1 (1990): 71. Billings and Blee also mention that "hints of an agricultural crisis abound in the ethnographic literature" (p. 81). On the agricultural crisis of the 1870s–90s in central West Virginia, see James P. Mylott, *A Measure of Prosperity: A History of Roane County, West Virginia* (Charleston, W.Va.: Mountain State Press, 1984), pp. 101–6.

36. J. S. Otto and M. E. Anderson, "Slash-and-Burn Cultivation in the Highland South: A Problem in Comparative Agricultural History," *Comparative Studies in Society and History* 24 (1982): 131–47; U.S. Bureau of the Census, *Census of 1880* (Washington, D.C.: Government Printing Office, 1883), vol. 3, tab. 7. Interestingly, the Ozarks' two subregions share the pattern found in Appalachia's three subregions. First settled were what could be called the older Ozarks (southern Missouri). There, by 1880, average farm size had fallen only to 130 acres. But in the hillier and later-settled newer Ozarks (northern Arkansas), average farm size had already fallen to 109 acres by 1880. (For a map of the areas involved, see Otto and Anderson, "Slash-and-Burn Cultivation," p. 135.) Coal underlay a small portion of the newer Ozarks, as it underlay virtually all of newer Appalachia. But Arkansas coal was not significantly mined until long after 1880. See U.S. Bureau of the Census, *Census of 1910* (Washington, D.C.: Government Printing Office, 1913), vol. 9, p. 208 (tab.). Thus, the newer Ozarks' smaller average farm size prior to 1880, like newer Appalachia's prior to 1880, could not yet have been fostered by much industrialization.

37. In the early 1930s Homer Morris interviewed 956 unemployed coal miners in southern West Virginia and eastern Kentucky. One of his questions asked for their occupational preference. Whereas 460 answered "farmer," only 107 answered "miner"; see Homer Lawrence Morris, *The Plight of the Bituminous Coal Miner* (Philadelphia: University of Pennsylvania Press, 1934), p. 187 (tab.). Despite the depression then at its worst, 32.1 percent of those 956 unemployed miners said that they would not return to the mines even if they had the chance (p. 70 [tab.]).

38. See, for example, Durwood Dunn, *Cades Cove: The Life and Death of a Southern Appalachian Community, 1818–1937* (Knoxville: University of Tennessee Press, 1988), p. 74.

39. Public opposition ended the giving of federal land to railroads in 1871, but it could not prevent the damage that had already been set in motion. For a concise accounting, see Samuel Trask Dana, *Forest and Range Policy: Its Development in the United States* (New York: McGraw-Hill, 1956), pp. 36–38.

40. Willard W. Cochrane, *The Development of American Agriculture: A Historical Analysis* (Minneapolis: University of Minnesota Press, 1979), pp. 94, 340–41 (including tab.).

41. Smith and Phillips, *North America*, p. 379 n. 23.

42. On Appalachian farm products replaced by midwestern farm products in late nineteenth-century Appalachian markets, see Joe Cummings, "Community and the Nature of Change: Sevier County, Tennessee, in the 1890s," *East Tennessee Historical Society's Publications* 58–59 (1986–87): 70–75; William D. Barns, *The West Virginia State Grange: The First Century, 1873–1973* (Morgantown: William D. Barns, 1973), pp. 19–24; Nat T. Frame, *West Virginia Agricultural and Rural Life*, 2 pts. in 1 vol. (N.p., n.d.), pt. 1, p. 15.

43. Smith and Phillips, *North America*, p. 236.

44. Richard M. Simon, "The Labour Process and Uneven Development: The Appalachian Coal Fields, 1880–1930," *International Journal of Urban and Regional Research* 4 (1980): 56–57; Keith Dix, *What's a Coal Miner to Do?: The Mechanization of Coal Mining* (Pittsburgh: University of Pittsburgh Press, 1988), pp. 176–81. This

"comparative advantage" enjoyed by coal operators in Appalachia—thanks to lower wages there—was common knowledge in the early twentieth-century U.S. coal industry. See, for example, Frederick E. Saward, *The Coal Trade, 1917* (New York: Frederick E. Saward, 1917), pp. 40–41.

45. Within this 1897–1926 comparison of earnings from coal mining, the 1897–1909 data appears in Jerry Bruce Thomas, "Coal Country: The Rise of the Southern Smokeless Coal Industry and Its Effect on Area Development" (Ph.D. diss., University of North Carolina, 1971), p. 200 (tab.). The 1910–26 data is calculated from Paul H. Douglas, *Real Wages in the United States, 1890–1926* (Boston: Houghton Mifflin, 1930), p. 143 (tab.), and from West Virginia Department of Mines, *Annual Report, 1924* (Charleston, W.Va.: Tribune Printing, n.d.), pp. 249–50 (tabs.); *Annual Report, 1925*, p. 206 (tab.); *Annual Report, 1926*, pp. 198–99 (tab.).

46. Richard Mark Simon, "The Development of Underdevelopment: The Coal Industry and Its Effect on the West Virginia Economy, 1880–1930" (Ph.D. diss., University of Pittsburgh, 1978), pp. 271–72 (tab.). West Virginia's miners averaged 6.325 more workdays per year between 1897 and 1924 than U.S. miners overall.

47. *Census of 1910*, vol. 11, pp. 208, 209 (tab. 36), 219 (tab. 51). By 1909 Appalachian Kentucky as yet mined relatively little coal, and east-central Tennessee's output, although it had begun early, was never very large. These West Virginia figures thus roughly approximate the overall position of newer Appalachia.

48. James H. Thompson, *Significant Trends in the West Virginia Coal Industry, 1900–1957* (Morgantown: Bureau of Business Statistics, West Virginia University, May 1958), p. 6 (tab.); Richard G. Wilkinson, *Poverty and Progress: An Ecological Perspective on Economic Development* (New York: Praeger, 1973), p. 5.

49. J. W. Paul, "Institutes: What They May Accomplish," in *West Virginia Mining Institute: Proceedings, 1908* (Fairmont, W.Va.: Free Press Printing Co., 1908): 19–20 (incl. tab.). The West Virginia figure here does not include that state's Monongah mine explosion that killed at least 359 miners a few months later, in December 1907. In that general period West Virginia miners were producing about half again more coal per miner than were the rest of the nation's coal miners (p. 20 [tab.]).

50. Quoted in David Alan Corbin, *Life, Work, and Rebellion in the Coal Fields: The Southern West Virginia Miners, 1880–1922* (Urbana: University of Illinois Press, 1981), p. 34.

51. Ibid.

52. Ibid., p. 33. Often the land farmed or gardened by wage-earning families did not qualify as a farm under the census definition. Had all of the plateau's landholdings that yielded agricultural products been counted as farms, the plateau's average twentieth-century farm sizes at each census would have been far smaller than the average sizes listed in Table 3.2.

53. Ibid.

54. Morris, *Plight of the Bituminous Coal Miner*, p. 52 (tab.). The overall U.S. average in 1920 was 3.3 children born per mother. The average mother married to a U.S. farmer had given birth to 3.8 children, and the average mother married to a U.S. miner had given birth to 4.3 children.

55. Morris, *Plight of the Bituminous Coal Miner*, pp. 196–200; West Virginia Department of Agriculture, *Third Biennial Report, 1917–1918*, pp. 36–39; *Fourth*

Biennial Report, 1919–1920, p. 23. In several southern West Virginia coal towns, estimates placed the average value of gardens between 10 and 20 percent of the average miner's wages, even during the high-wage era of World War I. Livestock further supplemented mine families' incomes. Average mining wages in southern West Virginia calculated from West Virginia Department of Mines, *Annual Report, 1917–1918*, pp. 237–39; *1918–1919*, pp. 249–51; *1919–1920*, pp. 262–64.

56. Lemon, "Weakness of Place and Community," p. 197.

57. A pathbreaking exposition of this approach is Jay Gitlin, "At the Boundaries of Empire," in *Under an Open Sky: Rethinking America's Western Past*, ed. William Cronin, George Miles, and Jay Gitlin (New York: Norton, 1992), esp. pp. 71–80.

58. Winifred B. Rothenberg demonstrates this in "The Market and Massachusetts Farmers, 1750–1855," *Journal of Economic History* 41 (1981): 300–312, as does Donald R. Adams, Jr., in "Prices and Wages in Antebellum America: The West Virginia Experience," *Journal of Economic History* 52 (1992): 206–16, esp. pp. 206–7.

59. John Chapman, *The Bank of England: A History*, 2 vols. (Cambridge: Cambridge University Press, 1958), vol. 1, chaps. 1 and 2; Eugen von Philippovich, *History of the Bank of England and Its Financial Services to the State*, U.S. Senate, 61st Cong., 2nd sess., document 591, National Monetary Commission (Washington, D.C.: Government Printing Office, 1911), pp. 96–143.

60. R. D. Richards, *The Early History of the Bank of England* (London: Frank Cass, 1958), pp. 202–8.

61. John Brewer, *The Sinews of Power: War, Money, and the English State, 1688–1783* (Cambridge, Mass.: Harvard University Press, 1990), p. 169; see also pp. 168–76.

62. I am distinguishing here between goals and values. People are more likely to share economic goals than they are to share economic values. Economic goals are rooted in human nature, whereas economic values (i.e., evaluations) always arise in reaction to specific conditions and also always arise within the specific context of how a given economic system works. I appreciate Jonathan Prude pointing out that this distinction between goals and values (evaluations) overlaps with Max Weber's distinction between ideas and ideal interests. (See Bendix, *Max Weber*, pp. 42–48, 257–68.)

63. Lemon, "Weakness of Place and Community," p. 197.

64. On this issue, see ibid., pp. 201–7; Robert A. Dodgshon, *The European Past: Social Evolution and Spacial Order* (London: Macmillan Education, 1987), pp. 20–23. Nonetheless, some colonial Americans were seeking profits *before* the age of paper money. This is documented by John Frederick Martin, *Profits in the Wilderness: Entrepreneurship and the Founding of New England Towns in the Seventeenth Century* (Chapel Hill: University of North Carolina Press, 1991); see esp. p. 67.

65. Richard Sylla, "American Banking and Growth in the Nineteenth Century: A Partial View of the Terrain," *Explorations in Economic History* 9 (1971–72): 214–16.

66. Robert P. Sharkey, "Commercial Banking," in *Economic Change in the Civil War Era*, ed. David T. Gilchrist and W. David Lewis (Greenville, Del.: Eleutherian Mills and Hagley Foundation, 1965), p. 27.

67. Jonathan Hughes, *The Vital Few: The Entrepreneur and American Economic Progress* (Boston: Houghton Mifflin, 1966), p. 360.

Race and Racism in Nineteenth-Century Southern Appalachia

Myths, Realities, and Ambiguities

David Whisnant, one of the premier chroniclers of Appalachia, recently noted that whenever he read books that generalized about "the South," he amused himself by checking their generalizations against what he knows of the mountain South. Rarely, he said, was the congruence very great. Nowhere, in fact, has the incongruence between the highland and lowland South been more apparent than on matters of race. In one of the most celebrated regional generalizations, U. B. Phillips in 1928 argued that racism—or more specifically the quest for white supremacy—was the central theme of southern history. While that claim has been debated ever since, few scholars have objected to the basic premise behind it: that, as Phillips put it quite simply, the Negro was an essential element in "the distinctive Southern pattern of life."[1]

For a significant section of the South, the southern Appalachians, however, the African American presence has not been central, perhaps not even essential, to its distinctive pattern of life. That so integral a factor to southern life elsewhere is peripheral to highland society no doubt accounts for the fact that, despite increasingly sophisticated analysis of the complexities of both southern race relations and Appalachian society, the two fields have not yet intersected to any significant degree. Perhaps as a result, no other aspect of the Appalachian character has been as prone to as much myth, stereotype, contradiction, and confusion as has the matter of race relations and racial attitudes among mountaineers.

Historians have often skirted the question, but none have yet tackled it nearly so directly as have literary interpreters of the region. Two works of early twentieth-century fiction are particularly striking in their portrayals of the contradictory assumptions regarding racism among southern high-landers. Both works, one a short story and one a novel, use the Civil War as a catalyst through which mountain whites confront not only blacks for the first time, but their own racist proclivities as well. In so doing, they give dramatic form to the deep-seated discrepancies that have long plagued popular and scholarly ideas regarding the relationship between these two groups of southerners.

In his immensely popular 1903 novel, *The Little Shepherd of Kingdom Come*, John Fox chronicled a young orphan boy's move from Kentucky's Cumberland mountains to the Bluegrass. Chad Buford had never seen a black person until he left his home and moved to a nearby valley, where he encountered two slaves. Dazed, he stared at them and asked his companion Tom, "Whut've them fellers got on their faces?" "Hain't you nuver seed a nigger afore?" his friend asked. When Chad shook his head, Tom said, "Lots o' folks from yo' side o' the mountains nuver have seed a nigger. Sometimes hit skeers 'em." "Hit don't skeer me," Chad replied. A few years later, when the outbreak of the Civil War forced Kentuckians to take a stand for or against the Union, Chad, by then a teenager fully exposed to slavery and plantation society as they existed in central Kentucky, chose to fight for the Union, despite pressure from his Confederate guardians. Yet his attitude toward slavery or blacks was not central to his decision. His exposure to it had been brief, and the defense of slavery, Fox wrote, "never troubled his soul. . . . Unlike the North, the boy had no prejudice, no antagonism, no jealousy, no grievance to help him in his struggle."[2]

Nearly thirty years after the publication of Fox's novel, William Faulkner examined highland racial attitudes from another, far more dramatic angle. In a 1932 short story, "Mountain Victory," he wrote of a Confederate major from Mississippi and his slave, who in heading home from Virginia just after the end of the Civil War, came upon a Tennessee mountain family and asked to spend the night in their cabin. The bulk of the story involves the varied reactions of members of this family to their two strange guests and their racial identity. Only well into the story does it become apparent that the Tennesseans assumed that Major Weddel, of French and Creole ancestry, was black as well, which prompted him to taunt his hosts as to the source of their hostility: "So it's my face and not my uniform. And you fought four years to free us, I understand." Ultimately their revulsion toward the black and the close relationship he enjoyed with his master led to a violent denouement, an ambush by the mountain men that left both Mississippians and one of the Tennesseans dead.[3]

This powerful but little-known Faulkner story and Fox's far more widely read saga of Civil War Kentucky offer enlightening comparisons on a number of levels. Both are studies of the culture clashes between plantation aristocrats and poor white mountaineers, and both examine the tensions between Confederate and Unionist values that set southerner against fellow southerner. But perhaps most significantly, both Faulkner and Fox depicted highlanders' ignorance—or to use Faulkner's term, innocence—of the biracial character of the rest of the South and described very different responses by highlanders suddenly exposed to the reality of another race.

While more subtle in delineating the reactions of their mountain characters than many, Faulkner and Fox both relied on one of the most basic assumptions regarding preindustrial Appalachian society—the absence of blacks. This essay explores the implications of that demographic given in terms of both the myths and realities of a far more elusive factor—the racial attitudes of white southern highlanders resulting from that minimal or nonexistent contact with blacks and what, if anything, made their brand of racism unique. Which was a more accurate reflection of mountain racism: John Fox's young humanitarian hero or Faulkner's vicious and violent Tennesseeans?

Part of the romanticization of Appalachia that accompanied its "discovery" in the late nineteenth century lay in its perceived racial and ethnic homogeneity. "Nowhere will be found purer Anglo-Saxon blood," a journalist wrote of the northern Georgia mountains in 1897.[4] Ethnogeographer Ellen Semple extolled the mountain populace of Kentucky on the same grounds. Not only had they kept foreign elements at bay, she observed in 1901, but they had "still more effectively . . . excluded the negroes. This region is as free from them as northern Vermont."[5] After geological expeditions through the Blue Ridge and the Alleghenies in the late 1880s, Harvard professor Nathaniel S. Shaler wrote that there were "probably more white people who have never seen a negro in this part of the United States than in all New England." He was amused at the intense curiosity his own black servants evoked among highland men and women, some of whom traveled over twenty miles to stare at them.[6]

Appalachian residents contributed to the myth. In 1906 East Tennessee minister Samuel Tyndale Wilson, then president of Maryville College, stated categorically that the mountain region is "the only part of the South that is not directly concerned with the race problem." He even suggested that the commonly used term "mountain whites," which he found pejorative (too much like "poor white trash"), be replaced with simply "mountaineer," with no need for any designation by race. In *The Hills Beyond*, his semifictional interpretation of his region's history, Asheville native Thomas Wolfe claimed that the mountain people had not owned slaves and that in many counties, "Negroes were unknown before the war."[7]

Even Flannery O'Connor based one of her most celebrated stories, "The Artificial Nigger," on the premise that mountaineers had no contacts with blacks. The 1950 story, which O'Connor once said was her favorite, centers on an elderly northern Georgia man who brings his ten-year-old grandson on an excursion to Atlanta in order to expose him to the world beyond their isolated backwoods existence. The experience becomes one of continual encounters with blacks, which alternately baffle, intrigue, repel, and traumatize the two highlanders, whose backgrounds have left them totally unprepared for this strange race of people. Once safely back home, the young boy sums up his introduction to the biracial urban South: "I'm glad I've went once, but I'll never go back again."[8]

While O'Connor (like Faulkner and Fox) drew upon the assumption of a pure white mountain South to explore more universal racial themes, more recent scholars have made much of the propagandistic effects of that image. James Klotter has argued convincingly that it was the region's perceived "whiteness" that so appealed to northern interests at the time and inspired them to divert their mission impulses toward deserving highlanders after their disillusionment with similar efforts on behalf of southern blacks during Reconstruction. More recently, Nina Silber has suggested that northerners found postwar reconciliation more palatable with the mountain South, due to its racial purity and its loyalty to the Union during the war. These traits provided northerners with identifying links less apparent in poor whites elsewhere in the South, still unreformed rebels caught up in the biracial complexities of the lowland South.[9]

This basic demographic assumption, which Edward Cabbell has called Appalachia's "black invisibility" factor, is simple enough to refute and a number of studies in recent years have effectively demolished the myth that African Americans were a negligible presence in Appalachia.[10] Slavery existed in every county in Appalachia in 1860, and the region as a whole included a black populace, free and slave, of over 175,000. Freedmen and

-women continued to reside in most areas of the mountain South by century's end, when their numbers totaled over 274,000.[11] Most of the region's few urban areas, such as Chattanooga, Knoxville, Asheville, and Bristol, saw a dramatic influx of blacks in the decades following the Civil War, and communal experiments, such as North Carolina's "Kingdom of the Happy Land" and Kentucky's Coe Ridge, were established by freedmen and -women moving into the region from antebellum plantation homes elsewhere.[12] From the 1880s on, the coalfields of Kentucky, Virginia, Tennessee, and especially West Virginia attracted thousands of southern blacks and drastically changed the racial demographics of substantial areas of central Appalachia.[13]

There were, however, rural areas of the southern highlands from which former slaves drifted away. At least ten Appalachian counties lost their entire black population between 1880 and 1900, due to a combination of push (scare tactics) and pull (economic opportunity elsewhere) factors.[14] Thus by the end of the century there were large numbers of mountain residents whose contacts with blacks were negligible. It was they who served as the models of racial purity—or to use Faulkner's term, "innocence"—to both contemporary observers and later generations. But the nature of the racial attitudes spawned by this void, whether real or perceived, has proven a difficult aspect of the mythology to come to terms with. Like W. J. Cash's *The Mind of the South*, most treatments of mountain racism have characterized it as a single and simple mentality. But unlike Cash, who took over 400 pages to describe the regional "mind" as he saw it, most of what has been written about southern highlanders' racial views has been consigned to slight and usually casual references, based on conjecture, exaggeration, and overgeneralization. More often than not, the topic is mentioned only in passing in works with other concerns or priorities. Much is taken for granted, and no one to date has subjected the issue to either serious scrutiny, systematic analysis, or substantial documentation.

What makes the topic so intriguing is the sharp dichotomy that characterizes opinions as to how white mountaineers viewed blacks. On the one hand is the assumption on which Faulkner drew heavily—highlanders' inherent fear of and intense hostility toward the race that they alone among southerners did not know or control. Conversely there is the more extensively supported notion that the mountains were a southern oasis of abolitionism and racial liberality. Despite the pervasiveness of both schools of thought, proponents of one never seem to have acknowledged the other, much less made any direct effort to discredit it.

Cash's *Mind of the South* had much to do with giving widespread credence to the idea of mountain hostility to blacks. At least his one relevant statement is among the most often quoted. "Though there were few slaves in the mountains," Cash wrote, the mountaineer "had acquired a hatred and contempt for the Negro even more virulent than that of the common white of the lowlands; a dislike so rabid that it was worth a black man's life to venture into many mountain sections."[15] This was a belief to which mountain residents and chroniclers of the region had long adhered. Just after the Civil War, John Eaton, as commissioner of Tennessee's Freedmen's Bureau, noted that even though there were far fewer blacks in the state's eastern highlands, "the prejudice of the whites against the Negro was even more acute" there than in areas overrun with "colored" refugees, such as Memphis or Vicksburg.[16]

John Campbell, perhaps the region's most influential twentieth-century chronicler, presented a somewhat more judicious view of its racism but confirmed that there were counties "without a single Negro inhabitant and where it was unpleasant if not unsafe for him to go." Muriel Shepherd quoted a North Carolina highlander who, in explaining why there were no blacks, free or slave, in the Rock Creek section of Mitchell County, stated that "colored people have a well-founded belief that if they venture up there they might not come back alive."[17]

The idea of a more intense highland racism was widespread even in other parts of the South. In his recent memoir of his sharecropping childhood in middle Georgia, for example, black author Raymond Andrews wrote of a particular overseer: "Mister Brown and his family were mountain folks, or 'hillbillies,' but were considered unusual for the breed, as it was often said that folks from up in the hills had no use for lowlanders, particularly colored folks." William Styron made a similar point in *The Confessions of Nat Turner*, perhaps the most insightful portrait of the slaveholding South in modern fiction. In attempting to explain why Joseph Travis split a slave family by selling a mother and child south, he noted that Travis had moved to Southampton County from "the wild slopes of the Blue Ridge mountains." Styron, in Nat's voice, speculates: "Maybe it was his mountain heritage, his lack of experience with Tidewater ways, that caused him to do something that no truly respectable slaveowner would do."[18]

But while there is evidence of intense negrophobia among southern highlanders, the diminished presence of slavery there led many to far different conclusions as to the reasons behind the institution's relative absence. The belief has long held sway that "Appalachians have not been saddled with the same prejudices about black people that people of the deep South have," as Loyal Jones, one of the region's most perceptive interpreters, has expressed it.[19] This idea of a moral superiority among highlanders in regard to their racial attitudes is deep rooted and is based in large part on the stereotypical "rugged individualism" credited to mountain men. That perception, along with the reality of comparatively fewer slaves in the region, led many to the conclusion that the rejection of slavery was a conscious choice.

The concept of Appalachia as a bastion of liberty was well developed by the time the Civil War broke out, largely because the area was seen as a refuge for escaped slaves. The region was considered part of the Underground Railroad route out of the South, where according to one contemporary source, "rugged mountaineers forfeited life for the furtherance of the means of justice, and mingled blood . . . with the blood of millions of slaves."[20] More recently, Boston social worker Leon Williams described the region as "settled to a substantial degree by slaves and indentured white servants fleeing from exploitation and angry with established colonial America." "The hills, in their exquisite isolation," he continued, "became havens for the disenchanted black and white . . . who needed to escape burdensome drudgery and slavery."[21]

Historian Barbara Fields has even suggested that the movement of yeomen into the backcountry can be viewed as a southern counterpart to the northern free-soil movement. They migrated into the hills, she maintains, "to escape the encirclement of the plantation and create a world after their own image." Highlanders themselves often extolled the slavelessness of their region in Calvinistic terms later adopted by the abolitionist movement. "We are more moral and religious and less absorbed . . . than the people of West Tennessee," noted East Tennessean David Deaderick in his journal in 1827, virtues he credited to the fact that "where slaves exist in large numbers and where all the work, or nearly all, is performed by slaves, a consequent inaction and idleness are characteristics of the whites."[22]

John Brown long saw the southern highlands as central to his abolitionist schemes. As early as 1847, in a meeting with Frederick Douglass, Brown pointed on a map to the "far-reaching Alleghenies" and declared that "these mountains are the basis of my plan," both as an escape route out of the South and a base of operations from which uprisings against the plantation South could be directed. Douglass quoted Brown as saying, "God has given the strength of the hills to freedom; they were placed here for the emancipation of the negro race; they are full of natural forts . . . [and] good hiding places, where large numbers of brave men could be concealed, baffle and elude pursuit for a long time."[23] When Brown finally enacted his attack on Harpers Ferry twelve years later, the highlands were still crucial to his aims.

He hoped to move south through Virginia and the Carolinas, liberating the slaves of the plantation piedmont and sending them to a chain of fortresses established in the mountains to their west, from which they would hold their opponents at bay as reinforcements, black and white, gathered to form an army of liberation. "The mountains and swamps of the South," Brown reiterated to a fellow conspirator a year before his 1859 raid on that western Virginia arsenal, "were intended by the Almighty for a refuge for the slave and a defense against the oppressor."[24]

In the early months of the Civil War a Minnesota journalist suggested that the key to putting down the southern rebellion lay in the federal government embracing and utilizing the support it enjoyed within the South, particularly among southern Appalachians. The reason, he maintained, was that "within this Switzerland of the South, Nature is at war with slavery." Bondage, he implied, was incompatible with high altitudes: "Freedom has always loved the air of mountains. Slavery, like malaria, desolates the low alluvials of the globe. The sky-piercing peaks of the continents are bulwarks against oppression; and from mountain valleys has often swept the most fearful retribution to tyrants," and thus the Appalachians remained loyal to the Union and a "golden opportunity . . . to strike for Liberty and Union in all the Highlands of the South."[25]

Such sentiments became even more prevalent after the war, as northerners acknowledged the Union loyalty of much of the region. In an 1872 sermon William Goodrich, a minister from Cleveland, Ohio, was among those who extolled the virtues of the highland South. "Explain it as we may," he preached, "there belongs to mountain regions a moral elevation of their own. They give birth to strong, free, pure and noble races. They lift the men who dwell among them, in thought and resolve. Slavery, falsehood, base compliance, luxury, belong to the plains. Freedom, truth, hardy sacrifice, simple honor, to the highlands."[26]

So the creation of "Holy Appalachia"—as Allen Batteau has termed it in his recent study of the region's "invention" by outside interests—was under way. It was a creation sometimes based on rather convoluted reasoning. The admiration for the Anglo-Saxon purity of mountaineers' identity carried with it the implication that a conscious rejection of slavery on ideological grounds played a major part in their lack of racial or ethnic contamination. Abraham Lincoln himself was worked into this increasingly idealized formula and became to a later generation of mountain residents a patron saint of Appalachia.[27]

Even Harry Caudill, whose haves-versus-have-nots analysis of Kentucky's Cumberlands extended to antebellum tensions between the area's few slaveholders and its vast majority of nonslaveholders, believed that the latter's Unionist stance during the Civil War stemmed not so much from class resentment as from the fact that in some vague way "these poorer mountaineers, fiercely independent as they were, found something abhorrent in the ownership of one person by another." John Fox's idealistic young hero in *The Little Shepherd of Kingdom Come* was not, Caudill maintained, "the only mountaineer to risk or endure death on the battlefields because of a sincere desire to see the shackles stricken from millions of men and women."[28]

Another major factor in the image of Appalachia as "holy" ground was the establishment of several abolitionist footholds in the region. The frequently touted claim that the abolition movement began in the mountains rests on early efforts in Wheeling, Virginia; in East Tennessee; and later at Berea, Kentucky. As early as 1797 a Knoxville newspaper advocated the forming of an abolition society, and the next decade saw Benjamin Lundy fulfilling that charge in Wheeling. Lundy later moved to northeastern Tennessee, where he joined a number of "New Light" Presbyterians and Quakers from Pennsylvania and Ohio, who established what were among the nation's first manumission societies and produced the earliest antislavery publications. By 1827, according to one claim, East Tennessee had one-fifth of the abolition societies in the United States and almost a fifth of the national membership.[29] But most organized efforts were phased out or moved elsewhere within a few years, so that Maryville College in Blount County remained the only substantial base of antislavery activity for the rest of the antebellum period.[30]

Other forms of highland antislavery were more sectional in nature. In 1847 Henry Ruffner, a Presbyterian minister and president of Virginia's Washington College with small slaveholdings in Rockbridge County, stirred debate over—and for a brief period, considerable support for—a proposal that slavery, while firmly entrenched in eastern Virginia, could be gradually abolished west of the Blue Ridge "without detriment to the rights or interests of slaveholders." He proposed that all slaves in the Shenandoah Valley and surrounding mountains be transported to Liberia and that future importation of blacks into the region be banned. But much of Ruffner's agenda and the basis for much of the initial enthusiasm for his proposal grew out of resentment of sectional inequities that benefited a Tidewater slaveholding elite at the expense of westerners. Once constitutional reforms in 1851 alleviated many of those perceived abuses, support for Ruffner's emancipation scheme evaporated.[31]

Though less explicitly abolitionist in purpose, Berea College stood as a model of interracial education from its origins in the 1850s until almost the end of the century, the product of Kentucky-born, Ohio-educated abolitionist John Fee's quest for "a practical recognition of the brotherhood of man." Ellen Semple cited Berea as an example of "the democratic spirit characteristic of all mountain people" and concluded that its location on the western margin of the Cumberland Plateau was "probably the only geographic location south of the Mason and Dixon line where such an institution could exist."[32] As unusual as this experiment was in the postbellum, much less the antebellum, South, one can hardly credit its existence to Appalachian liberality. The school's turn-of-the-century shift to an exclusive mission aimed at mountain whites and preservation of their folk arts bestowed on Berea a reputation as a cultural center of Appalachia. Fee himself never thought of it as even located in the mountains. "We are in the 'hill country,'" he wrote in 1867, "between the 'blue grass' & the mountains. From the former region we now draw our colored men, from the latter the young white men & ladies."[33]

Merely on the basis of these rather limited or regionally marginal efforts, however, the concept of Appalachia as a solid bastion of freedom and equality has been difficult to shake, as scholars from Carter Woodson in the 1910s to Don West in the 1970s have implied that Appalachia was thoroughly and deeply abolitionist. Yet they have all distorted the evidence to make such a case, and their treatments of the subject are deceptive. Woodson, himself a black Appalachian native, published his landmark 1916 essay, "Freedom and Slavery in Appalachia," in the very first issue of the *Journal of Negro History*, which he founded and edited. He maintained that the Scotch-Irish who settled the southern highlands, a "liberty-loving, and tyrant-hating race," exhibited "more prejudice against the slave holder than against the Negro," and he stressed their antislavery sentiment in the region as pervasive and ongoing. Woodson's geographic scope was deceptively broad, however, and encompassed far more than the southern highlands, so that as much of his essay deals with abolitionist activity in piedmont North Carolina and central Kentucky as it does with those short-lived efforts in East Tennessee.[34]

West, a northern Georgia native and cofounder of the Highlander Folk School, has used only scattered evidence—from the East Tennessee abolitionists to incidents of Confederate disaffection in northern Georgia—to draw even more generalized conclusions regarding mountain liberalism on racial matters. From these few examples he claimed to demonstrate that the mountain South "consistently opposed slavery" and "refused to go with the Confederacy." The southern mountaineer, West wrote, "may be said to have held the Lincoln attitude generally."[35]

There was more than a touch of presentism in both Woodson's and West's historical claims. Each maintained that the racial tolerance of the antebellum period was part of a legacy still very much in evidence in the Appalachia in which they were raised. Woodson concluded his essay claiming that "one can observe even day-to-day such a difference in the atmosphere of the two sections, and in passing from the tidewater to the mountains it seems like going from one country into another. . . . In Appalachian America the races still maintain a sort of social contact," working, eating, and worshiping together. West, too, drew on his own childhood memories to make the same case. He recalled that he never saw a black person until he was fifteen years old and his family had moved from Georgia's mountains to sharecrop in the cotton country of Cobb County. Unfamiliar with the racial mores of the lowland South, the Wests welcomed their black neighbors as guests in their home and at their dinner table, much to the chagrin of local whites. When asked about it, his mother replied that she had always been taught to treat people equally, an attitude West claimed "was indicative of the sentiment of many people in the Appalachian South."[36]

So what is one to make of these extreme contradictions regarding highland attitudes toward blacks? Both contain significant elements of truth and perhaps even accurately convey the sentiments of certain pockets of southern highland society. However, there is another body of evidence that, while by no means either comprehensive or systematic, can be mustered in support of the idea that southern mountaineers were first and foremost southerners and that they viewed slavery and race in terms not unlike those of their yeoman or even slaveholding counterparts elsewhere in the South.

Certainly the most useful contemporary source on the subject is Frederick Law Olmsted. As a New York journalist he spent fourteen months traveling through the South in 1853 and 1854, observing and reporting on the region and its peculiar institution. The final month or so of his "journey through the back country," as he called the latter part of his tour, was spent in the highlands of Georgia, Tennessee, North Carolina, and Virginia. Although Olmsted was not completely objective in what he sought and how he reported it, his account of highlanders' opinions on slavery and race are invaluable for two reasons: first, unlike numerous other travel accounts on the region, his alone focused specifically on the issues of slavery and race; and second, he moved through so remote a section of the mountains that he was able to give voice to the most obscure and yet probably typical segment of the Appalachian populace.

While Olmsted noted some differences in slavery as it existed in the mountains, the comments he evoked from residents in many ways reflected attitudes not unlike those of nonslaveholding yeomen or poor whites elsewhere in the South at the time. Most seemed to be equally contemptuous of slaves, their masters, and the system itself. But given the option of eliminating slavery and the privileged class it supported, they consistently deferred to what they saw as the lesser evil. Few advocated abolishing the institution, and most were blatant in demonstrating that racism dominated their rationales for tolerating its perpetuation. Olmsted said of one Tennessee mountaineer, "He'd always wished there had n't been any niggers here . . . but he would n't think there was any better way of getting along with them than that they had." A highland woman reacted with "disgust and indignation on her face" when Olmsted informed her that blacks in New York were free. "I would n't want to live where niggers are free," she said. "They are bad enough when they are slaves. . . . If they was to think themselves equal to we, I do n't think white folks could abide it—they're such vile saucy things." An East Tennessee farmer found the mere presence of blacks to be the system's worst feature and refused to be a part of it. Slaves were "horrid things," he said, insisting that he "would not take one to keep if it should be given to him."[37]

Olmsted and others after him recognized the degree to which class resentment was also at the core of whatever opposition mountaineers felt toward slavery and its beneficiaries. In his 1888 paean to the "loyal mountaineers" of Tennessee, Thomas Humes echoed a major theme of Olmsted's by noting that slavery, "even in the modified, domestic garb it wore" among these highlanders, had "a depressing, degrading influence" on them.[38] Slave labor and the plantation system forced yeomen from their seaboard and piedmont homes up into the mountains, where they were somewhat insulated from the system's direct competition but were nevertheless denied the greater economic opportunity the outside world had to offer. Southern highlanders, according to a 1903 analysis, "were penned up in the mountains because slavery shut out white labor. . . . It denied those that looked down from their mountain crags upon the realm of King Cotton a chance to expand, circulate, and mingle with the progressive elements at work elsewhere in the republic."[39] As northern Georgia's Lillian Smith even more eloquently phrased it, "A separation began in minds that had already taken place in living: a chasm between rich and poor that washed deeper and deeper as the sweat of more and more slaves poured into it."[40]

At least some mountain masters sensed the potential for lower-class resentment to transform itself into antislavery sentiment. Former Virginia governor David Campbell, a Washington County slaveowner, cautioned fellow slaveowners in the state's southwestern corner about how tenuous the commitment to the institution was among their nonslaveholding neighbors. Most Virginians west of the Blue Ridge, he observed, "never expect or intend to own" slaves and were thus not susceptible to the fervent proslavery defenses to which they were subjected during the sectional debates of 1850. While he recognized the common bonds of white supremacy that bound whites of all classes, he urged owners to tone down their impassioned rhetoric to their yeoman constituencies, since "they are not at all interested—so far from it [that] many of them feel exactly like the men of Indiana and Illinois or any of the northwestern states."[41]

Yet whatever element of truth there was to these claims of yeoman indifference to slavery's survival—and Olmsted for one offers considerable firsthand verification—a part of the cultural baggage mountain settlers brought from the lowlands was an intense and deeply rooted racism. In that sense they were very much like their "plain folk" counterparts throughout the South. Even nonslaveholding whites living closer to slavery and feeling even more directly victimized by it kept their resentment of the institution in check by more dominant feelings of contempt, hostility, and social superiority toward all blacks, free or slave. Many, in fact, lumped "crackers" and "rednecks" together with "hillbillies" in describing these effects.[42] In short, antislavery sentiment among Appalachians did not mean that they, any more than other southerners, were what Carl Degler has labeled "enemies of slavery on behalf of blacks."[43]

The strong racial prejudices in areas without a black populace were not a phenomenon limited to the mountain South. Other Americans in nonslaveholding parts of the country were hostile to what little black presence, if any, they lived with and felt threatened by future prospects of a black influx. Alexis de Tocqueville had observed this racism without tangible targets during his visit to America in 1831. "In no part of the Union in which negroes are no longer slaves," he wrote, "they have in nowise drawn nearer to the whites. On the contrary, the prejudice of the race appears to be stronger in the states which have abolished slavery, than in those where it still exists; and nowhere is it so intolerant as in those states where servitude has never been known."[44]

Eugene Berwanger, in his study of attitudes toward slavery in the Old Northwest and other western frontiers, demonstrated that antislavery sentiment there was fueled far more by residents' prejudice against blacks and a desire to keep them out of their region than by any moral qualms about the peculiar institution. It took Rodger Cunningham to point out perhaps the most obvious link between Appalachia and other slaveless areas of the country. Dismissing moral components as causal factors, he stated that "the mountains were largely free of slavery 'only' because their climate, terrain, and soil were mostly unsuited to crops and plantation sizes for which slave labor was profitable." But this, he continued, "was also the reason the North had no slaves."[45]

Just as resentment of slavery was rarely based on humanitarian impulses toward its black victims, so there was little correlation during the war years between loyalty to the Union and abolitionist sentiment. Nevertheless, the degrees to which mountain men were committed to slavery's preservation has been a point of contention. Two nineteenth-century historians of East Tennessee (both natives of the region) have argued that its commitment to slavery was so strong as to endanger its place in the Union. Just before the state voted on 8 June 1861 to secede, Knoxville lawyer Oliver Temple laid out his priorities: "If we had to choose between the government on one side without slavery, and a broken and dissevered government with slavery, I would say unhesitatingly, 'Let slavery perish and the Union survive.'"[46] Thomas Humes contended that most "loyal mountaineers" would have agreed with Temple's choice. "Generally they looked upon slavery as something foreign to their social life," he wrote. "They would have been displeased at its coming near their homes in the imperious majesty it wore in the cotton States. At the same time they were satisfied to let men of the South keep serfs at pleasure, but they counted it no business of theirs to help in the work." Thus, he concluded, they would have had no hesitation in choosing "perpetuity of the Union over that of slavery."[47]

Most mountain Unionists were sensitive to charges that they opposed black bondage, however, and emphatically asserted their full support of the institution. In fact, highland spokesmen such as Zebulon Vance, William Brownlow, and Andrew Johnson argued against secession to their highland constituencies and readerships on the grounds that slavery was safer in, rather than out of, the Union. Alexander J. Jones of Henderson County, one of western North Carolina's most vocal Unionists, asserted that "by throwing off those guarantees—the Constitution and the Union—southern states have done the cause of slavery more injury than anyone else could have done." Others warned of the devaluation of slave property and the difficulties of reclaiming fugitive slaves who went north into what would be foreign territory.[48]

"Parson" Brownlow, whose Knoxville newspaper made him among East Tennessee's most visible opponents of secession, was quick to state that his "contempt for the Abolitionists of the North is only equaled by my hatred of the Disunionists of the South." Nevertheless, he expressed what were likely the sentiments of large numbers of mountain residents: "The Union men of the border slave states are loyal to their Government and do not regard the election of Lincoln as any just cause for dissolving the Union. . . . But, if we were once convinced that the Administration in Washington and the people of the North contemplated the subjugation of the South or the abolishing of slavery, there would not be a Union man among us in twenty-four hours." Many mountain Unionists felt betrayed by Lincoln's Emancipation Proclamation, and some even abandoned their loyalist stance as a result. Former congressman Thomas A. R. Nelson, one of East Tennessee's most influential antisecessionist voices in 1861, declared two years later that he would have advocated secession if he "had believed it was the object of the North to subjugate the South and emancipate our slaves." "The Union men of East Tennessee," he declared emphatically, "are not now and never were Abolitionists."[49]

The very fact that mountain slaveholders were among the most ardent Unionists is indication enough that abolition was hardly the basis of their anti-Confederate tendencies. Both Zebulon Vance and Andrew Johnson had modest slaveholdings, and many who owned far more slaves were equally as resistant to secession. Analysis of election returns in western North Carolina on a referendum to hold a secession convention indicates a fairly even split between slaveholders and little or no correlation between a county's slave population and its vote on secession.[50]

Perhaps the most striking example of this pattern—or lack of pattern— was the situation in Kentucky's Tug Valley. In her masterful study of the Hatfield-McCoy feud, Altina Waller noted the paradoxical fact that Harmon McCoy, one of the valley's few slaveholders, was also among the few residents who remained loyal to the Union when the war broke out. But in that area he was not alone. Slaveholders in Pike County were as a rule less likely to support the Confederacy than were most of its nonslaveholding farmers.[51] Studies of northern Georgia's mountain counties also indicate that the few residents with substantial slaveholdings were actively Unionist and in several instances served in the Union rather than the Confederate army.[52]

Likewise in those parts of southern Appalachia where support for secession was strong, highlanders' concerns about slavery's future under a Republican regime was a vital factor in shaping that support. In 1944 historian Henry Shanks argued that the strong secessionist vote in Virginia's southwestern corner (85 percent of its delegates voted to withdraw from the Union in May) was due to substantial ownership of slaves by local farmers and their bitter hostility to "abolitionism, to the Republican party, and to the election of Lincoln."[53] While such sentiments were taken for granted in most other parts of the South, much of the explanation for highland support of the Confederacy has generally been the independence and individualism inherent in mountaineers. Even more vaguely, as a western Carolinian wrapped in the romance of the "lost cause" explained in 1905, the mountain South seceded not as a defense of slavery but, rather, over "the real issue . . . a lofty and patriotic sense of duty which animated the Southern people of all classes."[54]

Until recently such rationales were accepted with little acknowledgment of how central slavery's survival was as a motivating factor for much of Appalachia's support of secession, despite evidence of considerable rhetoric to that effect. The crisis raised even greater fears as to the impact of slavery's abolition on the southern highlands, fears that mountain secessionists were quick and effective in exploiting. Georgia governor Joseph E. Brown, himself a native of the state's mountain region, appealed to the racial fears of his fellow northern Georgians in urging them to support their state's separation from the Union. Within the Union, slavery was no longer safe, he reasoned, and "so soon as the slaves were at liberty, thousands of them would leave the cotton and rice fields in the lower part of our State, and make their way to the healthier climate in the mountain region. We should have them plundering and stealing, robbing, and killing in all the lovely vallies of the mountains."[55] Western North Carolina politicians were just as vocal in raising the specter of such an influx among their constituents as they described "the terrible calamity of having three hundred thousand idle, vagabond free negroes turned loose upon you with all the privileges of white men." By the same token, in seceding from Virginia, West Virginians were sharply divided as to the future status of slavery in their new state constitution, but they had no problem in agreeing to a Negro exclusion policy that would ban either slave importation or free black migration into the state.[56]

There are other indications that some sections of Appalachia could claim no exemptions from the evils of southern racial prejudice. Slave markets existed in a number of mountain communities, such as Wheeling, Winchester, and Abingdon in Virginia; Bristol, Jonesboro, Knoxville, and Chattanooga in Tennessee; and London and Pikeville in Kentucky. (Witnessing the cruelties of the slave trade in Wheeling, in fact, set Benjamin Lundy on his abolitionist course.)[57] Slave auctions elsewhere in the upper South were apparently dependent on slaves supplied from highland areas, and it was not an uncommon sight, according to British geologist George Featherstonaugh, to see slave coffles moving through southwest Virginia and East Tennessee headed for deep South markets. On an 1844 trip through the southern highlands, he expressed amazement at the sight of slavedrivers with over 300 men, women, and children in chains, which he encountered both along the New River valley and then again in Knoxville as they moved their human cargo toward Natchez, Mississippi.[58]

At least one observer saw the mere living conditions of mountain slaves to be intolerable and was skeptical of claims for their well-being. Joseph John Gurney, a British Quaker traveling through the Virginia mountains in 1841, encountered black workers at White Sulphur Springs and was distressed at the "miserable manner in which the slaves were clad." After chiding their master, a physician, on their appearance, Gurney reported, "he assured me that the slaves were among the happiest of human beings; but it was nearer the truth, when he afterwards observed that they were remarkably able to endure hardships." He concluded from this encounter that "certain it is, that the negroes here, as elsewhere, are an easy, placid, and long-suffering race."[59]

Former slaves themselves bore witness to the fact that bondage in the southern highlands was not necessarily any less abusive than elsewhere. Sarah Gudger recalled the visits of a "specalator" to a neighboring plantation near Old Fort, North Carolina. He and "Old Marse" would pick out a slave from the field, and then "dey slaps de han'cuffs on him and tak him away to de cotton country." Mary Barbour, from the same county, testified that her master sold almost all of his slaves, including at least twelve of her brothers and sisters, when they reached age three. Aunt Sophia, a former slave from eastern Kentucky, contended that though her master "wuzn't as mean as most," a nearby owner "wuz so mean to his slaves that I know two gals that kilt themselfs."[60]

After the war the racial violence that plagued so much of the South was evident in the mountains as well. The influx of blacks into such cities as Knoxville, Chattanooga, and Asheville led to open unrest not unlike that in other southern cities. In Asheville, the attempt by a black man to vote in 1868 led to a race riot that left one black dead and several blacks and whites wounded. In his study of this and other such incidents, Eric Olson noted that in terms of reactions expressed in the local newspaper, there was little to differentiate Asheville from Savannah.[61]

Several studies of the northern Georgia mountains make the case that racial violence was no less apparent there than in other parts of the state during the postwar decades. Edward Ayers has noted that although blacks in Whitfield and other mountain counties posed little political or economic threat to white residents during Reconstruction, the Ku Klux Klan in that area was notorious for the brutal treatment it and other mobs inflicted on the relatively few blacks in their midst. "Honor reigned," Ayers observed, "with as much volatility among the whites of the hills as among their low-country brethren."[62] Yet Ayers argued that the postemancipation abuse of highland blacks was distinguished from that elsewhere in the South by the fact that it was integral to a long tradition of group violence and extralegal retribution among mountaineers, the majority of which was inflicted by whites on other whites. In analyses of the whitecapping that plagued Georgia's mountain counties during the moonshine wars of the 1880s and 1890s, both Will Holmes and Fitzhugh Brundage confirm the biracial makeup of whitecappers' targets but note that blacks were whipped and murdered for offenses that included insolence or miscegenation as well as any threat they might have posed to moonshiners' security.[63]

In his statistical analysis of racial violence in late nineteenth-century Kentucky, George Wright noted that while mountain residents lynched fewer blacks than did other Kentuckians, they did so at a rate proportionate to the region's African American populace.[64] In a more broadly cast statistical study of racial violence in Appalachia, Robert Stuckert suggests that blacks were more often victimized by white mobs in mountain areas than elsewhere. Though only 6 percent of the black population of seven southern states lived in the highlands, over 10 percent of the blacks lynched in those states were Appalachian residents.[65] Brundage confirms these findings with his rather startling discovery that no area of Virginia saw more lynchings than did its mountain counties. Of a total of seventy blacks lynched in Virginia between 1880 and 1930, no less than twenty-four lost their lives in southwestern counties, a phenomenon Brundage credits to the "furious pace" of the region's postwar social and economic transformations, particularly the influx of itinerant black and foreign workers into mining and lumber camps. The fact that most occurred in towns, the centers of this change, rather than in the hills or countryside, confirms the economic roots of this particular expression of mountain racism.[66]

Although some Appalachians exhibited the same violent and abusive treatment toward blacks as other southerners, there are also indications of "kinder and gentler" race relations in the region. I have suggested elsewhere that slaveholders in the Carolina highlands exhibited more benevolent attitudes and lenient treatment toward their black property than was usual in the lowland South. Despite the conclusions of British Quaker Joseph John Gurney that slaves in southwestern Virginia were no better off than those in other parts of the South, other outside observers have provided among the most explicit testimony that there was indeed a qualitative difference in the treatment of highland bondsmen. Charles Lanman, for example, wrote in

1849 that "the slaves residing among the mountains are the happiest and most independent portion of the population." Olmsted noted that in the southern highlands, slavery's "moral evils . . . are less, even proportionately to the number of slaves." He detected that they were "less closely superintended. . . . They exercise more responsibility, and both in soul and intellect they are more elevated."[67] I also detected among mountain masters in North Carolina what seemed to be a preponderance of acts of goodwill, affectionate references to their slaves, unusual efforts—including on occasion financial sacrifice—to ensure their welfare and happiness, and even occasional pangs of conscience about the system.[68]

Other scholars have also noted greater moderation or leniency in highland race relations. In an analysis of political divisiveness in Virginia from 1790 to 1830, Van Beck Hall demonstrated the degree to which western legislators, while fully supportive of slavery itself, often differed from their eastern counterparts on more peripheral issues regarding blacks. On various occasions Appalachian delegates blocked proposals to toughen manumission procedures, to pass retaliatory measures against blacks after Gabriel Prosser's aborted 1800 rebellion, and to ban the distribution of abolitionist publications in the state. At the same time they supported measures to liberalize restrictions on the state's free black population, to end compensation for masters of slave criminals who were executed or banished, and to support Richmond free black efforts to establish their own church.[69]

Even during the intense racist repression of the Reconstruction era, some highlanders showed more restraint in dealing with the new freedman population than southerners elsewhere. In his comprehensive study of the Republican Party in the southern highlands, Gordon McKinney credited at least part of the explanation for its success there to "the relative lack of hostility between mountain whites and blacks," though he noted that it was an alliance based far more on political pragmatism than humanitarian ideals.[70] Despite John Eaton's observations regarding racism in Reconstruction Tennessee, a recent study has suggested that emancipation was accepted more quickly in East Tennessee than was true elsewhere in the occupied South.[71] Eric Olson concluded his study of racial postwar violence in Asheville with the suggestion that the incidents he described were more the exception than the rule; the disruptions remained more isolated and their effects more easily contained than was the case in similar incidents in Atlanta, for example.[72] J. Morgan Kousser, in documenting racial disfranchisement in the turn-of-the-century South, noted that hill country whites were among the few who opposed denying blacks the political rights they had gained a generation earlier, though such resistance had less to do with any benevolence toward blacks than with the realization that they were often the unacknowledged secondary victims of such measures as literacy tests, poll taxes, and understanding clauses.[73]

So where are we left in terms of characterizing the racism of nineteenth-century Appalachians? The reality seems almost as contradictory and confusing as the myths. If the evidence presented here does not span quite the extremes of the popular assumptions laid out in fictional form by Fox and Faulkner, it fills in much of the intervening space along that vast spectrum of opinion. The nature of the evidence on racism at the grassroots level of any populace is and must remain scattered, speculative, and circumstantial, so that any definitive or comprehensive statement on how mountain whites viewed blacks remains elusive. But the sheer range of experiences—lynchings and race riots occurring in areas where abolitionism had thrived; blacks moving quickly into some parts of the region when given the option, while deserting others just as rapidly; some highlanders willing to leave the Union to protect slavery while others proved relatively receptive to emancipation—all demonstrate the dangers of generalizing about highland attitudes and of drawing any hard and fast conclusions about a society that has been subjected to far more than its share of homogenization, stereotyping, and image-making.

Barbara Fields has warned us of the dangers of according race "a transhistorical, almost metaphysical, status," noting that "ideas about color, like ideas about anything else, derive their importance, indeed their very definition, from their context."[74] The variety of white responses to blacks in southern Appalachia serves as a vivid reminder of the fact that racial attitudes and actions are indeed functions of other social, economic, political, or even sectional forces. The power struggles between a state's mountain region and its state government or lowland elite; the politicalization of slavery, emancipation, and later disfranchisement and segregation; the demographic shifts, often dramatic, of populations black and white into or out of highland areas; the effects of poverty and other forms of material stagnation or deprivation; the new dynamics of community and class, and accompanying tensions, brought on by colonialism, industrialization, urbanization, and other forces of modernization—all of these were very real aspects of the Appalachian experience that could, and often did, affect racial attitudes. The actual contacts between mountain whites and blacks were of course a crucial—but far from consistent or predictable—factor in shaping race relations in the region. But these other factors were equally significant, if more subtle, determinants of highlanders' perceptions and treatment of blacks. The variations in pace and degree at which these changes were felt throughout the region may be the key to explaining the quiltlike character of highland racism.

Fields reminds us, too, that racism can be a slippery concept to pin down. "Attitudes," she maintains, "are promiscuous critters and do not mind cohabiting with their opposites."[75] Such was certainly true of racism's highland manifestations. The fluidity and often contradictory expressions of racial opinions among mountaineers reflect the diversity and complexity of experience rarely acknowledged about Appalachia and its historical development. Once that range of experience is recognized, it may be that the most that one can draw from this admittedly sketchy overview is that there was nothing truly unique about Appalachian racial attitudes. The region's residents were first and foremost southerners. Despite demographic deviations in their racial makeup and their political alienation from the South's dominant slaveocracy, white highlanders' views of African Americans in theory and treatment of them in practice were for the most part well within the mainstream of attitudes and behavior elsewhere in the South, a mainstream that was in itself by no means monolithic. Likewise those views manifested in the few areas of Appalachia without a significant black presence were not so different from those of Americans in other nonslaveholding parts of the country. On either side of the Mason-Dixon line, nineteenth-century white America was racist, varying only in degree and in form of expression. The same was true of Appalachia.

It is one thing simply to chronicle or to categorize the varieties of ways in which white mountaineers viewed or treated blacks, and that is all that has been attempted here. It is quite another to sort out, identify, and explain the more elusive causal factors behind such views. That formidable task still looms large as one of the more exciting challenges confronting Appalachian scholars and can perhaps proceed once the debris of myth and misconception that has for so long obstructed the route to such insights is at long last cleared away.

Notes

The author is grateful for very helpful critiques of this essay by Fitzhugh Brundage, Durwood Dunn, James Klotter, William McFeely, and Gordon McKinney.

1. U. B. Phillips, "The Central Theme of Southern History," *American Historical Review* 34 (1928): 30–43. On the debate among historians since, see John David Smith and John C. Inscoe, eds., *Ulrich Bonnell Phillips: A Southern Historian and His Critics* (Westport, Conn.: Greenwood Press, 1990). David Whisnant statement from a book review, *Journal of Southern History* 56 (1990): 566.

2. John Fox, Jr., *The Little Shepherd of Kingdom Come* (1903; reprint, Lexington: University Press of Kentucky, 1987), pp. 28, 119, 239.

3. William Faulkner, "Mountain Victory," in *Collected Stories*, by William Faulkner (1950; reprint, New York: Vintage, 1977), pp. 745–80; quote, p. 751. For a more extensive analysis of this story, see John C. Inscoe, "Faulkner, Race, and Appalachia," *South Atlantic Quarterly* 86 (Summer 1987): 244–53.

4. William Brewer, "Moonshining in Georgia," *Cosmopolitan* 23 (June 1897): 132, quoted in Nina Silber, *The Romance of Reunion: Northerners and the South, 1865–1900* (Chapel Hill: University of North Carolina Press, 1993), p. 144.

5. Ellen Churchill Semple, "The Anglo-Saxons of the Kentucky Mountains: A Study in Anthropogeography," in *Appalachian Images in Folk and Popular Culture*, ed. W. K. McNeil (Ann Arbor, Mich.: U.M.I. Research Press, 1989), pp. 150–51.

6. Nathaniel S. Shaler, "The Peculiarities of the South," *North American Review* 151 (October 1890): 483–84. See also Margaret Ripley Wolfe, "The Appalachian Reality: Ethnic and Class Diversity," *East Tennessee Historical Society Publications* 52 and 53 (1980–81): 40–60.

7. Samuel Tyndale Wilson, *The Southern Mountaineers* (New York: Presbyterian Home Missions, 1906), pp. 42, 20–21; Thomas Wolfe, *The Hills Beyond* (1935; reprint, New York: Plume, 1982), p. 263.

8. Flannery O'Connor, "The Artificial Nigger," in *The Complete Stories*, by Flannery O'Connor (New York: Farrar, Straus and Giroux, 1971), quote, p. 129. Curiously, analysts of this story fail to recognize or acknowledge the mountain context of the two characters' background. See, for example, Miles Orvell, *Flannery O'Connor: An Introduction* (Jackson: University of Mississippi Press, 1991), pp. 152–60; Kathleen Feeley, *Flannery O'Connor: Voice of the Peacock* (New York: Fordham University Press, 1982), pp. 120–24; Jill P. Baumgaertner, *Flannery O'Connor: A Proper Scaring* (Wheaton, Ill.: Harold Shaw, 1988), pp. 56–62.

9. James C. Klotter, "The Black South and White Appalachia," *Journal of American History* 66 (March 1980): 832–49; Silber, *Romance of Reunion*, pp. 143–58. See also Allen W. Batteau, *The Invention of Appalachia* (Tucson: University of Arizona Press, 1990), pp. 59–63, on other uses of Anglo-Saxonism in romanticizing Appalachia.

Even more recent studies have focused on turn-of-the-century mission work to Appalachian blacks. See Conrad E. Ostwalt, Jr., "Crossing of Cultures: The Mennonite Brethren of Boone, North Carolina," in *Environmental Voices: Cultural, Social, Physical, and Natural*, ed. Garry Barker, *Journal of the Appalachian Studies Association* 4 (1992), pp. 105–12; Conrad E. Ostwalt, Jr., and Phoebe Pollitt, "The Salem School and Orphanage [in Elk Park, N.C]: White Missionaries, Black School," *Appalachian Journal* 20 (Spring 1993): 265–75.

10. Useful and varied anthologies on the black experience in the southern highlands, most of which focus on the twentieth century, include William H. Turner and Edward J. Cabbell, eds., *Blacks in Appalachia* (Lexington: University Press of Kentucky, 1985); Edward J. Cabbell, guest ed., "Black Appalachians," special issue of *Now and Then* 3 (Winter 1986); Lenwood Davis, *The Black Heritage of Western North Carolina* (Asheville: Southern Highlands Research Center, University of North Carolina, 1986); William H. Turner, guest ed., "Blacks in Appalachia," special issue of *Appalachian Heritage* 19 (Fall 1991).

11. On the distribution of slaves in Appalachia, see Robert P. Stuckert, "Black Populations of the Southern Appalachian Mountains," *Phylon* 48 (June 1987): 141–51; Richard B. Drake, "Slavery and Antislavery in Appalachia," *Appalachian Heritage* 14 (Winter 1986): 25–33; James B. Murphy, "Slavery and Freedom in Appalachia: Kentucky as a Demographic Case Study," *Register of the Kentucky Historical Society* 80 (1982): 151–69; John C. Inscoe, *Mountain Masters: Slavery and the Sectional Crisis in Western North Carolina* (Knoxville: University of Tennessee Press, 1989), pp. 59–63, 84–86; Wilma A. Dunaway, "Southern Appalachia's People without History: The Role of Unfree Laborers in the Region's Antebellum Economy," paper presented at the annual meeting of the Social Science History Association, November 1989, Washington, D.C., tabs. 2–5. For a nineteenth-century perspective, see William E. Barton, "The Cumberland Mountains and the Struggle for Freedom," *New England Magazine* 16 (1897): 65–87.

We are still sadly lacking in scholarly treatments of antebellum free black highlanders. Among the few works dealing with the subject are Stuart Sprague, "From Slavery to Freedom: African-Americans in Eastern Kentucky, 1864–1884," in *Diversity in Appalachia: Images and Realities*, ed. Tyler Blethen, *Journal of the Appalachian Studies Association* 5 (1993): 67–74; Marie Tedesco, "Freedman and Slave Owner: The Strange Case of Adam Waterford," paper presented at the Sixteenth Appalachian Studies Conference, March 1993, Johnson City, Tenn.

12. Sadie Smathers Patton, "The Kingdom of the Happy Land" (Asheville: Stephens, 1957); Sam Gray and Theda Perdue, "Appalachia as the Promised Land: A Freedmen's Commune in Henderson County, North Carolina, 1870–1920," paper presented at the meeting of the American Anthropological Association, 1979, Lexington, Ky.; William Lynwood Montell, *The Saga of Coe Ridge: A Study in Oral History* (Knoxville: University of Tennessee Press, 1970).

For other treatments of the postwar black population in Appalachia, see William H. Turner, "The Demography of Black Appalachia, Past and Present," in Turner and Cabbell, *Blacks in Appalachia*, pp. 237–61; Michael A. Cooke, "Race Relations in Montgomery County, Virginia, 1870–1990," in Barker, *Environmental Voices*, pp. 94–104; Sprague, "From Slavery to Freedom," pp. 72–73; and Wilson, *Southern Mountaineers*, pp. 41–42.

13. On the migration of blacks in Appalachian coalfields, see Ronald L. Lewis, *Black Coal Miners in America: Race, Class, and Community Conflict, 1780–1980* (Lexington: University Press of Kentucky, 1987), chap. 7; Ronald L. Lewis, "From Peasant to Proletarian: The Migration of Southern Blacks to the Central Appalachian Coalfields," *Journal of Southern History* 55 (1989): 77–102; Emily Jones Hudson, "The Black American Family in Southeastern Kentucky: Red Fox, Kodak, and Town Mountain," in *Reshaping the Image of Appalachia*, ed. Loyal Jones (Berea, Ky.: Berea College Appalachian Center, 1986), pp. 136–45; Joe William Trotter, Jr., *Coal, Class, and Color: Blacks in Southern West Virginia, 1915–1932* (Urbana: University of Illinois Press, 1990), pt. 1; Wayne Flynt, *Poor but Proud: Alabama's Poor Whites* (Tuscaloosa: University of Alabama Press, 1989), chap. 5. None of these works speaks to the issue of local reaction of white Appalachians to this influx of black migrants, though Flynt has a perceptive discussion of race relations between black and Appalachian white workers in northern Alabama's coalfields (pp. 121, 136–38, 257–61).

14. Stuckert, "Black Populations of Southern Appalachian Mountains," pp. 141 (tab. 1), 145.

15. W. J. Cash, *The Mind of the South* (New York: Knopf, 1941), p. 219.

16. John Eaton, *Grant, Lincoln, and the Freedman: Reminiscences of the Civil War* (New York: Longmans, Green, 1907), p. 119. See also John Cimprich, "Slavery's End in East Tennessee," *East Tennessee Historical Society Publications* 52 and 53 (1980–81): 85.

17. John C. Campbell, *The Southern Mountaineer and His Homeland* (New York: Russell Sage Foundation, 1921), p. 95; Muriel E. Sheppard, *Cabins in the Laurel* (Chapel Hill: University of North Carolina Press, 1935), p. 60.

18. Raymond Andrews, *The Last Radio Baby: A Memoir* (Atlanta: Peachtree, 1990), p. 79; William Styron, *The Confessions of Nat Turner* (New York: Random House, 1967), pp. 326–27.

19. Loyal Jones, "Appalachian Values," in *Voices from the Hills: Selected Readings of Southern Appalachia*, ed. Robert J. Higgs (New York: Ungar, 1975), pp. 507–17.

20. Quoted in William H. Turner, "Between Berea (1904) and Birmingham (1908): The Rock and Hard Place for Blacks in Appalachia," in Turner and Cabbell, *Blacks in Appalachia*, p. 13. The whole notion of Appalachia as a center of Underground Railroad activity is suspect. Most major treatments of the Underground Railroad make no reference to southern highland locales. See Larry Gara, *The Liberty Line: The Legend of the Underground Railroad* (Lexington: University Press of Kentucky, 1961); William Still, *The Underground Railroad* (Philadelphia: Porter and Coates, 1872); Eber M. Pettit, *Sketches in the History of the Underground Railroad* (Fredonia, N.Y.: W. McKinstry and Son, 1879). The only such account to refer to even the possibility that Appalachians provided regular routes is Wilbur H. Siebert, *The Underground Railroad from Slavery to Freedom* (New York: Macmillan, 1899), pp. 118–19, but its map (facing p. 113) indicates no routes anywhere in the region.

21. Leon F. Williams, "The Vanishing Appalachian: How to 'Whiten' the Problem," in Turner and Cabbell, *Blacks in Appalachia*, p. 201.

22. Barbara J. Fields, "Ideology and Race in American History," in *Region, Race, and Reconstruction: Essays in Honor of C. Vann Woodward*, ed. J. Morgan Kousser and James M. McPherson (New York: Oxford University Press, 1982), p. 157; Samuel C. Williams, ed., "Journal of Events (1825–1873) of David Anderson Deaderick," *East Tennessee Historical Publications* 8 (1936): 121–37.

23. Frederick Douglass, *The Life and Times of Frederick Douglass* (1892; reprint, New York: Macmillan, 1962), pp. 273–74. See also William S. McFeely, *Frederick Douglass* (New York: Norton, 1991), pp. 186–87, 190–92.

24. Richard Hinton interview with John Brown and John Kagi in August 1858, in *John Brown*, ed. Richard Warch and Jonathan F. Fauton (Englewood Cliffs, N.J.: Prentice-Hall, 1973), p. 54 (second quote). For other treatments of the southern highlands as central to Brown's insurrection plan, see Siebert, *Underground Railroad*, p. 118; and Jules Abel, *Man on Fire: John Brown and the Cause of Liberty* (New York: Macmillan, 1971), pp. 245–48.

25. James W. Taylor, *Alleghania: A Geographical and Statistical Memoir* (St. Paul, Minn.: James Davenport, 1862), pp. 1–2, 15–16.

26. William Goodrich, *God's Handiwork in the Sea and the Mountains: Sermons Preached after a Summer Vacation* (Cleveland, Ohio: Privately published, n.d.), quoted in Jan Davidson's introduction to Frances Louisa Goodrich, *Mountain Homespun* (Knoxville: University of Tennessee Press, 1989), p. 13.

27. Batteau, *Invention of Appalachia*, p. 78.

28. Harry M. Caudill, *Night Comes to the Cumberlands: A Biography of a Depressed Area* (Boston: Little, Brown, 1962), pp. 38–39.

29. Asa Earl Martin, "The Anti-Slavery Societies of Tennessee," *Tennessee Historical Magazine* 1 (1915): 261–81; Cratis D. Williams, "The Southern Mountaineer in Fact and Fiction" (Ph.D. diss., New York University, 1961), 1:74–75; North Callahan, *Smoky Mountain Country*, ed. Erskine Caldwell (New York: Duell, Sloan, and Pearce, 1952), pp. 37–49; Thomas W. Humes, *The Loyal Mountaineers of Tennessee* (Knoxville: Ogden Bros., 1888), pp. 31–33; David W. Bowen, *Andrew Johnson and the Negro* (Knoxville: University of Tennessee Press, 1989), pp. 15–16.

30. Durwood Dunn, *Cades Cove: The Life and Death of a Southern Appalachian Community, 1818–1937* (Knoxville: University of Tennessee Press, 1988), pp. 124–25. On opposition to East Tennessee abolitionists, see Chase C. Mooney, *Slavery in Tennessee* (Bloomington: Indiana University Press, 1957), pp. 70–73; Bowen, *Andrew Johnson and the Negro*, p. 16; Drake, "Slavery and Antislavery in Appalachia," pp. 31–32. On postwar commitment to biracial education at Maryville, see Lester C. Lamon, "Ignoring the Color Line: Maryville College, 1868–1901," in *The Adaptable South: Essays in Honor of George Brown Tindall*, ed. Elizabeth Jacoway et al. (Baton Rouge: Louisiana State University Press, 1991), pp. 64–89.

31. Henry Ruffner, *Address to the People of West Virginia: Showing That Slavery is Injurious to the Public Welfare and That It May Gradually Be Abolished Without Detriment to the Rights and Interests of Slaveholders* (Lexington, Va.: R. C. Noel, 1847), cited and discussed in Fitzhugh Brundage, "Shifting Attitudes towards Slavery in Antebellum Rockbridge County," *Rockbridge Historical Society Proceedings* 10 (1980–89): 333–44. There is no indication that the abolition of slavery was ever a factor in intrastate sectional battles waged by highlanders in antebellum legislatures in North Carolina, Kentucky, or even Tennessee.

32. Richard D. Sears, *"A Practical Recognition of the Brotherhood of Man": John G. Fee and the Camp Nelson Experience* (Berea, Ky.: Berea College Press, 1986), p. 46; Semple, "Anglo-Saxons of the Kentucky Mountains," p. 151. See also Richard D. Sears, *The Day of Small Things: Abolitionism in the Midst of Slavery* (Lanham, Md.: University Press of America, 1986). Broader studies of abolitionism in Kentucky include Asa Earl Martin, *The Anti-Slavery Movement in Kentucky Prior to 1850* (Louisville, Ky.: Filson Club Publication no. 25, 1918); Lowell H. Harrison, *The Antislavery Movement in Kentucky* (Lexington: University Press of Kentucky, 1978); Gordon E. Finnie, "The Antislavery Movement in the Upper South before 1840," *Journal of Southern History* 35 (1969): 319–42; Jeffrey Brooke Allen, "Were Southern White Critics of Slavery Racists? Kentucky and the Upper South, 1791–1824," *Journal of Southern History* 44 (1978): 169–90; Stanley Harrold, "Violence and Nonviolence in Kentucky Abolitionism," *Journal of Southern History* 57 (1991): 15–38. None of these works acknowledges any significant abolitionist activity in the state's eastern mountain region. (Another Appalachian institution that embraced biracial educa-

tion after the war was Tennessee Wesleyan College in Athens, under the auspices of the Northern Methodist Church.)

33. Quoted in Sears, *"Practical Recognition of the Brotherhood of Man,"* p. 46. On Berea's move away from its commitment to black education, see Klotter, "Black South and White Appalachia," pp. 846–48; Turner, "Between Berea and Birmingham," pp. 13–14; Jacqueline G. Burnside, "Suspicion Versus Faith: Negro Criticisms of Berea College in the Nineteenth Century," in Jones, *Reshaping the Image of Appalachia,* pp. 102–25.

34. Carter G. Woodson, "Freedom and Slavery in Appalachia," *Journal of Negro History* 1 (April 1916): 132–50. Much the same ground is covered in Finnie, "Antislavery Movement in the Upper South." See also Barton, "Cumberland Mountains and the Struggle for Freedom."

35. Don West, *Freedom in the Mountains* (Huntington, W.Va.: Appalachian Movement Press, 1973), pp. 3–4, 9.

36. Woodson, "Freedom and Slavery in Appalachia," p. 147; Don West interview in *Refuse to Stand Silently By: An Oral History of Grass-Roots Social Activism in America, 1921–1964,* ed. Eliot Wigginton (New York: Doubleday, 1992), p. 68.

37. Frederick Law Olmsted, *A Journey through the Back Country in the Winter of 1853–54* (New York: Mason Brothers, 1860), pp. 239, 237, 263–64. On Olmsted's schedule and route, see Charles E. Beveridge, ed., *The Papers of Frederick Law Olmsted,* vol. 2, *Slavery and the South, 1852–1857* (Baltimore: Johns Hopkins University Press, 1981), pp. 309 (map), and 481–82 (itinerary). For a fuller discussion of his mission and findings, see John C. Inscoe, "Olmsted in Appalachia: A Connecticut Yankee Encounters Slavery and Racism in the Southern Highlands," *Slavery and Abolition* 9 (September 1988): 171–82.

38. Humes, *Loyal Mountaineers,* p. 30.

39. Julian Ralph, "Our Appalachian Americans," *Harper's Monthly Magazine,* June 1903, p. 37.

40. Lillian Smith, *Killers of the Dream,* rev. ed. (New York: Norton, 1961), p. 171.

41. Kenneth W. Noe, *Southwest Virginia's Railroad: Modernization and the Sectional Crisis* (Urbana: University of Illinois Press, 1994), p. 17.

42. See, for example, Smith, *Killers of the Dream,* p. 170; Daniel R. Hundley, *Social Relations in Our Southern States* (1860; reprint, Baton Rouge: Louisiana State University Press, 1979), pp. 258–60; Eugene D. Genovese, "Yeomen Farmers in a Slaveholder's Democracy," *Agricultural History* 49 (1975): 331–42; Steven Hahn, *The Roots of Southern Populism: Yeoman Farmers and the Transformation of the Georgia Upcountry, 1850–1890* (New York: Oxford University Press, 1983), pp. 88–91; J. William Harris, *Plain Folk and Gentry in a Slave Society: White Liberty and Black Slavery in Augusta's Hinterlands* (Middleton, Conn.: Wesleyan University Press), pp. 72–77; F. N. Boney, *Southerners All* (Macon, Ga.: Mercer University Press, 1984), chap. 2. On the commonality of southern and Appalachian values, see Richard B. Drake, "Southern Appalachia and the South: A Region within a Section," in *Southern Appalachia and the South: A Region within a Region,* ed. John C. Inscoe, *Journal of the Appalachian Studies Association* 3 (1991): 18–27.

43. Carl N. Degler, *The Other South: Southern Dissenters in the Nineteenth Century* (Boston: Northeastern University Press, 1982). Quote is title of chap. 2.

44. Alexis de Tocqueville, *Democracy in America*, 4th ed. (New York: Henry G. Langley, 1845), 1:389–90.

45. Eugene H. Berwanger, *The Frontier against Slavery: Western Anti-Negro Prejudice and the Slavery Extension Controversy* (Urbana: University of Illinois Press, 1967); Rodger Cunningham, *Apples on the Flood: The Southern Mountain Experience* (Knoxville: University of Tennessee Press, 1987), p. 99.

46. Oliver P. Temple, *East Tennessee and the Civil War* (Cincinnati, Ohio: Robert Clarke, 1899), pp. 196–97.

47. Humes, *Loyal Mountaineers*, p. 31. See also Arthur W. Spaulding, *The Men of the Mountains: The Story of the Southern Mountaineer and His Kin of the Piedmont* (Nashville: Southern Press, 1915), pp. 40–41.

48. Alexander H. Jones, *Knocking at the Door* (Washington, D.C.: McGill and Witherow, 1866), p. 14; Inscoe, *Mountain Masters*, pp. 236–38.

49. Vernon M. Queener, "William G. Brownlow as an Editor," *East Tennessee Historical Society Publications* 4 (1932): 80; W. G. Brownlow, *Sketches of the Rise, Progress and Decline of Secession* (Philadelphia: George W. Childs, 1862), p. 109; Nelson quoted in Richard Current, *Lincoln's Loyalists: Union Soldiers from the Confederacy* (Boston: Northeastern University Press, 1992), p. 50. For a comparison of attitudes in two sections of Appalachia, see John C. Inscoe, "Mountain Unionism, Secession, and Regional Self-Image: The Contrasting Cases of Western North Carolina and East Tennessee," in *Looking South: Chapters in the Story of an American Region*, ed. Winfred B. Moore, Jr., and Joseph F. Tripp (Westport, Conn.: Greenwood Press, 1989), pp. 115–29.

50. Inscoe, *Mountain Masters*, pp. 244–46.

51. Altina L. Waller, *Feud: Hatfields, McCoys, and Social Change in Appalachia, 1860–1900* (Chapel Hill: University of North Carolina Press, 1988), p. 30.

52. Etheleve Dyer Jones, *Facets of Fannin: A History of Fannin County, Georgia* (Dallas: Curtis Media, 1989), p. 32; Jonathan Sarris, "Anatomy of an Atrocity: The Madden Branch Massacre and the Guerrilla War in North Georgia, 1861–1865," *Georgia Historical Quarterly* 77 (Winter 1993): 679–710.

53. Henry T. Shanks, "Disloyalty to the Confederacy in Southwestern Virginia, 1861–1865," *North Carolina Historical Review* 21 (1944): 118–19. For more recent confirmation of Shanks's conclusions, see Kenneth W. Noe, "Red String Scare: Civil War Southwest Virginia and the Heroes of America," *North Carolina Historical Review* 59 (1992): 301–22.

54. Theodore F. Davidson, "The Carolina Mountaineer: The Highest Type of American Character," in *First Annual Transactions of the Pen and Plate Club of Asheville, N.C.*, by Theodore F. Davidson (Asheville: Hackney and Mole, 1905), pp. 84–85. For variations of this theme, see Spaulding, *Men of the Mountains*, pp. 41–43; Humes, *Loyal Mountaineers*, pp. 30–31; Caudill, *Night Comes to the Cumberlands*, pp. 37–39; Waller, *Feud*, pp. 30–31.

55. Quoted in Michael P. Johnson, *Toward a Patriarchal Society: The Secession of Georgia* (Baton Rouge: Louisiana State University Press, 1977), p. 50.

56. Circular by W. W. Avery and Marcus Erwin, quoted in Inscoe, *Mountain Masters*, p. 226; Richard O. Curry, *A House Divided: A Study of Statehood Politics and the Copperhead Movement in West Virginia* (Pittsburgh: University of Pittsburgh Press, 1964), chap. 9, esp. pp. 91–92.

57. Drake, "Slavery and Antislavery in Appalachia," 28. For more extensive discussion of the slave trade in Appalachia, see Dunaway, "People without History," pp. 4–8; Noe, *Southwest Virginia's Railroad*, chap. 1.

58. G. W. Featherstonaugh, *Excursion through the Slave States* (New York: Harper and Brothers, 1844), pp. 36–37, 46.

59. Joseph John Gurney, *A Journey in North America, Described in Familiar Letters to Amelia Opie* (Norwich: J. Fletcher, 1841), pp. 53–54.

60. Sarah Gudger and Mary Barbour interviews in *The American Slave: A Composite Autobiography*, ed. George P. Rawick, vol. 14, *North Carolina Narratives* (Westport, Conn.: Greenwood Press, 1972), pt. 1, pp. 354–55 (Gudger), p. 79 (Barbour). Aunt Sophia quoted in Drake, "Slavery and Antislavery in Appalachia," p. 27. For other examples of Appalachian ex-slave testimony, see Dunaway, "People without History," pp. 5, 7, 36–37.

61. Eric J. Olson, "Race Relations in Asheville, North Carolina: Three Incidents, 1868–1906," in *The Appalachian Experience: Proceedings of the 6th Annual Appalachian Studies Conference*, ed. Barry M. Buxton (Boone, N.C.: Appalachian Consortium Press, 1983), pp. 153–56.

62. Edward L. Ayers, *Vengeance and Justice: Crime and Punishment in the Nineteenth-Century American South* (New York: Oxford University Press, 1984), pp. 159–61.

63. William F. Holmes, "Moonshining and Collective Violence: Georgia, 1889–1895," *Journal of American History* 67 (December 1980): 589–611; W. Fitzhugh Brundage, *Lynching in the New South: Georgia and Virginia, 1880–1930* (Urbana: University of Illinois Press, 1993), chap. 5. See also Wilbur R. Miller, *Revenuers and Moonshiners: Enforcing Federal Liquor Law in the Mountain South, 1865–1900* (Chapel Hill: University of North Carolina Press, 1991), pp. 52–53. It is perhaps noteworthy that the only black informant Miller cites as a victim of whitecappers was a Georgian.

64. George C. Wright, *Racial Violence in Kentucky, 1865–1940: Lynchings, Mob Rule, and "Legal Lynchings"* (Baton Rouge: Louisiana State University Press, 1990), chap. 2 (see particularly tab. 4, p. 73).

65. Robert P. Stuckert, "Racial Violence in Southern Appalachia, 1880–1940," *Appalachian Heritage* 20 (Spring 1992): 35–41.

66. Brundage, *Lynching in the New South*, chap. 4.

67. Charles Lanman, *Letters from the Alleghany Mountains* (New York: Putnam, 1849), p. 314; Olmsted, *Journey through the Back Country*, pp. 226–27. It is worth noting that the mountain slaves to whom Gurney reacts are the first he encountered during his tour of the United States, whereas both Lanman and Olmsted moved into the southern highlands after extensive travel elsewhere in the South and thus had a basis for comparison of slave life that Gurney lacked.

68. Inscoe, *Mountain Masters*, chap. 5. Some reviewers of the book found this section less than convincing. See Shane White, "Feeling 'Awful Southern' or Slavery on the Periphery," *Reviews in American History* 18 (June 1990): 197–201; and reviews by Altina L. Waller, in *Register of the Kentucky Historical Society* 88 (1990): 346–48; John Schlotterbeck, in *Journal of Southern History* 57 (1991): 330–31; and Lynda Morgan, *American Historical Review* 96 (1991): 262–63. It is admittedly a slippery

point to prove, and the evidence must remain, by its nature, circumstantial and impressionistic.

69. Van Beck Hall, "The Politics of Appalachian Virginia, 1790–1830," in *Appalachian Frontiers: Settlement, Society, and Development in the Preindustrial Era*, ed. Robert D. Mitchell (Lexington: University Press of Kentucky, 1991), pp. 184–86.

70. Gordon B. McKinney, "Southern Mountain Republicans and the Negro, 1865–1900," *Journal of Southern History* 41 (1975): 493–96.

71. Cimprich, "Slavery's End in East Tennessee," pp. 84–85. Cimprich also indicated that antiblack sentiment among East Tennesseeans did indeed intensify after emancipation, just as Eaton had complained.

72. Olson, "Race Relations in Asheville," pp. 163–64.

73. J. Morgan Kousser, *The Shaping of Southern Politics: Suffrage Restriction and the Establishment of the One-Party South, 1880–1910* (New Haven: Yale University Press, 1974), pp. 112, 224, 248, 264.

74. Fields, "Ideology and Race in American History," pp. 144, 146. For further expansion of her arguments, see Fields, "Slavery, Race, and Ideology in the United States of America," *New Left Review*, no. 181 (1990): 118. See also John B. Boles, "Cycles of Racism in Southern History," paper presented at conference, "Black and White Perspectives on the American South," 29 September 1994, University of Georgia, Athens.

75. Fields, "Ideology and Race in American History," p. 155.

CHAPTER 5   RALPH MANN

Diversity in the Antebellum Appalachian South

Four Farm Communities in Tazewell County, Virginia

I n recent years historians of the Appalachian South have been under-
mining the common image of the egalitarian, self-sufficient mountain
community. While there were mountain communities that approxi-
mated Jeffersonian expectations, there were others that exhibited sharp
social distinctions, contained large numbers of landless families, and were
strongly oriented toward markets. We have also learned that these diverse
social communities were shaped by a variety of economic, topographic, and
social factors, including the timing and persistence of permanent settlement, the ease with which settlers found access to land, the cost of overcom-
ing mountain barriers, and the changing availability of markets.[1]

This essay examines one of the roots of Appalachian diversity by looking
at the linkage between families and land from 1820 to 1850 in four neighborhoods in Tazewell County, Virginia. In 1850, Jeffersonville, the county seat,
served a very diverse agricultural landscape. Thirteen miles west from the
courthouse lay Maiden Spring, the entrance to a section known simply as
the Cove. Maiden Spring had been named in 1772 by Rees Bowen for a doe

deer he had shot beside it. Deeply impressed by the beauty and fertility of the site, Bowen entered a claim to all the land watered by the stream that issued from the spring. In the 1770s and 1780s Bowen was joined by a handful of families, also making large claims to the unusually level and well-watered 15,000 acres of Cove lands. Mostly still resident and dominant in 1850, these families had made the Cove known for large farms, progressive agriculture, and good society.[2]

Beginning four miles northwest of Jeffersonville and running west for ten miles was Baptist Valley. Also first settled in the early 1770s, but by men who soon moved on, it later became, according to local tradition, dominated by the humble members of a Baptist congregation seeking to escape religious oppression in eastern Virginia. In 1850 the valley's residents were largely descended from the Baptist settlers. Here small farms, devoted to simple production, were scattered along the narrow valley; many of its 6,400 acres were unclaimed.[3]

A similar valley, known as Abb's for its white discoverer, Absalom Looney, ran from twelve to twenty-two miles northeast of the courthouse. Celebrated for the Indian massacre and captivity of its pioneer family, the Moores, in the mid 1780s, Abb's Valley had lain abandoned until the surviving Moores moved back in 1798. With its land held by the Moores and a few other, mostly absentee owners, Abb's Valley, approximately 7,000 acres isolated against the edge of the Allegheny Plateau, contained a sparse population dominated by tenants and squatters. Most of its farmland lay undeveloped.[4]

Southeast twelve miles from the seat of government was the Gap, the entrance to Burkes Garden. The largest of the four sections discussed here, containing 25,000 acres, the Garden was a high oval valley completely encircled by Garden Mountain. While the Garden was known for its beauty and good limestone soil, its high altitude, short growing season, and restricted access prevented the easy development of commercial agriculture. Speculative outside ownership had slowed settlement. In 1845 a speculator from Washington County named Joseph Meek had celebrated the acquisition of a large tract in the Garden with a prodigious meal, during the course of which he suffered a coronary and died. Litigation among his heirs tied up the land for ten years, during which time it was farmed by tenants. Still, in 1850 the Garden contained a thriving population of large and small landholders as well as a large proportion of tenants.[5]

The first part of this chapter uses land tax records at ten-year intervals to describe early patterns of residential and absentee landownership. The second part sketches the four communities' family, class, and racial structures

Map 5.1. Four Tazewell Communities, 1860

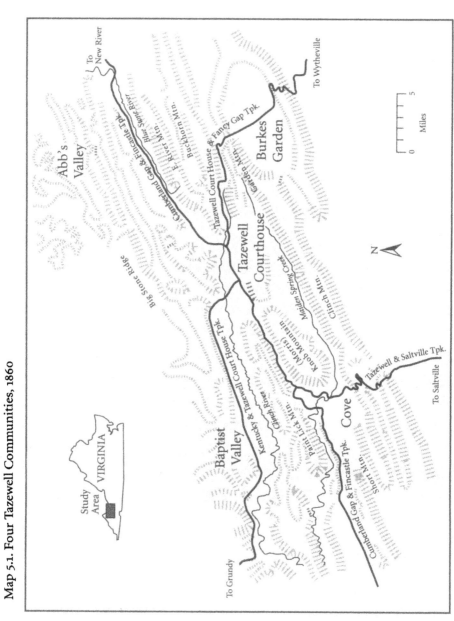

Source: Adapted from a map prepared by the cartographic staff of the Geography Department, University of Colorado.

in 1850, drawing on land tax records and on federal free population, slave, and agricultural censuses to judge the long-term social effects of land markets, family persistence, and access to markets.

In 1855 the Virginia and Tennessee Railroad was built to Wytheville, within reach of much of Tazewell. During the 1850s, inside Tazewell itself a network of new turnpikes linked communities and connected them to the new railroad. It is commonly argued that the railroad contributed to a commercial revolution in southwestern Virginia, as in other parts of the mountain South, that promoted slavery; forged trade links to the Valley of Virginia and the Tidewater; and helped ensure the southwest's loyalty to Virginia during secession.[6] Granted, the coming of the railroad did not long precede the coming of the Civil War, so there was not time for a major change in the relationship of land and people in Tazewell. Still, we can gauge the impact of improved access to markets by looking at families, land-ownership, and social structure in the four communities once again, in 1860. Thus the third part of the chapter will try to answer this question: On the eve of the Civil War, to what extent were these communities shaped by new commercial opportunities, and to what extent by long established patterns of landholding, relative isolation, and family persistence?

The Bowens, Wards, Youngs, Barnses, and Gillespies who arrived in the 1770s and 1780s in the Cove laid a lasting claim to much of the available land. A few early settlers moved on, and a few smaller landholders seem to have been squeezed out; but the central feature of Cove life in the first half of the nineteenth century was the dominance by approximately twenty farmers, representing six or seven large families, whose names appeared in an unbroken progression over the years. The Cove was widely recognized as "the garden spot of Tazewell County," its lands among the most valuable and its prominent families firmly a part of the county elite, serving on the county court and in the state legislature.[7]

First comer Rees Bowen was remembered as a literally larger-than-life figure, not as an aristocrat, but as an archetypical pioneer. A member of a westering landed family, he knew the way to prestige on the frontier. As first on the scene, he could claim Maiden Spring if he could hold it. A tall, muscular man, he was able, it was said, to let his wife stand on his hand and hold her at arm's length. Combining strength, industry, and purpose, he cleared land, multiplied his horses and cattle, and raised an unusually large, strong log house, stockading it in 1773 when the Shawnees threatened. While his fort served as refuge for the neighborhood, he served at Point

Pleasant in 1774, was lieutenant in the militia protecting the Clinch and Holston settlements in 1776, and died a hero's death at King's Mountain in 1780. Along the way he gained legendary status as a fist and skull fighter. Hearing of his prowess, a giant Pennsylvanian named Fork left his home and journeyed to Maiden Spring to "whip Rees Bowen." Refusing to yield or give up the struggle, Fork died in the attempt.[8]

His children consolidated the position Rees Bowen had won as land-holder and community power. His daughters and the daughters of his eldest sons, John and Rees, who had no sons, married into similar first comer landed families. His third son, Henry, played the part in a more settled Cove and Tazewell that the first Rees had played in the pioneer region. As county sheriff, county representative to the Virginia House of Delegates, member of the first county court of Tazewell, and militia colonel in the War of 1812, Henry Bowen was one of the most visible men in the county. Like his father, he continued to add land to his holdings and to raise horses and cattle. His two sons, Rees T. and Henry, dominated the Cove during the mid-century, living more comfortably than anyone else in the county. This second Henry had no children, so Rees T. passed to his sons both consolidated landhold-ings and unrivaled prestige.

Rees T. Bowen, a grazier and farmer and a general in the Virginia militia, was Tazewell's first citizen elected to Congress. His sons were officers in the Confederate army, along with their uncle leading the "Tazewell Troopers," and one of them, another Henry—another farmer/stock raiser, twice elected to the Virginia legislature and twice congressman (in 1882 and 1886)—was called the most beloved and most honored man in Tazewell's history. An early arrival and a fortuitous lack of sons both reinforced the family's ability to concentrate land and thus play a major part in the county's main eco-nomic activity, stock raising. Family prestige and talent as well allowed some Bowens to hold political positions worthy of a near-mythological ancestor.[9]

The Cove of the Bowens and their connections was nearly a closed so-ciety; although a few new names appeared over time, the land was over-whelmingly in the hands of residents, and little was ever on the market. In 1840, for the only time before 1860, the proportion of resident landholders fell below 90 percent. The absentee landholders, however, had very familiar names: they were heirs of the established families who had elected to move on to Missouri or Arkansas. By 1850 landholdings had reconsolidated into resident hands once more; 95 percent of those paying land tax on Cove land lived in the Cove. Changes in landholding represented a generational, life-cycle shift, not a loosening of control, and family strategies that included migration and the sale of inheritances within the family circle ensured long-term family influence. In 1820 eighteen resident farmers paid land tax; in 1850, twenty farmers, nineteen resident, paid land tax (see Table 5.1). Overwhelmingly, the surnames were the same.

A few miles to the north, the small farmers of Baptist Valley lived in a more fluid society. Names did appear early and stay in the records: Hankins, Brewster, Dailey, Lockhart. The heads of established families did serve as justices of the peace, constables, and other local political officials—though rarely did a man from Baptist Valley become sheriff or represent the county in Richmond.[10] Unlike the early settlers in the Cove, however, the first families in the valley did not claim all the available land. The land was less good; the settlers, few; the claims, small. In 1820 only eleven households paid land tax in Baptist Valley. Nine were resident. Over time, both the numbers of people owning land and the proportion of landholders living outside the valley slowly grew. The outsiders were usually not heirs to Baptist Valley land but were Tazewell families investing in land for future family use or for resale. By 1850 only 67 percent of the eighteen payers of land tax were local, although, again, their names were mostly constant (see Table 5.1). Residents' life had changed little. The arrival of outside buyers did not seem to prevent local families from establishing their sons on the land. In any case, similar land and similar neighborhoods lay all around Baptist Valley. Farms were available.

To the northeast, the people of Abb's Valley may have lived in a similar style, but the landholding situation was quite different. After the Moore tragedy, there had been little movement to settle there, at first because of fears of Indians and then probably because Abb's Valley was so far off the beaten path, with much more accessible land available for farmers in Tazewell County. While the returned Moores dreamed of buying up all valley land, speculators, again mostly local, took control of much of it, leaving it vacant. George Peery followed James Moore, Jr., into the little valley, and several members of his large family connection also invested in Abb's Valley land. It is not clear whether any of these Peerys besides George settled in Abb's Valley, as they all had holdings in other parts of the county. In any case, most of the Peerys who had bought land in Abb's Valley soon moved west to Missouri or Kentucky.[11] At no time between 1820 and 1850 did the majority of the handful of families—usually ten or eleven—paying tax on valley land actually live there (see Table 5.1).

Burkes Garden was similarly dominated by nonresident speculators, at least at first. Visited by James Burk before 1750, it was included in the extensive claims of the Patton family. Complicated family suits and the later attempts of a number of absentee landholders—such as Joseph Meek—to

Table 5.1. Residence of Land Tax Payers

	Resident		Nonresident	
	No.	%	No.	%
		1820		
Cove	18	100	0	0
Baptist Valley	9	82	2	18
Abb's Valley	5	45	6	55
Burkes Garden	22	54	19	46
		1830		
Cove	20	95	1	5
Baptist Valley	13	81	3	19
Abb's Valley	4	40	6	60
Burkes Garden	27	55	22	45
		1840		
Cove	15	79	4	21
Baptist Valley	10	77	3	23
Abb's Valley	5	45	6	55
Burkes Garden	35	65	19	35
		1850		
Cove	19	95	1	5
Baptist Valley	12	67	6	33
Abb's Valley	2	22	7	78
Burkes Garden	33	59	23	41
		1860		
Cove	19	86	3	14
Baptist Valley	10	53	9	47
Abb's Valley	4	57	3	43
Burkes Garden	43	67	21	33

Source: All figures are derived from the Virginia Land Tax, Tazewell, Virginia State Library, Richmond.

put together large claims retarded settlement, as did the difficulty of climbing Garden Mountain and the altitude of the Garden floor. For a long time it was thought that wheat and corn could not ripen during the Garden's short growing season. Tenants were an important part of the early population, but gradually, after 1800, a variety of farmers filtered into the Garden. As the major land suit was settled and land came onto the market, the numbers increased.[12] By 1820 twenty-two landowning families lived in Burkes Garden, and they constituted a slight majority of those paying taxes on Garden land. Speculators continued to arrive in the Garden, but as their children and other independent farmers moved in, the number of landed families resident and the proportion of taxpayers living on the land gradually increased, although usually over 40 percent of the taxpayers lived outside the Garden. As in all these communities, families early settled tended to stay—Greevers, Goses, Sprachers, Halls—and play a dominant role in community life. Since Burkes Garden was more prosperous than Baptist or Abb's Valley, its early families played an important part in county life. Unlike the Cove, however, Burkes Garden attracted a constant stream of new families—Floyds, Vails, Mosses—who, as large farmers often connected to prominent families in Wythe or Washington Counties that had held Garden land, also quickly assumed a central place in Garden life. In 1850 Burkes Garden had the largest resident population and the most fluid and diverse social structure of the four communities (see Table 5.1).

By 1850, patterns of settlement and landholding had created four distinct agricultural communities. In the Cove over half of the thirty-five resident white household heads reported over $1,000 in real estate; almost one-fourth operated large farms. At the same time almost 40 percent of the household heads claimed no real estate (see Table 5.2). When that proportion is reduced by the number of landless who were members of landed families, and therefore likely to inherit land, about three in ten were landless, with little prospect of getting land and little likelihood of staying long in the Cove. Listed as farmers, without land, they were tenants on the land of the first families. The same proportion—three in ten of all householders—were slaveholders; of those reporting landholdings, 40 percent also held slaves. Three families could claim to be planters with twenty slaves, and the average holding was fourteen. The slave population was over one-third of the total population of the Cove (see Table 5.5).[13]

In the Cove in 1850 the modal farm size was between 200 and 500 acres, of which between 100 and 200 acres were improved. Three in ten would be classified as large farms. Thirty percent of the Cove lands were improved, but that figure rises to over half if we exclude the lands of the Bowen brothers, by far the largest local landholders, who owned over 8,000 largely unimproved acres around Maiden Spring.[14]

Conspicuously absent from this community of solid yeomen, large landholders, tenants, and slaves were small farmers. None of the farms listed in the agricultural census was under 100 acres, and only two had less than 100 acres of improved land. Only three of the twenty-five household heads who reported real property had less than yeoman holdings (see Tables 5.2 and 5.3).

A representative Cove household, then, would be that of John Barns. A member of a family that had settled in the early 1780s, living in a cove

Table 5.2. Value of Real Estate

	1850		1860	
	Household Heads	%	Household Heads	%
		Cove		
$0	13	37	11	36
$1–999	3	9	3	10
$1,000–4,999	11	31	7	23
$5,000+	8	23	10	32
Total	35		31	
		Baptist Valley		
$0	10	37	6	21
$1–999	9	33	6	21
$1,000–4,999	8	30	13	46
$5,000+	0	0	3	11
Total	27		28	
		Abb's Valley		
$0	15	52	13	52
$1–999	6	21	4	16
$1,000–4,999	7	24	5	20
$5,000+	1	3	3	12
Total	29		25	
		Burkes Garden		
$0	29	35	22	29
$1–999	19	23	9	12
$1,000–4,999	28	34	34	45
$5,000+	7	8	11	15
Total	83		76	

Sources: Figures drawn from the *Seventh Census of the United States, 1850,* schedule 1, Free Population, Virginia, Tazewell, National Archives, microfilm publications, microcopy M432, roll 979; *Eighth Census, 1860,* schedule 1, Free Population, Virginia, Tazewell, National Archives, microfilm publications, microcopy M653, roll 1381.

bearing his family name, Barns farmed 500 acres, 200 of which were improved. He owned fourteen slaves; surrounding his home farm were four other farms, occupied by men without real estate, who were probably his tenants. A walk through the Cove starting at Barns's home would reveal the same pattern repeated: a large slaveholding farm—perhaps owned by Barns's kin or in-laws—tenants, and then another large farm. Not all of the landed were well-to-do. The Lesters were a long-established family but

Table 5.3. Improved Land and Farm Size, 1850

Acres	Improved Land		Farmland	
	Farms	%	Farms	%
		Cove		
0–25	0	0	0	0
26–50	0	0	0	0
51–100	2	15	0	0
101–200	7	54	2	15
201–500	2	15	7	54
501–1,000	2	15	2	15
Over 1,000	0	0	2	15
Total	13		13	
		Baptist Valley		
0–25	3	19	0	0
26–50	5	31	3	19
51–100	5	31	2	13
101–200	3	19	7	44
201–500	0	0	3	19
501–1,000	0	0	1	6
Over 1,000	0	0	0	0
Total	16		16	
		Abb's Valley		
0–25	8	50	0	0
26–50	3	19	0	0
51–100	4	25	3	19
101–200	1	6	5	31
201–500	0	0	4	25
501–1,000	0	0	4	25
Over 1,000	0	0	0	0
Total	16		16	
		Burkes Garden		
0–25	7	14	2	4
26–50	23	45	2	4
51–100	11	22	9	18
101–200	8	16	18	35
201–500	2	4	11	22
501–1,000	0	0	8	16
Over 1,000	0	0	1	2
Total	51		51	

Source: All figures drawn from the *Seventh Census,* schedule 4, Productions of Agriculture, Virginia, Tazewell, Virginia State Library, Richmond.

farmed moderate holdings. In the Cove, however, slaveholders outnumbered small farmers, as did tenants, and slaves outnumbered the family
members of the thirteen households of small farmers and tenants combined. By Tazewell standards the Cove was an elite community.[15]

Nearby Baptist Valley—an area of small, fairly homogeneous landholdings—was home to a community almost the antithesis of the Cove. The
twenty-seven households of Baptist Valley were almost equally divided in
1850 between yeomen, small farmers, and the landless. No one claimed large
farmer status, and of the landless, only three of ten lacked landed family
nearby. There was thus a permanent tenant class of at most 11 percent, and
these tenants were the only residents who did not bear long-established
names. Only one farm, that of James Cecil at the mouth of the valley near
Tazewell Court House, totaled more than 500 acres. Cecil's family connections lived mostly in the Clinch Valley, and although Cecil served as a squire
for Baptist Valley, many of his ties were elsewhere. There were only two
slaves resident in the valley; each lived alone in a white household (see Table
5.5).[16] Almost half the farms in Baptist Valley contained between 100 and
200 acres, and there were more very small farms than middle-sized ones.
Opinion in the county seat said that Baptist Valley farmers were backward;
only 35 percent of Baptist Valley farmland was improved (see Tables 5.2 and
5.3). Forty-four-year-old John Lockhart was a representative farmer there.
Like John Barns a member of a family that had arrived in the 1780s, Lockhart farmed 150 acres with the help of his four sons. With this workforce he
was able to improve seventy acres, roughly twice the neighborhood average.
He valued his farm at $900. His immediate neighbors, who included his
father, had farms pretty much like his, the exceptions being a blind widow
without property and two propertyless men in their twenties. One of these,
James Whitt, was a member of another local family that was long established and by local standards prosperous. Wilbern Whitt, James's father,
lived nearby, with another landless son immediately adjacent. Family ties,
family workforces, small farms: it seemed right that Baptist Valley's courthouse town was called Jeffersonville.[17]

In 1850 Abb's Valley seemed to be a section waiting for something to
happen. Twenty-nine households resided in an area somewhat larger than
Baptist Valley, but over half the household heads of Abb's Valley claimed no
real estate. Of these, at best two may have been nonlanded members of
landowning families; the records are contradictory. Thus at least 45 percent
of Abb's Valley residents were tenants or squatters, often on lands owned by
men who lived elsewhere. On the other hand, over one in four households
would qualify as yeoman landholders. Four of the fourteen resident land-

owning families were small slaveholders, and almost 10 percent of the valley's residents were black slaves (see Table 5.5). Abb's Valley's small population included individuals of sharply differing social status.[18]

Even the resident landholders seemed to live on speculative hopes; only 14 percent of Abb's Valley land was improved. Farming was carried out on a very small scale. Most of the landed farmers cultivated or grazed less than twenty-five acres, even though they owned middle-sized farms (see Tables 5.2 and 5.3). The area's relative isolation severely limited farming. Several residents did not claim to farm but listed themselves as artisans. Landowners contented themselves with placing tenants on their land, hoping for minimal returns while waiting for the value of their farmlands to rise. The tenants, of course, had little reason to improve someone else's holdings.[19]

Abb's Valley remained in thrall to a small group of speculative landholders. Some were resident, such as the Moore brothers, William and Andrew, who continued to be the dominant voices in the valley. Preeminent in wealth and, except for his brother, almost alone as a link to the early history of the valley, William Moore served as local justice of the peace. Importantly, he was also the only resident of Abb's Valley visible in courthouse affairs. He was easily the largest local farmer, claiming to own, with his brother, 900 acres. His 100 improved acres and eight slaves made him not only the largest operator but the only farm operator in Abb's Valley clearly concerned with markets and commerce. Most of Moore's neighbors were landless; some were obviously his tenants, and tenants and small farmers alike were newcomers.[20]

Despite William Moore's commitment to farm development, much of the Moores' land was almost worthless. The other two most important large landholding families, the Peerys and the Taylors, were no longer resident, despite their local roots and marriage ties with the Moores. Less tied to Abb's Valley by family experience than the Moores, they saw no reason to stay.[21] A core of first comers, a small group of middling farmers, and a predominance of tenants made up Abb's Valley, and its history was still entwined with the fortunes of the Moore family.

Burkes Garden, like Abb's Valley, had long been divided between residents and speculators, and tenancy had long been important. By 1850, however, change in the form of a resident landowning majority had already come to the Garden. The diverse Garden population contained almost equal numbers of landless families and solid yeoman farmers. Together these groups included nearly seven in ten Burkes Garden households. Slightly fewer than 1 in 10 of the 83 households could be called large farm families; 2 in 10 were small farmers. But just over half of the nonlanded farmers were members of local landed families. Fewer than 20 percent of Garden households were unlikely to inherit land; these were probably long-term tenants. The center of gravity in the Garden, therefore, lay with the 28 yeoman households (see Table 5.2).[22]

Among Tazewell communities, Burkes Garden clearly ranked behind the Cove in prestige, though well ahead of Baptist Valley and Abb's Valley. But in terms of opportunity for settlers, it ranked first despite its mountain wall. Compared with the Cove, it had much more available, and improvable, land. In area the Garden was 10,000 acres larger than the Cove, but in 1850 the two communities had very similar amounts of land that had been taken up into farms. Prime farmland still came onto the market in the Garden. The Garden also stood out from the other neighborhoods in its diverse population. There were about as many small farmers as large farmers and, similarly, roughly the same numbers of very small and very large farm operations, and not many of either. The modal number of improved acres was between twenty-five and fifty. Only one family held over 1,000 acres, and only two farms had over 200 improved acres. The proportion of improved acreage in the Garden, a little over 30 percent, was roughly equal to that of Baptist Valley and of the Cove, if the Bowens' speculations were included in the Cove totals. While the Garden could not match the level of development of the Cove's large working farms, it supported a population approaching twice that of the Cove and included two and three-fourths times as many whites (see Tables 5.3 and 5.5).[23]

One-third of the landowners in the Garden owned slaves; the average owner held four slaves. But the sixty-five slaves, 10 percent of the Garden's total population, did not approach the number of whites living on small farms or as permanent tenants. All these groups were less important—numerically and socially—than the middle-rank landholders. While the Cove was dominated by very large farmers and slaves, Baptist Valley by small farmers, and Abb's Valley by absentees and tenants, in the Garden, yeoman family farms made up the plurality (see Table 5.5).[24]

Philip Heninger can be taken as a representative 1850 farmer. A member of the first group of interrelated, middling families to come into the Garden in the early 1800s when settlement began to open up, he had in-laws and siblings among his immediate neighbors, who were farmers much like himself. A few tenants and very small farmers lived nearby. Some of these probably worked on the lands of Joseph Meek, son of the ill-fated speculator and the wealthiest landholder in the Garden; others were members of families connected to Heninger. He claimed $2,000 in real estate on a farm of around 140 acres, including 65 improved. He farmed this land with the help of one son. His one adult slave was a woman, who probably helped his wife care for her nine children, five of whom were under twelve.[25]

The diverse society of the Garden illustrates the social relations in mid-century Tazewell County. The Floyds—Laetitia, widow of Governor John Floyd and mother of governor-to-be John B. Floyd; son Colonel George R. C. Floyd; daughter Lavalette; and son-in-law George F. Holmes—had more statewide prestige and connections than anyone in the county. Chronically short of money and constantly seeking speculations in land and business to retrieve their fortunes, the members of the Floyd clan both arrived in the Garden and departed from it attended by landless dependents. Gentlemen and paternalists, they treated their entourage with a combination of concern and contempt, using Floyd family networks to get work or supplies for them and defending them in court despite strong suspicions of their guilt. But the Floyds also suggested in family correspondence that an incorrigibly lazy farm laborer should be whipped and on one occasion referred to "catching" youthful dependents and setting them to work—language usually associated with attitudes toward slaves.[26]

The Floyds and the Holmeses were in constant contact with a variety of large and small landholders, tenants, and farm laborers who lived near the Floyd holdings in the eastern end of the Garden. The quality of that contact varied considerably, however. Although any of these people might feel free to walk in on the Floyds, be fed, and stay the night, the landless came to work, to sell or trade, or to receive advice or charity, while others came to make deals or to pass the time. George Holmes's diary evinces clearly different conventions to be used with different classes of visitors. Although laborers often ate at Holmes's, they never "dined" there; although they often discussed work with him, he never "conversed" with them; and while transient employees clearly spent the night, he never recorded the fact.

In a society where a tenant might be the younger son of a landed family, or even a wealthy man leasing grazing land, and where some ties with dependents stretched over two generations, status lines were permeable. Andy Brewster was a member of the long-established, smallholding but prosperous Brewster family of Baptist Valley. In the early 1850s he was overseer and chief tenant of the Floyd holdings in and outside Burkes Garden. Although the Floyds were very aware that he was "in service" to them, he and his family were treated as equals. Holmes and the Floyds depended on his expertise with animals and traded with him on an equal basis. His family ate Christmas dinner with the Holmeses; his wife accompanied Lavalette Holmes on social calls; and when smallpox threatened Tazewell, Homes obtained vaccine for his family and Brewster's. When

Holmes broke with Andy Brewster, it was over how Brewster had used his almost total freedom to direct Holmes's property. The Floyds were confident that they possessed some of the "best blood" of Virginia, but they treated small farmers and tenants with respect. Dependents and landless laborers were another matter.[27]

During the 1850s a transportation revolution affected Tazewell. Before then, all the roads out of the county were nearly impassable much of the year, and any improvements to them were short lived at best. The only real exception was a turnpike connecting Jeffersonville to the east with Fincastle in the Valley of Virginia and to the west with Cumberland Gap. Until 1851 most of Tazewell's agricultural trade flowed along this one artery. The prime farm interest in Tazewell was buying cattle coming from Kentucky and Tennessee in autumn drives, wintering them, fattening them on Tazewell bluegrass until the following fall, and then sending them on to markets in the Shenandoah. The return of the cattle brokers from the Shenandoah markets was Tazewell's one annual transfusion of capital. Of the four communities studied here, only the Cove had direct access to this turnpike.[28]

By the mid-1850s, however, the Virginia and Tennessee Railroad reached first Wytheville and then Saltville and Bristol, effectively replacing the old Fincastle Pike. Even before that, a new turnpike, the Kentucky and Tazewell Court House Turnpike, had connected Jeffersonville with Grundy through the length of Baptist Valley, and a second, the Tazewell Court House and Fancy Gap Turnpike, had linked the county seat to Wytheville via an old trace through Burkes Garden. In 1858 a third new pike, the Tazewell and Saltville, connected the Cove to the Saltville spur of the railroad. By 1860, then, only Abb's Valley had no good, new connection to the outside. The railroad, of course, greatly strengthened a preexisting trade nexus. More of Tazewell had access, but the direction and destination remained the same, as did the main article of commerce, cattle. George Bickley, in his boosterish 1852 *History*, expected the railroad to revolutionize Tazewell agriculture, promoting scientific farming; making new crops, especially wheat, potentially profitable; and dragging the reluctant mountain yeomen into the modern age. By 1860 that had not yet taken place, but the four communities did show some clear marks of change.[29]

One of the clearest evidences of change was the arrival, in each of the four communities, of wealthy farmers from surrounding counties, usually counties already more committed to markets. In Abb's Valley, John Taylor, who had long held a large tract there, moved near his kinsman, William Moore, and began a large farming operation. Taylor's brother, Charles, who was a large farmer and landholder in nearby Wright's Valley and at Five Oaks, leased a large farm in Burkes Garden. Anthony Lawson, a farm entrepreneur from Wythe County, also began an aggressive program of buying up Garden land, buying out, among others, the Floyds. But unlike many outsiders speculating in the Garden, Charles Taylor immediately moved in and began farming, while Anthony Lawson became a part-time resident.[30]

Even in the Cove, landed newcomers appeared. The proportion of land tax paid by nonresidents went up slightly, and by 1860, almost all of the Cove's 15,000 acres were included in farms. As the number of farms increased, along with the pressure on the land market from speculation, the value of Cove land rose even higher. The most common farm size stayed at 500 acres, and, in part because of speculation, the modal amount of improved land per farm declined to 100 acres; but those figures disguised the real changes taking place. The total amount of improved land increased by over 1,000 acres, and two farms claimed over 1,000 acres of improved land each. In particular, the Bowens sold off some of their speculative holdings and improved their remaining property, so that their proportion of improved land was now greater than that of the community in general. Speculation and local improvement almost balanced out, so that in 1860 one-third of Cove farmland was improved, only a slight increase since 1850. But in 1860 five very large farms stood above the rest. As in 1850, over half the landowners in the Cove claimed over $1,000 in real property, but the proportions of large farmers and solid yeomen reversed, so that the former dominated these ranks numerically as they already had socially and financially. Large farmers were now one-third of all farm operators, landed and landless included. The Bowens were still the largest operators, but now several other old landed families—Wards and Barnses, for example—began to live and farm on the same scale (see Tables 5.2 and 5.4).

Social structure in the Cove was being stretched in both directions. On the surface, little change was taking place among the humbler residents, as almost the same proportion of small farmers and landless lived there in 1860 as in 1850. But the number of very small farms increased, mostly because of the division, through inheritance, of some of the smaller established family holdings. The real change, however, occurred among the landless. The proportion of landless farmers who were members of landed families went up slightly. The number of tenant households had been reduced from ten to seven—a small, but appreciable change in a community of thirty-one farming households. Most strikingly, twelve household heads were listed in the census as farm laborers. No farm laborers had been identified as such in

Table 5.4. Improved Land and Farm Size, 1860

Acres	Improved Land		Farmland	
	Farms	%	Farms	%
		Cove		
0–25	2	10	0	0
26–50	5	25	1	5
51–100	5	25	2	10
101–200	4	20	2	10
201–500	2	10	7	35
501–1,000	0	0	3	15
Over 1,000	2	10	5	25
Total	20		20	
		Baptist Valley		
0–25	7	37	0	0
26–50	4	21	2	11
51–100	6	32	2	11
101–200	1	5	8	42
201–500	1	5	5	26
501–1,000	0	0	1	5
Over 1,000	0	0	1	5
Total	19		19	
		Abb's Valley		
0–25	2	18	0	0
26–50	4	36	0	0
51–100	1	9	1	9
101–200	4	36	3	27
201–500	0	0	2	18
501–1,000	0	0	4	36
Over 1,000	0	0	1	9
Total	11		11	
		Burkes Garden		
0–25	11	19	1	2
26–50	13	22	4	7
51–100	25	42	5	8
101–200	6	10	21	36
201–500	4	7	21	36
501–1,000	0	0	4	7
Over 1,000	0	0	3	5
Total	59		59	

Source: All figures drawn from the *Eighth Census*, schedule 4, Productions of Agriculture, Virginia, Tazewell, Virginia State Library, Richmond.

1850. Pressure on the land had reduced the numbers of permanent tenants; more Cove lands were operated as large family farms. However, tenants were more than replaced by farm laborers, none of whom had local ties. In 1860 over half of the household heads engaged in farming had no land; four in ten of these also had no kin ties to the Cove's landed families and—at least in the Cove—little prospect of getting land.[31]

The numbers of slaves declined. Roughly the same proportion of white households held black slaves in 1860 as in 1850, and two families still held over twenty slaves. Increases in the cattle trade did not call for more slave labor, however, and white farm laborers would be more able to fill the diverse roles formerly played by tenants than slaves would be. So the average size of slaveholdings declined, and while a quarter of the Cove's people were black, and only two of these were free, white farm labor was increasing at the expense of both slaves and tenants (see Table 5.5).[32]

In the Cove of 1860, John Barns, now an old man, was considerably richer than he had been in 1850. He had expanded his landholdings and, unlike most, had increased his numbers of slaves. He had improved more of the lands on his two Cove farms and doubled the amount of undeveloped land that he held close by. He had hired an overseer and had placed farm laborers on his lands. His one son, William, although listed as a farmer, attended school and obviously was not counted on as farm labor. A walk through Barns's section would bring you to his brother's farm, to the farm of his brother's son, and eventually to the lands of other established, although somewhat less prosperous, families. But the landed lived in the midst of newcomers: farm laborers with names like Carter and Spence, most of whose kin in Tazewell lived, like them, on lands not their own. They were even less likely to become a part of Cove society than the tenants they had superseded.[33]

Baptist Valley was likewise affected by improved transportation. It was invaded by outsiders. Almost half of those paying land tax in 1860 in Baptist Valley resided elsewhere, usually in the more developed portions of Tazewell County. The number of residents grew, mostly through the arrival of new families. The size and number of farms increased slightly; now 35 percent were over 200 acres in size, and one included over 1,000 acres. But the proportion of improved land went down sharply, from 35 percent to 15 percent, as more land was being held for speculative purposes. Even farmers long resident invested in land, some buying land that lay along the valley's dividing ridge and had not previously been thought worth claiming (see Table 5.4).[34]

Consequently, wealth in land went up. Almost half of the farming house-

Table 5.5. Slave Population by Total Population

1850			1860		
Slaves	%	Total	Slaves	%	Total
		Cove			
142	35	357	111	27	421
		Baptist Valley			
2	1	207	4	1	227
		Abb's Valley			
20	9	228	45	18	248
		Burkes Garden			
65	10	666	62	8	739

Sources: All figures derived from the seventh and eighth censuses, schedule 1, Free Population, Virginia, Tazewell; *Seventh Census, 1850,* schedule 2, Slave Population, Virginia, Tazewell, National Archives, microfilm publications, microcopy M432, roll 993; *Eighth Census, 1860,* schedule 2, Slave Population, Virginia, Tazewell, National Archives, microfilm publications, microcopy M653, roll 1397.

holds could now be called solid yeoman, and three large farming families were resident. More importantly, the proportion without land dropped to two households in ten, the same as the proportion of small property holders. Only one of these landless households lacked landed kin in the valley, and that family, the Packs, had kin in a neighboring valley. The tenant class, never important in Baptist Valley, had almost disappeared. Furthermore, although farm laborers began to be listed in the Baptist Valley census in 1860, their presence did not signal the kind of shift implied by the arrival of laborers in the Cove. Only three farm laborer families were listed, and two of these had landed kin. The numbers of tenants and farm labor households together meant that almost three in ten of the resident families of Baptist Valley had no land. But only 7 percent of the households in the valley had no family links to the land and no prospects of inheritance, and only four slaves lived in the valley (see Tables 5.2 and 5.5).[35]

Baptist Valley, then, changed from a neighborhood of small farmers to a somewhat more speculative community of yeomen. Newcomers had joined its ranks, and land values were up; but the 1850s had, in the main, reinforced social relationships already in place. Outsiders were buying in, but there was not enough pressure on the land from this source to limit access. A representative farmer in 1860, though more wealthy than most, was James Brewster, older brother of Andy, with several sons farming in the section and one full-grown son to help on the home farm. He valued his 380 acres—100 improved—at $3,420. A walk through his neighborhood would have shown farms held by old Baptist Valley families and a moderate range of farm sizes; neither large estates nor marginal holdings appeared, and the most important covariant of farm size was the age of the household head. Young men with smallholdings had little reason to fear the future, so long as they could expect to follow the example of James Brewster. More prosperous than in 1850, with all but one of his sons settled on their own land, and with a reserve for the future, the sixty-year-old Brewster had used the 1850s to establish his family in the most traditional manner, maintaining the ways of a community rooted in small family farms. In Brewster's section, even the farm laborers bore established local names like Whitt and Hankins.[36]

Abb's Valley life also changed little in the 1850s. The farthest of the four communities from the new transportation lines, it was unlikely to have been deeply affected by commercial farming. The newly arrived Taylors, with the Moores, created a tiny elite of planters, together holding forty-five slaves. Other landed newcomers were attracted by somewhat better hopes than before, so that for the first time since 1820 a majority of those paying tax on Abb's Valley lands lived there (see Table 5.1). But most aspects of Abb's Valley society were constant. The number of families resident in Abb's Valley changed little. Over half of those farming still had no land, and most of these were tenants or possibly squatters, although a handful of families were headed by farm laborers. Only a quarter of the landless had local connections, so four in ten residents of Abb's Valley were probably permanently outside the circle of the landed.[37]

Social distances had increased, largely because of the arrival of John Taylor. The addition of his slaves to those of William Moore meant that almost 2 in 10 of the Valley's 248 residents were enslaved. A middle group—5 yeoman landholders—occupied about the same social position as a similar group had in 1850. Between the Moores, Taylors, and their tenants, landholdings scattered in size as they did spatially. Farming quality advanced slightly as smaller farmers had improved somewhat more of their lands. But the new land purchases meant that still the overwhelming bulk of Abb's Valley land, now almost 90 percent, was unimproved. There was more wealth, and slightly more of the landless had some hope of inheriting at least some land in Abb's Valley. But although the landowners were now more likely to be resident, most land awaited a reason for development.

Kiah Billups represented the possibilities in underdeveloped Abb's Valley. In 1850 he had held 40 acres, 15 of which were improved. In 1860 he had 120 acres, 30 of them improved. There was no land shortage, but since Billups's children at home were too young to help out on the farm, he probably had expanded his farm as far as he could. Further growth would have to wait for the maturation of his last young son at home. Like Abb's Valley, Billups had made gains in the 1850s, but for both, life was essentially the same.

As the census taker moved down the valley from Kiah's place, he passed a cluster of farm laborers and tenants before reaching John Taylor's farm. One of these landless people, probably employed by Taylor, was Augustus Billups, Kiah's newly independent and newly wedded son. The pattern of small farmers, farmers without farms, small farmers—punctuated by the Taylor and Moore places—was repeated the length of the valley. The Moores had prospered; the value of William Moore's real estate had more than tripled. But in the valley as a whole the number of working farms had declined in the 1850s, and several cabins stood unoccupied. Evidently only a few well-placed families could overcome Abb's Valley's limitations to grasp the new opportunity available in Tazewell County.[38]

The Burkes Garden community stood to gain most from the expanding transportation grid. The Garden was the section closest to Wytheville and the railroad and was well known to have fertile land available. Once the mountain wall was less daunting, Burkes Garden should thrive. The arrival of men like Taylor and Lawson did signal change; these experienced farmers knew the opportunities they might grasp. Another sign of change was that in 1860 residents of Burkes Garden dominated among those paying taxes on Garden land; after a slight slowdown between 1840 and 1850, the gradual move from absentee to local ownership had accelerated in the 1850s (see Table 5.1).

During the 1850s the size of the modal farm increased, as did the amount of land improved. Now as many farms contained between 200 and 500 acres as contained between 100 and 200. Almost half the Garden's farms were middle sized or larger, while the number of small farms had declined by over one-third. Over half the farms, roughly double the figure for 1850, now had over 50 improved acres. But because so much new land had been bought or claimed, the proportion of improved land to total land in farms actually had declined very slightly from 1850.[39] Three farms now contained more than 1,000 acres. As in the Cove and Baptist Valley, the scale of Garden farming had increased (see Table 5.4).

The place of the landless had also changed. The number of tenants had gone down very slightly, while farm laborers had appeared in such numbers that the twenty-eight laborers' households were now the largest group among the white landless. As demand for land went up, the importance of resident landed families and their farm laborers went up in Burkes Garden, just as in the Cove. Slightly more than half of the farmers without farms had no family ties to Burkes Garden land, a slight increase since 1850. As over four of five farm laborers had no family ties to land in the Garden, the landless had fewer prospects and fewer ties to the landed community than before. One-third of the farming households in the Garden were without land and with little hope of getting land—twice as many as in 1850.[40]

At the same time, the ranks of landholders had also polarized. Almost three of five landholders (up from two in five) could claim yeoman or large estates, and the proportion of large operators had doubled. The number of small farmers had been halved, and the few very small holders were linked by family and probably status to the tenants and laborers. The thriving solid yeoman farmers dominated numerically more than ever, and there was a visible shift to larger, more valuable spreads. But larger farms did not equal a greater dependency on slavery; the number of slaves had declined marginally. Slave labor was not basic to the changes in Garden society. As in the Cove, cattle raising did not demand large numbers of slaves, and no farmer held more than ten slaves. The vital changes were in the ranks of white labor and in the growing value and concentration of land (see Tables 5.2 and 5.5).

These changes had not come at the expense of established Garden families. On the contrary, most long-term families had done well, increasing their holdings even though the valuation of land was rising. There was no loss of status among the farmers and tenants of 1850 who persisted to 1860 in Burkes Garden. Half of the tenants—mostly members of landed families—who stayed became landholders, and half of the persistent smallholders became yeomen. Most of the laborers and tenants of 1860 were newcomers, and they were entering a different Burkes Garden.[41] Social distances had increased and links between landed and landless had weakened as farms grew in size and value and as farm laborers became more important than either tenants or slaves. Certainly, Burkes Garden had not become as closed a community as the Cove, and it had always been more diverse than the small farmer society of Baptist Valley, even though the Garden's yeoman farmers were very like the valley's core group in wealth and landholding. But by 1860 the Garden was both richer and poorer than Baptist Valley, as a group of large, resident landholders, employing transient farm laborers, increasingly dominated society.

In 1860 Philip Heninger owned a farm of 110 acres, 70 of which were improved. His holdings had not changed in ten years; he was sixty, and his oldest sons were gone. But the value of his property had gone up by nearly one-third. As before, a walk through his neighborhood would have shown nearby siblings and in-laws and many names long associated with the Garden—Greevers, Hanshoes, and Heningers—as well as families who had come in the 1850s—Mahoods and Vails. Middle-sized farms and young farmers without farms who bore familiar names predominated. But in the neighborhoods of larger holdings, owned by families such as the Meeks and Lawsons, clusters of farm laborers and tenants appeared. The farm laborers were new, as was the wealth represented in these large farms. Heninger had done well and had bought slaves and land for speculation. Burkes Garden had likewise thrived with the coming of the turnpike and railroad. Philip Heninger's social world was still in place, but newcomers above and below him in status signaled deep changes.[42]

In the mid-1850s the Floyds had given way to Joe Meek and Anthony Lawson as the dominant spirits in the Garden. Despite expedients, the Floyds had been unable to meet their debts. Losing all but honor, they had been sold out like gentlemen. Lawson was the primary purchaser. He took over debts and guaranteed Laetitia Floyd's legacies to her children, but he drove hard bargains, expected quick compliance, and easily fended off Floyd attempts to win better terms after the agreement had been signed. By 1870 Lawson and Meek, between them, would own one-ninth of the Garden. Successful businessmen rather than gentlemen paternalists, Meek and Lawson were celebrated for giving young men of character and ambition their starts in life by granting loans with no collateral. Their goal was to create more businessmen like themselves.[43]

A grim counterpoint to the Bowens's successful establishment of an elite landed family in the Cove is provided by the downward trajectory of the Burrass family of Burkes Garden. In 1804 Thomas Burrass became one of the earliest landowning settlers of Burkes Garden by claiming 300 acres on the waters of Wolf Creek in the Garden's eastern end. Although essentially land poor—his personal tax records usually list only one horse as taxable—he took an active part in Tazewell society, witnessing on one occasion the will of the wealthiest member of the pioneer generation. In 1806 Burrass became an ensign in the militia; in 1810, like the first Rees Bowen, lieutenant. But evidence of his debts began to appear in suits at law; in 1814 he held his land, but by 1820, he had lost it and served Burkes Garden as a post rider. He continued to try to establish himself and by 1830 once again owned land, this time 165 acres outside the Garden on Clear Fork. By 1840, however, he was back in the Garden, and he and his oldest son, Jim, were tenants and dependents of the Floyds, who had bought much of the part of the Garden where Burrass had originally located. Tom Burrass lived until 1867, spending his last years with his son-in-law, landless carpenter John Thompson.

He had failed to hold his land but had not lost all respect; like Andy Brewster's, his opinions and advice were taken seriously by the Floyds.[44]

Jim Burrass never got land. Maturing in the 1840s, he remained a tenant of the Floyds as long as they remained in the Garden. Illiterate (unlike his father), he participated actively in the local economy, trading work, young stock, or seed for meal or flour. Never quite trusted, sometimes drunk, and never escaping poverty, he first appears in George Holmes's diary walking to the courthouse to protest his ejection from Floyd land. Successful in this instance, he soon disappeared from Burkes Garden to reappear as a farm laborer near Jeffersonville.[45]

Jim's sons—Bill; Tom, Jr.; George; and Rans—were farm laborers and transients, sometimes in, sometimes outside the Garden. Tom, Jr., was counted trustworthy and had accumulated a little personal property, but Bill was considered dishonest and was automatically arrested for, though acquitted of, a local robbery. Bill's associates were members of families long dependent on local charity, and he was accused of drinking, gambling, and brawling with slaves. The Burrasses of his generation may well have become alienated from the society around them. In 1863, Union general Toland's cavalry raided through Burkes Garden in an attempt to cut the railroad at Wytheville. Repulsed at Wytheville, Toland's men were guided over the mountains, down Clear Fork, and into West Virginia and safety by a man named Burrass, who was later sent to Richmond as a traitor and executed.[46]

The growing access to markets had caused changes in all four communities, primarily by making land more valuable and attracting newcomers intent on taking advantage of newly accessible Tazewell lands. But new transportation had had little time to transform society in the direction of Bickley's commercial dreams. While Bill Burrass was an extreme case, the 1850s clearly pointed the way to sharper distinctions between landed and landless. However, there was no evidence that any of the four communities had been turned in a new social direction. The shape of each community had long been established by a combination of early settlement patterns, fertility, and accessibility. The communities most affected, Burkes Garden and the Cove, were the communities already most tied to markets and large-scale agriculture. That is, the increased access to markets merely ratified social structures already in place or reinforced established patterns of development— most strikingly the Cove's concentration of landholding and the Garden's movement toward resident large landholders. The market in land was promoted, and the valuation of lands was increased. In Burkes Garden and the

Cove the labor system was changed, as farm laborers began to replace tenants in importance. Well-to-do farmers and their sons took over the land; they would need labor, not surrogate farmers. Slavery was not promoted, however, and small farmers were rarely displaced. Baptist Valley and Abb's Valley were really not changed at all, although outside interest in their land increased.

Further, the four Tazewell communities illustrate the difficulty of identifying a "typical" Appalachian community. In 1860, Tazewell contained three different kinds of communities that various Appalachian scholars have demonstrated were central to the social experience of the mountain South. The Cove was the kind of bottomland, first comer society that Cratis Williams first suggested formed the basis of a native elite, an idea systematically developed by Mary Beth Pudup. As Pudup's work would predict, family persistence, the control of local resources, and the ability to respond to changes kept the Cove's dominant families at the focus of Tazewell political influence. If the experience of the Brewster family is typical, then Baptist Valley closely resembled the family-based subsistence farming communities that Ronald Eller believes were at the core of preindustrial Appalachian life. The experience of Baptist Valley suggests that at least the first stages of market farming could reinforce, not damage, this traditional society. Abb's Valley—identified with the Moores, largely populated by tenants, and waiting for change—looks much like the Georgia mountain communities described by Frederick Bode and Donald Ginter: heavily populated by tenants and dependent on a developing land market. Abb's Valley demonstrates, as Bode and Ginter argue, that the landless played a major role in Appalachian history. The diversity of Burkes Garden, where all these social groups lived and worked in close proximity, suggests that we cannot overlook any part—elite, yeomen, tenants, slaves—if we want to understand how antebellum Appalachian society worked. In Tazewell, as farming began to be commercialized, common pressures on the land affected all four communities, but Appalachian diversity, established long before, was still in place.[47]

Finally, while the very diversity of the four neighborhoods precludes easy comparisons with other counties and communities, a few speculative generalizations can be made about the place of Appalachian Tazewell in antebellum rural America. The proportion of landless people resembles the proportions found in studies of upland and mountain agricultural communities in Virginia, Kentucky, Georgia, and South Carolina. More directly, the high proportion of tenants—and perhaps squatters—in Abb's Valley, as in other undeveloped sections on northern and southern frontiers, suggests that tenancy as well as squatting was a common strategy on newly opened or inaccessible lands. If Abb's Valley's tenancy rates suggest a frontier survival there, the low ratio of improved to unimproved lands suggests a further frontier condition in all four communities. In Virginia, only in the furthest reaches of the mountain southwest and northwest were farms less improved. In the balance of the North and the South, only in the newly settled states did similar or lower rates of farm improvement obtain. Together, tenancy rates and low levels of land improvement indicate that Appalachian Tazewell, and Abb's Valley in particular, were emerging very slowly from the agricultural patterns of the early frontier.[48]

The widening social distances between landholding families of early settlers and the transient landless as Burkes Garden and the Cove (the two Tazewell neighborhoods furthest from frontier experiences) moved firmly into commercial farming are paralleled in studies by John Mack Faragher of Sugar Creek, Illinois, and by Martin Crawford of Ashe County, North Carolina, where societies at similar stages of development also stretched out at the top and bottom.[49] The experiences of Sugar Creek and Ashe County hint that while the direction society in each of the four neighborhoods took in the 1850s had been set long before, the future would be with the large landholders of the Cove and the Garden.

Notes

1. For a summary statement concerning the literature that undermines more traditional views of the mountain South, see Dwight B. Billings and Kathleen M. Blee, "Appalachian Inequality in the Nineteenth Century: The Case of Beech Creek, Kentucky," *Journal of the Appalachian Studies Association* 4 (1992): 114–15. Other important contributions include Paul J. Weingartner, Dwight Billings, and Kathleen M. Blee, "Agriculture in Preindustrial Appalachia: Subsistence Farming in Beech Creek, 1850–1880," *Journal of the Appalachian Studies Association* 1 (1989): 70–80; Lee Soltow, "Land Inequality on the Frontier: The Distribution of Land in East Tennessee at the Beginning of the Nineteenth Century," *Social Science History* 5 (1981): 275–91; Mary Beth Pudup, "The Boundaries of Class in Preindustrial Appalachia," *Journal of Historical Geography* 15 (1989): 139–62; Mary Beth Pudup, "The Limits of Subsistence: Agriculture and Industry in Central Appalachia," *Agricultural History* 64 (1990): 61–89; Durwood Dunn, *Cades Cove: The Life and Death of a Southern Appalachian Community, 1818–1937* (Knoxville: University of Tennessee Press, 1988), pp. 23–98; John C. Inscoe, *Mountain Masters: Slavery and the Sectional Crisis in Western North Carolina* (Knoxville: University of Tennessee Press, 1989), pp. 11–58; Altina L. Waller, *Feud: Hatfields, McCoys, and Social Change in Appalachia, 1860–1900* (Chapel Hill: University of North Carolina Press, 1988), pp. 34–52.

2. William C. Pendleton, *History of Tazewell County and Southwest Virginia, 1748–1920* (Richmond, Va.: W. C. Hill, 1920), pp. 407–10, 509–10; George W. L. Bickley, *History of the Settlement and Indian Wars of Tazewell County, Virginia* (Cincinnati, Ohio: For the Author, 1852), reprinted in John Newton Harman, Sr., *Annals of Tazewell County, Virginia*, 2 vols. (Richmond: W. C. Hill, 1922), 1:355–57.

3. Pendleton, *Tazewell County*, pp. 512–13; Bickley, *History*, p. 354; Louise Leslie, *Tazewell County* (Radford, Va.: Commonwealth Press, 1982), p. 110.

4. James Moore Brown, *The Captives of Abb's Valley: A Legend of Frontier Life* (Staunton, Va.: McClure, 1942), pp. 23–39; Pendleton, *Tazewell County*, p. 514.

5. Jim Hoge and Louise Hoge, "Burkes Garden," in Leslie, *Tazewell*, pp. 422–24; Bickley, *History*, pp. 357–58; interview with J. M. and Louise Hoge, 4 August 1988, Burkes Garden, Va.

6. For a strong statement of this point of view, see Kenneth W. Noe, "Southwest Virginia's Iron Road to Secession: A Reappraisal of Civil War Appalachia," *Appalachian Heritage* 17 (Spring 1989): 31–35. See also Inscoe, *Mountain Masters*.

7. Bickley, *History*, p. 357: Pendleton, *Tazewell County*, pp. 410–11, 427–28.

8. Leslie, *Tazewell*, pp. 725–26; Harman, *Annals*, 2:342–45; Jamie Ault Grady, "Bowens of Virginia and Tennessee," unpublished manuscript, Tazewell County Public Library, Tazewell, Va., 1969, p. 6-a; Pendleton, *Tazewell County*, pp. 407–9.

9. Pendleton, *Tazewell County*, pp. 408, 410, 624, 636; Harman, *Annals*, 2:344–48; Grady, "Bowens," pp. 7, 15–16.

10. Pendleton, *Tazewell County*, p. 645.

11. Ibid., pp. 422–24; Robert B. Woodworth, *The House of Moore* (Staunton, Va.: McClure, 1942), pp. 42, 67–68, 145; George B. Gose, *Pioneers of the Blue Grass* (Radford, Va.: Commonwealth Press, 1967), pp. 89–93.

12. Hoge and Hoge, "Burkes Garden," pp. 410, 419–24; Bickley, *History*, p. 358.

13. The heads of 13 of the 35 households in the Cove (37 percent) claimed no real estate; 3 of these were members of landed families, leaving 29 percent as likely tenants. Ten households, also 29 percent, contained slaves; 142 slaves were resident, making an average holding of 14. See U.S. Bureau of the Census, *Seventh Census of the United States (1850)*, schedule 1, Free Population, Virginia, Tazewell County, National Archives, microfilm publications, microcopy M432, roll 979; schedule 2, Slave Population, Virginia, Tazewell, microcopy M432, roll 993. For the purpose of this essay, I will refer to household heads claiming over $5,000 in real estate as large farmers, those claiming between $1,000 and $5,000 as yeomen, and those reporting some real estate, but less than $1,000, as small farmers. A planter will be someone holding twenty or more slaves.

14. In 1850 Cove farmers claimed 2,663 acres of improved land and 8,735 acres unimproved (30 percent improved). Eliminating the Bowens leaves 2,263 acres improved, 2,135 unimproved (51 percent improved). See *Seventh Census*, schedule 4, Productions of Agriculture, Virginia, Tazewell, Virginia State Library, Richmond. When comparing farms by acreage, I have called farms over 500 acres large, farms between 200 and 500 acres middle-sized, and farms between 100 and 200 acres small. Farms less than 100 acres are called very small; those over 500 acres, very large.

15. The descriptions of Barns's property and his neighborhood are drawn from

the *Seventh Census*, schedule 1, Virginia, Tazewell, microcopy M432, roll 979, p. 254; schedule 2, Virginia, Tazewell, microcopy M432, roll 993, p. 993; schedule 4, Virginia, Tazewell, p. 567; Virginia Land Tax, Tazewell, 1850, Virginia State Library.

16. Ten of the 27 heads of household in Baptist Valley claimed no real estate; 7 of these were members of landed families, leaving 3 of 27 (11 percent) as likely tenants. See *Seventh Census*, schedule 1, Virginia, Tazewell. Several of the outsiders holding Baptist Valley lands held slaves, but only 2 resided in the valley. See schedule 2, Virginia, Tazewell.

17. Farmers resident in Baptist Valley claimed 1,277 improved acres and 2,397 unimproved, making 35 percent improved. See *Seventh Census*, schedule 4, Virginia, Tazewell. The description of Lockhart is drawn from *Seventh Census*, schedule 1, Virginia, Tazewell, p. 298; schedule 4, Virginia, Tazewell, p. 565; Virginia Land Tax, Tazewell, 1850.

18. Fifteen of the 29 household heads resident in Abb's Valley (52 percent) claimed no real estate; 2 were related to the Osborne family, which claimed no property on the population census but claimed land on the agricultural census. If the Osbornes owned land, then 13 of 29 (45 percent) had no link to the land and were probably tenant class. See *Seventh Census*, schedule 1, Virginia, Tazewell; schedule 4, Virginia, Tazewell.

19. Abb's Valley farmers claimed just 795 improved acres and 4,728 unimproved, so 14 percent of the land was improved. See *Seventh Census*, schedule 4, Virginia, Tazewell.

20. *Seventh Census*, schedule 1, Virginia, Tazewell, p. 274; schedule 2, Virginia, Tazewell, p. 997; schedule 4, Virginia, Tazewell, p. 577; Virginia Land Tax, Tazewell, 1850.

21. On the Moores, see Pendleton, *Tazewell County*, p. 415; Bickley, *History*, p. 410. Family ties among the large landholders can be seen in Gose, *Pioneers of the Blue Grass*, pp. 89–90; Woodworth, *House of Moore*, pp. 68–69, 97.

22. Twenty-nine of Burkes Garden's 83 household heads claimed no real estate (35 percent), but 15 of these landless had family with land, so only 14 (35 percent) were probably long-term landless. See *Seventh Census*, schedule 1, Virginia, Tazewell.

23. Burkes Garden farmers claimed 4,176 acres of improved and 8,922 acres of unimproved land, making 32 percent improved. See *Seventh Census*, schedule 4, Virginia, Tazewell.

24. Fifteen Garden farm families held slaves, 18 percent of all farm families; 65 slaves were held, so the average number held was 4. See *Seventh Census*, schedule 2, Virginia, Tazewell.

25. *Seventh Census*, schedule 1, Virginia, Tazewell, p. 259; schedule 2, Virginia, Tazewell, p. 995; schedule 4, Virginia, Tazewell, p. 571; Virginia Land Tax, Tazewell, 1850.

26. For an account of Floyd family social attitudes, see Ralph Mann, "Mountains, Land, and Kin Networks: Burkes Garden, Virginia, in the 1840s and 1850s," *Journal of Southern History* 58 (1992): 420–22, 426–27.

27. George Frederick Holmes Agricultural Diary, George Frederick Holmes Papers, Manuscripts Department, Perkins Library, Duke University, Durham, N.C., pp. 24 (28 May 1856), 44 (20 September 1856), 53 (25 December 1856), 69 (11 May 1857), 77 (20 August 1857), 80 (4 September 1857), 94 (29 December 1857).

28. Pendleton, *Tazewell County*, pp. 530–34; Bickley, *History*, pp. 348, 362–70.

29. Pendleton, *Tazewell County*, pp. 534–35; Bickley, *History*, pp. 339, 378.

30. This information is drawn from the *Eighth Census of the United States (1860)*, schedule 4, Productions of Agriculture, Virginia, Tazewell, Virginia State Library, Richmond. For references to Charles Taylor and Anthony Lawson, see Holmes Agricultural Diary; E. L. Greever and A. S. Greever, "Burke's Garden: A Sketch," unpublished manuscript, Tazewell, 1897, in Virginia State Library, Richmond, p. 34.

31. Eleven of 31 farm household heads claimed no real property (35 percent); 7 (20 percent) had no family ties to land. Adding the 12 household heads listed as farm laborers, none of whom have local ties, means that 23 of 43 farm families were landless (54 percent), and 19 of 43 farming heads (44 percent) had neither land nor family links to land. See *Eighth Census*, schedule 1, Free Population, Virginia, Tazewell, Maiden Spring, microcopy M653, roll 1381.

32. In 1860 14 slaveholders held 111 slaves, for an average of 8 slaves, down from 14 in 1850. Twenty-seven percent of all white households held slaves. See *Eighth Census*, schedule 2, Slave Population, Virginia, Tazewell, Maiden Spring, microcopy M653, roll 1397. On the cattle trade, see Pendleton, *Tazewell County*, pp. 525, 658.

33. *Eighth Census*, schedule 1, Virginia, Tazewell, Maiden Spring, pp. 121–22, 140; schedule 2, Virginia, Tazewell, Western District, p. 9; schedule 4, Productions of Agriculture, Virginia, Tazewell, Maiden Spring, p. 13, Virginia State Library; Virginia Land Tax, Tazewell, 1860.

34. In Baptist Valley, farmers claimed 1,283 improved acres and 7,095 unimproved acres, making 15 percent of the claimed land improved. Ridge lands account for the fact that the total, 8,378 acres, was greater than the amount of land on the valley floor, approximately 6,400 acres. See *Eighth Census*, schedule 4, Virginia, Tazewell, Baptist Valley.

35. Six of the 28 resident farm household heads in Baptist Valley in 1860 (21 percent) claimed no real estate, and 1 (5 percent) had no family ties. One of the 3 farm labor families had no local ties, so 2 of 31 (7 percent) farm families had neither land nor ties to the land. See *Eighth Census*, schedule 1, Virginia, Tazewell, Baptist Valley.

36. Ibid., pp. 201–2; schedule 4, Virginia, Tazewell, Baptist Valley, p. 39; Virginia Land Tax, Tazewell, 1860.

37. In Abb's Valley, 13 of 25 farm household heads (52 percent) claimed no real estate; 3 farm labor household heads also claimed no real estate. Three of the tenant families and 1 farm labor family had local ties, so 12 of 28 (43 percent) of all families engaged in farming had neither land nor local ties. See *Eighth Census*, schedule 1, Virginia, Tazewell, Abb's Valley.

38. Ibid., pp. 34, 37; schedule 2, Virginia, Tazewell, Eastern District, p. 4; schedule 4, Virginia, Tazewell, Bluestone, p. 5; Virginia Land Tax, Tazewell, 1860.

39. Burkes Garden farmers claimed 4,667 acres of improved land and 12,084 acres of unimproved, so 28 percent of farmland was improved. See *Eighth Census*, schedule 4, Virginia, Tazewell, Burkes Garden.

40. Twenty-two of 76 farm household heads in Burkes Garden in 1860 (29 percent) reported no real estate. Twelve (55 percent) of these 22 had no family ties to Burkes Garden land, so 16 percent of farm household heads were permanent ten-

ants. Five of the 28 farm labor household heads (18 percent) had no ties to the Garden, so 35 of 104 farm household heads (34 percent) had neither land nor family ties. See *Eighth Census*, schedule 1, Virginia, Tazewell, Burkes Garden.

41. Five of the 9 persisting tenants owned real property in 1860; 7 of the persisting small farmers (under $1,000 in real estate) held real estate valued at more than $1,000 in 1860. Of the 27 tenant households I can trace, 18 left Burkes Garden between 1850 and 1860. See *Seventh Census*, schedule 1, Virginia, Tazewell; *Eighth Census*, schedule 1, Virginia, Tazewell, Burkes Garden.

42. *Eighth Census*, schedule 1, Virginia, Tazewell, Burkes Garden, pp. 107–9; schedule 2, Virginia, Tazewell, Eastern District, p. 8; schedule 4, Virginia, Tazewell, Burkes Garden, p. 19; Virginia Land Tax, Tazewell, 1860.

43. Holmes Agricultural Diary, pp. 26 (10 June 1856), 57 (12 January 1857), 65 (25 March 1857), 74 (19 July 1857), 81 (11 September 1857); Contracts between Anthony Lawson and John Warfield Johnston, William Lewis, and George F. Holmes (spouses of the three Floyd daughters), n.d., John Warfield Johnston Papers, Manuscripts Department, Perkins Library, Duke University, Durham, N.C.; G. R. C. Floyd to J. W. Johnston, 6 January 1876, Johnston Papers; Greever and Greever, "Burke's Garden," pp. 34–35.

44. Thomas Burrass's condition can be traced by looking at Virginia Personal Tax, Tazewell, for the years 1803, 1806, 1810, 1815, 1820, 1830; Virginia Land Tax, Tazewell, 1810, 1820, 1830, 1840, 1850, 1860; *Sixth Census of the United States (1840)*, schedule 1, Virginia, Tazewell, microcopy M704, roll 579, pp. 3–4; *Seventh Census*, schedule 1, Virginia, Tazewell, p. 85; *Eighth Census*, schedule 1, Virginia, Tazewell, Burkes Garden, p. 102; and in the court orders, wills, and patents collected by Netti Schreiner-Yantis, ed., *Archives of the Pioneers of Tazewell County, Virginia* (Springfield, Va.: Privately published, 1973), pp. 70, 91, 104, 169, 178, 186; Holmes Agricultural Diary, p. 46 (6 October 1856); Laetitia Floyd to Nicketti Johnston, 7 February 1848, Floyd Papers, Wylie Library, Clinch Valley College, Wise, Va.

45. Holmes Agricultural Diary, pp. 5 (26 January 1856), 14 (3 April 1856), 36 (26 July 1856); *Seventh Census*, schedule 1, Virginia, Tazewell, p. 96; *Eighth Census*, schedule 1, Virginia, Tazewell, Tazewell Court House, p. 164; Laetitia Floyd to Nicketti Johnston, 21 February 1846, Floyd Papers.

46. Holmes Agricultural Diary, pp. 11 (8 March 1856), 17 (19 April 1856), 27 (14 June 1856); *Eighth Census*, schedule 1, Virginia, Tazewell, Baptist Valley, p. 168; Hicksville, p. 85; Mann, "Mountains, Land, and Kin Networks," pp. 429–30; Gary G. Walker, *The War in Southwest Virginia: 1861–1865* (Roanoke, Va.: Gurtner, 1985), p. 57.

47. Cratis D. Williams, "The Southern Mountaineer in Fact and Fiction," *Appalachian Journal* 3 (1975): 9–25; Pudup, "Boundaries of Class," pp. 147–59; Ronald D. Eller, *Miners, Millhands, and Mountaineers: Industrialization of the Appalachian South, 1880–1930* (Knoxville: University of Tennessee Press, 1982), pp. 9–38; Frederick A. Bode and Donald E. Ginter, *Farm Tenancy and the Census in Antebellum Georgia* (Athens: University of Georgia Press, 1986), pp. 114–46.

48. Findings of proportions of the landless in Appalachian and piedmont communities are summed up in Billings and Blee, "Appalachian Inequality," pp. 118–19, and Mann, "Mountains, Land, and Kin Networks," p. 131. For general comparisons,

see Jeremy Atack, "Tenants and Yeomen in the Nineteenth Century," *Agricultural History* 62 (1988): 18–20. Sources for ratios of improved and unimproved lands include Sam Bowers Hilliard, *Atlas of Antebellum Southern Agriculture* (Baton Rouge: Louisiana State University Press, 1984), pp. 39–41, and Jeremy Atack and Fred Bateman, *To Their Own Soil: Agriculture in the Antebellum North* (Ames: Iowa State University Press, 1987), p. 112.

49. Martin Crawford, "The Farm Economy, the Market Economy, and Antebellum Social Relations in a Southern Mountain Community: Ashe County, North Carolina, 1850–1860," paper presented at the meeting of the Southern Historical Association, 1991, Fort Worth, Tex., pp. 6–7; John Mack Faragher, *Sugar Creek: Life on the Illinois Prairie* (New Haven: Yale University Press, 1986), pp. 184–87.

Economy and Community in Western North Carolina, 1860–1865

T he historical relationship between economic development and the community in Appalachia has been at the center of scholarly debate for at least three decades. These two terms have often been perceived as descriptions of two significantly different ways of life in opposition to each other as the market economy impinged on the life of the southern mountain people.[1] In trying to understand how the highland population adjusted to the changes, investigators have been handicapped by the absence of direct testimony from the non-elite population. The Civil War period, however, offers a brief glimpse into that world as the demands of modern warfare required people from all economic and social strata to express themselves about the way they lived. This study will take advantage of this unique opportunity to investigate how people in western North Carolina were adjusting to economic and social change in their world. Their comments and actions during the war years confirm the importance of both the community and the market economy in the region and suggest that western North Carolinians saw no necessary conflict between them. Additional evidence appears to indicate that although the community was a significant economic entity, the coexisting social community was not as securely based.

This study of western North Carolina is part of a much broader scholarly undertaking. Historians with a variety of specializations have sought to explain the transformation of the United States from an agricultural and rural country into an urban and industrial society. Some point to the post–Civil War period as the time when the most decisive changes took place.[2] But the greatest concentration of new studies has been in the colonial period. Reacting to earlier studies that saw colonial America as a largely undifferentiated area where the inhabitants shared common economic, political, and intellectual preconceptions, the more recent historians have challenged the prevailing orthodoxy by providing detailed social and economic analyses of individual communities. Concentrating primarily on the New England and Middle Atlantic colonies, investigators have disagreed over the motivations of early American farmers while agreeing on many of the particulars of colonial farm life.[3] Other writers have extended the debate past 1776 and have used the insights from the earlier period to examine the Early National and Jacksonian eras.[4]

The general agreement on the tasks performed by northern farmers before the American Revolution has destroyed the stereotype of the independent family farm. The new studies confirm the earlier picture of the nuclear family homestead as the most basic economic unit. They point out, however, that the farms were never individually self-sufficient.[5] While the families may have lived on a subsistence level, they still required the services of skilled craftsmen such as millers, blacksmiths, and wheelwrights to survive. While a family farm might produce most of its own food, all members of a community would be involved in a minimal trading system.[6] Even in this early period of exchange, there were merchants who purchased surplus produce from individual farmers and sent these goods into the broader market system. In return the merchants purchased and resold a variety of external goods to local farmers. Even when these transactions involved solely a transfer of commodities, a monetary value was assigned to each exchange. Many of these imported goods were essential to the continued success of the individual family units.[7] The major disagreement among scholars of the period is whether these exchanges were motivated by market pressures or by personal relationships developed at the community level.

Other historians have extended this analysis to a later period. Winifred Rothenberg has analyzed the convergence of market-center prices and local prices and concluded that by 1820 at the latest Massachusetts farmers were part of a market economy.[8] Clarence Danhof, in his study of innovation in northern agriculture, sees a steady increase of change that made commercial farming the dominant mode of operation by 1860.[9] But Danhof did note that some "backwater" communities in the mountains of New England remained outside the network because of the absence of modern transportation.[10] An economic study of one of these communities confirms his analysis.[11] Extensions of this model have been offered by other scholars who have sought to transfer the setting outside the Northeast. John Mack Faragher demonstrated that the same relationships could be found on the "open country" farms of Illinois.[12] Faragher's analysis indicates that the debate about the relationship between the community and market-based economies could be carried on in a variety of geographical settings.

Increasingly this analysis is being extended to the South. Gavin Wright's investigation of the cotton South has demonstrated that the local community economy was tied to a regionwide labor market for slaves.[13] But Wright's later work confirmed that the region was something of a backwater by Danhof's definition. The area as a whole was poorly served by railroads and was almost entirely rural—even more open country than Faragher's Illinois.[14] Steven Hahn's innovative work on antebellum upcountry Georgia depicts a region devoid of railroad facilities in which personal contacts and concerns dominated a community-based economy. Lacy K. Ford has reached a different conclusion in his analysis of the South Carolina upcountry. While agreeing that yeoman farmers practiced "safety-first" farming by insuring that they produced a subsistence for their families, Ford finds most of them actively involved in a market economy after the arrival of the railroad in the 1850s.[15] A further study of antebellum Georgia has challenged the notion that these small farmers were all independent landowners who shared a common economic base. Instead, it concludes that at least one-quarter of the free farmers in the state were tenants of some type.[16] In addition, there was a constant influx and departure of population that often resulted in the change of half of a community's population in a decade.[17] These findings suggest that southern upcountry communities were more complex economic entities than previously thought.

Following the lead of Hahn and Ford, several scholars of the mountain South have examined the preindustrial agricultural economy and society of the region in detail. Like their counterparts in the broader fields of American colonial and early national history, Appalachian scholars are reacting to a description of their subject region and its inhabitants as an undifferentiated society and economy. These yeomen were thought to live on independent subsistence farms that were geographically and economically isolated from the remainder of the South and the nation. Sustaining these farms and the families that lived there were powerful kinship and community ties that shielded the mountaineers from the intrusion of the outside world. Challenging this portrait of a static and harmonious world in southern Appalachia, the more recent Appalachian community studies have posited a much more complex society and economy. While they do not agree on all points, a general picture of the region has emerged. The earliest settlers into the mountains made their way from southern Pennsylvania and western Maryland into the Shenandoah Valley of Virginia. In both locations, the frontier farmers sought inexpensive land and freedom from economic domination. As the population increased in Pennsylvania and Virginia, the farm families began to spread into present-day West Virginia, southeastern Kentucky, eastern Tennessee, northern Georgia, and western North Carolina. These earliest European inhabitants of the highland South brought with them the experiences of living in more developed agricultural regions.

As these new migrants secured land and started to farm, a complex regional economy and society began to appear. A small commercial elite developed almost immediately. As Tyler Blethen and Curtis Wood have documented, merchants and livestock drovers were as much a part of the frontier economy as subsistence farmers.[18] The presence of this leadership when combined with a rapid growth of white population and the importation of African slavery insured that the mountain South would have a significantly differentiated society. While the highlands contained virtually no planters who survived primarily by the sale of a staple crop, the region did contain a small but powerful middle class of large landowners, merchants, doctors, lawyers, and political leaders.[19] These persons were usually directly involved in the market economy and acted as mediators between the larger American economy and the small farming communities of the Appalachian South.

At the same time, the small farm population of the southern mountains has also been carefully investigated and found not to be as homogeneous as previously thought. Paul Salstrom has pointed out that the region can be divided into three sections that experienced quite different growth and development patterns.[20] The work of Durwood Dunn and Tracy McKenzie in eastern Tennessee, Ralph Mann, Warren Hofstra, Robert Mitchell, and Kenneth Noe in Virginia, and Mary Beth Pudup in southeastern Kentucky confirms the basic point that different parts of the highlands developed at varying speeds and patterns.[21] Blethen and Wood have taken this analysis even further by pointing out that there were substantially different economic and social relationships to be found within the same county.[22] Thus, any investigation of the region must carefully describe the complex social and economic setting.

The Civil War offers an unusual opportunity to study open country agriculture in a Appalachian community setting. First, there is an abundance of correspondence available from all segments of the white population concerning economic activities. The hardships created by the federal blockade and the disruptions caused by the war prompted both the elite and the barely literate to document their activities. Since the governor of North Carolina for most of this period was fellow mountaineer Zebulon Baird Vance, the highland population was encouraged to seek government assistance for its distress. In addition, dislocations caused by the war created conditions that allow for testing hypotheses advanced to explain the nature of community-based agriculture. Individuals—usually the husband—were removed from the family, and this unit was forced to function without one or more of its major workers. Skilled craftsmen including blacksmiths, tanners, and millers volunteered for military service or were conscripted. The removal of these key persons from the community can therefore be studied in a manner not usually available to historians. In addition, the war disrupted normal trade patterns and created economic conditions that revealed the significance of the market in ways that could not be duplicated in peacetime.

The war also offers an opportunity to examine the significance of the community beyond its purely economic role. As Darrett Rutman has observed, a community economy presupposes a minimum amount of goodwill within the group.[23] But the Civil War period in the southern mountains was a time of savage internal warfare in which deserters and draft evaders challenged law enforcement officials and regular army units. Loyalties were divided throughout the highlands, and in some localities civilian neighbors attacked one another with a ferocity usually reserved for the battlefield. The presence of Confederate troops living off the land only served to further exacerbate the hostile feelings directed toward the authorities who brought on these hardships. Thus, the strength of community ties and the cohesion of the group was tested under extreme conditions during the war.

While there are few community studies available for western North Carolina for the antebellum period, the general outline of life in the region seems clear. Studies by John Inscoe and Martin Crawford have identified a distinct mountain elite who usually owned relatively large numbers of slaves.[24] Thus like the surrounding lowland areas, mountain society had an identifiable top made up of slaveowners and a bottom made up of human chattel. There is also substantial evidence that the middling group of whites was as divided economically as it was in other parts of the mountain South. Studies of Haywood and Jackson Counties indicate that there was a significant tenant farming population in the western counties. What is particularly striking in these two counties is the fact that tenancy was most pronounced in sections where slaveholding was most prominent. In certain communities such as the Tuckasegee Valley of Jackson County, a virtual duplication of lowland farming arrangements was created.[25] In the more remote coves of the same county, subsistence farming prevailed.

Even in areas where slaves were a significant part of the community, western North Carolina was quite distinct from farming areas dominated by staple crop production. The numbers of both slaves and slaveowners were substantially smaller proportions of the population than elsewhere in the South. Although Burke County's enslaved population was 25 percent of all residents, the black population of western North Carolina as a whole was only 10 percent of all inhabitants. Slaveowners were an even greater minority, and in most counties the owners of more than twenty slaves numbered only a handful.[26] Even those "planters" who owned more than twenty slaves rarely owned a plantation in the strictest sense; they were more likely to rent out their workers as skilled craftspeople than they were to use them in gang labor in agriculture. Despite these differences from other parts of the South, it would be inaccurate to overemphasize these distinctions. The mountain area was part of the slave South, and social and economic features that characterized much of the lowlands were found in the highlands as well.

As the existence and expansion of slavery indicates, contact with the larger southern economy was readily available to mountain residents. While railroads were absent in all western counties except sections of Burke and Rutherford, travel by foot, wagon, and horseback was quite extensive. Two major overland routes passed through western North Carolina: the Knoxville, Tennessee, to Greenville, South Carolina, road—known as the Buncombe Turnpike—passing from north to south; and the Western North Carolina Turnpike, running from east to west from Salisbury, North Carolina, to the Georgia border. Written communication with the outside world was maintained through a large number of community post offices in each county.[27] Merchants in each county had contacts with adjoining communities, neighboring states, and the urban North.[28] Forest McDonald and Grady McWhiney have documented the active livestock trade through western North Carolina and how local agricultural surpluses were sold to supply these stock drives.[29] Thus, the geographic isolation of the North Carolina mountain population was not as great as usually portrayed, and many individuals had substantial dealings with people in the outside world.

The coming of the Civil War tested the strength and durability of the economy and community in western North Carolina. The most immediate point that was settled beyond a doubt was that the nuclear family was the most basic unit of production and consumption. The dislocations caused by the war illustrated the importance of each productive member of the family. As a Cherokee County correspondent explained, "Our people . . . have learned to subsist mainly on the immediate productions of their own labor. Deprive us of that labor and the innocent & helpless must perish. . . . What consolation or encouragement can come to a mans [sic] heart in an hour of trial from a home where the helpless are perishing for want of his hand to provide."[30] The authorities were constantly reminded by highland residents that the absence of men from their families was often an economic disaster because "we have very few slaves in Western North Carolina."[31] Husbands were not the only crucial members of the household, however. A crippled father in McDowell County asked that his two sons be returned from the army to help him with his work.[32] The death of a wife was as devastating to the family as that of her spouse, as the following Wilkes County petition indicates: "Mr. Burgess has within the last few days lost his wife leaving him six little children[,] the youngest only a few days old & the largest not able to do anything in the shape of work and without any assistance in the world save the father[.] . . . [W]e most humbly pray your excellency to do whats [sic] in your power to get a discharge for Mr. Burgess that he may save his little children from starvation."[33] This suffering was quite widespread and was considered to be the major cause of desertion among Confederate troops from western North Carolina.

The situation became so critical that state and Confederate officials were forced to alter established policies. While conditions worsened throughout the conflict, disruption of the mountain society and economy began as early as 1862. One solution proposed by local and state officials was an end to conscription so that enough men could be retained in the area to feed the population. That option was firmly rejected by the Confederacy.[34] A second means to alleviate distress was to provide some form of government assistance to those in need. This the state government attempted to do. In an unprecedented series of actions, the state provided money, food, and other necessities to county committees to distribute to the needy.[35] When the Confederacy introduced the tax in kind in 1863, some of the supplies collected were distributed at home rather than being sent to the front.[36] Despite these innovative measures, a letter from Jackson County reported that the wives and families of Cherokee Indian soldiers were "living on weeds and the bark of trees."[37] While most families in the mountains never reached this level of desperation, suffering and deprivation were widespread.

Economic difficulties faced by families during the war were also caused by the disruption of the broader community. While most western North Carolina farm families were subsistence farmers—that is, they sought to provide for their own needs as their primary objective—they were constantly involved in an exchange of goods and services. While many households sought to be self-sufficient in food, they required a miller to grind their grain and corn into flour and meal. In the same manner, salt purchased from the local merchant was a necessity to preserve the meat that the family raised and slaughtered. While the 1860 census revealed that mountain families were more likely to meet their own manufacturing needs at home than in other parts of North Carolina, the specialized skills of the tanner, the wheelwright, the miller, and the blacksmith were essential to every family.[38] Even the most isolated family was dependent at some point on outside labor for survival.

While this system of trade has usually been portrayed as simple exchanges of goods, it was often based on a monetary value being assigned to each part of the transaction. Even under the pressure of war, barter trades were handled on an approximate cash basis. A Wilkes County businessman received the following offer from a local farmer: "We received a note from you stating that you was anxious to swap beef hides for leather. We will swap at the old prices if that will suit."[39] Not only was cash the basis of commodity exchange, but it also was the measure of value for the most basic economic good—land. Unlike real property in other parts of the South where land was treated as a disposable resource—an attitude found in the mountains as well—landholdings were usually the measure of a highlander's wealth and a source of speculative investment.[40] In addition, the value of slaves had a regionally determined monetary value.[41] But rather than invest in hundreds of slaves, many members of the western North Carolina elite purchased tens of thousands of acres of wooded land.[42] As a result, all aspects of a mountain farm family's life, including its land, crops, livestock, and labor, were computed in monetary terms.

The existence of these cash exchanges confirmed that the most critical of the services purchased by mountain families were those of the blacksmith and the miller. Surviving letters and petitions from many parts of western North Carolina testified to the impossibility of continuing to produce goods without the help of a smith.[43] A Haywood County correspondent noted that his area was "disorganized" without a blacksmith, and a Caldwell County petition asserted, "We are laboring under grate [sic] disadvantage in our neighborhood for want of a Blacksmith."[44] A petition from McDowell County asked that the Broad River District be provided with a miller since the farm families had to transport their grain over five miles of poor roads to be ground.[45] A Haywood County correspondent informed the governor that miller Elisha P. Hyatt had been unexpectedly conscripted. The writer continued, "He is absolutely necessary in this neighborhood as a miller. We cannot get along well without him."[46] The author of the letter was speaking for all western North Carolina families in their need to purchase the services of skilled craftsmen.

While smiths and millers were critical to the survival of mountain farmers, many other craftsmen were also essential for sustaining the highland economy. Tanners and shoemakers proved to be nearly as important to civilians as to the army. Particularly when preparing for the cold winter months, farm families were aggressive in expressing their concern about securing adequate footwear.[47] In addition, millwrights who could repair mill machinery and keep the mills running were considered as essential as the millers whom they kept in business.[48] Probably the most valuable single individual was the jack-of-all-trades. A Burke County petition described one of these men as follows: "We feel that his services are indispensible [sic] in the neighborhood where he resides—He is the only mechanic in the neighborhood—he makes looms, bed steads, trays, chairs[,] tables, chests, stocks[,] scythes, plows &c &c."[49] Clearly the loss of an individual such as this could cripple the productivity of any locality.

Although all of these expressed needs could fit into a subsistence and noncommercial pattern, there is abundant evidence that western North Carolina farmers were integrated into a market economy. The first indication of the importance of the market was the emphasis that the local population placed on adequate transportation. This concern was made manifest by mountain voters long before the Civil War. The Whig Party rode its commitment to the extension of the Western North Carolina Railroad to power in the highland counties.[50] One of the most successful Democrats west of the Blue Ridge was William H. Thomas, who endorsed the railroad extension in 1846—four years before the state party took its first tentative steps in that direction.[51] Despite their strong advocacy, mountain politicians were unable to obtain their coveted rail system before the fighting started.

Instead they had to make do with a road network that could not withstand the demands placed on it by the war. One correspondent reported in the spring of 1863 that many of the bridges on the turnpike between Macon County and Asheville were "entirely gone" and travel was quite hazardous.[52] Mitchell County citizens demanded that their wheelwright be returned to them and that a wagon-making factory be built in their county to insure that they could travel.[53] The solution to the problem of hauling heavy loads in Transylvania County was thought to be the return of a teamster from the army.[54] Even government officials were forced to admit that the normal pattern of transport to western North Carolina had been destroyed. Nicholas W. Woodfin, North Carolina salt commissioner at Saltville, Virginia, could not ship his precious cargo to many mountain counties.[55] Obviously these concerns would not have been viewed as critical if the region had not needed to trade with other parts of the South.

An even better indication of mountaineer dependence on commercial transactions was the unexpected demand for cloth-making equipment and yard goods. For those familiar with the "hillbilly" stereotype, the woman weaver has come to symbolize the continuity of the highland handcraft tradition. Every mountain home was reputed to contain a spinning wheel and a loom to turn wool from the farm's sheep into thread and yarn that was then woven into cloth. Abundant evidence from letters written during the Civil War, however, indicates that many western North Carolina families had stopped producing their own clothing. For example, many households lacked even the basic cotton and wool cards needed to prepare the fibers for the process of making thread and yarn.[56] Other weavers simply refused to consider starting from that basic level and insisted on obtaining commercially produced thread and yarn.[57] Still others disdained any use of the loom and demanded access to the finished product.[58] The demand for cloth became so great in the western counties that a group of businessmen wanted government assistance to construct a textile factory near Asheville.[59] Clearly, many mountain families had become dependent on the market for a product that had been previously a staple of home manufacture.

As conclusive as the above example is of market dependency, the expectation of some farm families that they could continue to rely on the availability of food for purchase is equally convincing. While the direct purchase of a large proportion of a family's food supplies was undoubtedly the result of wartime conditions, those involved did not find the practice unusual or unacceptable. In fact, they usually expressed more resentment about the prices they had to pay than the fact that they had to purchase the goods. One Cherokee County woman complained, "My husband has been taken away from myself & family as a disloyalist whitch I think has been caused by desyning men that wont go into the army themselves but prefer to stay at home & speculate by selling the wives of soldiers goods at 500 per cent."[60] Another family did not bother to request an allotment of food but asked for a direct cash stipend instead.[61] These and other examples suggest that some western North Carolina families had not been self-sufficient in foodstuffs before the war and were accustomed to purchasing food on a regular basis.

There is another historical development that indicates that these rural families and communities were part of the broader market economy. Rothenberg argues that price convergence on products sold in a market center and prices on the same goods in a rural community indicates that these two localities are part of the same market system.[62] Throughout the war, people in the western North Carolina counties faced the same problems of high commodity prices, speculation, and inflation suffered by urban Confederates. Despite desperate attempts by Governor Vance to regulate supplies and prices, the extraordinary cost of salt, shoes, and food left the mountaineers as defenseless as the most confirmed city resident.[63] Since these same conditions prevailed throughout the Confederacy, any claim that the citizens of western North Carolina were isolated from market forces seems hard to substantiate.

While the significance of the market in western North Carolina is obvious, the complex society of landed and commercial elite, yeoman farmers, tenants, and slaves insured that the market's impact would not fall equally on each person. For slaveowners and merchants, the local economy was tied directly to commercial transactions originating outside the mountains. These two groups used local products to trade with suppliers and businesses on a regional and national basis. While yeoman farmers and tenants rarely dealt directly with outside merchants, their correspondence during the war indicates that they had become dependent upon trade with the outside world for part of the goods they required to sustain themselves. At the same time, these same groups lived in an interdependent local economy in which local exchanges of goods and services provided much of their basic necessities. Even the merchants were dependent upon the community for the surpluses that provided them with the goods to be used in trading. Thus, it is difficult to separate the impact of local trade and the broader market in the economic life of western North Carolina.

Surviving manuscripts also confirm that these neighborhood ties helped to form a social community in the mountains. Friends and kin sought assistance for families that faced special difficulties, including the presence of elderly parents or small children.[64] These letters and petitions showed the importance of face-to-face relationships described by previous scholars of

American communities. In addition, neighbors sought to retain the services of persons who provided non-economic services to the community. One correspondent requested that the only physician in Madison County be returned to take care of the great needs of the people there.[65] Several localities pleaded for the return of their schoolteachers and expressed the fear that their children would grow up in ignorance.[66] These petitions are a striking refutation of the stereotype developed after the war that portrayed the mountain people as hostile to education. Finally, a number of persons begged for the restoration of the clergyman to their churches. A Wilkes County congregation requested, "We your petitioners . . . pray you release from the Army our dear Brother Emile Childers as he is a very useful minister of the Gospel. The Churches in the county is left allmost without ministers so many of them has gone volunteer in the service. We pray God that the sanctuary be not forsaken lest our cause and Country be lost."[67] These and other examples confirm that the social community was an important part of highland life.

But the war also revealed that this social community was quite fragile, because many formal institutions that could have provided great strength to mountain neighborhoods were not in a position to do so. This was often the case with local churches. Local congregations did act as centers of neighborhood activities, but the highland people were among the most "unchurched" Americans. The best records available indicate that only one in seven persons in western North Carolina was a church member.[68] Since most of the local congregations were either Methodist or Southern Baptist—both evangelical and missionary—there was no theological reason for this low level of membership. Neither was this gap in social institutions filled by other organizations usually found in American rural communities. For example, the numerous mountain schools were of such short duration that they did not play a major role in the life of any locality.

For the men in the community, however, the political party did act as an integrating institution. As Harry Watson has observed in his study of Cumberland County, North Carolina, loyalty to one partisan organization was very widespread and often distinguished one community from another.[69] The commitment to vote exclusively for either the Democrats or the Whigs was also a family tradition as well.[70] This pattern observed in Cumberland County was found throughout western North Carolina. With rare exceptions, mountain voters refused to deviate from past allegiances even when the second American party system broke up in the 1850s.[71] Even under the extreme pressure for nonpartisan conformity that accompanied the Civil War, the parties survived in modified form. Through 1863 much of the old

Democratic Party survived as the new Confederate party, while other Democrats and most former Whigs formed the Conservative Party.[72]

The political party served not only as an organizer of mountain males; it also divided them into hostile factions. For example, two Buncombe County cousins nearly fought a duel in 1855 over purely political differences.[73] This episode was prompted by extremely vituperative articles in partisan newspapers—the major means of communication in western North Carolina.[74] This type of activity created deep animosities that set some communities and families in permanent opposition to one another, and the pressure of war did not soften these attitudes. One Wilkes County correspondent reported, "It has been called a Democratic war & Whig fight."[75] Another mountain observer ended his analysis of a congressional race with the following exclamation: "Christ, how I hate [the] democracy."[76]

Political developments during the war revealed the depth of political animosities in western North Carolina. The 1863 campaign for Confederate congress in the mountain district was a classic example of the divisive impact of mountain politics on the mountain community. There were four candidates, and their partisan commitments ranged from ardent support of Jefferson Davis to acknowledged advocacy of peace.[77] The most blatant attempt to influence political behavior during the campaign occurred in Cherokee County. In that instance, several supporters of the incumbent congressmen were seized by Confederate troops from Georgia and were forced into the army despite having legitimate exemptions under the conscription law. Those accused of perpetrating this kidnapping were described by an outraged congressional candidate as "all Democrat and secessionist."[78] Following the incident, the candidate vowed revenge on his neighbors: "If nothing else is done, I am determined to write home to shoot Ramseur down in the road or any where else and get rid of him."[79]

The willingness of the supporters of peace candidate George W. Logan to question the basic policies of the Confederacy only exacerbated political differences. Their activities often seemed to challenge the legitimacy of the new nation. A speaker in Transylvania County supported reunion; a meeting in Wilkes County raised the American flag; a gathering in Rutherford County was willing to accept peace without Confederate independence. The hostility generated by these actions is captured in a letter that advised the governor to invite one man "to Raleigh & have him hanged."[80] The climax of partisan warfare came when Confederate troops closed down a peace party newspaper in Henderson County and refused to allow it to reopen until the editor agreed to change the content of his articles.[81] The bitter gubernatorial election of 1864 between Zebulon B. Vance and William

W. Holden insured that political divisiveness would endure to the end of the war and beyond.

Just as the political battles during the war confirmed earlier partisan divisions, the Confederate conscription policy revealed long-standing antagonisms within mountain neighborhoods. In addition to the obvious division between those enslaved and those free, mountain society contained a series of gradations that were recognized in all localities. Phillip Paludan in his analysis of the Shelton Laurel massacre in Madison County in January 1863 makes these social distinctions the basis for his interpretive framework. Paludan identifies the feeling of superiority felt by the pro-Confederate town dwellers of Marshall when they compared themselves with the isolated farmers in Shelton Laurel.[82] The idea that the well-to-do favored southern independence for selfish reasons was a common belief among yeomen and tenant farmers during the war. The peace party leaders appealed to this feeling to attract a large popular following.[83] Extant letters from the mountain elite tend to confirm the suspicions of the lower classes, including a reference by a Polk County correspondent to "the lower and meaner classes."[84]

A study of military service in seven Cherokee County communities confirms the absence of unity within mountain neighborhoods. As Paludan asserted in his Madison County study, the Cherokee County investigators discovered that Confederate recruits had substantially higher property evaluations than those who joined the Union army. Equally interesting was their finding that the largest number of eligible males in the county—44 percent—joined neither army. Thus, in this section of western North Carolina, there appeared to be at least a three-way division of loyalty. Most of the men who joined neither army were among the very poorest in these communities and apparently had no stake in the success of either side. Also significant was the investigators' discovery that Union volunteers were found in all seven neighborhoods. The percentage of men who escaped to Federal lines ranged from 5 to 20 percent.[85] Martin Crawford found these same divisions in his study of Ashe County as well. Two sections of the county had a substantial number of Unionists. Unlike in Cherokee County, however, Crawford found the greatest reluctance to join the Confederate service came from men who were married and headed a family farm.[86] While the precise divisions may have varied from county to county, there is little question but that conscription highlighted existing social distinctions in western North Carolina.

There is considerable evidence to suggest that these differences were not solely the result of war-related animosities. Paludan traces the genesis of the

Shelton Laurel–Marshall troubles to antebellum incidents.[87] This observation was confirmed by an 1863 report that stated, "Col. Allen's 64th N.C. Regt. and the men of his command are said to be hostile to the Laurel men and they to the former for a long time. A kind of feud existing before the war."[88] A similar situation existed in Jackson County, where five Hooper brothers shot and killed five men from the Watson family in an incident that took place before the war.[89] This family violence was not unique to the North Carolina mountains. James Klotter's broad study of Appalachian feuding notes that a variety of incidents took place before the fighting started.[90]

Although these incidents revealed deep fissures within communities, one could still argue that the violence reflected the solidarity of kinship groups. After all, the Sheltons and the Hoopers were simply acting on their exaggerated sense of family honor. One Henderson County correspondent captured this sentiment accurately. He stated that his son in the army knew that the father was deeply opposed to desertion, "but he also knows that if he were to desert and come home that I would feed and clothe him as heretofore and further—harbor and conceal him."[91] But even this feeling of solidarity was not universal. The investigator of the Hooper family incident noted, "Following the slaughter, two of the young men joined the federal forces; two went south and fought with the Confederacy; and it is said that one associated himself with the renegades."[92] Watauga County Unionist Keith Blalock ordered one of his subordinates to shoot Blalock's uncle.[93] The splits within families existed not only between the male members. A mother and daughter in Henderson County hid escaped Federal prisoners from their father and husband as well as local authorities.[94] While these examples may not have been typical, they do point out that social divisions within western North Carolina extended to the family level.

These divisions that devastated western North Carolina civilians during the war suggest that the community may have operated with differing degrees of effectiveness as an economic and as a social structure. The existence of an "economic community" was clearly demonstrated by the collapse of this system when important members of the local network were removed by conscription. At the same time, the growing dependence of the mountain people on the market economy was obvious as the disruption of trade created substantial hardship. Further evidence points to an important social dimension in this local community as well. Family, church, and schools provided means to tie local residents together. Unlike the community economy, however, the social community did not seem to be as tightly structured. Because the social community was divided by racial, class, and political rivalries that created enduring animosities, the region exploded into massive violence under the pressure of war. This inability of the community and the family to suppress local antagonisms and to hold mountain society together strongly suggests that economic interdependence was not sufficient to create an enduring relationship with neighbors. Thus the reality of Appalachian community life in the nineteenth century needs further investigation. The letters written by the people of the western counties of North Carolina during the Civil War suggest that there was considerable variation within preindustrial Appalachian neighborhoods that needs to be thoroughly explored before broad generalizations about mountain community life can be made.

Notes

A version of this chapter was delivered at the April 1988 Organization of American Historians convention in Reno, Nevada. The author would like to thank Professors Paul Johnson and Mary Anglin for their valuable comments on that paper. The author also wishes to acknowledge financial assistance from the National Historical Publications and Records Commission and Western Carolina University.

1. Examples include Phillip Shaw Paludan, *Victims: A True Story of the Civil War* (Knoxville: University of Tennessee, 1981); Ronald D. Eller, *Miners, Millhands, and Mountaineers: Industrialization of the Appalachian South, 1880–1930* (Knoxville: University of Tennessee Press, 1982); Michael J. McDonald and John Muldowny, *TVA and the Dispossessed: The Resettlement of Population in the Norris Dam Area* (Knoxville: University of Tennessee Press, 1982).

2. See Robert Wiebe, *The Search for Order, 1877–1920* (New York: Hill and Wang, 1967); Samuel P. Hays, "Political Parties and the Community-Society Continuum," in *The American Party Systems: Stages of Political Development*, ed. William N. Chambers and W. Dean Burnham (New York: Oxford University Press, 1967); Thomas Bender, *Community and Social Change in America* (New Brunswick: Rutgers University Press, 1978).

3. Charles S. Grant, *Democracy in the Connecticut Frontier Town of Kent* (New York: Columbia University Press, 1961); Philip G. Greven, *Four Generations: Population, Land, and Family in Colonial Andover, Massachusetts* (Ithaca: Cornell University Press, 1978); Robert A. Gross, *The Minutemen and Their World* (New York: Hill and Wang, 1976); James T. Lemon, *The Best Poor Man's Country: A Geographical Study of Early Southern Pennsylvania* (Baltimore: Johns Hopkins University Press, 1972); Kenneth A. Lockridge, *A New England Town: The First Hundred Years, Dedham, Massachusetts, 1636–1736* (New York: Norton, 1978); Michael Merrill, "Cash Is Good to Eat: Self-Sufficiency and Exchange in the Rural Economy of the United States," *Radical History Review* 3 (Winter 1977): 42–71; James A. Henretta, "Families and Farms: *Mentalite* in Preindustrial America," *William and Mary Quarterly*, 3rd. ser., 35 (January 1978): 3–32; Robert E. Mutch, "The Cutting Edge: Colonial America

and the Debate about the Transition to Capitalism," *Theory and Society* 9 (November 1980): 847–63; Joyce O. Appleby, "Commercial Farming and the 'Agrarian Myth' in the Early Republic," *Journal of American History* 68 (March 1982): 833–49.

4. Jonathan Prude, *The Coming of Industrial Order: Town and Factory Life in Rural Massachusetts, 1810–1860* (New York: Cambridge University Press, 1983); Christopher Clark, *The Roots of Rural Capitalism: Western Massachusetts, 1780–1860* (Ithaca: Cornell University Press, 1990); Robert A. Gross, "Culture and Cultivation: Agriculture and Society in Thoreau's Concord," *Journal of American History* 69 (June 1982): 42–61; John T. Schlotterbeck, "The 'Social Economy' of an Upper South Community: Orange and Green Counties, Virginia, 1815–1860," in *Class, Conflict, and Consensus: Antebellum Southern Community Studies,* ed. Orville Vernon Burton and Robert C. McMath (Westport, Conn.: Greenwood Press, 1982): 3–28; Hal S. Baron, "Staying down on the Farm: Social Processes of Settled Rural Life in the Nineteenth-Century North," in *The Countryside in the Age of Capitalist Transformation: Essays in the Social History of Rural America,* ed. Steven Hahn and Jonathan Prude (Chapel Hill: University of North Carolina Press, 1985), pp. 327–43.

5. Mutch, "Cutting Edge," p. 849; Gross, "Thoreau's Concord," p. 45; Rodney C. Loehr, "Self-Sufficiency on the Farm," *Agricultural History* 26 (1952): 41; Carole Shammas, "How Self-Sufficient Was Early America?," *Journal of Interdisciplinary History* 13 (Autumn 1982): 252–53; Bettye Hobbs Pruitt, "Self-Sufficiency and the Agricultural Economy of Eighteenth-Century Massachusetts," *William and Mary Quarterly* 41 (July 1984): 338.

6. Lemon, *Best,* p. 28; Shammas, "How Self-Sufficient," p. 267.

7. Lemon, *Best,* p. 28; Mutch, "Cutting Edge," p. 851; Schlotterbeck, "Upper South," pp. 14, 18.

8. Winifred B. Rothenberg, "The Market and Massachusetts Farmers, 1750–1855," *Journal of Economic History* 41 (1981): 302. For a differing view, see Michael A. Bernstein and Sean Wilentz, "Marketing, Commerce, and Capitalism in Rural Massachusetts," *Journal of Economic History* 44 (1984): 171–73.

9. Clarence H. Danhof, *Change in Agriculture: The Northern United States, 1820–1870* (Cambridge: Harvard University Press, 1969), pp. 21–22.

10. Ibid., p. 288.

11. Gordon B. McKinney, "The Land No One Wanted: An Economic History of Whitefield, New Hampshire," *Historical New Hampshire* 28 (Winter 1972): 185–209.

12. John Mack Faragher, "Open Country Community: Sugar Creek, Illinois, 1820–1850," in Hahn and Prude, *Countryside,* pp. 233–58.

13. Gavin Wright, *The Political Economy of the Cotton South: Households, Markets, and Wealth in the Nineteenth Century* (New York: Norton, 1978), pp. 144–54.

14. Gavin Wright, *Old South, New South: Revolutions in the Southern Economy since the Civil War* (New York: Basic Books, 1986), pp. 24, 40–41.

15. Steven Hahn, *The Roots of Southern Populism: Yeoman Farmers and the Transformation of the Georgia Upcountry, 1850–1890* (New York: Oxford University Press, 1983), pp. 50–57; Lacy K. Ford, Jr., *Origins of Southern Radicalism: The South Carolina Upcountry, 1800–1860* (New York: Oxford University Press, 1988), pp. 219–77. For other studies dealing with the South, see Schlotterbeck, "Upper South"; Lacy K. Ford, Jr., "Yeoman Farmers in the South Carolina Upcountry: Changing Produc-

tion Patterns in the Late Antebellum Era," *Agricultural History* 60 (1986): 17–37; Gwenda Morgan, "Community and Authority in the Eighteenth-Century South: Tidewater, Southside, and Backcountry," *Journal of American Studies* 20 (December 1986): 435–48; Donald L. Winters, "'Plain Folk' of the Old South Reexamined: Economic Democracy in Tennessee," *Journal of Southern History* 53 (1987): 565–86.

16. Frederick A. Bode and Donald E. Ginter, *Farm Tenancy and the Census in Antebellum Georgia* (Athens: University of Georgia Press, 1986); see also Dwight B. Billings and Kathleen M. Blee, "Appalachian Inequality in the Nineteenth Century: The Case of Beech Creek, Kentucky," *Journal of the Appalachian Studies Association* 4 (1992): 113–23. The large number of tenant farmers in the mountains may have been due to rapid population growth that limited landownership opportunities. See Crandall A. Shifflett, *Coal Towns: Life, Work, and Culture in Company Towns of Southern Appalachia, 1880–1960* (Knoxville: University of Tennessee Press, 1991), pp. 18–21.

17. H. Tyler Blethen and Curtis W. Wood, Jr., "The Pioneer Experience to 1851," in *The History of Jackson County*, ed. Max R. Williams (Sylva, N.C.: Jackson County Historical Society, 1987), p. 83. See also, Faragher, "Open Country," p. 237.

18. H. Tyler Blethen and Curtis W. Wood, Jr., "The Appalachian Frontier and the Southern Frontier," *Journal of the Appalachian Studies Association* 3 (1991): 36–47; H. Tyler Blethen and Curtis W. Wood, Jr., "A Trader on the Western Carolina Frontier," in *Appalachian Frontiers: Settlement, Society, and Development in the Preindustrial Era*, ed. Robert D. Mitchell (Lexington: University Press of Kentucky, 1991), pp. 150–65; H. Tyler Blethen and Curtis W. Wood, Jr., "The Antebellum Iron Industry in Western North Carolina," *Journal of the Appalachian Studies Association* 4 (1992): 79–87.

19. For western North Carolina, see John Inscoe, "Mountain Masters: Slavehold-ing in Western North Carolina," *North Carolina Historical Review* 61 (1984): 143–73; John Inscoe, "Diversity in Antebellum Life: The Towns of Western North Carolina," in *The Many Faces of Appalachia*, ed. Sam Gray (Boone: Appalachian Consortium Press, 1985), pp. 153–68; Gordon B. McKinney, "Preindustrial Jackson County and Eco-nomic Development," *Journal of the Appalachian Studies Association* 2 (1990): 1–10.

20. Paul Salstrom, *Appalachia's Path to Dependency: Rethinking a Region's Eco-nomic History, 1730–1940* (Lexington: University Press of Kentucky, 1994), pp. 1–59.

21. Durwood Dunn, *Cades Cove: The Life and Death of a Southern Appalachian Community, 1818–1937* (Knoxville: University of Tennessee Press, 1988); Robert Tracy McKenzie, "Wealth and Income: The Preindustrial Structure of East Ten-nessee in 1860," *Appalachian Journal* 21 (Spring 1994): 260–79; Ralph Mann, "Mountains, Land, and Kin Networks: Burkes Garden, Virginia, in the 1840s and 1850s," *Journal of Southern History* 58 (1992): 411–34; Ralph Mann, "Family Group, Family Migration, and the Civil War in the Sandy Basin of Virginia," *Appalachian Journal* 19 (Summer 1992): 374–93; Warren R. Hofstra and Robert D. Mitchell, "Town and Country in Backcountry Virginia: Winchester and the Shenandoah Valley, 1730–1800," *Journal of Southern History* 59 (1993): 619–46; Kenneth W. Noe, *Southwest Virginia's Railroad: Modernization and the Sectional Crisis* (Urbana: Uni-versity of Illinois Press, 1994); Mary Beth Pudup, "The Limits of Subsistence: Agri-culture and Industry in Central Appalachia," *Agricultural History* 64 (1990): 61–89;

Mary Beth Pudup, "Social Class and Economic Development in Southeastern Kentucky, 1820–1880," in Mitchell, *Appalachian Frontiers*, pp. 235–60.

22. Blethen and Wood, "Pioneer Experience," pp. 83–85.

23. Darrett B. Rutman, "Assessing the Little Communities of Early America," *William and Mary Quarterly* 42 (April 1986): 168–69.

24. John C. Inscoe, *Mountain Masters: Slavery and the Sectional Crisis in Western North Carolina* (Knoxville: University of Tennessee Press, 1989); Martin Crawford, "Political Society in a Southern Mountain Community: Ashe County, North Carolina, 1850–1861," *Journal of Southern History* 55 (1989): 373–90; Martin Crawford, "Confederate Volunteering and Enlistment in Ashe County, North Carolina, 1861–1862," *Civil War History* 37 (March 1991): 29–50.

25. Joseph D. Reid, Jr., "Antebellum Southern Rental Contracts," *Explorations in Economic History* 13 (1976): 69–83; Blethen and Wood, "Pioneer Experience," p. 85.

26. U.S. Bureau of the Census, *Eighth Census of the United States, 1860: Population* (Washington, D.C.: Government Printing Office, 1864), pp. 235–36.

27. See John R. Slater, "Communications," in Williams, *Jackson County*, p. 376.

28. See the extensive outside commercial contracts documented in the William Holland Thomas Papers, Perkins Library, Duke University, Durham, N.C., and the Calvin J. Cowles Papers, North Carolina Division of Archives and History, Raleigh.

29. Forest McDonald and Grady McWhiney, "The Antebellum Herdsmen: A Reinterpretation," *Journal of Southern History* 41 (1975): 161–62.

30. D. W. Siler to Zebulon B. Vance, 5 November 1862, reel 13, in *The Papers of Zebulon Baird Vance*, ed. Gordon B. McKinney and Richard M. McMurry (Frederick, Md.: University Publications of America, 1987).

31. Mary C. Williams et al. to Zebulon B. Vance, 27 January 1863, reel 16, ibid.

32. James Bailey to Zebulon B. Vance, 25 January 1863, reel 16, ibid.

33. Tyre York et al. to Zebulon B. Vance, 12 October 1862, reel 15, ibid.

34. James A. Seddon to Zebulon B. Vance, 23 April 1864, reel 13, ibid.

35. Paul Escott, "Poverty and Government Aid for the Poor in Confederate North Carolina," *North Carolina Historical Review* 61 (1984): 462–80.

36. Tod R. Caldwell to Zebulon B. Vance, 18 March 1864, reel 22, in McKinney and McMurry, *Papers of Vance*.

37. Margaret E. Love to Zebulon B. Vance, 10 May 1864, reel 23, ibid.

38. U.S. Bureau of the Census, *Eighth Census of the United States, 1860: Agriculture*, pp. 105–7, 109–11.

39. H. and H. J. Spicer to J. and C. J. Cowles, 26 January [18]63, Cowles Papers.

40. Wright, *Old South*, pp. 30–31; Blethen and Wood, "Pioneer Experience," p. 77.

41. Wright, *Cotton South*, pp. 144–54.

42. E. Stanly Godbold, Jr., and Mattie U. Russell, *Confederate Colonel and Cherokee Chief: The Life of William Holland Thomas* (Knoxville: University of Tennessee Press, 1990), pp. 17–35.

43. William Adkins, statement, n.d., R. F. Callaway et al. to Zebulon B. Vance, 11 November 1862, reel 15; W. Joiner et al. to Vance, 31 March 1863, reel 16; Hirum Green et al. to Vance, 16 May 1863, reel 17; J. J. Neal et al. to Vance, 4 June 1863, reel 18; Jno H. Addington to Vance, 31 March 1864, reel 22; Cynthia McDaniel et al. to Vance, n.d., reel 26, in McKinney and McMurry, *Papers of Vance*.

44. D. C. Shoop to Zebulon B. Vance, 24 March 1864, reel 22; W. M. Crisp et al. to Vance, 14 May 1863, reel 17, ibid.

45. John A. Coxey et al. to Zebulon B. Vance, n.d., reel 26, ibid.

46. R. E. A. Love to Zebulon B. Vance, 22 April 1864, reel 23, ibid.

47. Jas. Eller et al. to Zebulon B. Vance, 8 November 1862, reel 15; E. Morgan et al. to Vance, 17 October 1863, reel 20; N. A. Powell to Vance, 15 September 1864, reel 24; V. Ripley et al. to Vance, 3 October 1864, E. J. Aston et al. to Vance, 24 October 1864, Wiley T. Walker et al. to Vance, 1 November 1864, reel 25, ibid.

48. J. F. Shell to Zebulon B. Vance, [3 March 1863], James E. Wiseman, to Vance, 16 March 1863, reel 16, ibid.

49. Elizbeth Conley et al. to Zebulon B. Vance, 10 July 1863, reel 18; see also Benjamin Deboard et al. to Vance, 20 October 1863, reel 20, ibid.

50. Marc W. Kruman, *Parties and Politics in North Carolina, 1836–1865* (Baton Rouge: Louisiana State University Press, 1983), p. 10.

51. Campaign broadside reprinted in *Jackson County Journal*, 12 June 1912.

52. S. H. Miller to Zebulon B. Vance, 23 March 1863, reel 16, in McKinney and McMurry, *Papers of Vance*.

53. Moses Young et al., statement, 1 June 1863, Thomas Baker et al. to Zebulon B. Vance, 1 July 1863, reel 18, ibid.

54. B. C. Lankford to Zebulon B. Vance, 18 July 1863, reel 18, ibid.

55. Woodfin to Zebulon B. Vance, 1 October 1863, reel 20, ibid.

56. Thomas Atkinson to Zebulon B. Vance, 27 November 1863, reel 20; N. Bowen to Vance, 6 January 1864, reel 21; J. J. Erwin to Vance, 1 February 1864, [W.] Murdock to Vance, 7 February 1864, reel 3; J. A. Reagan to Vance, 15 February 1864, R. V. Welch to Vance, 20 February [18]64, reel 22; J. M. Warren to Vance, 16 March 1865, reel 26, ibid.

57. A. W. Cummings to Zebulon B. Vance, 14 April 1863, reel 17; R. T. Walker to Vance, 2 March 1865, reel 4, ibid.

58. Wm. Lankford to Zebulon B. Vance, 14 April 1863, reel 17; A. T. Summey to Vance, 20 May 1863, reel 7, ibid.

59. Wm. L. Henry to Zebulon B. Vance, 16 May 1864, reel 23, ibid. Some British historians maintain that scholars can identify capitalist modernization by locating a demand for consumer goods. See David Levine, "Consumer Goods and Capitalist Modernization," *Journal of Interdisciplinary History* 22 (Summer 1991): 67–77.

60. H. T. McLelland to Zebulon B. Vance, 22 February [18]63, reel 16, in McKinney and McMurry, *Papers of Vance*.

61. John Lono to Zebulon B. Vance, n.d., reel 26, ibid.

62. Rothenberg, "Market," p. 305.

63. Zebulon B. Vance, proclamation, 13 April 1863, reel 13, in McKinney and McMurry, *Papers of Vance*.

64. Examples of this include W. H. Bailey to Zebulon B. Vance, 18 February 1863, reel 16; J. P. Dula to Vance, 22 May 1863, reel 17; Thos. L. Cotton to E. J. Hale and Sons, [1864], reel 4, ibid.

65. G. C. Askew to Zebulon B. Vance, 17 July 1863, reel 18, ibid.

66. Jesse Sentell et al. to Zebulon B. Vance, 16 August 1863, reel 19; A. Glaty et al. to

Vance, 21 October [18]64, reel 25; Amos Hildebrand et al. to [Vance], [2 January 1865], reel 26, ibid.

67. J. K. Baldwin et al. to Zebulon B. Vance, 27 September 1862, reel 15, ibid.

68. Clifford R. Lovin, "Religion," in Williams, *Jackson County*, p. 265; U.S. Bureau of the Census, *Eleventh Census of the United States, 1890: Religion* (Inter-University Consortium for Political Research Data Base).

69. W. Dean Burnham, *Presidential Ballots, 1836–1892* (Baltimore: Johns Hopkins University Press, 1955), pp. 648–68.

70. Harry L. Watson, *Jacksonian Politics and Community Conflict: The Emergence of the Second American Party System in Cumberland County, North Carolina* (Chapel Hill: University of North Carolina Press, 1981), pp. 220, 304.

71. Kruman, *Parties*, pp. 53–54.

72. Ibid., pp. 222–40.

73. Asheville *News*, 28 June, 5 July 1855; J. T. S. Baird to Zebulon B. Vance, [9 July 1855], in *The Papers of Zebulon Baird Vance*, ed. Frontis Johnston (Raleigh: Department of Archives and History, 1863), pp. 29–30.

74. See Asheville *News*, July–August 1854, July–October 1860.

75. Calvin J. Cowles to Zebulon B. Vance, 19 October 1863, reel 3, in McKinney and McMurry, *Papers of Vance*.

76. Wm. L. Love to Zebulon B. Vance, 3 April [18]63, reel 3, ibid.

77. Wm. L. Love to Zebulon B. Vance, 29 August 1863, reel 19, ibid. Partisan reaction to the Civil War was not limited to communities in the southern mountains. A study of two rural New Hampshire towns notes important differences in volunteering between Republicans and Democrats. See Thomas R. Kemp, "Community and War: The Civil War Experience of Two New Hampshire Towns," in *Toward a Social History of the American Civil War: Exploratory Essays*, ed. Maris A. Vinovskis (New York: Cambridge University Press, 1990), p. 65.

78. A. T. Davidson to Zebulon B. Vance, 5 May 1863, reel 3, in McKinney and McMurry, *Papers of Vance*.

79. A. T. Davidson to Zebulon B. Vance, 11 March 1863, reel 3, ibid.

80. W. Murdock to Zebulon B. Vance, 12 August 1863, reel 19, ibid.

81. L. S. Gash to Zebulon B. Vance, 7, 11 September 1863, reel 19, ibid.

82. Paludan, *Victims*, pp. 25–34.

83. W. Murdock to Zebulon B. Vance, 12 August 1863, reel 19, in McKinney and McMurry, *Papers of Vance*.

84. Wm. E. Earle to George Little, 11 January 1865, reel 26, ibid.

85. Derrick Cheek and Mike Trammell, "The Great Divide," unpublished paper, Western Carolina University, 1987, pp. 3–4, 9–10.

86. Crawford, "Confederate Volunteering," pp. 37–48. A study of New Hampshire towns shows a similar reluctance of married men and farmers to volunteer. See Kemp, "Community and War," pp. 68–70.

87. Paludan, *Victims*, p. 22.

88. W. M. G. Davis to H. Heth, 20 January 1863, reel 13, in McKinney and McMurry, *Papers of Vance*.

89. J. Kent Coward, "Community in Crisis," in Williams, *Jackson County*, p. 438.

90. James C. Klotter, "Feuds in Appalachia: An Overview," *Filson Club History Quarterly* 56 (July 1982): 310.

91. L. S. Gash to Zebulon B. Vance, 1 June 1863, reel 18, in McKinney and McMurry, *Papers of Vance.*

92. Coward, "Community in Crisis," p. 438.

93. John P. Arthur, *History of Watauga County, North Carolina* (Richmond: Everett Waddy, 1915), p. 166.

94. Paludan, *Victims*, p. 74.

Lives on the Margin

Rediscovering the Women
of Antebellum Western
North Carolina

O n 12 July 1833 Francis Stewart Silvers was executed in Morganton, North Carolina, for the murder of her husband, Charles Silvers. She was the first woman to be executed in North Carolina and likely received that sentence because, on the advice of her attorney, she pleaded not guilty, despite abundant evidence found in her home that linked her to Charlie's death by the blow of an axe.

Frankie Silvers, as she was called, is one of the few female figures of nineteenth-century Appalachia to receive popular notice. She was, and still is, known as someone who killed her husband through violent means and then carefully and cold-bloodedly demolished his body in an effort to "destroy the evidence." As convention would have it, Frankie was jealous of her "two-timing" husband—often referred to in songs and stories as Johnnie rather than Charlie—and determined to even the score.

According to Alfred Silvers, brother of Charles, this clever woman killed her husband while he lay sleeping, having exhausted himself chopping firewood that day. Then, "in a conspiracy entered into by the whole Stewart family," Frankie disposed of Charles's body, using the wood he had so carefully chopped to cremate him.[1]

Another story, less often told, was that Frankie Silvers confessed to her attorney that she had killed Charles in self-defense while he was loading his gun to shoot her.[2] According to the clerk of the superior court at the time of her trial, the confession was accepted as truthful and would likely have warranted an acquittal had she told this to the court.[3]

The various renderings of Francis Stewart Silvers's life and death raise more questions than they address. Why, for example, did Francis Silvers not plead self-defense? What were the constraints that made it impossible for her to tell this story, even when it might have saved her life? Equally important, why do we know so little of her life, save the legends told concerning the murder of Charles Silvers and her own death by hanging?[4] And what makes the legend of "Frankie Silvers" so compelling, even now, that it distracts us from asking more substantive questions?

To return to Alfred Silvers's account of his cruel sister-in-law, "Franky Stewart (that was her maiden name) was a mighty likely little woman. She had fair skin, bright eyes and was counted very pretty. She had charms. I never saw a smarter woman. She could card and spin her three yards of cotton a day on a big wheel."[5] This mighty likely little woman was also a productive woman, skilled in the trades of her time. We do not know, however, if Francis Stewart Silvers's handicrafts were used as a barter at the local store or whether she wove the cotton and made it into clothing for the household. We can only speculate about how Francis, who came from a family of subsistence farmers, was received by the Silvers family, whose resources were sufficient to build a two-story cabin in the early nineteenth century and markedly increased after the Civil War as a result of their success in mining mica.[6]

We know little more about Nancy Silvers, "orphan daughter of Francis," who was "bound unto Barbara Stuart [sic] until she is eighteen years of age, to receive at her freedom one cow and a calf, two suits of clothes, one good bed and furniture and twelve months schooling."[7] Nancy Silvers ostensibly grew up in the care of her grandmother, Barbara Stewart, and then married and moved to another part of the North Carolina mountains. She was identified as a widow of the Confederacy.

As for Francis Stewart Silvers's own accounting of her life, we are told by witnesses that she appeared willing to tell her story from the gallows. However, her father shouted from the crowd, " 'Die with it in you, Franky [sic].' "[8] And she did.

It is the purpose of this essay to interrogate the silence surrounding nineteenth-century Appalachian women whose stories, like those of Francis Stewart Silvers and her daughter, remain largely untold. If the infamous Frankie Silvers proved memorable for her transgressions against gendered codes of the nineteenth century, her saga likewise offers a caution about the continued authority of such codes to present women's lives as, for the most part, unremarkable and irrelevant to historical accounts of the region.[9] Through an examination of women's productive activities and economic relations in antebellum western North Carolina, this essay seeks to complicate historical accounts and to suggest that in Appalachia, as elsewhere, gender is a problematic category.

Historians of Appalachia such as John Inscoe, Gordon B. McKinney, Jason Basil Deyton, and Martin Crawford have presented carefully documented analyses of antebellum western North Carolina as a region that was most assuredly *not* isolated unto itself.[10] Rather, western North Carolina was connected through economic transactions, political ties, and kinship affiliations to the eastern part of the state as well as to the markets of the lowland South and the Northeast where mountaineers sold agricultural produce and livestock valued in the millions.[11]

Merchants, slaveowners, mineral prospectors, and entrepreneurs sought various avenues to capitalize on the wealth of the mountains, from the early decades of the nineteenth century on.[12] Indeed, the establishment of land titles and county seats in western North Carolina provided the means through which local elites advanced their own causes and outside investors added to their profits.[13] If, by the close of the nineteenth century, western North Carolina was construed as a region set apart from the mainstream, this was largely the result of major developments in transportation and industry that targeted other parts of the state to the exclusion of the mountains in the aftermath of the Civil War.[14] However, in the antebellum years the mountains of North Carolina were a vital part of the state's economy and interstate commerce, and residents of western North Carolina actively promoted these assets.

In the Appalachia that McKinney, Crawford, and Inscoe present, there was not simply one yeoman class of self-sufficient producers but a range of class fractions and racial identities wherein individual households assumed different relationships to petty commodity production, agriculture, and merchant capital. In place of an ethos of egalitarianism, there were competing interests as landless farmers struggled to pay their rents while elites, who may well have been kin and/or neighbors, consolidated their holdings.[15]

These accounts fail to render gender relations with the same degree of complexity, however, at best offering a partial vision of women's activities.

Inscoe concedes that some of the "Mountain Masters" were, in fact, mistresses but leaves this important subject largely unexamined.[16] McKinney offers a problematic reading of gendered divisions of labor in the mountains, based on letters sent Governor Zebulon Vance by women in war-torn western North Carolina.[17] Referring to women as "the other victims" of the Civil War, McKinney presents their narratives as self-evident accounts of economic dependency, without consideration for the fragmentary character of the texts themselves or the destabilizing effects of life at war.[18] While McKinney and Inscoe acknowledge that women in war-torn western North Carolina applied themselves to an ever-increasing set of productive tasks, the proliferation of women's responsibilities is offered as further evidence of the disruptiveness of the Civil War.[19] We are left to conclude that, in antebellum Appalachia, rules about gender were underwritten by traditions of (nuclear) familism and that history was the province of men.[20] Where, then, do we place the observations made by Augustus Merrimon of a night spent in "a common log [c]abin" in 1853 while riding the court circuit of western North Carolina? "Several lasses, enlivened the scene. They were the daughters of our host. They relished the various topics of conversation, which were principally 'unmarked hogs,' 'wild hogs,' 'boars'[,] 'mountain boomers,' and the like. It was astonishing to me to see how eagerly every one heard the opinions of those around. The gravest senator could not be more interested in the most important interests of the County than was this group of ladies and gentlemen."[21]

In appreciation for Merrimon's astonishment at the interest of young women in livestock and other aspects of the local economy, this essay calls for a more expansive reading of women's lives in antebellum Appalachia. Such a reading argues, in other words, that constructions of gender, like class and ethnicity, were articulated through the web of economic and social relations that connected Appalachia to the rest of nineteenth-century America.[22] Drawing upon census manuscripts and other materials on Yancey County, North Carolina—home to Francis Stewart Silvers—the task here is not only to inquire about the productive activities in which women were engaged but equally to query the cultural discourse in which these activities were embedded, if not concealed.[23]

This inquiry is offered in the spirit of Virginia Yans-McLaughlin's research on Italian women in nineteenth-century New York, wherein she notes the gulf between women's work experiences and cultural perceptions of women's labor. Asking "whose definition and evaluation of work should the historian accept," Yans-McLaughlin calls for an intersection of ethnological and historical approaches to women's work.[24] It is not only a question of *which* interpretations prevail but rather *how* gendered interpretations are constructed that is of interest here.[25] Who has the authority to define gendered arrangements of labor, and how are these definitions instituted in nineteenth-century Appalachian life? Who contests these definitions and through what means?

Preliminary analysis of census manuscripts suggests that these sources of historical data were themselves encoded in the cultural scripts of the times. Prior to the 1850 census, only heads of households were named. Other members were enumerated and categorized according to status within the household and social or civil condition (for example, adult/child, daughter/son/wife, boarder/servant, free/unfree). Thus, for example, Francis Stewart Silvers would never have been named by the census manuscripts of her era but, rather, would have been cataloged in 1820 as "daughter" in the Blackstone Stewart household and in 1830 as "wife" in the Charles Silvers household.[26]

The 1880 census simply listed women as "keeping house" if they were wives and as "at home" if they were daughters, while the 1860 census did not provide even this cursory reference to women's productive activities.[27] By contrast, even as young men in their early teens, sons were routinely listed as farmers or farm laborers and were often titled to the personal and real estate of the household. The latter held true in almost all cases where mothers rather than fathers headed households.

Only in those instances where women were defined as holding public—and gender-appropriate—occupations such as teacher, seamstress, or domestic were their economic activities given notice. Through such strategies of depreciation, census takers rendered invisible the work performed by women for and in their own households. As Powers and Jensen have observed, these strategies continued into the twentieth century, for example, when census takers in 1920 were told to disregard the practice of keeping boarders as a form of employment.[28]

Census takers were not, of course, the sole or primary authors of the cultural scripts they implemented but rather participants in a drama whose origins are rooted in the principles of English common law.[29] The laws of North Carolina in the first half of the nineteenth century held that, upon marriage, a woman surrendered ownership of real and intangible property to her husband, was judged not capable of entering into contracts, and was not accountable for her actions.[30] She gave title to her husband for "the services of the wife, and likewise to the fruits of her own industry, whether they be exerted in his own affairs or in those of a stranger."[31] She could be disciplined by her husband with "such a degree of force as is necessary to control an unruly temper and make her behave herself."[32]

The Marriage Act of 1871–72 introduced the possibility that a married woman could function as a "free trader," provided that she obtained her husband's written consent, had her petition approved by the officer authorized to probate deeds, and filed the petition with the register of deeds. Prior to 1872 the only ways a woman could be a free trader were (1) if she were single and (2) after 1837, if she received a "divorce from 'bed and board,' " a form of legal separation that prohibited her husband from wielding control over any property or earnings acquired by her after the separation took effect.[33]

Returning to the matter of the census, census takers could thus be construed as operating upon assumptions that had been codified as law, namely that married women were dependents without legal rights or economic means. By the same token, one might venture the possibility that these assumptions also colored the kinds of petitions women made to the governor of North Carolina during the Civil War.[34] To restate the point, we can analyze these respective texts as instances of public discourse on gender, framed by legal codes and cultural perceptions. This leaves unanswered, however, Yans-McLaughlin's important questions about the nature of women's productive activities and the prospect of alternative or counterhegemonic discourses on gender.[35]

Nonetheless, with the proviso that we recognize census data as a set of normative assertions about gender formulated from the vantage point of those in authority, we can profitably use this material as a starting point for investigations of women's lives. Indeed, as Pudup suggests, in the study of preindustrial Appalachia, particularly in the study of non-elites, we have few other resources upon which to rely.[36]

From the population schedule of the 1860 census for Yancey County, for example, it is possible to ascertain numbers of women listed as heads of households, domestic servants, teachers, seamstresses, and the like as well as households containing boarders. The schedule on agriculture lists women as heads of farms, the size of their landholdings (or the lack thereof), and amounts and kinds of agricultural produce and livestock.

The schedule on slaves, a special census collected in 1860, lists slaveowners and slaves alike, affording a different slant on women's labor. Social statistics collected in 1860 provide some details about the value of women's labor in economic terms as well as general information about agricultural production and the value of real estate held in the county. The schedule on industry provides details on economic diversification and elite formation within the county, with their implications for women's productive activities. Finally, the schedule on union veterans and widows can be used as a partial index of the loss of economic productivity occasioned by the war as well as a listing of additions to the number of households headed by women in the 1860s.[37]

Before proceeding to a preliminary inventory of details thus obtained, a further cautionary note is in order. The census schedules listed above are not comparable in any strict sense, for individuals enumerated on one census schedule do not necessarily appear on another. For example, some heads of farmsteads listed in the schedule on agriculture are absent from the population schedule, and vice versa.[38] Rather than a data set on Yancey County, for example, the census schedules are best seen as jigsaw pieces belonging to parallel but not identical images—and with no single image complete.

In light of these constraints, the supplementary schedules should be regarded as source material for the county as a whole and the schedule on population as a resource through which to trace individual families. The families followed in this analysis are ten households headed by women, located in three towns or settlements: Burnsville, the county seat; Bakersville, which was to become the county seat for Mitchell County, established the following year (1861); and Ledger, a settlement in close proximity to mica mines.[39] These ten households represent roughly 22 percent of the farmsteads listed as headed by women in the county as a whole and 4 percent of the farms in Yancey County.[40] In terms of population figures, the 45 women comprise .5 percent of the 8,655 residents of the county and a little over 2 percent of the approximately 2,000 residents of the three communities.[41]

It is, in other words, a small sample representing only one dimension of women's lives. When we look at the population schedule for the three settlements under consideration, we find evidence of other productive activities, in addition to farming, in which women and girls were engaged. For example, nineteen households were noted as keeping boarders (in eleven of those instances, the boarders were listed as farm labor). Instructions to census takers notwithstanding, we can assume that the activity of caring for boarders required female labor.

Furthermore, twelve households kept female domestic servants, several with the same surname as the heads of households. Census takers listed two additional households with female servants, the difference in category of service indicating women and girls of "mulatto" ethnicity.[42] Three households in the settlements listed female schoolteachers among their inhabitants.[43] While two of the teachers boarded in the households of elite families, the third was head of her own household. Finally, in one craft household, the occupation of the wife was noted as "tailorist."[44]

In nineteen of the more than thirty households listed in the population schedule as being headed by women, there is no occupation listed for any of the inhabitants.[45] Typically this is the case when members of the household are elderly, when sons are under the age of fifteen, or when there are daughters and no sons. For those households not traceable to the schedule on agriculture, one can speculate that they are engaged in farming to some degree, since that is the primary occupation of the region, but that is hardly satisfactory as an answer.

What of the households headed by women that *are* listed on the schedule of agricultural production? The sample is small but revealing, it seems, of the varied conditions under which women lived. First, however, a little background is necessary. According to Inscoe, 69 percent of all farms in Yancey County had less than 50 acres, and only 10 percent contained over 100 acres.[46] Examination of the schedule on agricultural production indicates that the range of farm size extends from no acreage—presumably indicating a tenant farmer—to 15,000 acres, owned by the wealthiest farmer/merchant in the county, Milton Penland. Mean farm size, if such a concept has any merit, was approximately 40 acres of improved land and 200 acres of unimproved land or woodland, valued at $750.00.

Farms *listed* as being headed by women represented only 25 percent of the farmsteads headed by women. Of the 135 farmsteads listed as headed by women, eleven (8 percent) were "landless" or tenant farms. By contrast, the largest farm was owned by Rachel Banks and contained 200 acres of improved land and 350 acres of woodland. Mean farm size, for farmsteads headed by women, was roughly 27 acres of improved land and 100 acres of unimproved land, valued at $500.00.

Two of the farms listed were run by women who had slaves. Cecilia Lewis had two slaves—one male and one female—to provide labor on her farm of 100 acres. Her only son, Oscar, was listed as a physician, not a farmer, and her daughter, Mary, had no ostensible occupation.[47] Nonetheless the farm produced $25 worth of orchard products, $50 worth of produce for market, 240 pounds of butter, home manufactured goods valued at $12, and staple products for the household.

Cordelia Adams had a larger farm, although not as large as Rachel Banks's, and two male slaves to furnish labor. Her son, Joseph, was only nine at the time of the census. Her farm produced wheat, rye, oats, corn, and buckwheat as well as the predictable beans and potatoes. Orchard produce was valued at $5, and market gardens at $20. The farm also produced 150 pounds of butter and $80 worth of home manufactured goods.[48]

Rachel Banks had no slaves and no family, according to the fictions of the census.[49] Nonetheless, at age sixty-five she kept a productive farm. She invested in livestock, with 30 swine to Cordelia Adams's 20 and Cecilia Lewis's 2. She had a herd of 15 cattle (3 milk cows), while the others owned one or two cattle. Like Cordelia Adams's, Rachel Banks's farm produced a variety of grains. Of the three wealthy farmsteads, Rachel Banks's was the most diversified in the crops it produced: sweet potatoes (50 bushels); tobacco (30 pounds); flax (40 pounds); beeswax, honey, and molasses in amounts exceeding subsistence needs; $100 worth of orchard products; $20 of market produce; and $50 of home manufactures—to give a partial accounting of her produce.

At the opposite end of the spectrum were the farmsteads run by Sarah Webb and Eliza Caraway. Sarah Webb's family of six included no one save herself who was older than eleven. Sarah Webb owned no land, and her personal estate was valued at $100. She kept 10 swine and 2 milk cows, from which she produced 20 pounds of butter, and grew flax (9 pounds), corn (100 bushels), and sweet potatoes as well as Irish potatoes and beans. Except for the butter and $10 worth of market garden produce, her farm seems to have been geared toward subsistence levels of production—a considerable feat, given the shortage of labor.

Similarly, Eliza Carroway owned no land and had only $75 in her personal estate. She did have adult children: Caroline, age 28, and Henry, the "farmer," 21 and the possessor of an estate worth $177. Also in the household were a 3-year-old son, Merret, as well as David Anderson, age 9, and Clarissa Carroway—presumably her mother-in-law. Eliza Carroway had sheep and horses, 2 cows, and a herd of 19 swine. Her farm produced small quantities of flax, wool, and tobacco as well as what appear to have been subsistence levels of butter, peas, beans, and potatoes.[50] The 60 bushels of corn her farm produced may have included enough for market, and she produced $15 worth of produce from her orchards. The home-manufactured goods her farm produced were valued at $15 (as opposed to $6 for Sarah Webb's farmstead). Perhaps the difference was the handiwork of Caroline and Clarissa Carroway.

There were other farms headed by women that fell between these two extremes as well as farms that were even poorer than the ones described above. Some farms, such as that of Minerva Gouge, specialized in livestock production, while others concentrated on growing corn or orchard goods for sale.[51] Harriet Tucker, for example, kept a horse, two cows, and eight swine on her fifty-acre farm. Her principal crops appear to have been wheat (80 bushels) and Indian corn (200 bushels), although she produced $6 worth of market garden crops and home-manufactured goods valued at $25.[52]

What emerge from this schematic listing are the different strategies women used to run their farms. Critical to these decisions were amounts (and quality) of land and the available labor supply as well as resources such as farm implements, draft animals, and seed. However, it is also safe to assume that women and adult members of the households exercised judgment over what crops would produce well on their farmsteads and what kinds of produce they could sell to local merchants and to markets in Charleston and Savannah. Certainly, Rachel Banks's and Minerva Gouge's livestock herds would have found ready markets as part of the stock herds driven through nearby Asheville to the lowland South, and Harriet Tucker's extra corn might have been sold at the drovers' stands along the Buncombe Toll Road or access roads in Yancey County that led up to it.

By way of a preliminary conclusion, it would appear that farmsteads headed by women were viable concerns, even in the (formal) absence of male labor.[53] It is also true—Rachel Banks notwithstanding—that the most productive farms were those that relied on male as well as female labor. Perhaps more important still were the ages, rather than the genders, of members of the household. Further research is necessary to address the character of productive relations on antebellum farms, for these farmsteads—few in number though they may be—suggest that women's labor and decision making were more significant than conventional wisdom would have us believe.[54]

To develop this conundrum further, let us turn to the issue of slaveholding practices in antebellum western North Carolina. In terms of sheer numbers, slaveholding was not a major factor in the agricultural practices and social traditions of Yancey County.[55] The 1860 U.S. census (*Schedule Two: Slave Inhabitants*) lists 362 slaves owned by 62 owners.[56] Twenty-six slaveholders (or 42 percent) had 2 or fewer slaves, while 14 men (22.5 percent) reported ownership of 10 or more slaves.[57] Six of the 62 slaveholders (9.6 percent) inventoried were women, all but 2 of whom had 1 slave apiece. The other 2, described in the previous section, had 2 slaves in each of their households.

However, it is not only the gender of the slaveholders that is of interest, but equally the gender of the slaves. In Yancey County 206 (or 57 percent) of the 362 slaves were female. Lest one attribute that to high numbers of female offspring, it should be noted that approximately 60 percent of the female slaves were twelve years of age or older, and 21 percent were at least thirty years of age. By way of contrast, some 50 percent of the 156 male slaves were under the age of twelve.

What value were female slaves to slaveholders?[58] Besides procreation, clearly an important enterprise from the standpoint of slaveholding households, it can be presumed that female slaves provided domestic service. We can estimate the value of such labor, for the schedule on social statistics records domestic work as garnering weekly wages of $.75 to $1.25 in 1860. But the value of domestic work was even greater to those households that kept boarders, for the "price of board to 'laboring men'" was reported to be $1.25 per week, and doubtless more than that for the merchants, physicians, clergymen, and store clerks who boarded under more sumptuous conditions.[59] Seven of the nineteen households listed for the settlements of Burnsville, Bakersville, and Ledger as keeping boarders also relied on slave labor, and we may safely assume that the two factors were somehow connected.[60]

Beyond domestic service, female slaves likely worked in agricultural production and the production of what was termed "home-made" or "household manufactures." Slave labor was important to agricultural production in western North Carolina, especially on larger farms such as Milton Penland's or farms with few adult members available to provide farm labor.[61] However, given the relatively small size of mountain farms and the orientation of most farms around subsistence-based agriculture, supplemented by cash cropping, slave labor played a much less significant role on mountain farms than on the plantations of the lowland South.[62]

More notable was the value of slave labor to manufacturing and mercantile enterprises in western North Carolina. Not only did slaves perform general maintenance work in these operations, they also produced the goods to be sold—from bricks, furniture, wagon wheels, and plugs of tobacco to shoes, hats, and men's clothing. This last is of particular interest, for it illustrates the connection between household production and manufacturing activities in western North Carolina and other rural areas. According to Inscoe, "The wife of Ashe County merchant David Worth set up a cloth-making business and trained several of their seven slaves to sew men's and boys' clothing, which she then sold in her husband's store. Profits from that source led the Worths to establish a carriage and furniture factory in which their own slaves, along with several persons hired locally, were employed."[63]

Sewing clothes and, to a lesser extent, making cloth were part of the repertoire of many mountain households in the antebellum period. It was to this end that flax was grown and sheep were sheared. While mountain counties gave rise to increasingly complex occupational structures, this meant, for the most part, specialists such as tanners and shoemakers who offered services that supplemented but did not entirely replace household manufactures. In a similar vein, stores offered ready-made cloth and other factory goods for those who could afford them and, equally important, served as venues for locally produced goods, as in the example cited above.[64] Women who were not the wives of merchants would call upon members of their households to produce handiwork for barter or home use, and slaveholders employed slaves to this same end.

In other words, home manufactures, produced by women *and* men, can be seen as a form of petty commodity production akin to other economic strategies employed by the residents of the mountains.[65] As with farming, this form of production was flexible in terms of time and available labor, and even location of productive activities.[66] The goods thus produced found their way to markets in the lowland South as well as community stores and neighboring households. Zona Hughes, drafted by her aunt to live with her and her husband—ostensibly to get a good education—explains the system:

> When school was out, I spent my time at home with Aunt Susie working every waking hour. Aunt Susie was a good woman but her rule of life was hard work and lots of it. She was good to me in her own way, and taught me to do many things that would prove useful in my later life. She had several cows and usually milked five or six during the summer months. The milk was used for cheese, and it was Aunt Susie who taught me how to make homemade cheese. . . . The cheese, and butter also, was taken to Bakersville to be sold to merchants there, and cloth was purchased with the proceeds. I have known her to buy a whole bolt of domestic cloth as well as calico to be used for summer dresses.[67]

Susie Phillips was a busy woman who used her household as a workshop and her niece as a laborer.[68] Her principal activity was to produce coverlets, jeans, and blankets on order. This venture was quite profitable in the 1880s, for Zona notes that her aunt received as much as $25 for one of her coverlets and was kept too busy by her clientele to make good her promises to her niece.[69]

In effect, this form of production absorbed the shocks of an economy that was neither self-sufficient nor completely reliant on factory goods.[70] The majority of the 33 commercial enterprises recorded by the 1860 census

Table 7.1. Household Manufactures, Western North Carolina Counties (in dollars)

	Total Valuation			Per Capita Value		
	1840	1850	1860	1840	1850	1860
Counties						
Ashe	20,310	58,302	38,461	2.72	6.64	5.00
Buncombe	63,373	93,312	51,004	6.28	6.95	4.03
Burke	51,054	14,591	12,179	3.23	1.88	1.32
Cherokee	12,706	18,306	32,907	3.71	5.41	3.59
Haywood	8,605	30,027	28,590	1.73	4.24	4.93
Henderson	6,765	17,941	22,157	1.32	2.62	2.11
Macon	54,925	18,052	18,493	3.67	5.19	8.64
Wilkes	38,746	69,148	35,804	3.08	5.72	2.43
Yancey	4,688	64,279	43,316	0.79	7.83	5.00
North Carolina (per capita value only)				1.87	2.40	2.06
United States (per capita value only)				1.70	1.18	0.78

Source: Tryon, Household Manufactures in the United States, pp. 308–9, 326–29.
Note: Data not available for Alleghany, Caldwell, Jackson, Madison, McDowell, and Watauga Counties.

for Yancey County, for example, were grist mills and saw mills which manufactured moderate amounts of goods primarily for local consumption.[71] For goods not produced by local businesses nor obtainable from area merchants, households relied upon their own craft skills and, like Susie Phillips, transformed them into commercial endeavors when feasible.

As indicated by the example of the unnamed wife of Ashe County merchant David Worth, home manufacturing equally lent itself to what has been variously termed "putting-out systems" or "industrial outwork." These were informal arrangements where women and/or slaves fashioned commodities for local entrepreneurs who brokered the produce in other markets.[72] Such arrangements proved to be precursors to factory systems of labor, absorbing women's productive labor and further marginalizing rural households.[73]

In overlooking the significance of outwork and home manufactures to nineteenth-century America, Thomas Dublin argues, we are left with static theories that cannot explain the complexities and countertwists in the long road from agrarian life to industrial capitalism.[74] Returning to the central concern of this essay, we also fail to recognize the contributions and contradictory dimensions of women's labor and instead simply describe women as "keeping house" and "at home." Such an interpretation leaves us in need of extraordinary circumstances, other wars, to explain women's growing participation in waged work—for example, mica processing—at the turn of the century.

This cursory examination of free and unfree women's labors in antebellum Appalachia suggests, instead, that women were actively engaged in a variety of productive strategies that underwrote household subsistence and contributed to the growing commodification of regional economies. Such a perspective allows room for the amazing observations of Augustus Merrimon, while at the same time acknowledging the limits placed on women's agency by the legal and cultural codes of the day. Finally we can return to Francis Stewart Silvers and see someone other than the jealous, cunning woman who was the undoing of her (perhaps) wayward man.

Appendix

The Frankie Silvers Poem*

This dreadful, dark and dismal day
Has swept my glories all away
My sun goes down, my days are past
And I must leave this world at last.

Oh! Lord, what will become of me?
I am condemned you all now see
To heaven or hell my soul must fly,
All in a moment when I die.

Judge Donnell has my sentence pass'd
These prison walls I leave at last
Nothing to cheer my drooping head
Until I'm numbered with the dead.

But oh! that dreadful Judge I fear,
Shall I that awful sentence hear?
"Depart ye cursed down to hell
And forever there to dwell."

*Clifton Avery, *Official Court Record of the Trial, Conviction, and Execution of Francis Silvers, First Woman Hanged in North Carolina*, from the Minutes of the Burke County Superior Court (Morganton, N.C.: News-Herald, 1953), p. 12. Avery introduces the poem by noting that Silvers was "reputed to have recited [the poem] from the scaffold" (p. 10).

I know that frightful ghosts I'll see
Gnawing their flesh in misery,
And then and there attended be
For murder in the first degree.

There shall I meet that mournful face
Whose blood I spilled upon this place;
With flaming eyes to me he'll say:
"Why did you take my life away?"

His feeble hands fell gently down,
His chattering tongue soon lost its sound
To see his soul and body part
It strikes with terror to my heart.

I took his blooming days away,
Left him no time to God to pray
And if sins fall on his head
Must I not bear them in his stead?

The jealous thought that first gave strife
To make me take my husband's life,
For months and days I spent my time
Thinking how to commit this crime.

And on a dark and doleful night
I put this body out of sight,
With flames I tried him to consume
But time would not admit it done.

You all see me and on me gaze,
Be careful how you spend your days,
And never commit this awful crime,
But try to serve your God in time.

My mind on solemn subjects roll;
My little child, God bless its soul!
All you that are of Adam's race,
Let not my faults this child disgrace.

Farewell good people, you all now see
What my bad conduct's brought me—
To die of shame and of disgrace
Before this world of human race.

Awful indeed to think of death,
In perfect health to lose my breath,
Farewell my friends, I bid adieu,
Vengeance on me must not pursue.

Great God! how shall I be forgiven?
Not fit for earth, not fit for heaven,
But little time to pray to God,
For now I try that awful road.

Notes

For their insightful criticism and encouragement, the author thanks Dwight Billings, Jane Hatcher, Lois Helmbold, John Inscoe, Ralph Mann, Gordon McKinney, Mary Beth Pudup, members of her Bay Area writers' group, and the anonymous reviewers. Thanks also to Jody Higgins for offering material on the early history of Yancey County.

1. "Red Buck" Bryant, "Interview with Alfred Silver," in *Common Times: Written and Pictorial History of Yancey County*, ed. Jody Higgins (Burnsville, N.C.: Yancey Graphics, 1981), p. 17.

2. This version was offered by Henry Spainhour, who witnessed the trial and execution of Francis Silver. See "Francis Silvers' Confession," letter to the editor, *Lenoir Topic*, published in the *Morganton Star*, 7 May 1886; reprinted in Maxine McCall, *They Won't Hang a Woman*, Burke County Cultural Heritage Project (Morganton, N.C.: Burke County Public Schools, 1972), p. 50.

3. Higgins, *Common Times*, p. 18.

4. One ballad was alleged to have been written by Frankie Silvers while she was in prison and recited by her from the gallows (see Appendix). According to Spainhour, a resident of Morganton at the time of the trial, the ballad was composed by Thomas W. Scott and was based on the gallows confession/song of a man known only as "Beacham." To quote Spainhour, "Now, after nearly 53 years, some person had gotten hold of Scott's piece composed from Beacham's song" and made "the thing look as dark as the ingenuity of man could devise, when there is not the slightest evidence that it was a premeditated murder, but a matter of an instant" (Spainhour, "Francis Silvers' Confession").

5. Bryant, "Interview with Alfred Silver," p. 18.

6. Charlie's brother, Dave, would become known for his successful mica prospecting in the aftermath of the Civil War. See Frank G. Lesure, "Mica Deposits of the Blue Ridge in North Carolina," United States Geological Survey, Professional Paper 577, 1968, and United States Geological Survey, "Mine Descriptions," unpublished.

7. Clifton K. Avery, *Official Court Record of the Trial, Conviction, and Execution of Francis Silvers, First Woman Hanged in North Carolina*, from the Minutes of the Burke County Superior Court (Morganton, N.C.: News-Herald, 1953), p. 12. According to McCall, "Red Buck" Bryant traced Nancy Silvers in 1901 to Madison

County, North Carolina. However, the only information recorded was that Nancy Silvers lost her first husband, David Parker, to the Confederate cause and later remarried. See McCall, *They Won't Hang a Woman*, p. 59.

8. Bryant, "Interview with Alfred Silver," p. 18.

9. The most obvious transgressions were the murder of Charles Silvers and the efforts to dispose of his remains, as well as Francis Silvers's denial of culpability through a plea of "not guilty" to the charges of the state. However, even after her trial Francis Silvers continued to transgress the codes of her day, dressing in men's clothes, wearing her hair short like a man's, and temporarily breaking free of the Morganton jail. The accounts of her execution alternately describe Francis Silvers as unrepentant, carrying a piece of cake with her to the scaffold so that she might consume her last meal in full, and contrite, admitting her guilt through the recitation of the aforementioned ballad (see n. 4 above and Appendix). The alleged confession of Francis Silvers is noteworthy as a reflection of public sentiment, then and now, as the fictions of her life continue to be woven into songs and other artifacts of popular culture.

10. Martin Crawford, "Political Society in a Southern Mountain Community: Ashe County, North Carolina, 1850–1861," *Journal of Southern History* 55 (1989): 373–90; Martin Crawford, "The Farm Economy, the Market Economy, and Antebellum Social Relations in a Southern Mountain Community: Ashe County, North Carolina, 1850–1860," paper presented at the meeting of the Southern Historical Association, 1991, Fort Worth, Tex.; Jason Basil Deyton, "The Toe River Valley to 1865," *North Carolina Historical Review* 24 (1947): 423–66; John C. Inscoe, *Mountain Masters: Slavery and the Sectional Crisis in Western North Carolina* (Knoxville: University of Tennessee Press, 1989); John C. Inscoe, "Kinship, Wealth, and Political Power in Antebellum Western North Carolina," paper presented at the Appalachian Studies Conference, 1989, Morgantown, W.Va.; Gordon B. McKinney, "Subsistence Economy and Community in Western North Carolina, 1860–1865," paper presented at the meeting of the Organization of American Historians, 1988, Reno, Nev.; Gordon B. McKinney, "Women's Role in Civil War Western North Carolina," *North Carolina Historical Review* 69 (1992): 37–56.

11. Inscoe, *Mountain Masters*, pp. 46, 25–58, 115–30. See also McKinney, "Subsistence Economy and Community"; H. Tyler Blethen and Curtis W. Wood, Jr., "A Trader on the Western Carolina Frontier," in *Appalachian Frontiers: Settlement, Society, and Development in the Preindustrial Era*, ed. Robert D. Mitchell (Lexington: University Press of Kentucky, 1991), pp. 150–65.

12. Certainly one of the most celebrated entrepreneurs was Thomas Lanier Clingman. See his *Selections from the Speeches and Writings of Hon. Thomas L. Clingman of North Carolina, with Additions and Explanatory Notes* (Raleigh: John Nichols, 1887). One should also include such figures as A. S. Merrimon, who was—like Clingman—a United States senator and important figure in the political circles of North Carolina, and James Patton, a merchant and profiteer who developed one of the first major resort hotels of the region as an addition to his livestock stands and drovers' inns. See Blethen and Wood, "Trader on the Western Carolina Frontier"; Inscoe, *Mountain Masters*; A. R. Newsome, "The A. S. Merrimon Journal, 1853–54," *North Carolina Historical Review* 8 (1931): 300–330; James Patton, *Letter of James*

Patton, one of the First Residents of Asheville, North Carolina, to His Children (Racine, Wisc.: William Patton, 1845).

13. Mary Beth Pudup and Altina Waller make this argument in their important rewriting of the histories of eastern Kentucky. See Mary Beth Pudup, "The Boundaries of Class in Preindustrial Appalachia," *Journal of Historical Geography* 15 (1989): 139–62; Altina F. Waller, *Feud: Hatfields, McCoys, and Social Change in Appalachia, 1860–1900* (Chapel Hill: University of North Carolina Press, 1988).

14. In part this was due to the formidable mountain terrain; equally important, mountaineers felt their interests were not fairly considered by the state government. See William Way, Jr., *The Clinchfield Railroad: The Story of a Trade Route across the Blue Ridge Mountains* (Chapel Hill: University of North Carolina Press, 1931); Inscoe, *Mountain Masters*, pp. 152–76; Deyton, "Toe River Valley," pp. 442–46.

15. See Joseph D. Reid, "Antebellum Southern Rental Contracts," *Explorations in Economic History* 13 (1976): 69–83; Frederick A. Bode and Donald E. Ginter, *Farm Tenancy and the Census in Antebellum Georgia* (Athens: University of Georgia Press, 1986). *Eighth Census of the United States, 1860, Schedule 4: Production of Agriculture* (Washington, D.C.: Government Printing Office, 1864) lists 135 individuals in Yancey County as agents or managers of farms they do not own.

16. Inscoe leaves unexplored the nexus of activities and interactions that made up slaveowning households in general and women's lives in particular. For an example of the significance of this world, not just to the daily maintenance of southern households but to the way of life that characterized the antebellum South, see Elizabeth Fox-Genovese, *Within the Plantation Household: Black and White Women of the Old South* (Chapel Hill: University of North Carolina Press, 1988), and *Six Women's Slave Narratives*, ed. Henry Louis Gates and with an introduction by William L. Andrews (New York: Oxford University Press, 1988).

17. Women were left to grapple with the chaos caused in communities by divided loyalties (and their very real consequences), the conscription of adult males, and raids by deserters and enemy soldiers. In their letters they pleaded for the return of husbands and sons lest their farms go completely to ruin and they to starvation. What is problematic is the assumption that women did not and could not tend farmsteads in the absence of male labor. See McKinney, "Women's Role in Civil War Western North Carolina," pp. 49–50.

18. McKinney titled an earlier version of his essay "The Other Victims: Women in Civil War Western North Carolina" when he presented it to the Southern Historical Association in Norfolk, Va., 1988.

19. See John Inscoe's meticulously researched account of Mary Bell's life during the Civil War, "Coping in Confederate Appalachia: Portrait of a Mountain Woman and her Community at War," delivered to the Appalachian Studies Association, 1992, Asheville, N.C. I do not disagree with Inscoe and McKinney over the contention that the Civil War disrupted economic and social relations, but with the assumption that this extraordinary time serves as a marker of the limited sphere occupied by Appalachian women before and after the war. Ralph Mann provides the one dissenting note, observing that the frontier life of antebellum Sandy Basin, Va., allowed for the "relaxing [of] categories of male and female behavior" and served the area well during the Civil War. See Ralph Mann, "Guerrilla Warfare and

Gender Roles: Sandy Basin, Virginia, as a Test Case," paper presented at the meeting of the Appalachian Studies Association, 1992, Asheville, N.C., p. 7.

20. This interpretation is not unique to the historians of Appalachian North Carolina. See also Durwood Dunn, *Cades Cove: The Life and Death of a Southern Appalachian Community, 1818–1937* (Knoxville: University of Tennessee Press, 1988); Ronald D. Eller, *Miners, Millhands, and Mountaineers: Industrialization of the Appalachian South, 1880–1930* (Knoxville: University of Tennessee Press, 1982); Mitchell, *Appalachian Frontiers*.

For alternative readings of gender relations in Appalachia, although not in reference to the antebellum period, see Jacquelyn Dowd Hall, "Disorderly Women: Gender and Labor Militancy in the Appalachian South," *Journal of American History* 73 (September 1986): 346–82; Sally Ward Maggard, "Will the Real Daisy Mae Please Stand Up? A Methodological Essay on Gender Analysis in Appalachian Research," *Appalachian Journal* 21 (1994): 136–50; Kathleen C. Stewart, "Speak for Yourself: Gender as Dialogic in Appalachia," in *Uncertain Terms: The Negotiation of Gender in American Culture*, ed. Faye Ginsburg and Anna Tsing (Boston: Beacon, 1990).

21. Newsome, "Merrimon Journal," pp. 312–13. Merrimon spends much of his journal decrying the drunkenness and debauchery of women and men who attended his court. See, for example, p. 311.

22. For a similar reading of gender relations in the yeoman households of antebellum South Carolina, see Stephanie McCurry, "The Politics of Yeoman Households in South Carolina," in *Divided Houses: Gender and the Civil War*, ed. Catherine Clinton and Nina Silber (New York: Oxford University Press, 1992).

23. Technically, Yancey County cannot be called the home of Francis Silvers, for she died the year before Yancey would be formed from the considerably larger county of Burke, whose territory encompassed the foothills that extended into the North Carolina piedmont as well as mountainous terrain and whose county seat was several· days' travel by wagon from the mountains where the Stewarts and Silverses lived. Yancey County itself would split in 1861 over divided loyalties in the Civil War (cf. Deyton, "Toe River Valley").

24. Virginia Yans-McLaughlin, "Italian Women and Work: Experience and Perception," in *Sex, Class, and the Woman Worker*, ed. Milton Cantor and Bruce Laurie (Westport, Conn: Greenwood Press, 1977), pp. 104–5. See also Elizabeth Knowlton, "Women in the Archives: Women's Power and the Archivist's Responsibility," paper presented at the meeting of the National Women's Studies Association, 1987, Atlanta, Ga.

25. This essay is also indebted to the enormous scholarship on women and gender, the work of feminist historians for the past three or more decades. A partial listing of the important contributions of feminist historians would include Ava Baron, ed., *Work Engendered: Toward a New History of American Labor* (Ithaca: Cornell University Press, 1991); Elsa Barkley Brown, "African-American Women's Quilting: A Framework for Conceptualizing and Teaching African-American Women's History," *Signs* 14 (1989): 921–29; Clinton and Silber, *Divided Houses*; Thomas Dublin, *Women at Work: The Transformation of Work and Community in Lowell, Massachusetts, 1820–1860* (New York: Columbia University Press, 1979); John Fout and Maura Shaw Tantillo, eds., *American Sexual Politics: Sex, Gender, and Race since*

the Civil War (Chicago: University of Chicago Press, 1993); Carol Groneman and Mary Beth Norton, eds., *To Toil the Livelong Day: America's Women at Work, 1780–1980* (Ithaca: Cornell University Press, 1987); Jacquelyn Dowd Hall, James Leloudis, Robert Korstad, Mary Murphy, Lu Ann Jones, and Christopher B. Daly, *Like a Family: The Making of a Southern Cotton Mill World* (Chapel Hill: University of North Carolina Press, 1987); Dorothy O. Helly and Susan M. Reverby, eds., *Gendered Domains: Rethinking Public and Private in Women's History* (Ithaca: Cornell University Press, 1992); Jacqueline Jones, *Labor of Love, Labor of Sorrow: Black Women, Work, and the Family, from Slavery to the Present* (New York: Vintage, 1985); Alice Kessler-Harris, *Out to Work: A History of Wage-Earning Women in the United States* (New York: Oxford University Press, 1982); Suzanne Lebsock, *The Free Women of Petersburg: Status and Culture in a Southern Town, 1784–1860* (New York: Norton, 1984); Anne Firor Scott, *The Southern Lady: From Pedestal to Politics, 1830–1930* (Chicago: University of Chicago Press, 1970); Louise A. Tilly and Joan W. Scott, *Women, Work, and the Family* (New York: Holt, Rinehart, and Winston, 1978).

26. I am indebted to an anonymous reviewer for these observations.

27. Changes in enumeration procedures and the greater care with which the 1880 census recorded the activities of women wage earners were, at least, in part a response to growing criticism by groups such as the Association for the Advancement of Women. See Marjorie Abel and Nancy Folbre, "A Methodology for Revising Estimates: Female Market Participation in the U.S. before 1940," *Historical Methods* 23 (1990): 169; *Eighth Census of the United States, 1860, Schedule 1: Population* (Washington, D.C.: Government Printing Office, 1864); *Tenth Census of the United States, 1880, Schedule 1: Population* (Washington, D.C.: Government Printing Office, 1883).

28. Only as *sole* source of income for a given family could keeping boarders be listed as employment. See Marilyn Powers, "From Home Production to Wage Labor: Women as a Reserve Army of Labor," *Review of Radical Political Economy* 15 (1983): 88 n 1; Joan Jensen, "Cloth, Butter, and Boarders: Women's Production for Market," *Review of Radical Political Economics* 12 (1980): esp. 15.

29. See Albert Coates, *By Her Own Bootstraps: A Saga of Women in North Carolina* (Raleigh: Albert Coates, 1975), a treatise on the history of North Carolina laws as they pertain to women's rights.

30. See Coates, *By Her Own Bootstraps*, pp. 4–5, 8, 10–11, 15. See also Victoria E. Bynum's analysis of the laws of nineteenth-century North Carolina on the property rights and legal status of married women, *Unruly Women: The Politics of Social and Sexual Control in the Old South* (Chapel Hill: University of North Carolina Press, 1992), and also see Joseph S. Ferrell, "Notes and Comments," *North Carolina Law Review* 41 (1962–63): 604–16.

31. Coates, *By Her Own Bootstraps*, p. 19, quoting Justice Ruffin for the court in *Smyme v. Riddle* 88 NC 463 (1883).

32. Coates, *By Her Own Bootstraps*, p. 29, quoting the court in *State v. Black*, 60 NC 262 (1864).

33. Coates, *By Her Own Bootstraps*, pp. 11, 18. According to Coates, the Martin Act of 1911 made all women free traders, regardless of marital status.

34. This seems especially likely, given the fact that "many mountain women requested that male relatives and neighbors write these letters for them" (McKinney,

"Other Victims," p. 18). While McKinney attributes requests for male secretaries to the inherent conservatism of Appalachian women, these women might simply have been illiterate, which was true for many women enumerated in the 1860 census. These questions notwithstanding, the letters thus written asked not for the return of enlisted soldiers but for food, money, and the exemption of conscripts. Further, the petitions met with success. To quote McKinney again, "State and county governments provided approximately $25,000,000 [sic] in welfare assistance—a significant break with past policy" (p. 15).

35. James Scott advances the argument that public discourse invariably reproduces relations of authority, for those without power are not free to make their feelings known. To call for rebellion or openly to contest authority in this setting would be inviting defeat. Consequently, the powerless find alternative means—which Scott refers to as "hidden transcripts"—to express dissent and foster resistance. Translated into the context of this essay, if there were alternative discourses on gender and/or contested practices, we would not locate them in the aforementioned documents. See James C. Scott, *Domination and the Arts of Resistance: Hidden Transcripts* (New Haven: Yale University Press, 1990).

36. Mary Beth Pudup, "Social Class and Economic Development in Southeastern Kentucky, 1820–1880," in Mitchell, *Appalachian Frontiers*, pp. 243–44.

37. This information was collected in 1890 as provided by "the act of March 1, 1889," presumably a program of war reparations. No effort was made to collect comparable information for the veterans and widows of the Confederacy; where such information was taken down erroneously in this document, it was so noted and names were crossed out. The Civil War was referred to as "the war of rebellion," and Union veterans were classified as "U.S. soldiers."

38. In addition, names are misspelled, households listed as being in one locale in one list wind up in a different settlement on another list, and valuations of property for a given household may vary from one listing to the next.

39. Because of the problems in correspondence between the different schedules, one household is tentatively included that is listed as that of Mary Burleson in the population schedule and that of Merideth Burleson in the schedule of agricultural productions. The differences in spelling are within the range of error found in other instances, but the two might be separate households.

Ideally the next step would be to expand this initial sample to include ten families headed by men and to cover a range of occupations and levels of wealth and property. I would also like to include households headed by or containing women who were teachers in this expanded version.

40. The figure I derived from the schedule on agriculture is 1,183 farms for Yancey County as a whole, of which 45 were headed by women. There were 223 farms in Burnsville, 120 farms in Bakersville, and 80 farms in Ledger, or a total of 423 farms in the areas under study. See *Eighth Census, Schedule 4*. This figure differs from Inscoe's calculation of 1,050 farms for Yancey County in 1860 (*Mountain Masters*, p. 23). Whereas his figure is based on *Agriculture of the United States in 1860*, compiled by Joseph C. G. Kennedy (Wilmington, Del.: Scholarly Resources, 1973), p. 210, my estimate comes from raw census material and might slightly overreport the number of farms, insofar as some of the wealthiest families held ownership of more than one farm.

41. The total is 2,044, a rough estimate based on the population schedule that notes that some 74 households were either unoccupied or had no one available to talk with the census takers. Of the three areas, Burnsville had the largest population: 1,570 individuals and 295 households. See *Eighth Census, Schedule 1.*

42. This term belongs to the racialized classification scheme of the 1860 census that refers to the "color" of residents of the household. What is not clear from the census is whether the term *mulatto* refers to persons of Cherokee descent or those of mixed parentage (African American slave/European American master) or both. The significance of the term, and the coding of "servants" as another "color," is not in question inasmuch as it underscores the presence of racial as well as gender-based hierarchies in antebellum North Carolina.

43. All told, there were only five schoolteachers listed for the settlements under examination. The two male schoolteachers were sons residing in female-headed households. Ibid.

44. Ibid. A number of households contain elderly women (and men), some with the surname of the head of household. What their activities or their relations to the heads of households were we can only speculate, since the 1860 census did not record this information.

45. Ibid.

46. Inscoe, *Mountain Masters*, p. 23.

47. This, of course, was also true for Cecilia Lewis, as she was listed in the population schedule.

48. Jason Deyton valued butter at ten cents per pound in his discussion of agricultural production for 1850. That figure might have fluctuated during the intervening decade, but it gives some indication of the value of this commodity— i.e., 150 pounds of butter would equal or exceed the amount of market garden or orchard produce yielded by many of the farms under consideration. See Deyton, "Toe River Valley," pp. 451–53.

49. Had Rachel Banks been married and divorced or widowed more than once, she could easily have sons living next to her who would not be identifiable as such through the population schedule. The issue of tracing kin relations is equally a problem when one tries to locate married daughters, who likewise might be settled within the same community but not recognized as such. It is through circumstances such as these that gender/kin relations are obscured.

50. In his study of Cades Cove, N.C., Durwood Dunn notes that in addition to corn, wheat, oats, and rye, crops such as peas, beans, and Irish and sweet potatoes were produced for market as well as home use. Honey, molasses, and beeswax were shipped to Knoxville for sale, while butter and eggs were exchanged for goods at local stores. Tobacco was grown for home use and for sale. Dunn does not specify subsistence levels of production, so one is left to wonder how much of these various crops a given farm would have to produce in order to have enough to market. See Dunn, *Cades Cove*, pp. 75–76.

51. Minerva Gouge's farm also produced 300 bushels of corn, wheat, rye, oats, and buckwheat as well as flax, beeswax, and orchard products valued at $20 and home-manufactured goods worth $25. Her 100-acre farm was very productive—at least

partly because she had three teenaged sons, a 12-year-old son, an 8-year-old daughter, and Polly Stephens (age 10) to help her.

52. Her household included two sons, 17-year-old Zephamiah and 9-year-old Benjamen, and two daughters, 14-year-old Phebey and 12-year-old Aacey.

53. For the purposes of this discussion, male laborers are included as part of household productive forces only when formally specified in the census schedules. One can safely speculate that households that did not contain sons or borders relied, instead, on communitywide and intrahousehold patterns of labor pooling as well as casual day labor. Once again, the conventions of the census limit our vision of household patterns of production.

54. Dunn, *Cades Cove*, pp. 183–86, offers the usual formula: Women and girls tended vegetable gardens, which produced for market as well as for home. Men and boys worked crops such as corn and tobacco. He observes, however, that gendered divisions of farm labor were flexible enough to allow girls to hoe corn, for example, and for wives and "spinsters" such as Aunt Becky Cable to herd cattle and do fieldwork.

In his study of the settlement of the "backcountry" by émigrés from the borderlands of Great Britain, David Hackett Fisher makes a stronger claim than Dunn, proposing a "paradox" of gender distinctions: namely, that hard labor was routinely shared by women and men throughout growing seasons and harvest times, and that women participated in all forms of farm work, including forest clearing, ground breaking, and the slaughtering of cattle and other livestock. It could be argued that Hackett Fisher is talking about an earlier time period—the eighteenth versus the nineteenth century—and frontier life as opposed to settled farmland communities. However, Hackett Fisher argues that the cultural traditions had abiding influence, not only for the lives of the immigrants but for the communities they established in the New World. See David Hackett Fisher, *Albion's Seed: Four British Folkways in America* (New York: Oxford University Press, 1989), pp. 676, 783–898.

55. In 1860, Yancey County ranked ninth among the fifteen counties of western North Carolina in terms of size of the slave population, according to Inscoe, *Mountain Masters*, pp. 60–61.

56. Moreover, as Deyton tells us, part of Yancey County split off in opposition to the Confederacy and its plans for secession from the Union. In the newly formed Mitchell County there were only sixty-five slaves altogether and none in the northern section of the county. Slaveholding was seen as in competition with free labor and unfair to the working class. See Deyton, "Toe River Valley," p. 459.

57. Milton Penland headed the list with 32 slaves under his ownership.

58. It is beyond the scope of this essay to extend this discussion to the Cherokee Indians, whose territory was western North Carolina by royal proclamation. It was only in 1778 that the North Carolina legislature formally opened lands to white settlers, who had been covertly settling there for some time. (See Deyton, "Toe River Valley," p. 432.) While the region later known as Yancey County was used principally by the Cherokee for hunting, it is also possible that some of the Cherokee moved there in the 1830s to escape forced removal through the Trail of Tears. Residents of the area routinely acknowledge Cherokee ancestry, and the census of 1860 used the

term *mulatto* to describe the ethnic heritage of some county residents. Without more specific information, however, it is best to recognize Cherokee/white relations in antebellum Yancey County as a matter warranting study. The important analyses of Cherokee women's lives in the eighteenth and nineteenth centuries offered by Perdue and Hatley lend guidance to this future effort. See Theda Perdue, "From Public Roles to Private Lives: Cherokee Women in the Eighteenth Century," paper presented at "Private Lives/Public Roles: A Symposium on North Carolina Women's History," 1990, Raleigh, N.C.; Theda Perdue, *Slavery and the Evolution of Cherokee Society* (Knoxville: University of Tennessee Press, 1979); Thomas Hatley, "Cherokee Women Farmers Hold Their Ground," in Mitchell, *Appalachian Frontiers*, pp. 37–51.

59. Put another way, day laborers who boarded with families earned $.50 to $1.00 per day, while day laborers who did *not* board earned $.75 to $1.00. For carpenters who did not board, the daily wage was $1.25. Farm laborers (who typically boarded with their employers) earned $9.00 per month.

60. One household had a domestic servant.

61. I would venture to say that tenancy, casual labor, and use of slave labor were three strategies used interchangeably by western North Carolina farmers, depending on access. From the figures cited previously, one can estimate the value of slave labor in agricultural production as somewhere between $.35 and $1.00 per day. An important caveat here is that we need also to factor in the costs of maintaining households, including slaves. This is difficult to do, given the limits of the 1860 census. See Robert Tracy McKenzie, "Wealth and Income: The Preindustrial Structure of East Tennessee in 1860," *Appalachian Journal* 21 (Spring 1994): esp. 270–71, 278 nn 36 and 37.

62. This is Inscoe's major point in *Mountain Masters*. See esp. pp. 59–86.

63. Ibid., pp. 70–73; quote pp. 70–71.

64. According to McKinney, a number of the letters to Governor Vance were from women decrying the fact that they were forced to return to cloth making due to the closure of local stores during the Civil War. He contends that many of the women in mountain communities had lost the skills necessary to cloth production ("Other Victims," p. 15). Deyton argues just the opposite point, contending that the precipitous *increase* in homemade manufactures during the mid-nineteenth century was due to expanded levels of cloth production ("Toe River Valley," p. 453).

65. According to Rolla Milton Tryon, the categories of homemade manufactures included "1) wearing apparel and household textile supplies; 2) household implements, utensils, furniture, necessities, and comforts; and 3) farming implements, building materials, and general supplies" (*Household Manufactures in the United States, 1640–1860* [Chicago: University of Chicago Press, 1917], p. 188).

66. For example, individuals would gather at various farmsteads to collectively produce quilts, molasses, and other goods. See Dunn, *Cades Cove*, p. 188.

67. Arizona Hughes, *Aunt Zona's Web*, as told to Thomas C. Chapman (Banner Elk, N.C.: Puddingstone Press, 1976), p. 45.

68. Ibid., pp. 42, 45–46, 53–54. Zona's recollections run to other topics and forms of home manufacture: drying apples and cherries, carding wool, weaving, etc. For example, "In the evenings after school during the fall months, I would hitch a mule

to a sled and drive up on the mountain to bring back apples. We would peel these apples for drying—we dried apples all winter, and it took a great deal of time every evening to peel, cut and place these apples on dryers. The frame dryers were placed over the large fireplace in the big old-fashioned kitchen. Aunt Susie dried pounds and pounds of fruit every winter, and these were not only used by the family, but they were also used as trading items for coffee, sugar, and other staples" (p. 45).

69. Ibid., pp. 42–43.

70. This is a point that Tryon makes in her study of household manufactures throughout the United States. Whereas home manufactures had dropped to an average per-capita value of $.78 for the United States as a whole and $2.06 for the state of North Carolina, the per-capita value for Yancey County was $5.00. Indeed, in Yancey County the rate of production of home manufactures had risen dramatically from 1840 to 1850 and had fallen moderately by 1860. See Table 1.

71. There were also tanneries, smithies, a wool carder, and a linseed oil mill. In many instances, a single individual owned more than one enterprise. Milton Penland, for example, owned a tannery, a smithy, and a gristmill. Interestingly enough, one of the twenty-three entrepreneurs listed was a woman named Lucinda Bennett, who operated a gristmill of moderate size, producing 420 pounds of flour valued at $186 in 1860. See *Eighth Census, Schedule 5: Products of Industry.*

72. As part of the arrangement, the merchant would furnish raw materials and specify quantities and types of finished products. Laborers would work the materials and return the finished goods to the merchant. The advantage to the laborer was that such work was performed at home and could be fitted around the exigencies of farm work and other household duties.

73. In Yancey County one system of outwork was fashioned around the processing of mica for sale to area merchants. This was work performed by women at the turn of the century on farmsteads and later in factories.

74. See Thomas Dublin, "Women and Outwork in a Nineteenth-Century New England Town: Fitzwilliam, New Hampshire, 1830–1850," in *The Countryside in the Age of Capitalist Transformation: Essays in the Social History of Rural America*, ed. Steven Hahn and Jonathan Prude (Chapel Hill: University of North Carolina Press, 1985), esp. pp. 52–53.

Class, Section, and Culture in Nineteenth-Century West Virginia Politics

From its creation in 1863 the state of West Virginia has constituted the only Appalachian political unit above the county level that has provided a continuous focus for policymaking, electoral politics, and full arrays of executive, judicial, and legislative offices and functions. The achievement of West Virginia statehood is therefore a landmark event and has tended to dominate the state's political historiography. According to historians' traditional view, statehood represented a social as well as a political upheaval: the liberation of an Appalachian smallholder democracy from the rule of an oligarchy based in the plantation districts of Tidewater Virginia. I first challenged this view in 1972, in an article that argued, first, that western Virginia was dominated by an Appalachian version of the traditional Virginia oligarchy, an elite whose power was rooted in the economic circumstances of the mountains but also in the same inegalitarian constitutional features that sustained the plantation oligarchy of eastern Virginia; and second, that this western Virginia elite, having fought sectional battles with its counterpart in eastern Virginia for the better part of two generations, both opposed and survived the creation of West Virginia, fighting on with considerable success to preserve its leadership for a generation after 1863, at the expense both of the leaders who created the new state and of industrialists who asserted their own claim to leadership shortly after the Civil War. These findings are presented here in revised form, with annotations that suggest the relevance of my research to the subsequent investigations of social historians in other districts of the Appalachian region.[1]

The preindustrial or traditional political system in West Virginia relied on kinship, propinquity, and face-to-face communication as its organizational sinews and represented a blend of Virginia political institutions and practices modified by the circumstances of the "arrested frontier" of the Appalachian backwoods. It was strongest in mountainous districts beyond the reach of the emerging industrial centers and in the agricultural highland valleys adjacent and tributary to the Valley of Virginia. To understand the social basis of this system, it is necessary to go back well before 1863 or 1850 and to begin with two facts that are easily lost sight of if attention is fixed on the climactic achievement of statehood: first, West Virginia was then, as it is now, a mountainous country with the consequent impediments to the movement of people, goods, and information, and second, before 1863 it remained part of Virginia, notwithstanding premonitions of an eventual separation, and so remained subject to the influence of the Old Dominion's oligarchical political institutions.

The West Virginia hills, present in one form or another in nearly every corner of the state, are indeed majestic and grand, as noted in the official anthem, but they are not all of the same size, shape, or origin. The geological history of the Appalachian mountain system divided the future state between two physiographic "provinces." The Appalachian Plateau province (locally called the Allegheny Plateau) covers more than two-thirds of the state and slopes northward and westward from the highest peaks of the Allegheny Mountains. The plateau presented to travelers and settlers a labyrinth of razorback ridges and narrow valleys deeply incised by the Ohio River's easternmost tributaries, but the streams themselves created strips of fertile bottomlands that offered far greater possibilities for agriculture than the thin soils and precipitous slopes of the surrounding hills. East of the plateau, comprising the tier of counties that now form West Virginia's border with Virginia, lies the "ridge-and-valley" province of the central Appalachians. Here were to be found altitudinous but relatively broad valleys resembling the nearby Valley of Virginia and connected to the Great Valley by the watersheds of the Potomac and upper New Rivers and also by "wind gaps" following the beds of ancient eastward-flowing streams whose waters had been diverted by subsequent upheavals to the west. Thanks to the limestone substrata that underlie the ridge-and-valley province, the soils of these highland valleys are naturally fertile and afforded West Virginia's most attractive pasture and farmlands, although these highlands contained few of the state's deposits of commercially exploitable minerals and fuels.

Separating the two provinces in the northeast is the Allegheny Front, a central ridge that divides the Potomac watershed from that of the Monongahela (an Ohio tributary). In the southeast, the geological divide is not a watershed divide; here the boundary between plateau and ridge-and-valley provinces is less clearly demarcated, but in practical terms the high ridges extending north and south of the New River marked the limits of easy accessibility from the east. The canyon of the New River cuts an "intricate" path through these ridges, flowing northwest to link the present southeastern border counties with the Ohio via a major tributary, the Great Kanawha. But in practical terms, New River Gorge was as much a barrier as a link until the Chesapeake & Ohio Railroad (C&O) was completed in 1872–76. Virginia officials who earlier sought to exploit the route for water transportation found that the canyon's perpendicular cliffs and narrow channels made for splendid scenery. From the standpoint of navigation, however, the scene was "awful and discouraging."[2]

During the late colonial period, settlers who penetrated the western Virginia mountains established narrow ribbons of settlement in the valleys east of New River Gorge and the Allegheny Front or else took giant steps across the highlands to outposts along the Monongahela, Ohio, and Kanawha. Consequently two somewhat distinct regions developed, one in the ridge-and-valley province and one on the northern and western edge of the plateau. The former lay along the present border with Virginia and occupied the Bluestone, Greenbrier, South Branch (Potomac), and other highland valleys paralleling the border ridges, along with two Shenandoah Valley counties at the tip of the eastern panhandle. Here was to be found in 1860 a farming population that was for the most part drawn from the Valley of Virginia. These districts shared the valley's peculiar mixture of Virginian style and Pennsylvanian agriculture and reproduced its characteristic features of compact, stone-built market towns and roundhead religions mellowed by time and wealth. Another region lay northwest across the Alleghenies in the bottomlands and foothills bordering the western rivers. The northwest matured in the company of eastern Ohio and western Pennsylvania. Here, too, farming predominated, but the mid-nineteenth century saw a quickened pace of manufacturing and mining developed in river and railroad towns like Wheeling, Parkersburg, Clarksburg, Fairmont, and Grafton in the north and Charleston in the south. But while the differences between these two regions were important, so were the similarities. Both contained native Virginian populations of British, German, and Scotch-Irish descent, the majority of them small farmers and herdsmen, although large farms and slaveholding were more common in the east, as were manufacturing and (after 1850) mining and lumbering in the northwest. Both regions harbored divisions of interest, loyalty, and principle that produced in each a genuine civil war in 1861–65, although again, Confederates predominated in one, Union men in the other. Moreover, while the two regions were divided by mountain barriers in their midst, they were also united by the enduring circumstances of the Appalachian frontier.[3]

Between the eastern and northwestern settlements in antebellum western Virginia, and penetrating deep within each, lay a wildly beautiful "interior" consisting of the peaks and ridges of the Alleghenies and the rugged uplands of the plateau. Avoided by the earliest settlers, the highland coves, hollows, and tablelands were gradually occupied by their descendants and by newcomers from eastern Virginia and (in smaller numbers) from New England and Europe. These highlanders, alternately romanticized and excoriated by later observers as "contemporary ancestors" and "a god-forgotten race," established a "domestic economy" based on family farming, stock raising, and the harvesting of forest products. While travelers who visited remote highland districts regarded them as isolated, in fact they enjoyed a good deal of contact with the outside world, both through the visits of itinerants—merchants, peddlers, stock buyers and drovers, politicians, preachers, and the travelers themselves—and through episodic travel by backwoodsmen themselves, particular through moving livestock and forest products to markets. The isolation of the interior was therefore relative, but the difficulties of movement through the mountain terrain were sufficient to ensure that debate over transportation improvement would remain a focus of politics through most of the nineteenth century. "All our supplies come from tne head of navigation on the Kanawha over a road remarkable for the beauty and sublimity of its scenery, the depth of its mud, and the dizzy precipices which bound it on either side," wrote an Ohio soldier campaigning in the interior south of New River Gorge in the spring of 1862. Such problems made the Civil War in West Virginia "an affair of outposts" after the early battles that saved the northwest—and the Baltimore & Ohio Railroad (B&O)—for the Union in 1861. The same circumstances shaped peacetime social, economic, and political life in West Virginia, before and after the Civil War.[4]

Paradoxical though it seems, West Virginians were united in that they faced to a greater or lesser extent common obstacles to movement and communication posed by their mountainous home. The demands of the terrain created networks of settlement penetrating upward into the mountains along dividing streambeds until the spring at the head of the last hollow was reached. Neighbors who lived quite close in terms of air distance could be separated by an arduous journey across or around the intervening ridges. Thus internal differences were defined less by prominent ecological features than by subtler variations in the quality and accessibility of land and by the interpenetration of people who, as the sayings go, "live[d] on the bottom and look[ed] down on the people on top" with those who "raise[d] corn on the hillside and the devil in the valley."[5] During the preindustrial era, such conditions were present to some extent everywhere in West Virginia except in the most populous districts along the Ohio and the Potomac.

West Virginia history might have been very different had the B&O succeeded in its original plan to build to the Ohio via the Valley of Virginia and New River Gorge. But the influence of Richmond merchants first held up the railroad's Virginia charter and then forced it by law to follow the Maryland and Pennsylvania borders. The B&O reached Wheeling in 1853, too late to help in that city's struggle for commercial supremacy with Pittsburgh but exerting a transforming effect on older settlements such as Martinsburg and Clarksburg and calling into existence new ones such as Keyser, Grafton, and Fairmont. A subsidiary line, the Northwestern Virginia Railroad, joined Grafton and Parkersburg in 1857 and became the initial link in the B&O's southwestern branch to Cincinnati and St. Louis. South of the B&O, however, travel remained difficult until the completion of the C&O across southern West Virginia in 1873. Charleston, capital of the potentially rich Kanawha region and of the state after 1870, anxiously awaited the C&O and the coming of a long-anticipated but slow-to-materialize "Kanawha boom." Although it lay closer than any other West Virginia town to the heart of the great Appalachian coalfield and boasted steamboat connections to Wheeling, Parkersburg, and Cincinnati, Charleston remained remote and isolated, separated from northern West Virginia by a combination rail and river journey that under the best conditions could consume the better part of two days. The quandary of a West Virginia politician of 1870 was typical. "Are you going to Charleston?" he asked a fellow statesman. "The Ohio river is blocked with ice. How shall we get there?" A band of northern West Virginia legislators faced the same problem in 1871 and struck out overland to cover the eighty-odd miles between railhead and capital. Six days later "we arrived here on foot . . . , our wagon having broken down three miles out. . . . Some days we made 17 miles by [dint?] of traveling 18 hours. we ate things clean and unclean, and slept like sardines—heads and tails—." "It seems as if we were almost outside of the world here," wrote a member of the constitutional convention of 1872.[6] After two more years the authorities put their effects on a boat and returned the capital to Wheeling, where it remained until coming to final rest in Charleston in 1885. Even after the completion of the C&O through Charleston to the Ohio, northern and southern West Virginia remained without a direct rail connection east of the Ohio River until the end of the century. The Norfolk & Western's completion connected the southern counties along the Virginia and Kentucky borders with the Ohio in 1892. The Virginian Railway, which opened the coalfields of the southern interior counties, was not completed until 1907.

Communications development followed the pace of transportation improvement. In 1872 it took a week to ten days to get a letter from Charleston to Monongahela Valley communities, a distance of 150–180 miles. As late as 1879 no more than half of West Virginia's counties enjoyed daily postal connections, and there was no north-south through postal route save along the Ohio. Telegraph service followed the railroads. Daily newspapers were limited to Wheeling before 1880 and to Wheeling, Charleston, Parkersburg, Clarksburg, and Martinsburg before 1890. Weeklies, which scarcely existed before 1850, followed a similar pattern of development. Of the thirty secular weeklies published in 1860, fourteen were based in towns along the B&O or the Ohio; ten others were published in towns in the eastern valleys. In addition, both Wheeling dailies published weekly and triweekly versions of their newspapers. Six religious or agricultural-literary publications issued exclusively from railroad and river towns.

In these circumstances one would not expect to find a highly organized political system providing linkages along the axial lines of regularized transportation and communication but, rather, a loosely organized system based on the networks of settlements, roads, and rivers connecting the interior districts with the courthouse and market towns of the east and northwest. The system that prevailed in preindustrial West Virginia was in fact the system of antebellum Virginia, modified by the special circumstances of the mountain frontier.

"As every member of the Bar knows," wrote former governor William A. MacCorkle in 1928, "the land law of West Virginia is peculiar."[7] Peculiar indeed, the law reflected the activities of several generations of large and small speculators, spasmodic and inconsistent attempts at revision and reform, and a chaotic system of land registry inherited from Virginia. Land reforms during Thomas Jefferson's administration as governor (1779) quashed the most extravagant claims of colonial speculators to Appalachian land, but there remained land warrants issued to veterans of the Indian and revolutionary wars and the preemption rights of pioneer occupants guaranteed by the law of 1779. A lively trade in western Virginia land claims developed soon after the Revolution and contributed during the Federalist period to the granting of lavish titles to tracts of 500,000 acres or more. The commonwealth's inconsistent application of tax delinquency laws furthered confusion by creating a welter of overlapping and conflicting claims. Patient but costly adjudication of these claims eventually quieted titles in the more thickly settled districts during the antebellum decades. Elsewhere the confusion persisted into the industrial era. Webster County, for example, an interior county rich in untapped timber and coal resources, carried in 1880 claims on its land books accounting to five times the actual acreage available. In Nicholas County titles were not quieted until 1892.

Initially the most active speculators in western Virginia lands were nonresident merchants or politicians, but from the 1780s on a trend was evident whereby resident land agents, lawyers, surveyors, and other officials deputized by eastern authorities or speculators to handle the land alienation process began to acquire significant amounts of the land themselves. Of fifty-two Virginia legislators who received western land grants of 10,000 acres or more between 1775 and 1800, twenty-two represented western constituencies. Cases in point were George and Edward Jackson, founders of western Virginia's and West Virginia's most prominent political dynasty. George Jackson, a lawyer who represented western districts in the Virginia Convention of 1788, the general assembly, and Congress, led a successful fight to prevent recognition of the colonial Indiana Company's extensive claims in northwestern Virginia. He himself acquired title to more than 60,000 acres in Monongahela valley counties between 1797 and 1804. His brother Edward, a legislator, surveyor, and commissioner of lands, acquired 72,867 acres in his own name and 51,936 in partnership with others during the same period. The historian of Nicholas County provides an example of the networks of influence involved in such acquisitions in describing two large local tracts owned by Virginians resident in nearby older and more thickly settled counties. "McClung [legislator from Greenbrier County to the east] looked up the lands desired, Welch [public surveyor] surveyed and Moore [United States congressman and senator from Lexington in the valley] secured the grants."[8]

Important breakthroughs for resident western speculators came in 1831 and 1837, when the general assembly declared forfeit and liable to entry all previous grants returned delinquent for taxes and transferred the point of condemnation and sale from Richmond to the circuit courts of the counties wherein the lands were located. This legislation, accompanied by population growth and a mounting volume of litigation as settlers and speculators alike sought to clear their titles, enabled ambitious westerners to acquire land as a form of payment in kind for services as land agents or attorneys, while their direct access to local information about the value and availability of vacant or delinquent lands facilitated direct purchases of grants under the terms of the reforms. It was all perfectly legal. Writing of a series of deals involving the local commissioner of delinquent lands and two lawyer-legislators in the 1850s, a county historian remarks that "there is no evidence of sharp practices. . . . The old deeds show that the sales of forfeited lands at the Courthouse were always well-advertised."[9] But the relative isolation of most western districts, plus low literacy rates, poor roads, and limited newspaper circulation and postal service, would have ensured a minimum of competition at the courthouse sales. Equally important, these factors place a political premium on the itinerant nature of the lawyer's profession, which brought him into frequent personal contact with backwoods constituents and made him the principal bearer of political information and influence and the star performer at the sociable quarterly court days.

In these circumstances, there developed in western Virginia a resident ruling class that, as it emerged to maturity after 1830, drew its most influential leaders from lawyers who specialized in land litigation and speculation. Based in the larger courthouse towns and plying the backwoods judicial circuits where they enjoyed a monopoly of legal expertise, these same lawyers also provided political linkages between and within the isolated mountain settlements. Governor MacCorkle, who saw the system in operation as a young lawyer in the Kanawha region during the 1870s, described the political advantages of the circuit-riding lawyer: "[He] knew the condition, financial, social, political, and personal of almost every man in his circuit. He knew the lines and the corners of the land surveys. He was the confidant of a vast number of people. . . . He was continually meeting old friends and making new ones and he was the center of attention at the court."[10] The most successful practitioners retired from regular circuit work after becoming established but retained regional influence that extended outward through the interior from one of several courthouse towns: Clarksburg and Weston in north central West Virginia, Parkersburg and Charleston on the west, and Lewisburg, Union, Beverly, and Romney in the upland valleys of the east.

The attorneys who appeared at the bar of these and neighboring interior courthouses and who also appear on the published lists of antebellum land grants constitute a galaxy of West Virginia political leaders both before and after the Civil War. Moreover, the published grants constitute only those titles acquired directly from the commonwealth in public sales of vacant or delinquent land. They do not record acreage acquired privately from other purchasers or litigants. Allen T. Caperton's grants in Nicholas County amount only to 10,000 acres, for example, but the Caperton estate there consisted of over 90,000 acres when it was liquidated in 1879. Johnson N. Camden's 5,113 acres in grants in nearby Braxton County account for less that a quarter of the 22,000 he accumulated during his youthful speculating career.

Political and economic advantages of the antebellum western elite were cumulative and hereditary. Local offices, which were eligible to nonresidents and (until 1852) appointive, provided sinecures for impecunious relatives and training posts for younger ones. The more successful lawyers developed regional influence and competed with one another for judgeships and seats in the legislature and in Congress. Even after state and local officers became elective in 1852, the viva voce method of voting preserved habits of political deference to local notables, while of course lawyers retained the prerogatives of bench and bar. Among nineteen prominent antebellum politicians surveyed, seven men held appointive local offices at the outset of their careers; ten held elective posts. One started with a state appointment; one was beaten in his first try for office by another member of the group. All but one held office by the time they were thirty; eleven started between the ages of seventeen and twenty-five. Fourteen of the nineteen served as commonwealth's attorneys (prosecutors), seven of them in one or more counties in which they did not reside. The remaining five entered legislative or constituent assemblies directly. Seats in the legislature and in Congress went to well-connected men as young as twenty-six. The later offices of the group included one federal, four state, and eight circuit court judgeships; one federal and three state executive posts; and eight congressional and at least nineteen legislative seats, not to mention candidacies that ended in defeat. The list covers Whigs and Democrats, Virginia and West Virginia, before and after the Civil War.[11]

Some idea of how antebellum political institutions worked to promote oligarchy in western as well as in eastern Virginia may be had from the biographies of two West Virginians who are usually presented as self-made men. The biographers of Thomas Jonathan "Stonewall" Jackson usually present him as one bereft "of the traditional pose of fame. He was a mountain man [with] the blunt honesty, the firmness, and the self-reliance of a frontiersman from the remote western parts of Virginia."[12] In truth Jackson was a cadet of a powerful and "very clannish" family whose political eminence has already been noted. Before his untimely death at age thirty-six, Stonewall's father had already served two terms as federal commissioner of internal revenue for the district of western Virginia. His mother's remarriage to a ne'er-do-well lawyer in 1832 was promptly followed by the step-father's appointment to a clerkship in the newly formed interior county of Fayette. Stonewall himself held a local office in Lewis County at the extra-constitutionally early age of seventeen. Even his appointment to the United States Military Academy owed something to family influence. As his widow remarked of the future general's departure for West Point, "His friends had done for him all they could," which was a lot.[13] Jackson's military genius was his own, but without his "friends" the Confederate Cromwell, like the figure in Gray's "Elegy," might have lived longer and died guiltless of his country's blood.

Like Jackson, Johnson N. Camden was born into a cadet branch of a politically prominent family; unlike him, Camden lived to see and to shape the transition in West Virginia to an industrial political economy, but he too benefited from the older regime. Camden also held local office in his teens and won an appointment to West Point. But he returned to West Virginia after two disappointing years on the Hudson and took up the family avocation of law, politics, and land speculation. In 1850 Camden was admitted to the bar of Braxton County, an interior county south of Weston whose roster of clerks, deputies, and legislators included his father and two of his uncles. Braxton's appointed commonwealth's attorney at the time happened to be Samuel Price of Lewisburg. Upon Price's resignation a few months later, young Camden was appointed to succeed him. Then in 1852, the office having become elective, he won the prosecutor's job for Nicholas County, where he had never resided until be came to take up his duties. Shortly thereafter, Camden resigned his post to take up banking and law in Weston. Although his activities in politics languished at this point, his interest in land did not; it was though land speculation that Camden entered the new Burning Springs oil field and embarked on a new career as a captain of industry during the Civil War.

"I have had some experience in office," Samuel Price wrote in his bid for a

U.S. senator's seat in West Virginia in 1874; "nearly all the offices from an overseer of the road (I was never a constable) to that of Lieut Govr have been filled by me."[14] Apparently quite modest appointments could found or extend a family's influence. John J. Jackson, Sr., like his cousin Stonewall, got his start with an appointment to West Point. He was the illegitimate son of a congressman and the grandson of another; "Peculiar circumstances, not necessary to be stated in this letter, render his appointment desirable to me," his father wrote to the appointing official.[15] While Jackson subsequently served six terms in the Virginia general assembly, his principal office was that of prosecutor. He held the job in Wood County from 1826 to 1852 and served concurrently in the neighboring county of Ritchie from 1842 to 1852. All three of *his* sons held the same office in Wood (Parkersburg) and/or in one of the less populous neighboring counties, two of them after it became elective in 1852. The linchpin of the system, as elsewhere in the South, was a co-optative and omnicompetent county court. Having been "by the courtesy of the County Court, . . . permitted to [practice] before it almost as soon as he began to study [law]," Jackson, Sr., "remained a warm advocate of this court even to the end."[16]

The elite of western Virginia thus constituted a ruling class, in the sense that it sought and won governmental power to protect and advance its interests, to provide for its prosperity, and to regulate the admission of outsiders on appropriate terms. To be sure, it was a buckskin elite by comparison with the traditional model of Virginia gentility. The men who organized the county court of Nicholas in 1818 provided well for themselves and their progeny in the distribution of civil and militia offices. The group included this backwoods district's first slaveholder, small-scale rentiers and speculators, and other substantial citizens who, with Louise McNeill's quasi-fictional hero of *Gauley Mountain*, "Counted years by the harvest yield / And wealth by the surveyed line."[17] But the same men also combined these interests with such homely trades as milling and carpentry, the gathering of ginseng, and the harvesting of souls. If the land alienation system allowed large tracts to be held for speculation, others originally large were eventually parceled among numerous offspring. Oral voting and the large (and difficult) distances between polling places preserved the hegemony of local notables, even after offices became elective in 1852. This does not mean that ordinary people were wholly without leverage, however. The predominantly oral means of communication meant that the transmission of political information was a two-way process. Unlike those on the receiving end of modern mass communication, listeners at the court day hustings and political entertainment could talk back. Although we have lost the sense of the dialogue, we can be reasonably sure that it took place. Preindustrial constituents constituted a public, not a mass.

Backwoods notables in turn exercised a good deal of leverage on their counterparts in the courthouse towns. The Nicholas leaders forced reluctant Kanawha and Greenbrier speculators to support their quest for a separate county by a strategic withdrawal of votes. The politicians, themselves competing for favor at Richmond, were forced to submit. The founder of the Camden clan, a backwoods preacher who combined Methodist exhortation with land investments, helped carve Lewis from Harrison in similar circumstances in 1817. It is not unlikely that a similar process was involved in the thirty-one counties created in West Virginia between 1815 and 1861.

The western elite was open as well as flexible. In its higher echelons, able and ambitious young men launched careers via ancient though carefully regulated routes. One of the oldest western leaders was Joseph Johnson, an untrained but talented debater who took on and defeated a Harrison County legislator who had held the job for twenty-two years. This attracted the eye of one of the earlier Judge Jacksons, whose patronage launched Johnson on a long career in Congress and other high places. Samuel Price and Charles James Faulkner married close to the center of established wealth and standing in the Greenbrier and Shenandoah Valleys, respectively. In the northwest, Jonathan M. Bennett, himself the son of a prosperous farmer, married another Jackson and was one of those who helped send cousin Stonewall into the world. Johnson N. Camden of Weston married the daughter of a Wheeling judge. Evermont Ward, a locally celebrated jurist and land speculator in southwestern West Virginia, was the illegitimate son of the region's first congressman, while his maternal grandfather was the first sheriff of Cabell County. A West Virginia Namier could probably disclose hundreds of such "connections," linking the networks of local and regional influence in subtle but far-reaching ways. This is not to suggest that the linkages embraced all points of contention or access. Rather, they lent to the competitive stirring of early Appalachian capitalism the stability of extended families and cohesive communities.

The point should be made also that land speculation in advance of the transportation improvements that made West Virginia's natural resources exploitable was no more profitable than alternative forms of investment. But there is the further point that there were few alternative forms of investment under antebellum conditions. When the discovery of oil in the Parkersburg area presented an alternative on the eve of the Civil War, Camden seized it with alacrity and put his interior land accumulations on the shelf in favor of oil production and refining. For most of the governing class, however, its achievement lay in that it adapted successfully the political institutions of antebellum Virginia to the circumstances of the mountain environment and managed to obtain the dominant access to the region's premier resource, land. It is in this sense that the preindustrial political economy best reveals its class bias, notwithstanding the homely and mellow character of the elite.

Although West Virginia historians such as Charles Ambler interpreted it as a struggle between mountain Democrats and plantation oligarchs, much of the sectional tension that colors Virginia history can be read as an attempt by the western elite to expand its local autonomy.[18] The Democratic reforms of 1830 and 1851 did not disturb the basis of its local hegemony, while both enlarged the west's representation in statewide political balances. In this regard it is noteworthy that the first reform was followed by the land legislation that quashed the claims of nonresident capitalists to western land and placed control of its further distribution in the hands of resident lawyer-politicians. Their task after 1837 was twofold. First, they worked through the courts to quiet surviving land titles and to prevent the resurrection of eighteenth- and early nineteenth-century claims. This met the need of constituents in the thickly occupied districts and also served local speculators by strengthening the purchase appeal of western Virginia land. Second, they had to prevent the application of the same distraint and forfeiture proceedings to their own post-1837 acquisitions that the reforms applied to earlier claims. There seems to have been no threat of this happening under Virginia auspices, but the West Virginia statehood movement posed a serious threat indeed. The constitutional convention of 1861–62, in which land lawyers were notably underrepresented, entertained a proposal to apply forfeiture proceedings to tax delinquent grants irrespective of age. Benjamin Smith and James H. Brown of Kanawha County, two veteran land lawyers who had remained loyal to the Union, managed by appealing to the tangled nature of land matters and to their own expertise to have this measure amended and then recommitted and killed by a select committee on land titles headed by themselves. A potentially more dangerous situation arose from the application of proscriptive measures after the Civil War. Among the devices adopted by postwar Republican legislatures to purge the new state of rebel influence were attorney's and suitor's oaths that severely compromised former Confederates' ability to defend themselves from suits brought by Unionist neighbors seeking compensation for war damages or trespass. To what, if any, extent these measures resulted in the expropriation of rebel property cannot be determined without following an intricate trail through the courts. Most of the forfeited land sold under state auspices after the war, however, went to veteran speculators. The largest postwar grant, involving 23,264 acres in Logan County granted to former (and future) Circuit Court Judge Evermont Ward of Cabell in 1870–73, seems to have involved in part reacquisition of earlier grants. At the least, however, the proscriptive measures help to account for the furious unanimity with which veteran leaders determined to rewrite the West Virginia constitution and, in Price's words, to "get a good judicial system & a good county organization."[19]

Significantly, the antebellum leaders did not seek to abolish the new state after the war, only to control it. Members of the antebellum elite sought political power in part as a means to stimulate the transportation improvements that would unlock the treasures of their wilderness. At Richmond this aim translated chiefly as a drive to expand Virginia's program of state-sponsored internal improvements. It is noteworthy again that the reforms of 1851 were followed by a revitalization of this program under the administration (1856–60) of Virginia governor Henry A. Wise. Later, direct access to Washington as West Virginians opened to veteran speculators (as it did to their industrialist antagonists in post-Reconstruction politics) the prospect of federal expenditures and also private contacts with eastern and British capitalists.

It is open to question, however, whether this search for overhead capital would alone have led to a division of Virginia. The last antebellum decade was one of sectional reconciliation, east and west. Among the reasons already noted were the prospective achievement of western goals in the areas of legislative apportionment and transportation, and the west's growing influence in statewide politics. Another factor was growing eastern concern for internal unity in the face of the deepening crisis over slavery. Virginia's first popular gubernatorial vote in 1851 pitted two westerners, with Joseph Johnson, the Democrat, victorious over George W. Summers, the Whig. In 1855 Henry Wise launched his "successful and spectacular" gubernatorial campaign, appealing across earlier sectional and partisan lines. A Tidewater Whig turned Democrat, Wise had worked for sectional compromise in 1851 and initially presented himself as a moderate on national issues. But his efforts increasingly drew him and his followers into competition with the orthodox State's Rights faction led by Senator Robert M. T. Hunter. Westerners fell out on both sides of the Hunter-Wise rivalry, but since each leader sought increasingly to outbid the other as a champion of "Southern Rights," the effect beneath the surface division was to strengthen underlying loyalty to Virginia and to the South. The competition also recruited other Whig converts, further undercutting the potential appeal of separatism in the West.

The nature of antebellum western Virginia politics is further suggested by faintly glimpsed traces of opposition from below. To what extent was this opposition bound up with the statehood movement? This is one of the unresolved questions of West Virginia history. The separatist leaders, although they manifested their own kinds of social and economic conservatism, denounced "the court house cliques" of antebellum times and borrowed an Ohio broom to sweep away Virginian cobwebs. Despite lawyer Brown's best efforts, the new state constitution mandated universal free education, replaced the county courts with the township form of local government, established the secret ballot in place of oral voting, reorganized the judiciary, and buttressed these changes with annual elections and other democratic reforms. Meanwhile, as the Union armies probed deep into the interior, Union general Jacob D. Cox recruited two regiments of troops from among backwoodsmen in the upper Kanawha Valley, districts whose established leaders had by that time crept into neutrality or fled east across the Alleghenies with the armies of Floyd and Wise. Equally suggestive are islands of Republican voting strength that persisted long after the war in interior counties such as Upshur, Grant, and Wyoming. Upshur County, thoroughly sacked by land hunters from New York, Philadelphia, Clarksburg, Weston, and Beverly in the half-century before its creation in 1851, became a Unionist stronghold in the upper Monongahela region, offering refuge to loyalists fleeing the Confederate valleys nearby. In the east, Grant County, occupying the mountainous reaches west of the South Branch Valley, was apparently as Union-loving as the neighboring district was Confederate. After the war, Grant and neighboring Hardy County vied with each other as the "banner" Republican and Democratic counties in the state, respectively, while a similar though less drastic difference persisted between Upshur and neighboring Randolph. Less Republican, but even more anomalous by comparison with its neighbors, was Wyoming County in the southern interior. Here the remote tableland on the western flank of Flat Top Mountain sheltered local Unionists and refugees who, protected by the mountains' precipitous eastern front, formed an unintimidated outpost well in advance of Federal lines. Morgan County, occupying the ridges between the Shenandoah and South Branch counties, but unlike the others enjoying a connection with Federal garrisons via the B&O, was another outpost of backwoods Republicanism during the remainder of the century, this one in the staunchly Democratic eastern panhandle.[20]

One of the most suggestive hints of backwoods upheaval was the sudden emergence to political prominence of another itinerant profession with wide contacts in interior districts: circuit-riding preachers of the Methodist, Baptist, and other evangelical sects. No fewer than fourteen preachers or licensed lay exporters sat in the West Virginia constitutional convention, where they followed the leadership of Gordon Battelle. A Methodist and antislavery spokesman, Battelle was also the author of the aforementioned land reform proposal that the lawyers exerted themselves to defeat. Both Wyoming and Upshur were represented by minister delegates; Upshur's representative spoke against the practice of oral voting, giving as one of his reasons the instructions of his constituents. A contemporary places at twenty-nine the number of evangelists who served in the West Virginia legislature from 1863 to 1872. On the hustings, according to Ambler, "While the politicians and the elite who had so gratuitously assured their friends in the east that 'the Trans-Allegheny will be with you to a man' were either fighting to make good their promises or remaining neutral to save their hides and their property, Methodist Episcopal circuit riders and their allies were penetrating the remotest reaches of [the state] to preach the gospel of salvation to 'the people,' and rally them to fight for the Union."[21] In the Kanawha region, preachers acted as scouts for the Union armies and helped to recruit loyal regiments in the no-man's-land between Charleston and the Confederate territory east of New River Gorge. Suggestively, too, the lawyer-dominated constitutional convention of 1872 debated a proposal to ban ministers of the gospel from the further holding of office.

What obscure form of the class struggle, if any, do these portents reveal? It is impossible to say on the basis of existing evidence. As Ambler concedes, the men involved, like most of the rank-and-file separatists, were obscure. Many left West Virginia during or soon after the war; others, including "most of those from the central, southern, and eastern counties, dropped out of sight."[22] With them went most of the evidence of submerged radicalism during the statehood era, especially since Battelle's death in the field in August 1862 stilled the most eloquent ministerial voice. As for the anti-preacher reaction in 1872, an ex-Confederate lawyer, Samuel Woods, explained that "many people through the State are in favor of proscribing preachers [because] the M E preachers who got into the Legislatures behaved so shamefully."[23] But he did not say how they had offended. It is clear that at least in part the preachers' activities involved religious differences over slavery and jurisdictional struggles between northern and southern churches. "We have the Northern Methodist church to encounter," wrote a state-rights Democrat in 1860; "Although the members and ministers in general are sound on the slavery question, . . . their associating with the Northern Conference and getting their religious papers from the free states tend to create among them an anti-slavery feeling. We have the Southern branch of that church also. Its ministers and members take strong pro-slavery grounds, justifying and sustaining it by the precepts of the Bible and common humanity."[24] Otherwise the sudden emergence and disappearance of the preachers remain unexplained. The proposed ban in 1872 was defeated by a vote of 38 to 26. Republicans (of whom there were only seven voting) were unanimously against it, and Democrats were divided 55 to 45 percent. Lawyers in the convention divided on the issue in the same proportion as other members. Moreover, the vote does not correlate to any impressive extent with other roll calls in the convention, nor is it interpretable in terms of recognizable religious, sectional, or fractional alignments within the convention. Woods correctly predicted that even without the ban, preachers would be "effectually proscribed by public opinion" from politics thereafter.[25] Whether or not public opinion was in fact the agent, preachers certainly died a political death after 1872, except on issues (like prohibition) appropriate to their cloth. At the very least, however, the preachers' impact testifies to the importance of itinerancy and face-to-face communications in backwoods political life. "Our Southern methodist preachers who find their way into every neighborhood should be furnished with documents to enable them to . . . be well informed as to the controversy between the North and the South," a western supporter told Senator Hunter, "and in a quiet way infuse it into the minds of the people."[26]

While the preachers' behavior during the statehood era remains mysterious, that of the erstwhile rulers of western Virginia does not. As Francis H. Pierpont stated in his inaugural address as governor of Unionist Virginia, "The leading politicians of Virginia, both in the East and West, embarked on the scheme of secession . . . the Governor, Lieut.-Governor and all the State officials, and four out of five of the Judges of the Court of Appeals, all the judges of the circuit Courts except one, and as far as I am advised, nearly all the prosecuting attorneys and sheriffs."[27] Democrats, accepting the logic of their recent politics, led the parade south after Virginia's secession. Among those who still retained their Whig loyalties, Allen T. Caperton entered the Confederate senate, while Summers, having helped to organize the unsuccessful Washington Peace Conference, retired to his home near Charleston; "Cold, selfish, timid," scolded a Wheeling newspaper, "he loved his money, his house, and his lands more than he did the cause of the

Union."²⁸ The western defectors, a separatist leader scoffed in 1861, "will keep at a respectful distance from danger. They will fill the lucrative offices and secure the rich appointments which appertain to the new order of things . . . , while the Union-loving people will be called upon, for the honor of Virginia and two shillings a day, to do the fighting and undergo the hardships of war."²⁹ This was an unkind thought, but true. Of eminent western politicians who took an active part for Virginia, only one (Congressman Albert Gallatin Jenkins) was killed in the war.

The antebellum governing class had its proportion of Unionists, but these were notably lacking in their enthusiasm for a new state. Johnson N. Camden kept his head down and his mouth shut and concentrated on the oil business. His father-in-law, a former congressman and the solitary loyal circuit-court judge referred to by Pierpont, vacated the bench rather than take an oath to Pierpont's government. The John J. Jacksons, *pere et fils*, attended the First Wheeling Convention but clashed bitterly with separatist leaders and withdrew, the son to accept an appointment from Lincoln to the federal bench for the western Virginia district, the father to head Unionist opposition to statehood. James H. Brown and Benjamin Smith, as previously noted, attended the Third Wheeling (constitutional) Convention, but their cases are equally revealing. In addition to opposing land reform and "Yankeefied" innovations in government, they took a hand in boundary and economic matters. As a "large state" advocate in the boundary discussions, Brown worked to expand West Virginia's supplies of coal, timber, and·Confederates. The two also threatened to withhold the Kanawha region from West Virginia if the state were constitutionally forbidden to underwrite the construction of a railroad linking Charleston to the B&O. ("I thought the day of sectionalism had passed," remarked a Wheeling delegate.) The eventual compromise prohibited the state (but not counties or municipalities) from indebting itself for this purpose but left the way open to direct subventions from tax monies.³⁰ This work accomplished, Smith went over to the opposition and became in 1866 the first Democratic-Conservative candidate for governor. Brown, however, accepted a slot on the nonpartisan and unopposed "Union State Ticket" elected in 1863 and so became a charter member and presiding justice of the supreme court of appeals. He also adopted the Republican Party label assumed by the other statemakers, but he seems to have been neither an admired nor a trusted figure in Republican councils. In addition, he accepted the statemakers' overthrow in the state elections of 1870 with an equanimity to be found in few other Republican hearts. "There is at least consolation in the reflection that something has been accomplished," he wrote to Senator Waitman T.

Willey upon Willey's retirement in 1871, "when we contemplate the Union saved—a new state founded—peace restored—universal liberty proclaimed—the rights of man recognized & guaranteed & the land of Washington & Lincoln, of ourselves & our sires no longer trodden by the foot of a slave—."[31] Brown might also have added that, despite his several defeats at the hands of the other separatists, he had all but single-handedly managed to sustain the basis of antebellum politics by preserving the status quo in land matters and extending West Virginia's borders south and east.

The defeat of 1870 ended the brief rule of West Virginia's founding fathers. Although internal dissension contributed to Republican defeat and exile, a more fundamental reason for the party's predicament was that the statemakers had bitten off more of Virginia than they could govern through the instruments that underpinned their leadership in the state's emerging industrial cities and towns: newspapers, railroad excursions, permanently functioning party organizations, partisan patronage distribution, campaign contributions—all features necessary to mobilize a literate, town-dwelling electorate. Writing in 1876, a Wheeling correspondent of a New York Republican newspaper explained the GOP's enfeebled condition in West Virginia in revealing terms. "It is exceedingly difficult to reach the voting masses of the state," he wrote. "Thousands of the people live in remote and almost inaccessible mountain districts, where they have but few means of communicating with the outside world. Many of them are unable to read, and they are Democrats because they don't know any better. Of course among this class of people public speaking is the only kind of campaign work which accomplishes anything."[32] Republicans, he went on to say, were hampered by a lack of funds and of "home speakers." The Democrats, on the other hand, also lacked for funds but not for speakers. The twenty-five years of Democratic rule that followed Reconstruction in West Virginia were also characterized by party factionalism, but much of the contention can be explained as a persistent clash of competing political cultures, by which I mean the values and expressive behaviors involved in the formation and articulation of political choices, the character and cost of election campaigns, the means by which leaders recruit and communicate with followers, and the typical social and economic resources and personal attributes of successful leaders. A political culture based on modern forms of communication and political organization advanced southward and eastward through West Virginia with the spread of towns and industrialism, but a rival culture based on a blend of Virginia political customs modified by the social and economic conditions imposed by mountainous terrain persisted along the Virginia border and in those interior counties that remained undeveloped industrially.[33] This formulation explains the relationship of Democratic factionalism to the sectional and economic concerns of the day, as the political leadership of the state's industrialists and their agents was challenged with recurrent success by shifting coalitions of conservative "Bourbons" from the eastern border counties, by agrarian reformers adept at mobilizing market-oriented farmers and merchants in many parts of the state, and by "distinguished land attorneys" such as the circle of politicians known as the "Kanawha Ring," who were able to exploit the networks of backwoods connections and attitudes they encountered as they plied the state and federal judicial districts that fanned out from the capital city of Charleston. Even after Democratic rule gave way to a new generation of business-oriented Republicans at the end of the century, the political culture of old Virginia remained entrenched along the state's eastern border. Not until 1940, when labor-backed liberal Democrats wrested control of their party from Bourbons of the border counties, could West Virginia's political separation from the Old Dominion be regarded as complete.

Notes

1. This essay is adapted from a ninety-page article first published as "The New Dominion and the Old: Ante-Bellum and Statehood Politics as the Background of West Virginia's 'Bourbon Democracy,'" *West Virginia History* 33 (1972): 317–407. I felt at the time that such length was justified in view of the need to address four interrelated tasks: (1) to challenge prevailing interpretations of West Virginia's statehood movement in terms of new scholarly interests in the cultural dimensions of politics and the economic bases of Appalachian history, (2) to treat in detail (as background for a book I was then writing) the neglected political history of West Virginia between the Civil War and the end of the nineteenth century, (3) to relate both topics to the industrial transformation of the state that began during the last antebellum decade and that eventually penetrated almost the entire state by the end of World War I, and (4) to demonstrate the value of quantitative electoral and legislative voting analysis in clarifying historical issues. Addressing these concerns, which derived largely from my interest in the period after the Civil War, forced me to examine the antebellum period and eventually to see it in a strikingly different way from earlier historians of the state. The resulting reinterpretation of antebellum western Virginia sectionalism and its economic and cultural contexts is reproduced here. At the time the original was published, I considered myself to be breaking new ground. Now the ground is no longer new. Subsequent annotations will draw attention to points of convergence and divergence between my work and that of other scholars who followed. Otherwise, citations refer only to direct quotes or paraphrases; full documentation can be found in the original essay.

2. "Report of the Commissioners Appointed to View Certain Rivers within the

Commonwealth of Virginia in the Year 1812," reprinted in *The Thirty-fifth State: A Documentary History of West Virginia,* ed. Festus P. Summers and Elizabeth Commetti (Morgantown: West Virginia University Library, 1966), pp. 194–95.

3. Paul Salstrom distinguishes between an "old" and a "new" Appalachia, with the latter comprising the Appalachian Plateau and the former the ridge-and-valley province plus the Blue Ridge of Virginia (but not of the Carolinas or Georgia). This formulation may be useful for macroeconomic analysis, but it can obscure the similarities between the bottomlands found along plateau rivers and the highland valleys farther east, which leads in turn to a failure to recognize the interpenetration of mountainous and valley lands in both provinces. The term *interior,* widely used in nineteenth-century West Virginia, referred to the remoter reaches of the plateau and thus to a geographic area that shrank as railroads and industry spread during the course of the century. It should be added that geologists also draw a boundary between an old and a new Appalachia, but place it about 100 miles southeast of Salstrom's boundary. Related distinctions in economic and social geography are drawn between "valley" and "upland" (both Cumberland Plateau and Blue Ridge) in East Tennessee history by William Bruce Wheeler and Michael McDonald ("The Communities of East Tennessee, 1850–1940," *East Tennessee Historical Society's Publications* 58–69 [1986–87]: 5–8).

4. The question of how "isolated" and "arrested" communities were in backwoods Appalachia has become a symbolic issue in the debate over the origins of twentieth-century Appalachian poverty. My use of the term *isolation* is relative and is intended only to explain the circumstances that put a premium on itinerancy in preindustrial culture. For an early challenge to the notion that "traditional" Appalachia was isolated from the rest of the country in absolute terms, see Gene Wilhelm, "Appalachian Isolation: Fact or Fiction," in *An Appalachian Symposium: Essays in Honor of Cratis D. Williams,* ed. J. W. Williamson (Boone, N.C.: Appalachian State University Press, 1977), pp. 77–91. For a summary of the symbolic meanings of the issue and a use of the term *isolation* in the sense that I use it, see Dwight Billings, Kathleen Blee, and Lewis Swanson, "Culture, Family, and Community in Preindustrial Appalachia," *Appalachian Journal* 13 (Winter 1986): 154–55, 161.

5. Cf. Mary Beth Pudup, "Social Class and Economic Development in Southeast Kentucky, 1820–1880," in *Appalachian Frontiers: Settlement, Society, and Development in the Preindustrial Era,* ed. Robert D. Mitchell (Lexington: University Press of Kentucky, 1991), pp. 245–50, on the crucial difference between the owners of alluvial bottomlands and other owners and landless residents of mountain counties in that state.

6. Gideon Camden to Jonathan M. Bennett, 20 December 1870, Jonathan M. Bennett Papers, West Virginia and Regional History Collection, West Virginia University, Morgantown (hereinafter cited as WVU); John M. Hagans to Waitman T. Willey, 17 January 1871, Waitman T. Willey Papers, WVU; Samuel Woods to Isabella Woods, 21 January 1872, typed copy in Charles Henry Ambler Papers, WVU.

7. William A. MacCorkle, *Recollections of Fifty Years of West Virginia* (New York: Putnam, 1928), p. 169.

8. William Griffee Brown, *History of Nicholas County, West Virginia* (Richmond, Va.: Dietz, 1954), p. 151.

9. Edward Conrad Smith, *A History of Lewis County* (Weston, W.Va.: Edward Conrad Smith, 1920), pp. 231–32.

10. MacCorkle, *Recollections*, pp. 227–28.

11. Cf. Pudup on "the intersection of professional occupation, political office, county-seat residence, and property ownership" in Appalachian Kentucky ("Social Class and Economic Development," p. 250). John C. Inscoe describes a similar elite in the leadership of western North Carolina in *Mountain Masters: Slavery and the Sectional Crisis in Western North Carolina* (Knoxville: University of Tennessee Press, 1989). See also Wheeler and McDonald on the leadership roles of "town elites" in East Tennessee ("Communities of East Tennessee," pp. 5–8).

12. Frank E. Vandiver, *Mighty Stonewall* (New York: McGraw Hill, 1957), p. 2.

13. Mary Anna Jackson, *Memoirs of "Stonewall" Jackson* (Louisville, Ky.: Courier-Journal, 1895), pp. 6, 9–11.

14. Samuel Price to David Goff, 22 October 1874, David Goff Papers, WVU.

15. Quoted in Dorothy Davis, *John George Jackson* (Parsons, W.Va.: McClain, 1976), p. 245.

16. George W. Atkinson and Alvaro F. Gibbens, *Prominent Men of West Virginia* (Wheeling, W.Va.: W. L. Callin, 1890), p. 247.

17. Louise McNeill, "Cornelius Verner," in *Gauley Mountain*, by Louise McNeill (New York: Harcourt, Brace, 1931).

18. Inscoe makes a similar point about North Carolina, where a "dual sectionalism" led western leaders to press the general assembly for state-funded transportation improvements in the mountain districts while drawing closer to eastern leaders in their allegiance to slavery and its defense. An important difference, however, was that, according to Inscoe, the economic interest of western land developers and businessmen lay with southern markets, especially with the plantation districts of South Carolina, while in western Virginia the most favorable commercial opportunities lay in markets to the west, north, and northeast. See Inscoe, *Mountain Masters*, esp. pp. 177–210.

19. Samuel Price to Gideon Camden, 29 January 1872, Gideon Draper Camden Papers, WVU.

20. Table 1 (p. 344) in "The New Dominion and the Old" illustrates in statistical terms the differences in voting behavior that distinguished these counties from their immediate neighbors. These counties exceeded their neighbors' deviations from statewide average Republican voting by factors ranging from .6 standard deviation to 3.7. Since West Virginians tended to "vote as they had shot" until partisan balances were affected by an influx of new voters accompanying industrialization, the persistence of such differences among adjacent counties is noteworthy, but they do not correspond neatly to geographic divisions between valley and plateau. Wyoming and Upshur were interior Republican counties surrounded by strongly Democratic neighbors. Grant and Morgan were eastern border counties occupying mostly ridges adjacent to Confederate (and Democratic) valleys.

21. Charles H. Ambler, "The Makers of West Virginia," *West Virginia History* 2 (1941): 272–73.

22. Ibid., p. 271.

23. Samuel Woods to Isabella Woods, 25 February 1872, typed copy in Ambler Papers, WVU.

24. Gideon Camden to Robert M. T. Hunter, 14 February 1860, in *Correspondence of Robert M. T. Hunter, 1826–1876*, ed. Charles H. Ambler (American Historical Association, *Annual Report* [1916], vol. 2 [Washington, D.C.: Government Printing Office, 1918]).

25. Samuel Woods to Isabella Woods, 25 February 1872, typed copy in Ambler Papers, WVU.

26. Gideon Camden to Robert M. T. Hunter, 14 February 1860, in Ambler, *Correspondence of Hunter*.

27. Speech of 17 June 1861 in Virgil A. Lewis, *How West Virginia Was Made. Proceedings of the First Convention of the People of Northwestern Virginia at Wheeling May 13, 14, and 15, 1861 and the Journal of the Second Convention.* . . . (Charleston W.Va.: News-Mail, 1909), p. 164.

28. Wheeling *Intelligencer*, 29 November 1861, quoted in Roy Watson Curry, "The Newspaper Press and the Civil War in West Virginia," *West Virginia History* 6 (1945): 236.

29. John S. Carlile, speech of 14 May 1861, in Lewis, *How West Virginia Was Made*, pp. 73–74.

30. Charles H. Ambler, Francis H. Atwood, and William B. Mathews, eds., *Debates and Proceedings of the First Constitutional Convention of West Virginia (1861–1863)*, 3 vols. (Huntington, W.Va.: Gentry Bros., 1939), 1:166–67, 317–547; 2:455, 460–61; 3:128–29, 155–56, 175, 231–39, 253, 277.

31. James H. Brown to Waitman T. Willey, 7 March 1871, Willey Papers, WVU.

32. *New York Times*, 8 October 1876.

33. I have elaborated on the theme of competing political cultures and their relationship to the changing political economy in West Virginia after the Civil War in *West Virginia: A History* (New York: Norton, 1976), pp. 115–23. Altina Waller provides an excellent case study of conflict between newer and older elites and the displacement of the latter by the former in Logan County, W.Va., in *Feud: Hatfields, McCoys, and Social Change in Appalachia, 1860–1900* (Chapel Hill: University of North Carolina Press, 1988), pp. 140–50.

Agriculture and Poverty in the Kentucky Mountains

Beech Creek, 1850–1910

L ike so many other aspects of the region's preindustrial social life, farming in Appalachia has received but scant attention until very recently. Early, casual observers from Frederick Law Olmsted to Horace Kephart undoubtedly exaggerated the "rude and destructive" character of mountain farming.[1] Such stereotypes have been carried over into cultural interpretations that link Appalachian poverty to the presumed backwardness of mountain culture, including its agriculture, often without systematic ethnographic evidence.[2] Subsequent scholars, advancing the model of Appalachia as an internal colony, attributed the decline of the Appalachian farming economy to the intrusion of absentee land and mineral ownership and to the corporate domination of the region by multinational energy businesses. Thus Ronald Eller claimed that "the small, marginal farm usually associated with the stereotyped picture of Appalachia was in fact a product of modernization" and the Appalachian Land Ownership Task Force asserted that "with th[e] intrusion [of coal and timber interests] began the decline of mountain agriculture."[3] Yet these scholars, too, failed to devote sufficient attention to the history, internal dynamics, and developmental consequences of Appalachian farming.

New studies, however, are beginning to focus more directly on Appalachian agriculture and its impact on the economic and social development of the region. Following up on the earlier work of L. C. Gray, Forrest McDonald and Grady McWhiney have shown the importance and economic viability of animal husbandry throughout the nineteenth-century South, including open-range herding in the upland, backcountry, and mountain regions.[4] Horticultural practices in the southern mountains, too, have begun to be reappraised, appearing in a far more favorable light than as stereotyped in traditional accounts. Thus John Otto and his coauthors have shown that the "slash-and-burn" technique of "forest farming," commonly practiced throughout the Appalachian and Ozark highlands in the nineteenth and early twentieth centuries, was a viable and effective form of agriculture within certain ecological and demographic limits.[5]

Although historical research is beginning to portray the region's farming as more viable than traditional accounts supposed, considerable controversy remains, however, in regard to the relative balance between subsistence-oriented agricultural production and commercial farming in Appalachia.[6] Recent studies have emphasized the importance of commercialism in the settlement and early development of eastern Tennessee, western Virginia, and southwestern Virginia.[7] For example, John Inscoe has described the mountains of North Carolina as "a thriving, productive, and even [economically] progressive society" where slaveholding and commercial agriculture predominated during the antebellum period. He suggests that "only slowly and reluctantly have historians recognized that antebellum society in the southern Appalachians shared much in common with the rest of the South."[8] On the other hand, studies of preindustrial life in the more isolated sections of eastern Kentucky and West Virginia, such as Altina Waller's analysis of the Tug River Valley, describe farming there as having been largely subsistence oriented prior to 1900, a finding supported by an early U.S. Department of Agriculture study that reported that 58.4 percent of all farms in the Allegheny-Cumberland Plateaus were still noncommercial in 1935.[9]

Nevertheless, even in the Kentucky mountains the predominance of subsistence agriculture and the extent of market involvement have been debated. Thus Tyrel Moore claims that "clearly, the pioneer economy and isolation of the Appalachian frontier did not dominate eastern Kentucky throughout the period between 1800 and 1860." Emphasizing economic development, including iron manufacturing along the Ohio River in northeastern Kentucky, he concludes that "Appalachian Kentucky, on the eve of the Civil War, was not unlike other areas of the country between northern New York and central Alabama that possessed similar kinds of economic resources."[10] But Mary Beth Pudup, examining a later period in southeastern Kentucky, claims that the years from 1850 to 1880 "witnessed the progressive isolation of the area's economy from the paths of deepening [national] commercialization and locally generated capitalist transformation, as economic production [in eastern Kentucky] became oriented toward simple household subsistence."[11]

The Beech Creek Study

In order to examine further the role of agriculture in the social and economic development of the Allegheny-Cumberland plateau region, we have based our approach on the prior ethnographic observations of James S. Brown and his colleagues in the Beech Creek neighborhoods of Clay County, a nonmining community in eastern Kentucky.[12] By analyzing data from manuscript censuses and tax rolls for the years 1850 to 1910 on the ancestors (and their neighbors) of families that Brown first studied in 1942, we have tried to examine the social origins of farming patterns Brown described in his classic study of rural Appalachian social life and to situate them in the context of that area's economic development and poverty.[13] Since Beech Creek was not directly affected by the development of coal mining, a study of long-term agricultural trends in agriculture there enables us to examine developmental tendencies in a mountain farming community in isolation from the effects of industrialization.

The people living along Beech Creek were already poor when Brown first entered the area on horseback to observe them fifty years ago. Their tiny farms averaged less than 10 acres in crops in 1942. Nine of the 29 farms (31 percent) that Brown studied exhaustively averaged fewer than 30 total acres of improved and unimproved land—a figure comparable to Clay County as a whole, where 34 percent of all farms were less than 30 acres and 50 percent were less than 50 acres. These 29 Beech Creek farms combined to only 273 acres in cultivation, 226 of these acres in corn. Productivity was low, averaging only 10 to 20 bushels of corn per acre. Although some good bottomlands remained, many portions "[had] been cultivated since the early days and [were] so exhausted by continual cropping and erosion [that by 1942 they were] rocky, unproductive, and thin."[14] "Evidence of erosion [was] everywhere—slips, slides, gullies, rock-choked stream beds, washed banks and bare, scarred fields."[15] Yet subsistence farming continued to play a central role in the lives of Beech Creek families.

"In 1942, the farm was still the chief source of income for the Beech Creek family."[16] Brown's analyses of thirty family budgets revealed that the total value of farm products for all families was only $12,405, more than two-thirds of which ($8,660) was consumed at home. Less than one-third was sold for a combined total of only $3,745 of income that was shared by all thirty families. This small amount of cash represented one-fourth of the families' entire cash income. The rest came from nonfarm employment in forestry, Civilian Conservation Corps and Works Projects Administration jobs, government subsidies, and pensions. A small portion of income was derived from family members working "outside" in southern Ohio factories, indicating that extraregional migration and employment were already becoming important factors in the life of Beech Creek.

Thus by the time of the Second World War, Beech Creek farms were far from the islands of self-sufficiency that were once stereotypic of remote, nonindustrialized sections of the Cumberland Plateau.[17] "The data on expenditures," according to Brown, revealed both "the decreasing self-sufficiency and the relative poverty of the Beech Creek farm family."[18] Brown observed that earlier, "when lumbering came to the area and made more money available, [Beech Creekers] gave up such domestic crafts as weaving and shoemaking and bought clothing and shoes. Eventually they spent large portions of cash income for flour, sugar, lard, and meat, which they had formerly produced."[19] By 1942 numerous Beech Creek families were forced to supplement even their home consumption of corn with additional purchases. The goals of this chapter are to ascertain how this situation came about by examining historical trends in Beech Creek's agriculture and, more generally, to suggest long-term developmental implications for tendencies internal to subsistence farming in the Allegheny-Cumberland Plateau.

Early Settlement and Development of Clay County

It would be a mistake simply to project Brown's description of Beech Creek's twentieth-century social isolation and economic marginality backward onto Clay County's past, since our research suggests that the county was more closely incorporated into interregional trade networks and less geographically isolated in the 1840s than were the Beech Creek neighborhoods when Brown first observed them 100 years later. During the frontier settlement of Kentucky, both population and commerce entered central Kentucky primarily through the Cumberland Gap and radiated outward from there, up toward the three headwaters or "forks" of the Kentucky River in the Cumberland mountains and down toward the river's mouth on the Ohio River. Space does not permit a full explication of this thesis, but we believe that to understand the early settlement and development of Clay County, one must deconstruct or "un-think" the modern concept of "Appalachia"—as well as the related notion, popularized in nineteenth-century local-color writing, of there having been "Two Kentuckies"—in order to grasp Clay County's early place in the unified development of the social order that came into being up and down the Kentucky River.[20]

At the same time that central Kentucky, and especially the Blue Grass region, were growing in population and wealth at the center of the state's trade that extended down the Mississippi to New Orleans and up the Atlantic Coast from there to mercantile centers in Baltimore and Philadelphia, Clay County was also beginning to experience significant growth as a consequence of making the state's first important manufactured product, salt—a crucial commodity in Kentucky's otherwise predominantly agricultural economy.[21] Many nonslaveowning, yeoman farmers pushed into the Kentucky hills when the price of land rose and its availability declined in central Kentucky, but so too did the representatives of wealthy slaveowning families who built Clay County's salt industry along Goose Creek, a tributary of the Southfork of the Kentucky River.

James White, a Virginian whose estate was valued at $1 million when he died in 1838, began to purchase land and manufacture salt in Clay County in cooperation with his brother Hugh White (and Hugh's sons), who moved to Clay County during the first decade of the nineteenth century. By 1860 the White family controlled approximately 20,000 acres of land in Clay and other mountain counties.[22] James Garrard, the second governor of Kentucky, patented more than 45,000 acres of land in Kentucky before and after Kentucky's statehood. Although most of his lands were in the Blue Grass region, Garrard also bought thousands of acres in southeastern Kentucky and sent his son Daniel to Clay County to establish salt wells and furnaces there early in the century. Daniel Garrard and his sons owned 15,000 acres in southeastern Kentucky before the Civil War. The Whites and the Garrards, along with a few other families, thus established economic and political dynasties in Clay County based on slave labor, salt manufacturing, commerce, and large-scale farming that persisted throughout the antebellum and early postbellum periods and, in some cases, even into the modern era.

Early life in Clay County thus revolved around two very different systems of production, the subsistence-oriented system of forest farming, based predominantly on family labor, that was practiced by the vast majority of the population and a smaller, slave-based manufacturing and mercantile economy controlled by a few wealthy families. The county's fifty-eight slaveowners, representing only 7 percent of household heads, owned 10 percent of the total population (515 slaves), but slaveownership did not touch directly the lives of most farm households in Clay County. The result of this dual system was a highly stratified community.[23] The ten wealthiest individuals in Clay County in 1860—all slaveowners—averaged personal estates worth $45,890 in a county where the mean estate was worth only $859, or 53 times less. In fact, the wealthiest individual, salt manufacturer Francis Clark, was 200 times richer than the mean, with an estate worth $175,000 in 1860.

By 1817 Clay County salt had become one of Kentucky's leading exports, reaching as far west as the Missouri Valley, south to Tennessee, and east to Virginia. The industry reached its peak of production between 1835 and 1845 when as much as 250,000 barrels of salt were produced annually from eight to fifteen saltworks.[24] Salt sales benefited manufacturers but also created opportunities for local farmers to supplement their incomes by engaging in well drilling, barrel making, boat building and navigation, and coal digging.[25] State expenditures for highway construction and river improvements, although targeted at the salt industry, also benefited local farmers as did the mercantile activities of salt manufacturers who stimulated local trade by exchanging salt, nonlocal manufactured products, and money for farm commodities.[26] Salt manufacturers operated self-sufficient farms with slave labor, but their large landholdings also created opportunities for tenant farmers and farm laborers as well. Overland roads built for the salt trade linked Clay County farmers to southern markets via the Wilderness Road (some twenty miles away), and local court litigation reveals that as early as 1807 drovers from the Blue Grass were adding livestock to their herds from Clay County as they passed nearby on their way through the Cumberland Gap.[27]

At the peak of the salt industry's influence, entrepreneurs from Clay County outlined a bold scheme to the Kentucky legislature that proposed a $10 million interstate canal, lock, and damn system that eventually would have linked the Goose Creek saltworks to the Atlantic coast.[28] But the Panic of 1837 and the national depression of 1839–41—along with opposition from central Kentucky railroad interests—relegated this plan to a footnote in Kentucky history. Soon thereafter, the Clay County salt industry began to decline as salt manufacturing elsewhere in regions with better locations prospered. Furthermore by 1850, after earlier extensions of the National Road and improvements in navigation and safety on the Ohio River had been made, the "Wilderness Road . . . lost practically all significance as a transmontane route and was of mere local importance."[29] Whereas mountain roads had been "not much inferior to those of central Kentucky" prior to 1830, the macadamization of roads in central Kentucky from 1830 to 1850 created "a magnificent system of highways" in the Bluegrass region.[30] According to Verhoeff, "it was during this period that the rugged mountain region, left henceforth to shift for itself in the matter of highways, became isolated to such a marked degree."[31]

Elsewhere we will discuss how deepening isolation affected the lives of slaves and slaveowners in Clay County. The vast majority of African Americans left Clay County during the late nineteenth century. Former slaveowners engaged in internecine struggles (known popularly as "family feuds" and locally as "wars") at the turn of the century to control Clay County's political and economic life. In their roles as landowners, merchants and local boosters, lawyers, and corporate partners, they served as the indigenous agents of outside capital in the modern exploitation of local labor, land, timber, and coal resources.[32] In the remainder of this chapter, however, we will examine trends in the quality of life among the majority of Clay County residents who were engaged in agricultural subsistence and independent commodity production.

Clay County Agriculture in 1860

Tables 9.1 and 9.2 report farm sizes and values, corn production, and livestock inventories for Clay County in 1860 (along with comparable values for Beech Creek farms) for three categories of farm operators: owners, tenants, and slaveowners.[33] (The Beech Creek community included no slaveowners.) The designation of slaveowners is straightforward in the census manuscripts, but the determination of owners and tenants and their relationship to a third category (farm laborers) is problematic, as are the social dynamics of tenancy in the mountains. At best, tenancy levels are estimates.[34]

Using techniques suggested by Bode and Ginter, we estimate that no less than 22 percent and perhaps as many as 41 percent of the 230 farmers who headed their own households in our Clay County sample were tenants in 1860.[35] Higher estimates, according to Bode and Ginter, are less certain yet more likely to be correct. Our higher estimate includes 44 "farmers without farms" as well as the 22 "farm laborers" in our sample who headed their own households in 1860. (Most farm laborers, however, were not tenants but, rather, members of farm households related by kinship to the household head; 80 percent of these were sons of the household head.) Since the analysis that follows, however, is necessarily restricted to farm families and individuals listed in the census of agriculture, Tables 9.1 and 9.2 compare the

Table 9.1. Farm Size and Values in Clay County, 1860

	Owner/Operators			Tenants		
	Mean	No.	%	Mean	No.	%
Improved acres	52	92	100	35	28	97
Unimproved acres	424	92	100	463	11	40
Cash value of farm	$ 935	91	99	–	–	–
Cash value of livestock	$ 410	91	99	$210	29	100
Cash value of machinery	$ 38	92	100	$ 19	29	100
Cash value of home manufacturing	$ 28	82	89	$ 18	16	55

Source: Eighth Census of the United States, 1860: Agriculture (manuscripts).

farms operated by owners (75 percent) with tenant farms defined as those operated by individuals with no property and/or missing values for improved acres and cash value of farms (25 percent).

Contrary to stereotypes about Appalachian farms, Table 9.1 shows that most farms in Clay County, even those operated by tenants, were extremely large in comparison with other regions. Owner-operated farms in 1860 averaged 476 total acres in the county at a time when farms in the northern United States, including the Midwest, averaged only 129 acres (see Table 9.3). Farms operated by slaveowners were even larger, averaging 1,150 acres —almost ten times the size of average northern farms (though small in comparison with large southern slaveholding operations). But because land in the mountains of Kentucky was comparatively cheap, the cash value of Clay County farms in 1860 was low. Owner-operated farms averaged only one-fourth of the value of farms in the North's eastern subregion, and even the large farms owned by slaveholders—these, presumably, occupying some of the best bottomlands in the county—were less than 25 percent more valuable than average farms in the Northeast one-tenth their size. In fact, the largest farms in Kentucky were those of the Kentucky mountains. Farm sizes increased and the value of farms decreased as one traveled east from the Blue Grass region across the rugged Cumberland Mountains, reflecting both the patterns of large landholding and low level of commercialization in Appalachia.[36]

Consistent with the model of slash-and-burn forest farming described by Otto, Clay County farmers, including slaveowners, improved only small portions—roughly 10 percent—of their farmlands, allowing "old ground" to return to forest or to be used for pasture and leaving much of their total acreage unimproved.[37] On the 121 owner-operated and tenant farms in our

Slaveowners			Beech Creek Farms		
Mean	No.	%	Mean	No.	%
109	37	100	60	59	100
1,041	34	92	679	46	78
$4,419	32	86	$1,437	47	80
$ 880	37	100	$ 373	59	100
$ 83	36	97	$ 38	59	100
$ 54	26	70	$ 26	45	76

1860 agricultural sample, improved lands averaged only 48 acres, ranging from only 3 acres (the minimum for inclusion in the census) to one large farm operation with 300 improved acres. Almost half of all farmers in Clay County (48 percent) cultivated 30 acres or less in 1860, despite owning large amounts of unimproved hillside forestland, while the largest farms—the top 10 percent—cultivated 100 or more acres. Owner-operated farms cultivated, on average, only 52 acres—an area roughly three-fourths that of farms in the North (see Table 9.3).

Because enumerators did not report the cash values and unimproved acreage of tenant farms (see Table 9.1), it is impossible to know exactly what resources tenants had at their disposal; but their farms, too, were large. The tenant farms with known values averaged 498 total acres. Nonetheless, tenants cultivated even less acreage than farm owners, averaging plots of only 35 acres. This size difference, in part, probably reflected life-cycle differences between tenants and owners. Some tenants rented farmlands in addition to pursuing other occupations—our sample included a cooper, a blacksmith, a coal digger, a constable, a gunsmith, and a salt maker—but most were young farmers. Tenants, averaging thirty-three years old, were an average of six years younger than farm owners, and they were more likely to head simple (nuclear) families. Forty-one percent of the farm owners in our sample headed extended and multiple family units or had others living in their households, but only 27.5 percent of the tenant farmers headed such households. Consequently, tenant farmers commanded fewer labor resources from family members and others in their households than did owners to clear lands and cultivate crops, and their younger ages allowed them less time to have accumulated other farm resources such as livestock and machinery.

Table 9.2. Farm Production in Clay County, 1860

	Owner/Operators			Tenants		
	Mean	No.	%	Mean	No.	%
Bushels of corn	406	92	100	420	29	100
Cash value of slaughtered animals	$ 91	90	98	$ 62	29	100
Number of cows	3.6	92	100	2.9	29	100
Number of cattle	6	80	87	3.3	21	72
Number of oxen	2.7	55	60	2.3	12	41
Number of sheep	15.3	77	84	8.8	11	38
Number of hogs	23	83	90	16	27	93
Cash value of garden products	$145	7	8	—	—	—

Source: Eighth Census of the United States, 1860: Agriculture (manuscripts).

Other than the fact that Beech Creek farms were small in 1942—necessitating at least periodic off-farm employment to supplement income—it is unlikely that farm activities in 1860 differed greatly from the daily and seasonal work rhythms and the age and sex division of labor that Brown described so well for the Beech Creek farms he observed in 1942. Farmers in Clay County as well as in Beech Creek pursued forms of general (or diversified) subsistence-oriented farming in 1860 that stressed meeting the needs of their households first before bartering or selling whatever surplus in crops and animal products were left over.

Comparison of Clay County farm production (Tables 9.1 and 9.2) with data from northern farms the same year (Table 9.3) reveals the surprising finding that these Appalachian farms—including farms in the Beech Creek neighborhoods—were on average at least as productive as their northern counterparts and even surpassed them in important farm products such as corn.[38] Clay County farm owners, on average, produced 340 percent more corn on their farms than did farmers in the Northeast and only 22 percent less than midwestern farmers, the nation's leading grain producers. Their livestock inventories included roughly the same number of cows, cattle, and sheep but considerably more hogs and more oxen (important for the heavy work of clearing and hauling in a rugged environment) than northern farms. Owner-operated farms in Clay County and all farms in Beech Creek averaged higher returns (in cash or kind) for slaughtered animals than did farms in either the Northeast or the Midwest. Although corn was by far the most important field crop in Appalachia, the comparison of Beech Creek farm values for 1860 (see Table 9.6) with northern farms suggests that farmers'

Slaveowners			Beech Creek Farms		
Mean	No.	%	Mean	No.	%
831	35	95	450	59	100
$ 270	36	97	$ 98	58	98
7	37	100	3.8	56	95
16	30	81	5.1	48	81
5	29	78	3.9	38	64
26	25	68	14.1	31	53
27	35	95	21.2	56	95
$ 67	4	11	—	—	—

production of other crops in Clay County was also reasonably competitive with other regions. Beech Creek farmers produced more wheat than northeastern farmers and more wool than midwestern farmers. They produced considerably less oats than both subregions of the North, but the Appalachian practice of allowing livestock, especially hogs and cattle, unrestricted range to feed on forest masts is likely to have compensated for this deficiency.

The relative self-sufficiency of mountain farms, and their ability to reproduce themselves without heavy reliance on store-bought commodities, is indicated by the high per-farm values of home manufacturing reported in Table 9.4. Rolla Tryon, an authority on household manufacturing, concluded that "as a factor in the economic life and prosperity of the country as a whole," home manufacturing "was practically nil at the end of the sixth decade of the nineteenth century."[39] Northeastern farms manufactured on average only $4 worth of goods at home in 1860, and midwestern farms produced only a little more, valued at $9. (See Table 9.3.) In sharp contrast, however, Clay County farm owners produced considerably more homemade goods that year, valued at $28. Farms benefiting from slave labor manufactured still more goods ($54 worth), valued at almost eight times the northern average. Tenant farmers had less labor time to devote to home manufacturing—only 55 percent made goods at home, perhaps increasing their dependence on merchants or landlords—but those that could afford the time to do so also produced considerably more goods ($18) than did northern farmers.

Beech Creek farmers manufactured $26 worth of products at home in 1860. By the time that Brown interviewed Beech Creekers in 1942, home

Table 9.3. Average Sample Farm Characteristics for Northern U.S. Farms with Three or More Improved Acres, 1860

| State/Region | Farm Statistics | | | | Livestock | | | | |
	Farm Value ($)	Value of Implements ($)	Improved Acreage	Unimproved Acreage	Horses	Oxen	Milk Cows	Cattle	Sheep
Eastern region	3,581	125	79	39	2.4	0.8	4.9	4.2	15.8
Western region	2,367	90	65	72	3.1	0.8	3.0	4.9	9.2
North	2,819	103	70	59	2.9	0.8	3.7	4.6	11.6

Source: Atack and Bateman, *To Their Own Soil*, pp. 111–12.
Note: Eastern region = Connecticut, New Hampshire, New Jersey, New York, Pennsylvania, Vermont; Western region = Illinois, Indiana, Iowa, Kansas, Michigan, Minnesota, Ohio, Wisconsin.

manufacturing had diminished, but some of the oldest people there could still recall how important home manufacturing had once been to their way of life.

> Farm life at the time of the Civil War [was] still well remembered by one old man still living on Beech Creek [in 1942], Preston [Johnson]. His father . . . owned most of the creek, and the [Elisha Johnsons] were considered "good livers." They lived in a log house with three or four rooms and a "lean-to" kitchen. Most of their furniture and kitchen utensils were homemade. . . . Wheat and corn, grown exclusively for use at home, were ground in the early days at a mill down-river. . . . Beef cattle and sheep were slaughtered for home use. . . . They bought salt from wells not too far away and produced their own sugar from groves of maple trees ("sugar orchards," they were called). Wild honey was not uncommon, and most families had beegums on the hill behind the house. Sorghum molasses were made in the fall. Sheep were numerous; their wool was spun into thread and woven into cloth for winter clothes. Some people raised cotton, but flax seems to have been commoner, and women took pride in the linen they wove. (The oldest woman on the creek remembered the whole process of linen-making and recalled with nostalgia how stiff and hard new linen was and how soft and white it became with long, hard use.) [Elisha Johnson] tanned hides and made shoes for his family (and his youngest son, Preston, remembered the last shoes he had made, probably in the 1880s.) About the only things the [Johnsons] had to buy were needles and coffee.[40]

Inventories			Output of Principal Crops and Products (rounded to whole numbers)							
		Value of								
	Value of	Livestock					Irish			Home
	Livestock	Slaughtered	Wheat	Corn	Oats	Wool	Potatoes	Butter	Cheese	Manufactures
Hogs	($)	($)	(bu.)	(bu.)	(bu.)	(lbs.)	(bu.)	(lbs.)	(lbs.)	($)
4.7	493	88	38	139	169	57	82	421	221	4
15.7	420	77	105	520	58	26	37	166	22	9
11.6	447	80	80	378	99	37	54	261	96	7

Home manufacturing persisted throughout the nineteenth century and contributed to the craft revivals that spread across the Appalachian region in the 1920s.[41]

While the data in Tables 9.1 and 9.2 do not take into account, as below, the size of farm families that had to be supported in the region, they nonetheless suggest the viability of agriculture in this section of the Kentucky mountains at the midpoint of the nineteenth century. Even to other Kentuckians at the time, however—probably because these were in large measure subsistence rather than wholly commodity-producing units—the productivity of mountain farms was largely overlooked. Thus in 1854, when the Kentucky Agricultural Society was organized for the improvement of farming in the commonwealth, the mountains of eastern Kentucky were excluded from its three farm districts and, later in the century, the University of Kentucky Agricultural Experiment Station largely ignored the problems of mountain farmers by devoting exclusive aid and research to commercial farm interests in the central and western sections of the state.[42] Geographical isolation, ignorance about mountain farming, and the prevalence of subsistence practices, rather than economic insufficiency, contributed to erroneous impressions about eastern Kentucky farming during the middle of the nineteenth century that would contribute to twentieth-century stereotypes about Appalachia.

Before turning to a discussion of long-term agricultural trends, however, it is important to note that although the majority of farm owners in 1860— and perhaps many tenants as well—were, in the language of contemporary

Table 9.4. Beech Creek Farm Values, 1850–1880

	1850			1860		
	Mean	No.	%	Mean	No.	%
Improved acres	41	41	79	60	59	100
Unimproved acres	287	30	58	679	46	78
Cash value of farm	$ 527 ($596)	41	79	$1,437	47	80
Cash value of home manufacturing	$ 26 ($29)	45	87	$ 26	45	76
Cash value of machinery	$ 17 ($19)	49	94	$ 39	59	100

Sources: U.S. censuses of agriculture, 1850, 1860, 1870, 1880.
Note: Dollar values in parentheses are standardized to 1860 dollar values.

Beech Creekers, "good livers," there was additionally a small number of comparatively well-to-do farmers in the county. Tables 9.1 and 9.2 show that slaveowners operated relatively large farm enterprises worth nearly five times the cash value of other owner-operated farms in the county and owned livestock inventories worth twice as much. They grew twice as much corn and slaughtered animals worth three times as much as other farm owners.

The largest slaveowners in Clay County—those also involved in salt manufacturing and other commercial ventures—were quite wealthy. Besides the $20,000 capital invested in his salt manufacturing business, Daniel Garrard and his son, Theophilus, together owned about 12,500 acres of farmland worth $28,000 on which they produced more than 1,600 bushels of corn and slaughtered animals worth $850 in 1860. The salt manufacturers Alexander White, Daugherty White, and James White, Sr., owned farms totaling about 5,000 acres and valued at almost $45,000 on which they grew more than 4,000 bushels of corn and raised livestock valued at more than $9,000 in 1860. Furthermore, the fact that one elderly salt manufacturer, Francis Clark, owned lands worth $120,000 in 1860 but, according to the farm census, operated only a 1,000-acre farm with very limited production suggests that at least some, and perhaps a good amount, of the value of farm products raised by tenant farmers may have gone to such large landowners as well.

1870			1880		
Mean	No.	%	Mean	No.	%
39	106	80	24.9[a]	60	71
			14.6[b]	48	56
221	110	83	168[c]	57	67
$ 782	111	84	$ 582[d]	61	72
($524)			($442)		
			$ 474[e]	85	100
			($360)		
$ 31	115	87	—	—	
($21)					
$ 23	130	98	$ 23	81	95
($15)			($17)		

[a]Acres in tillage. [b]Acres in pasture. [c]Acres in woodland.
[d]Owners only. [e]All farmers.

Trends in Beech Creek Agriculture, 1850 to 1880

The comparison of Beech Creek and Clay County farms in 1860 (see Tables 9.1 and 9.2) suggests that trends on Beech Creek farms can be taken as representative of countywide trends even though, on average, Beech Creek farms—including tenant operations—were slightly larger, more valuable, and more productive in 1860 than owner-operated farms in the rest of the county.[43] If the picture of Clay County and Beech Creek farming in 1860 was one of relatively high agricultural production in comparison with farm operations in the northern United States, the story of farming there over the next two decades, however, is one of dramatic and rapid agricultural decline. Whereas farms in the North—especially but not only in the Midwest—increased the value, productivity, and efficiency of their operations through improvements in transportation, mechanization, specialization, and the use of chemical fertilizers, Beech Creek—and, by extension of our findings, Clay County—farms decreased dramatically in size and productivity throughout the remainder of the nineteenth century.[44]

Tables 9.4, 9.5, and 9.6 document dramatic declines in the size and value of farms, livestock inventories, and crop production in Beech Creek from 1860 to 1880. By almost all measures, 1860 was a peak year of agricultural abundance. Between 1850 and 1860 the average farm in Beech Creek had more than doubled in size from a total of 328 improved and unimproved

Table 9.5. Beech Creek Livestock Inventories, 1850–1880

| | 1850 | | | 1860 | | |
	Mean	No.	%	Mean	No.	%
Hogs	26.2	51	98	21.1	56	95
Milk Cows	2.9	52	100	3.8	56	95
Cattle	9.7	41	79	5.1	48	81
Oxen	2.8	16	31	3.8	38	64
Sheep	17.6	40	77	14.1	31	53
Horses	2	48	92	2.1	49	83
Value of livestock	$ 192	51	100	$374	59	100
	($217)			—		
Value of slaughtered animals	$ 60	48	92	$ 98	58	98
	($68)			—		

Sources: U.S. censuses of agriculture, 1850, 1860, 1870, 1880 (manuscripts).
Note: Dollar values in parentheses are standardized to 1860 dollar values.
ᵃEstimated by the formula ((((livestock value × .3) 10.04) × 0.76) /7.6), where .3 is the

acres to 739 total acres in 1860. The value of farms increased by 240 percent from $596 in 1850 (as expressed in 1860 dollars) to $1,437 in 1860 (see Table 9.4). Although the average number of animals on each farm actually fell somewhat between 1850 and 1860, the values of livestock holdings and slaughtered animals rose considerably (see Table 9.5). Crop production, too, reached peak levels (see Table 9.6). Corn, the most important crop in the mountains, increased by 25 percent. The production of oats fell; but more farms grew wheat in 1860 than in 1850, and the number of farms making butter, and their quantities, had skyrocketed by 1860.

During the next two decades, however, these improvements vanished as livestock holdings, production levels, and farm values fell precipitously. Most farm variables fell to levels even lower than those of 1850. By 1880 Beech Creek farms averaged only 208 acres and were only 28 percent as large and 31 percent as valuable as farms had been in 1860. Livestock inventories— valued at only 29 percent of 1860 holdings—declined for all animals except sheep, with hog production falling most dramatically from twenty-one hogs per farm in 1860 to only thirteen in 1880. Even more dramatic than the decline in the numbers of animals was the increase in the proportion of farms that no longer owned certain species of livestock. Hogs, for instance, were nearly universal on farms in 1860 (95 percent), but only half of the farmers in Beech Creek (51 percent) owned hogs by 1880. Oxen were present on 64 percent of the farms in 1860, but only 21 percent of the farmers owned

1870			1880		
Mean	No.	%	Mean	No.	%
9.8	114	86	12.8	44	51
2.3	125	95	1.9	73	85
3.8	80	61	3.1	58	67
2.9	48	37	2.3	18	21
12.0	99	75	14.3	46	53
1.5	87	66	1.4	47	55
$ 257	131	99	$ 142	84	98
($172)			($108)		
$ 88	123	93	$ 107[a]	84	98
($59)			($81)		

average ratio of the value of slaughtered animals to
value of livestock for 1850 to 1870 and 0.04 is average price per pound.

them two decades later. Farm products derived from livestock fell proportionately. Milk cows, for instance, declined by 50 percent, and butter production fell far below the 1860 level. Because sheep holdings were held
constant, the average production of wool did not drop as dramatically as
butter, yet fewer farms produced wool in 1880 than in 1870. Crop production, too, fell more or less in proportion to the decrease in farm sizes, while
the smaller size of farms forced a reallocation of acreage allotments among
crop mixes. The number of farmers growing wheat and potatoes declined,
but oat production increased by a modest amount (perhaps necessitated by
the impact of timbering on livestock grazing). Most importantly, corn production averaged only 247 bushels per farm in 1880, an amount only 55
percent of the 1860 corn crop that had averaged 450 bushels.

Because the manuscripts of the 1890 census were destroyed by fire, the
manuscript record for U.S. farms ends in 1880. This is especially unfortunate for the study of Appalachian agriculture since mountain farms were
obviously undergoing considerable changes during the last decades of the
nineteenth century. Clay County tax rolls for 1892, however, extend a partial
view of Beech Creek farms another dozen years beyond 1880. But because
inclusion in the county tax rolls was based on less stringent criteria than
inclusion in the federal census of agriculture—in 1860, for instance, we
could locate seventy Beech Creek farmers in the tax rolls but only fifty-nine
in the census that year—caution must be exercised in comparing data from

Table 9.6. Output of Principal Crops and Products in Beech Creek, 1850–1880

	1850			1860		
	Mean	No.	%	Mean	No.	%
Corn (bu.)	362	51	98	450	59	100
Wheat (bu.)	35	8	15	60	31	53
Oats (bu.)	111	23	44	34	12	20
Irish potatoes (bu.)	20	27	52	27	25	42
Beans (bu.)	9	37	71	7	57	97
Butter (lbs.)	28	6	12	373	53	90
Wool (lbs.)	21	37	71	26	28	47

Sources: U.S. censuses of agriculture, 1850, 1860, 1870, 1880 (manuscripts).

Table 9.7. Corn Production and Livestock in Beech Creek, 1860 and 1892

Year	No. of Taxpayers	Corn (bu.)	%	Horses Value	No.	%	Mules Value	No.	%
1860	70	504	71	$116	1.8	70	$91	1.5	11
1892	56	246	71	$69	1.3	39	$93	1.3	21

Source: Clay County tax rolls.
Note: The dollar values for 1892 are expressed in 1860 dollars.
aCattle in 1892 is cattle plus bulls.

tax lists with census data from earlier years. Also, the absence of 1890 census manuscript data prevents us from assessing the reliability of 1892 tax reports. These reservations aside, however, the data on agricultural holdings reported for purposes of county tax assessments suggest further, modest declines in farm production, especially livestock, from 1880 to 1892.

Comparison of Table 9.7 with Tables 9.5 and 9.6 suggests that average corn production in Beech Creek held steady between 1880 and 1892, but the number of cattle (milk cows, oxen, and other cattle) and hogs per farm fell along with the proportion of farmers owning each. Only 41 percent of the farmers listed in the tax rolls, for instance, owned hogs in 1892 (down from the 1880 census level of 51 percent). The average number of horses per farm remained relatively steady, but the proportion of farmers owning horses

1870			1880		
Mean	No.	%	Mean	No.	%
234	129	98	247	76	88
36	51	39	39	37	43
48	40	30	37	26	30
18	103	78	13	8	9
8	106	80	—	—	—
72	100	76	78	71	83
22	95	72	20	45	52

Cattle[a]			Hogs			Total Personal and Real Estate
Value	No.	%	Value	No.	%	
$97	8.8	77	—	9.5	59	$1,183 (n = 60) (% = 86)
$70	5.8	46	$12	5	41	$427 (n = 41) (% = 73)

declined from 55 percent in 1880 to 39 percent in 1892. A portion of such decreases may reflect the fact that marginal farmers excluded from the agricultural censuses were included on the county tax lists, but the comparison of data from 1860 and 1892 tax lists confirms the unmistakable conclusion that Beech Creek farmers in 1892 were significantly poorer than those of a generation earlier. On all variables except ownership of mules, the monetary values (in constant dollars), the amounts produced, and—except for corn growing—the proportion of farmers reporting production fell dramatically between these years. Most significantly of all—as a reflection of the declining prosperity of agriculture—Beech Creek farmers in 1892 were far less wealthy than their ancestors of the previous generation, their estates valued at only 36 percent (in standardized dollars) of those of the earlier era.

Table 9.8. Surplus Agricultural Production in Clay County, 1860

Size of Farm Unit					Land	
Number of Improved Acres	Mean Surplus (bu.)	% Producing Surplus	No.	Tenure	Mean Surplus (bu.)	
Below or equal median of 35 acres	150	79	63	Owners	314	
Above median of 35 acres	508	95	56	Tenants	334	
Above 100 acres	684	100	8			
All farms	318	87	119			

Source: Eighth Census of the United States, 1860: Agriculture (manuscripts).
ªLarge slaveowners operated farms with more than 100 improved acres.

Trends in Surplus Production

Thus far we have examined aggregate trends in animal and crop production, but the data indicating these trends have not been standardized to take into account the changing nutritional needs of Beech Creek farm households or the variable feed requirements of their livestock. As we have demonstrated elsewhere, the average size of Beech Creek households declined during the years under investigation.[45] This factor, along with the decreasing size of farms and their diminished livestock inventories, implies that, over time, Beech Creek farmers may have needed to grow less food and feed. The changing mix of crop allocations, too, suggests the importance of standardization, but since Beech Creek farms did not primarily produce agricultural commodities, the monetary value of products sold does not capture variations in output. Consequently, we have utilized well-documented techniques developed by economic historians to measure the output of nineteenth-century farms in order to assess changes in the productivity of Beech Creek farms.[46]

Table 9.8 reports surplus agricultural production in Clay County for 1860. It shows surprisingly high levels of production on even the smallest farm units. Even those below the median of 35 improved acres averaged 150 bushels of produce above and beyond the subsistence and reproduction requirements of their households and farms. Only 21 percent of these small units failed to meet their own needs. Larger farms did even better, those

Tenure		Slaveowners			
% Producing Surplus	No.	Slaveowners	Mean Surplus (bu.)	% Producing Surplus	No.
87	92	Large[a]	1,512	94	18
85	27	Small[b]	501	85	13
		All	1,087	90	31

[b]Small slaveowners operated farms with less than 100 improved acres.

above the median producing 508 bushels of surplus and those cultivating more than 100 acres producing 684 bushels. Perhaps not surprisingly, since tenant farm families were smaller and had fewer members to feed than households headed by farm owners, farms operated by owners and tenants were almost identically productive, although it should be noted that a few of the largest farms in our sample—including one with 300 acres of improved lands—were operated by nonowners, implying that some "tenants" were actually professional farm managers.

In addition to the sample farms, Table 9.8 also reports data on all farms in the county that were operated with slave labor. These too were able to produce large food surpluses that went well beyond the consumption requirements of their own households as well as the needs of their slaves. The largest of these, with improved acreage greater than 100 acres, averaged 1,512 surplus bushels. The existence of large surpluses on such farms confirms the existence of potentially marketable quantities of foodstuffs in Clay County during the late antebellum period, just as the production of modest surpluses on smaller units confirms the latters' self-sufficiency. Additionally, the production of surpluses on the farms of the largest slaveholders suggests that these operations produced ample food for slaves employed in off-farm enterprises such as salt making. Thus, for example, the salt manufacturers Daugherty White, Alexander White, and James White, Sr., produced 8,697 surplus bushels of food beyond the consumption needs of their combined eighty slaves, and Daniel and Theophilus Garrard produced a surplus of

Table 9.9. Surplus Production in Beech Creek, 1850–1880

	1850	1860	1870	1880
Tenant farmers	51 bu.	331 bu.	108 bu.	17 bu.
	(n = 29)	(n = 16)	(n = 32)	(n = 23)
Farm owners	327 bu.	414 bu.	247 bu.	139 bu.
	(n = 23)	(n = 37)	(n = 100)	(n = 61)
Small owners	158 bu.	223 bu.	102 bu.	85 bu.
	(n = 12)	(n = 20)	(n = 52)	(n = 24)
Large owners	512 bu.	639 bu.	404 bu.	174 bu.
	(n = 11)	(n = 17)	(n = 48)	(n = 37)
All farmers	173 bu.	389 bu.	213 bu.	106 bu.
	(n = 52)	(n = 53)	(n = 132)	(n = 84)

Sources: Calculated from U.S. censuses of agriculture, 1850, 1860, 1870, 1880 (manuscripts).

Table 9.10. Beech Creek Farms Not Producing Agricultural Surpluses

	1850	1860	1870	1880
Percentage	36.5	9	20	36
Number	19	5	26	30
Total number of farms	52	53	132	84

Sources: Calculated from U.S. censuses of agriculture, 1850, 1860, 1870, 1880 (manuscripts).

4,093 bushels of food in excess of the amount they needed to feed the twenty-one slaves they owned.

In comparison with other farm regions, Clay County farms were surprisingly productive. Atack and Bateman report average farm surpluses of 359 and 175 bushels, respectively, for owner-occupied farms in the Midwest and the Northeast in 1860.[47] Assuming that hogs were fed entirely on forest masts, both tenants and farm owners in Clay County produced, on average, surplus levels roughly comparable to those of farm owners in either subregion of the northern United States at the time of the Civil War. Clay County slaveowners produced three times as much surplus as midwestern farm owners and six times as much as northeastern farm owners.

Table 9.9 and Figure 9.1 report trends in surplus production among Beech Creek farmers from 1850 to 1880. All categories of farmers, tenants as

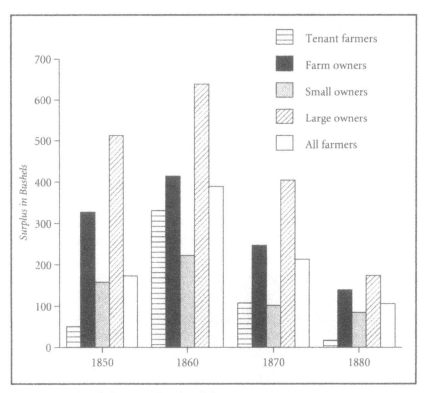

Figure 9.1. Trends in Farm Productivity

well as large and small owners, improved production significantly between 1850 and 1860 but saw these improvements reversed by 1880 when surpluses fell to levels well below those of 1850. Surpluses on owner-operated farms fell 66 percent from 1860 to 1880, and all farmers experienced declines that averaged almost 300 bushels (73 percent). Tenant farmers were more severely affected. Their surplus production fell by almost 95 percent to an average of only 17 bushels, suggesting that oral history recollections of particularly hard times among this group in the twentieth century are probably quite accurate.[48] Table 9.10 shows that the number of farms experiencing food deficits rose from only 9 percent in 1860 to 36 percent in 1880. As argued above, the most realistic way to model Appalachian farm practices is to assume that farmers did not give their hogs significant quantities of feed throughout the year. Nevertheless, the fact that simply adding hog consumption to farm requirements in 1880 would have lowered the average surplus for all farms to only thirty-five bushels and created food deficits for 48 percent of Beech Creek's farmers suggests how economically vulnerable Beech Creek farms were becoming by 1880.[49]

Reasons for the Decline of Surplus Production

A number of possible factors may explain the decline in Beech Creek farming between 1860 and 1880. Even though Clay County was not a major battleground, some reductions in livestock holdings may have been caused by conflict that occurred there during the Civil War. The South as a whole experienced vast declines in its livestock supply because of the destruction of animals during the war. Eight former slave states, for example, produced nearly 3 million fewer hogs in 1880 than 1860 because of wartime losses.[50] Minor battles and raids in Clay County undoubtedly caused some hardship, including the murder of one resident of Beech Creek by Confederate cavalry. In addition to the destruction of salt-making facilities by Federal troops, Confederate troops are known to have captured 150 head of cattle during a raid on Goose Creek, and the guerrilla forces of John Hunt Morgan are said to have "stole[n], robbed, and burned nearly everything [owned by] the people of Red Bird Creek, Goose Creek and South Fork."[51]

Declining soil fertility, too, may have reduced farm output, but this is difficult to determine since the agricultural censuses did not report acreage allotments by crop before 1880. Beech Creek's soil was almost certainly less fertile in 1942 when Brown observed the community than it had been in 1860. But an analysis of county-level aggregate census data shows that per-acre yields of corn did not fall between 1880 and 1910, suggesting that the worst impacts of soil erosion in Clay County probably occurred during the twentieth century rather than during the period immediately after the Civil War.

A more likely explanation for the decline of Beech Creek farming in the nineteenth century is the changing balance of land and population. The Appalachian population experienced one of the highest reproduction rates in the United States during the period covered by our investigation.[52] The effect of rapid population growth on limited land resources—in this case due largely to the reproduction of only a handful of families—can be illustrated by its impact on farming along the rugged creek bed portion of Beech Creek, one of the three neighborhoods that made up the whole Beech Creek community.

Beech Creek itself—that is, the creek from which the Beech Creek community derives its name—runs only five miles from its headwaters to its mouth at the south fork of the Kentucky River. The creek flows through hilly terrain where valley bottoms are rare, amounting to less than 10 percent of the basin's total land area. "From the air the Beech Creek basin looks like a great gully with many subsidiary ditches branching off in vine-like fashion."[53] Unlike the broad valleys that run alongside a few sections of the

Kentucky River in Clay County, the Beech Creek basin is not an area in which a large population can sustain itself through the practice of subsistence farming.

In 1810 only one household lived on the creek itself, Daniel Johnson's family with six members. According to Brown, 26 people lived along the creek in 1850, all of them located near the mouth of the stream. By 1880 49 people in seven households lived along the creek from its mouth almost to its headwaters in the rugged hills high above the river. Population on the creek increased further from 86 in 1900 to 164 in 1920, after which it remained almost stationary until 1942 because of the outmigration of 95 people.[54]

Such population growth directly influenced the quality of Beech Creek agriculture through its impact on farm size. The custom of equitable partible inheritance meant that mountain farms had to be divided and redivided to accommodate new generations of farm families. Thus it seems likely that by 1880, Beech Creekers were already beginning to approach a point of diminishing returns as they subdivided their farms to provide a means of livelihood for their children and grandchildren.

An intergenerational analysis of two original Beech Creek farm families, the Andrewses and the Johnsons, confirms the diminishing prospects that Beech Creek farmers faced from 1850 to 1892 as a consequence of the declining scale of their farm operations.[55] Adoniram Andrews (1734–1838) came to the Kentucky mountains from New England after serving in the Continental army during the American Revolution and fighting in the Battle of King's Mountain in North Carolina. He traveled through the Cumberland Gap to the Beech Creek section of Clay County, where he established a farm on the Southfork of the Kentucky River and built a sawmill on the river. He was elected to serve on the first grand jury that was formed in Clay County in 1805. "Squirrelman" Job Andrews, believed to be his brother, settled nearby. Soon afterward, Daniel Johnson patented 100 acres on the river at the mouth of Beech Creek in 1816, not far from the more extensive landholding of Adoniram Andrews. In 1826 his brother, Richard Johnson, purchased 50 of his acres and also began to raise a family. Andrews descendants, along with those of a few other settlers, soon populated the Laurel neighborhood of Beech Creek along the Kentucky River, while descendants of the Johnsons populated adjacent tributaries of the river in the Beech Creek basin. Much of the history of the Beech Creek community revolved around the activities of these two families, and members of both families still live in or near Beech Creek today.

The changing patterns of landownership and farm production among the Andrews and Johnson families in Beech Creek between 1850 and 1880 are evident in a comparison of five fathers with their same-age sons thirty years later which reveals that the sons were unable to accumulate as much land or grow as much food as their fathers had done before them at a comparable age, simply because they had to share their fathers' estates with other siblings. Thus in 1850, at age 51, Adoniram Andrews III—the wealthiest farmer in Beech Creek—owned 5,603 acres. Thirty years later his son Daniel, age 48, owned 600 acres. Elisha Johnson owned 1,400 acres in 1860 when he was 47, but his son Alex owned only 400 acres at age 51 in 1892. Abel Johnson owned 700 acres at age 48 in 1860, but his son Samuel owned only 100 acres when he was the same age in 1892. Job Andrews owned 350 acres in 1860 when he was 35, but his son, Morris, age 33, owned only 50 acres in 1892. William Johnson owned 500 acres in 1870 at age 55, but his 51-year-old son, Squire—faring better than many of his generation, given the extent of his father's possessions—owned 350 acres in 1892.

Analysis of farm outputs for eighteen additional fathers and their adult children in Beech Creek from 1850 to 1892 reveals that in no case did members of the younger generation of farmers—the third generation in Beech Creek after its initial settlement—produce surpluses in the 1880s as great as those produced by their fathers at the peak of their productivity in the earlier period from 1850 to 1860.[56] Although this generation was not poor, the diminished levels of its landholding, wealth, and farm production point to the social origins of the poverty of subsequent generations.

Family size, the quantity of initial landholdings, and the acquisition of additional acres influenced how well the fathers of each generation could position their sons and daughters for the next generation of farm life in Beech Creek. Both the effects of life cycle and family formation on farming outcomes, as well as the long-term impacts of farm subdivision, can be shown by a detailed examination of the Elisha Johnson family, a family that for several years dominated the Beech Creek basin area. Indeed, the experience of this single family summarizes the whole journey from prosperity to poverty that marks the history of Beech Creek from 1860 to 1942.

Elisha Johnson, whose home manufacturing was described above, was a son of one of the original settlers of Beech Creek. According to Brown, he married in 1836 and had eight children, including Preston Johnson, with whom Brown lived in 1942 while he carried out his first fieldwork. In 1850, at age thirty-seven, Elisha operated a farm of 250 acres (30 improved) that included $200 worth of livestock. He slaughtered $35 worth of meat that year, grew 500 bushels of corn, and managed to produce a good surplus of food (equivalent to 254 bushels) beyond the immediate needs of his family.

During the next decade he managed to buy many additional tracts of land from neighbors and relatives, enabling him both to increase his farm production and to prepare for his children's future. By 1860 his household had increased in size but so too had his farming operation, which would soon comprise virtually the entire basin area of Beech Creek from its mouth to its headwaters. He still only cultivated about 35 acres but owned more than 1,400 acres in 1860. His livestock inventory had increased considerably to include three horses, five cows, six oxen, six cattle, four sheep, and twenty hogs worth nearly $600. He slaughtered $120 worth of animals that year and produced a surplus that was the equivalent of 430 bushels of food.

By 1870 Elisha still produced a sizable food surplus (334 bushels), but he farmed only 300 acres, having begun to distribute his property among his sons and daughters who were establishing their own farms and families on portions of his lands, though he still retained legal title to their farms. Some sons and daughters left Beech Creek, but a married daughter and two sons, Alex and John, were listed in the agricultural census in 1880. Elisha, age sixty-seven, produced a good surplus (186 bushels) in 1880, as did his daughter, Mary Polly, and his son Alex. Another son, John, also operated a farm that was reported in the census, but he was unable to produce a surplus on his smaller holding, producing only enough food for his family and livestock.[57]

According to Brown, when Elisha Johnson died, sometime after 1880, his widow, a second wife, retained 280 acres as a "widow's dower" that was subsequently divided into seven tracts, each containing about 40 acres, at the time of her death. Several of Elisha's children passed on land to their children, but the eldest, John, had conflicts with his siblings and sold his property to nonkin, thus opening up lands within the creek basin to nonkin for the first time since the days of original settlement.[58]

By 1942 Elisha Johnson's lands—which according to Brown's estimate may have totaled as much as 2,200 acres at their peak—had been subdivided into twenty-four tracts owned by twenty-one different owners. "*At that time, 21 families lived on parts of the original farm, on which only one family was living in 1860.* Three of these families lived on what was the widow's dower; one lived on the part Preston was given; seven lived on what was John's; two on Eliza's; three on Alex's; and four on James' farm."[59]

Only one of Elisha's children, Preston, was still alive when Brown first observed Beech Creek. Brown wrote,

The youngest son of Elisha Johnson (Preston) was still living in 1942. Unlike his brother Alex, Preston never had a civil war pension, and unlike his brother James, who had only two children, Preston had a family of 16 children. To support this big family, Preston sold parts of his original farm. By far the biggest block, some 350 acres, was sold to Calvin Andrews, a Laurel neighborhood man who bought it for the timber. Two small tracts—one of 35 acres and the other of 15 acres—he sold to his daughter Sarah Johnson Williams and to his son-in-law Ernest West. The farmhouse itself, which Preston built [around 1880] and the 75 acres surrounding it, were deeded to his daughter Ellen J. West [in 1932] in return for her assuming care for her old parents as long as they lived. In 1942, Preston himself owned only one steep, forested tract of some 66 acres.[60]

Thus by 1942 156 people in 32 impoverished households lived in an area (the Beech Creek basin) where only 26 people in 3 households had lived 90 years earlier in relative plenty.

The same high rate of population growth that eventually destroyed the balance of people, land, and resources in Beech Creek had its impact throughout the rest of Clay County. For each decade from 1850 to 1900 the county's population grew by 22 to 25 percent, primarily through natural increase. Only the decade between 1900 and 1910 registered a slower rate of growth (with an increase of 16 percent) when many young people had begun to leave the county to search for opportunities elsewhere.[61] Such population growth resulted in reduced farm sizes and more intensive land-use practices.

In 1880 1,414 Clay County families farmed a total of 239,896 improved and unimproved acres for an average of 170 acres per farm. By 1910 more than twice as many families (2,916) farmed only slightly more space (244,214 acres) on farms that averaged only 86 acres. Per capita farm acreage declined in the county from 38 acres in 1860 to less than 14 acres in 1910.

The consequences of enormous population growth and farm subdivision were undoubtedly worsened by the inherent limitations of forest farming. Forest farming was an effective adaptation that substituted land for labor and capital, but its continued success "required an abundance of woodlands for new fields and range."[62] Time and space both worked against the long-term success of successive generations of mountain farmers, even in a locality such as Beech Creek, which was relatively sheltered from the impact of coal mining and related industrialization. The effects of population growth and farm subdivision were even more pronounced in those counties where absentee landownership and mining were drastically diminishing cultivable land, thus placing the long-term needs of forest farming and the corporate capitalist form of industrialization on a historical collision course.[63]

In regard to space, it has been estimated that "omnivorous hogs required less range land than cattle . . . [but] even a small herd of cattle required hundreds of acres of unfenced range in order to find sufficient native forage."[64] Farm subdivision reduced the space available for livestock foraging by forcing farmers to use their increasingly scarce lands ever more intensely. Thus the proportion of each farm that was improved in Clay County rose steadily from 12 percent in 1860 to 42.4 percent in 1910, bringing more and more woodland into cultivation. Additionally the commercial timber industry further accelerated forest clearances during the logging boom that occurred between 1890 and 1925.[65] These changes were registered in declining livestock inventories. The average Clay County farm had 13.4 hogs and 5.1 cattle (of all types) in 1880 but only 5.8 hogs and 3.9 cattle in 1910. (As reported in Table 9.5, the average Beech Creek farmer had 21 hogs and 12.7 cattle of all types fifty years earlier in 1860.)

Time requirements, too, worked against later generations of Appalachian farmers. The practice of "forest fallowing" required long amounts of time, usually a generation or more, for reforestation to restore old soil to its original productivity. "After an old field was reforested, it could be cleared and farmed anew. But if the field was again cultivated before reforestation and restoration of nutrients in the forest growth was completed, then declining yields, soil exhaustion, and soil erosion resulted."[66] When farms began to shrink in Clay County as a consequence of intergenerational subdivision and, as less "new grounds" became available, farmers became pressured both to cultivate steeper and poorer quality acreage as well as to shorten the length of time their lands remained out of production. Thus an informant, Hubert Collins, recalling Beech Creek farming during his youth in the 1930s, told our interviewer that his parents and their neighbors would typically "let their old grounds lay out . . . a couple or three years." When asked if the landscape he recalled as a boy looked different from today's, he replied, "Wouldn't be no trees. Everything'd be in corn."

The long-term limitations of forest farming in Appalachia were apparent even to contemporary observers during the nineteenth century. In 1873 J. B. Killebrew noted that "the people in no portion of the state [of Tennessee] live so well or have their tables so bountifully furnished" as the farmers of the Cumberland Mountains of East Tennessee; yet Killebrew foresaw what would soon become the Achilles' heel of mountain farming when he pointed out that already by the 1870s "in the matter of the subdivision of farms, East Tennessee ha[d] gone quite as far as seems desirable."[67] Sixty years later, Tennessee farmers, like their counterparts in the hills of Kentucky, were impoverished.[68]

The consequences of slow economic growth, population increase, land shortage, and soil depletion in the nonmining counties of Appalachia were obvious to twentieth-century ethnographers. In Beech Creek, scarce bottomland remained in the control of a few families, but "by the time the grandchildren of the original landowners were grown, the area was so thickly populated relative to the agricultural potential of the land that families had moved up hollows and coves until the entire length of Beech Creek and its tributary valleys was inhabited."[69] In the Tennessee community of Little Smoky Ridge, likewise, "successive divisions of property and loss of soil fertility" had made cultivable land "scarce even by local standards." Family tracts of 100 to 600 acres had been reduced by inheritance to small plots of only 15 to 40 acres in the 1950s.[70]

Ethnographers were wrong, however, to attribute this structural limitation to a flaw in Appalachian culture. Pearsall, for instance, contributed to the erroneous assumption of Appalachian exceptionalism when she wrote that mountain farmers "were committed to the destructive extensive methods of their forbearers, and they could be successful only so long as the supply of new land was unlimited. The result is the *cultural blind alley* in which they find themselves."[71] But mountain farmers were no more led down a blind alley than were their predecessors in other American farm regions. What occurred in the nonindustrial sections of Appalachia in the late nineteenth century was simply the repetition of events that had already happened in older regions such as New England during the late eighteenth century when "mounting [population] pressure on the land supply" had led to "sharply diminished landholding and a greater cultivation of marginal lands."[72] The only things that were exceptional in these Appalachian localities were the timing of the demographic upheaval—since the lack of modern means of transportation and extensive market linkages permitted the relatively late survival of subsistence agriculture in the mountains—and the fact that trained social scientists were on hand to observe firsthand and to record the outcome of processes that had occurred earlier and been forgotten elsewhere.

In early New England, as later in Appalachia, "family lands were divided again and again to accommodate the increasing numbers of young men."[73] Charles Grant, for instance, reports that the "economic opportunity" that had once been "exceptionally bright" for the first generation that peopled the town of Kent, Connecticut, from 1740 to 1770 became "darkened . . . by the pressure of population . . . against a limited supply of land" by the time of its third generation.[74] The regionwide result was a massive exodus of population from New England between 1790 and 1830. It was during this period that Adoniram Andrews left New Hampshire to settle in the Kentucky mountains, and it was his great-grandchildren's generation in Beech Creek—the third generation after settlement—whose way of life was becoming "darkened" by the increasing scarcity of land.

New Englanders adapted to the crisis of their agricultural society by sending many of their sons and daughters into the new factories that had begun to dot their rural landscape. Many more people moved to new lands on the western frontier, however, including Kentucky, where, like Adoniram Andrews, they were able to continue farming as their ancestors had done before them with little cultural discontinuity. East Kentuckians, too, moved into the mines and mills that sprang up in Appalachia almost overnight as railroads—necessarily built by outsiders, since the local Appalachian economy by itself could not generate the millions of dollars in investments that transportation improvements required—opened the region to capitalist industrialization early in the twentieth century. Even more people moved to new urban and industrial frontiers in the cities of the Midwest, where they were forced, or able, to adapt to an altogether new way of life. As the follow-up studies of Beech Creek in the 1960s demonstrated, the success of that cultural adjustment is as striking a story as that of the poverty in the hills that had forced their departure.[75]

Notes

Support for this research was provided by grants from the Rural Economic Policy Program of the Aspen Institute, the University of Wisconsin Institute for Research on Poverty, Berea College, and the University of Kentucky. We especially wish to thank Jane Bagby, Gloria Beeker, Roberta Campbell, Gail Holman, Jack Thigpen, and Paul Winegartner for assistance collecting and coding data from manuscript census records. Above all, we thank James S. Brown for his help in our carrying further his "Beech Creek" studies.

1. H. Kephart, *Our Southern Highlanders* (1913; reprint, Knoxville: University of Tennessee Press, 1976), p. 37. For a discussion of the stereotyping of Appalachian agriculture, see J. T. Kirby, *Rural Worlds Lost* (Baton Rouge: Louisiana State University Press, 1987), esp. pp. 80–111.

2. For an example of such attributions made without the systematic investigation of farm practices, see M. Pearsall, *Little Smoky Ridge* (Birmingham: University of Alabama Press, 1959).

3. R. D. Eller, *Miners, Millhands, and Mountaineers: Industrialization of the Appalachian South, 1880–1930* (Knoxville: University of Tennessee Press, 1982), p. 6;

Appalachian Land Ownership Task Force, *Who Owns Appalachia? Landownership and Its Impact* (Lexington: University Press of Kentucky, 1983), p. 81. Also see D. Pierce, "The Low-Income Farmer: A Reassessment," *Social Work in Appalachia* 3 (1971): 8.

4. See F. McDonald and G. McWhiney, "The Antebellum Southern Herdsman," *Journal of Southern History* 41 (1975): 147–66. On the impact of the closing of the range, see J. C. King, "The Closing of the Southern Range: An Exploratory Study," *Journal of Southern History* 48 (1982): 53–70. On early livestock droves in Appalachia, see P. Salstrom, "The Agricultural Origins of Economic Dependency, 1840–1880," in *Appalachian Frontiers: Settlement, Society, and Development in the Preindustrial Era*, ed. R. D. Mitchell (Lexington: University Press of Kentucky, 1991), pp. 261–83.

5. J. S. Otto, "The Decline of Forest Farming in Southern Appalachia," *Journal of Forest History*, January 1983, pp. 18–26; J. S. Otto, "The Migration of the Southern Plain Folk: An Interdisciplinary Synthesis," *Journal of Southern History* 51 (1985): 183–200; J. S. Otto and N. E. Anderson, "Slash-and-Burn Cultivation in the Highland South: A Problem in Comparative Agricultural History," *Comparative Studies in Society and History* 24 (1982): 131–47. For evidence that forest farming was recently practiced in some parts of Appalachia, see J. F. Hart, "Land Rotation in Appalachia," *Geographical Review* 67 (April 1977): 148–66.

6. These debates follow years of research and controversy about the relative importance of market embeddedness and moral economy in early New England. For an overview of these issues, see A. Kulikoff, "The Transition to Capitalism in Rural America," *William and Mary Quarterly*, 3rd ser., 46 (January 1989): 120–44. S. Hahn, in *The Roots of Southern Populism: Yeoman Farmers and the Transformation of the Georgia Upcountry, 1850–1890* (New York: Oxford University Press, 1983), has stressed the importance of subsistence production in the southern upcountry during the antebellum period. For an early comparison between subsistence farming in preindustrial Appalachia and New England, see D. Billings, K. Blee, and S. Swanson, "Culture, Family, and Community in Preindustrial Appalachia," *Appalachian Journal* 13 (Winter 1986): 154–70.

7. See D. Dunn, *Cades Cove: The Life and Death of a Southern Appalachian Community, 1818–1937* (Knoxville: University of Tennessee Press, 1988); J. C. Inscoe, *Mountain Masters: Slavery and the Sectional Crisis in Western North Carolina* (Knoxville: University of Tennessee Press, 1989); R. D. Mitchell, *Commercialism and Frontier: Perspectives on the Early Shenandoah Valley* (Charlottesville: University Press of Virginia, 1977); R. Mann, "Mountains, Land, and Kin Networks: Burkes Garden, Virginia, in the 1840s and 1850s," *Journal of Southern History* 58 (1992): 411–34. For an important and provocative effort to locate the interplay of Appalachian subsistence production and commercialization in spatial and temporal dimensions, see Salstrom, "Agricultural Origins."

8. Inscoe, *Mountain Masters*, pp. 12, 11.

9. A. Waller, *Feud: Hatfields, McCoys, and Social Change in Appalachia, 1860–1900* (Chapel Hill: University of North Carolina Press, 1988); United States Department of Agriculture, *Economic and Social Problems and Conditions of the Southern Appalachians* (Washington, D.C.: Government Printing Office, 1935). Also see M. B.

Pudup, "Social Class and Economic Development in Southeastern Kentucky," in Mitchell, *Appalachian Frontiers*, pp. 235–60.

10. T. Moore, "Economic Development in Appalachian Kentucky, 1800–1860," in Mitchell, *Appalachian Frontiers*, pp. 232, 234.

11. M. B. Pudup, "The Limits of Subsistence: Agriculture and Industry in Central Appalachia," *Agricultural History* 64 (1990): 74.

12. Brown's ethnographic observations of farming, family patterns, and community stratification in 1942 are reported in J. S. Brown, *Beech Creek: The Social Organization of an Isolated Kentucky Mountain Neighborhood* (1950; reprint, Berea, Ky.: Berea College Press, 1988). See also J. S. Brown, "The Conjugal Family and Extended Family Group," *American Sociological Review* 17 (1952): 297–305; "The Family Group in a Kentucky Mountain Farming Community," *Kentucky Agricultural Experiment Station Bulletin 588* (1952). Outmigrants from Beech Creek and their urban relocation were studied in H. Schwarzweller, J. Brown, and J. Mangalam, *Mountain Families in Transition* (University Park: Pennsylvania State University Press, 1971), and they were resurveyed in V. McCoy, "Solidarity and Integration of Migrant Family Groups" (Ph.D. diss., University of Cincinnati, 1986).

13. For a discussion of methodological problems involved in asking new questions about past ethnographic studies and utilizing their findings to answer questions not originally asked by their authors, see K. Blee and D. Billings, "Reconstructing Daily Life in the Past: An Hermeneutical Approach to Ethnographic Data," *Sociological Quarterly* 27, no. 4 (1986): 443–62.

14. Brown, *Beech Creek*, p. 28.

15. Ibid.

16. Ibid., p. 30.

17. See M. McDonald and J. Muldowny, *TVA and the Dispossessed: The Resettlement of Population in the Norris Dam Area* (Knoxville: University of Tennessee Press, 1982), for a reconstruction of typical farming, family, and community patterns in eastern Tennessee's Cumberland Plateau in the 1920s that closely parallels Brown's description of Beech Creek in the 1940s.

18. Brown, *Beech Creek*, p. 31.

19. Ibid., p. 33.

20. The misleading notion that the Appalachian and Blue Grass regions of Kentucky developed independently from each other from the days of their earliest settlement, resulting in two separate Kentuckies, was advanced by local-color writers such as J. L. Allen, "Through the Cumberland Gap on Horseback," reprinted in *The Blue-Grass Region of Kentucky and Other Kentucky Articles* (New York: Harper and Brothers, 1899), and J. Fox, Jr., *Blue Grass and Rhododendron* (New York: Charles Scribner's Sons, 1901). For a history of the settlement and development of the Kentucky River, see T. Clark, *The Kentucky*, bicentennial ed. (Lexington: University Press of Kentucky, 1992).

21. See E. Parr, "Kentucky's Overland Trade with the Ante-bellum South," *Filson Club History Quarterly* 2 (January 1928): 71–81; E. Perkins, "The Consumer Frontier: Household Consumption in Early Kentucky," *Journal of American History* 78 (September 1991): 486–510; R. Wade, *The Urban Frontier: Pioneer Life in Early Pittsburgh, Cincinnati, Lexington, Louisville, and St. Louis* (Chicago: University of

Chicago Press, 1964); T. Clark, "Salt, a Factor in the Settlement of Kentucky," *Filson Club History Quarterly* 12 (January 1939): 42–52; J. F. Smith, "The Salt-Making Industry of Clay County, Kentucky," *Filson Club History Quarterly* 1 (April 1927): 134–41; M. Verhoeff, *The Kentucky River Navigation* (Louisville, Ky.: John P. Morton, 1917).

22. Data on the landholdings of the White and Garrard families reported here are compiled from W. Jillson, *The Kentucky Land Grants* (Baltimore, Md.: Genealogical Pub. Co., 1971), and county tax rolls.

23. Data on social stratification are from D. Billings and K. Blee, "Appalachian Inequality in the Nineteenth Century: The Case of Beech Creek, Kentucky," *Journal of the Appalachian Studies Association* 4 (1992): 113–23.

24. Verhoeff, *Kentucky River Navigation*, p. 154.

25. Evidence for local opportunities created by salt making is contained in numerous cases of litigation brought before the antebellum Clay County Circuit Court that will be presented elsewhere.

26. See the merchant's day book of salt maker B. F. White for the years 1844 to 1854 (Kentucky State Library and Archives, Frankfort) and the earlier ledger of Hugh and James White for the Goose Creek Salt Works in 1806–7 (Filson Historical Society, Berea, Ky.).

27. See case of *Andrew Craig v. Conley Findley and Company* (1808), Records of the Clay County Circuit Court (Kentucky State Library and Archives).

28. Verhoeff, *Kentucky River Navigation*, pp. 103–7.

29. Verhoeff, *The Kentucky Mountains: Transportation and Commerce, 1750 to 1911* (Louisville, Ky.: John P. Morton, 1911), p. 126.

30. Ibid., pp. 169.

31. Ibid., p. 170.

32. K. Blee and D. Billings, "Appalachian Feuding: A Longitudinal Case Study of Violent Disputing," final report to Fund for Research on Dispute Resolution, 1992.

33. Data on Clay County is based on a population sample of every fourth household listed in the 1860 manuscript census of Clay County (approximately 250 households). We matched as many as possible of these households with individuals listed as operating farms in the 1860 manuscript census of agriculture ($n = 122$), and we matched individuals identified in the 1860 manuscript schedules of slaveholding with farm operators in the agricultural census ($n = 37$). Agricultural data for farmers in Beech Creek from 1850 to 1880 was assembled separately from census manuscripts. For information on how we located "Beech Creekers" in these records, see D. Billings and K. Blee, "Family Strategies in a Subsistence Economy: Beech Creek, Kentucky, 1850–1942," *Sociological Perspectives* 33, no. 1 (1990): 63–88.

34. Case studies report antebellum tenancy levels ranging from as high as 55 percent in one eastern Tennessee county (Dunn, *Cades Cove*) to as low as 3.6 percent in a southeastern Kentucky county (Pudup, "Limits of Subsistence"), while the author of a regionwide study of manuscript farm census records concludes that 25 percent of all farmers in Appalachia were landless in 1860 (W. Dunaway, "Southern Appalachia's People without History: The Role of Unfree Laborers in the Region's Antebellum Economy," paper presented at the annual meeting of the Social Science History Association, November 1989, Washington, D.C.). Researchers also dispute

how to interpret the social relations of farm tenancy in Appalachia. Pudup, in "Limits of Subsistence," suggests that tenant status largely reflected age, gender, and family status rather than social class, but Dunaway, in "People without History," p. 4, argues that tenants "comprised a sizeable sector of the farm population and provided a coerced labor supply for the region's agricultural production." Since Brown found that between 50 and 75 percent of all the possible relationships within the three Beech Creek neighborhoods in the 1940s were kin relationships to some degree, it is likely that tenancy within Beech Creek was shaped more by family than by social class relations, but it is also true, as county court records reveal, that elite landowners in Clay County rented lands to tenant farmers. In the latter situation, social class relations were predominant. For an oral history account of the harshness of such arrangements in Clay County and elsewhere in eastern Kentucky, see Jim Garland, *Welcome the Traveler Home* (Lexington: University Press of Kentucky, 1983), pp. 27, 31; L. Shackelford and B. Weinberg, *Our Appalachia: An Oral History* (Lexington: University Press of Kentucky, 1977), p. 197.

35. F. Bode and D. Ginter, *Farm Tenancy and the Census in Antebellum Georgia* (Athens: University of Georgia Press, 1986).

36. T. Arcury, "Agricultural Change in the Mountain South at the Turn of the Century," Center for Developmental Change Report #8, University of Kentucky, 1989.

37. See n. 5 above.

38. Northern rather than southern farms provide the most appropriate comparison for Clay County and Beech Creek farms, since both groups of farmers (including Clay County's slaveowning farmers) practiced general (diversified) farming rather than the production of staple crops such as cotton, tobacco, and—in other parts of Kentucky—hemp that characterized much of southern agriculture. Data on northern farms is from J. Atack and F. Bateman, *To Their Own Soil: Agriculture in the Antebellum North* (Ames: Iowa State University Press, 1987).

39. Quoted in ibid., p. 205.

40. Brown, *Beech Creek*, p. 6.

41. See D. Whisnant, *All That Is Native and Fine: The Politics of Culture in an American Region* (Chapel Hill: University of North Carolina Press, 1983), pp. 105–79. See also H. Shapiro, *Appalachia on Our Mind: The Southern Mountains and Mountaineers in the American Consciousness, 1870–1920* (Chapel Hill: University of North Carolina Press, 1978), pp. 213–43.

42. S. Maggard, "From Farmers to Miners: The Decline of Agriculture in Eastern Kentucky," in *Science and Agricultural Development*, ed. L. Busch (Totowa, N.J.: Allanheld, Osmun, 1981), pp. 25–56.

43. Farmers in the Beech Creek neighborhoods were, however, somewhat wealthier than the countywide average; 26 percent owned estates valued at more than $2,000, but only 11 percent of Clay County farmers owned farms that valuable in 1860, suggesting that far from being an economically marginal section of Clay County as it is today or when Brown first studied it, Beech Creek was a typical, even thriving, rural farm community in 1860.

44. See R. Hunt, "Northern Agriculture after the Civil War, 1865–1900," pp. 53–74, and D. Winters, "The Economics of Midwestern Agriculture, 1865–1900," pp.

75–96, both in *Agriculture and National Development,* ed. L. Ferleger (Ames: Iowa State University Press, 1990).

45. Elsewhere we have reported that households declined in size from a mean of 6.87 members in 1850 to 5.18 members in 1910. See Billings and Blee, "Family Strategies in a Subsistence Economy."

46. Our analysis utilizes methods reported in J. Atack and F. Bateman, "Self-Sufficiency and the Marketable Surplus in the Rural North, 1860," *Agricultural History* 58 (1984): 296–313, and in Atack and Bateman, *Their Own Soil.* The equations are based on calculations of the nutritional needs of each farm household, adjusting for age and gender of its members, as well as feed requirements of livestock and variable proportions of crops assumed to have been held back for the next year's seed. Caloric needs as well as crop and livestock production are each translated in "corn equivalent units." A surplus is defined as any production of corn equivalent units (in bushels) over and beyond the consumption (and seed) requirements of the farm household (including slaves and laborers when present) and its livestock. We modified the Atack and Bateman equations in one important respect, however, by not including the feed requirement for hogs in our calculations, since the feeding of hogs on forest masts is assumed to have been universal among mountain farmers, an option not available in many areas of the North.

47. Atack and Bateman, *Their Own Soil,* p. 220.

48. In his published autobiography, labor organizer and folk singer Jim Garland (*Traveler,* p. 31) recalls that during his boyhood in Clay County around the turn of the century, "My mother said that during the years my father sharecropped, the family literally became naked. When someone had to go to the store, all the families garments were pooled so this one person would have enough to wear."

49. Adding hog feeding to the 1860 equations would have increased the proportion of farmers failing to produce surpluses from 9 percent to 30 percent for that year.

50. See McDonald and McWhiney, "Southern Herdsmen."

51. K. Morgan and K. Morgan, *History of Clay County, Kentucky,* bicentennial ed. (Manchester, Ky.: Morgan Book Co., 1976), p. 168.

52. We estimate that with children under age ten constituting 37 percent of the 1860 population in Clay County, natural increase there was remarkably high even by Third World standards today. As late as 1930 only 10 of 190 Appalachian counties are estimated to have had higher general fertility rates than did Clay County, according to G. DeJong, *Appalachian Fertility Decline* (Lexington: University Press of Kentucky, 1968).

53. Schwarzweller et al., *Mountain Families,* p. 4.

54. Brown, *Beech Creek,* pp. 12, 229.

55. The family names are pseudonyms used by Brown in *Beech Creek.*

56. Full data is presented in D. Billings and K. Blee, "Causes and Consequences of Persistent Rural Poverty: A Longitudinal Case Study of an Appalachian Community," final report to the Ford Foundation and the Rural Economic Policy Program of the Aspen Institute, 1991. For similar findings in the Tug River Valley of Kentucky and West Virginia, see Waller, *Feud.*

57. Elsewhere we have shown that cooperation among households within the

larger "family groups" first described by Brown was crucial for the survival of units not producing sufficient quantities of food. See Billings and Blee, "Family Strategies."

58. Brown, *Beech Creek*, p. 266.

59. Ibid., p. 267; italics added.

60. Ibid., p. 268.

61. See Billings and Blee, "Persistent Rural Poverty," for demographic evidence on nineteenth-century outmigration.

62. Otto, "Migration," p. 195.

63. Since Clay County was the last county in Kentucky to be reached by railroads, it provides an excellent test case of the long-term developmental tendencies of the mountain subsistence agricultural system. For an excellent examination of the profoundly negative impacts of corporate capitalist development on farming in mining counties, see Alan Banks, "Labor and the Development of Industrial Capitalism in Eastern Kentucky" (Ph.D. diss., McMaster University, 1979).

64. Otto, "Migration," p. 196.

65. On the extent, timing, and impact of timbering in Appalachian Kentucky, see Eller, *Miners, Millhands, and Mountaineers*, pp. 28–127.

66. Otto, "Decline of Forest Farming," p. 24.

67. Quoted in McDonald and Muldowny, *TVA*, p. 121.

68. According to McDonald and Muldowny, *TVA*, many farmers in the Norris Basin of eastern Tennessee were impoverished by 1930 when their farms averaged only 23.7 acres in crops, and gross farm incomes (including in-kind home consumption) averaged less than $100 per capita.

69. Schwarzweller et al., *Mountain Families*, p. 3.

70. Pearsall, *Little Smokey Ridge*, p. 48.

71. Ibid., p. 49; italics added.

72. K. Lockridge, "Land, Population, and the Evolution of New England Society, 1630–1790," *Past and Present* 39 (April 1968): 69.

73. Ibid.

74. Quoted in ibid.

75. The best study of urban migration and adjustment of rural Appalachians remains Schwarzweller et al., *Mountain Families*. For other reports on Appalachia's urban experience, see W. Philliber, *Appalachian Migrants in Urban America* (New York: Praeger, 1981); W. Philliber, C. McCoy, and H. Dillingham, eds., *The Invisible Minority: Urban Appalachians* (Lexington: University Press of Kentucky, 1981); P. Obermiller and W. Philliber, eds., *Too Few Tomorrows: Urban Appalachians in the 1980s* (Boone, N.C.: Appalachian Consortium Press, 1987).

A fuller understanding of the relationship between the town, economic growth and economic improvement in the pre-industrial world, and of the same relationship during and after the industrial revolution would go far towards explaining the nature of the great change from the traditional to the modern world.

—E. A. Wrigley

Town and Country in the Transformation of Appalachian Kentucky

Asingle log cabin stands boldly against a hillside littered with girdled tree stumps and recently shorn cornstalks. Two rush-seated rockers, strings of drying beans, and a large spinning wheel crowd the front porch. The curl of chimney smoke is barely discernible through a shroud of mist and fog.

A row of small frame houses huddles tentatively on another steep hillside. A would-be street disregards the slope and cuts straight up the hill, its dirt path packed hard underneath the daily footsteps of miners on their way to and from work. Perhaps fittingly, the company-owned houses all wear a uniform gray from repeated washings with coal dust.

The isolated subsistence farmstead and grimy coal camp are the two settlement ideals most closely identified with Appalachia in history, literature, and various other representations.[1] Their recurring images signal that the rural village, bustling city, or even prosaic small town did not gain significant presence in the region's settlement system. Indeed, the two pervasive settlement ideals are not complete fictions. Underpinning the still photographs is social and economic history meaningfully written in terms of enduring rurality and hasty, if not brutally careless, industrialization.[2]

A more nuanced understanding of Appalachian settlement includes the only urban forms that can claim ubiquity in the mountains, namely county seat towns.[3] New counties were created in Appalachia throughout the late eighteenth and nineteenth centuries along with the designated places where their courts would meet: these places became county seat towns. Understanding settlement requires more than discussion of physical forms, however. The growth of county seat towns betokened social differentiation within the population and, more generally, deepening social and spatial divisions of labor between town and country.

In this chapter I explore the nineteenth-century growth of county seat towns and settlement systems more generally in the distinctive Appalachian venue of southeastern Kentucky. Appalachian Kentucky was settled as an agricultural region and later became a principal locus of the region's bituminous coal industry. Both historical economic formations are central to the emergence and transformation of the region's settlement system. After enunciating a regional framework for conceptualizing the growth of settlement systems in Appalachian Kentucky, I go on to examine patterns of urban growth during industrializing decades when county seat towns took on many trappings of urban structure and function. I focus particularly on the coalfield counties of Floyd, Harlan, and Perry and their respective county seat towns of Prestonsburg, Harlan, and Hazard. The experience of these coalfield county seats suggests that the growth of towns in Appalachia, as elsewhere throughout the nation and the world, was symptomatic of regional capitalist economic growth. More pointedly, these towns disclose the specific capitalist forms taking hold in the surrounding countryside and their placement within the U.S. political economy.

It is axiomatic that towns and cities are centers of surplus and that, historically, rural surpluses have been the basis for urban growth. The extent and character of urban growth, moreover, has been shown to depend greatly upon the nature of surplus production in the countryside and the relations between the localized production system and wider ambits and structures of political and economic activity.[4] Towns and cities have no independent social agency *as towns*, a presumption that guided early urban history and sociology with unfortunate results. As Philip Abrams put it, "The material and especially the visual presence of towns seem to have impelled a reification in which the town as a physical object is turned into a taken-for-granted social object and a captivating focus of analysis in its own right."[5] Repeated quests for generalizations about "the town" as a generic social reality foundered on repeated discoveries that towns are "fields of action integral to some larger world."[6] Simply put, the search for a theory of towns (and cities) always and everywhere leads to wider theories of social change. The town survives as a worthy object of historical study precisely because it opens windows on the larger world through "which the interactions and contradictions of that larger world are displayed with special clarity."[7]

These simple precepts enjoy a dual relevance as both generalizations about urban growth and practical guides for understanding particular instances and patterns of urbanization. The movement from the general to the particular is accomplished by casting these precepts into regional frameworks, in recognition of the fact that rural surplus production and the concomitant presence or absence of towns are powerfully conditioned by historical geography. Questions of where, when, and what kind of rural surplus is created, along with crucial question of how it is produced, together suggest an approach to the study of settlement systems in which towns and cities are rooted in overlapping geographical contexts. A regional approach fully recognizes urbanization as a macrosociological spatial process of population concentration and economic centralization into towns and cities. Under this wide conceptual umbrella, the experiences of otherwise far flung reaches of the globe come together and avail themselves to comparative scrutiny. A regional approach makes room for comparative analysis by stipulating that urban growth is always context dependent and that town forms and social contexts are *both* the objects of analysis in any study of settlement systems.

David Goldfield's various studies of the U.S. South lie within the revisionist urban history movement linking town and country into an indissoluble whole. He ably demonstrates how regional frameworks illuminate the process and pattern of urbanization.[8] Southern cities may have been built with bricks and mortar like their northern counterparts, but Goldfield contends the similarities largely end there. "The southern city is different because the South is different."[9] It follows that "the most helpful perspective from which to study the southern city may be the southern region." He identifies three key features of southern regional history—an enduring rural lifestyle dominated by staple agriculture, race relations, and a colonial economy—and then demonstrates how distinctive regional history fostered distinctive urbanization.

Goldfield has not been alone in documenting southern difference. In their classic essay, Earle and Hoffman demonstrated how each of the South's colonial staple exports, tobacco, wheat, and rice, supported a somewhat different urban pattern according to "the weight and volume of each staple, its requirements for in-transit processing, and its market destinations."[10] Among these three staples, only wheat exerted what the authors call "linkage effects" sufficient to support towns and cities of varying size. The introduction and spread of cotton cultivation during the nineteenth century, coupled with the westward shift of wheat cultivation, suppressed urban development in the South during the antebellum era. Like tobacco before it, cotton required few centralized services because it was financed and processed outside the region. Absent in the South, therefore, was a wide distribution of towns and cities save for state capitals, a few seaports, and even fewer inland entrepôts. The pattern of southern urban growth, or lack thereof, had roots during the colonial era when staple export agriculture became the South's economic base.[11]

It was not the mere presence of staple export agriculture—the what, where, and when of the southern framework, as it were—that suppressed southern urbanization, however. The socially dominant form of staple production in plantation slavery—*how* tobacco, rice, and, later, cotton were produced—formed the keystone in the southern production system. As Bateman and Weiss, Eugene Genovese, Gavin Wright, Charles Post, and a host of others have shown, the plantation system proved antithetical to the emergence of linkages around the farm sector to specialized consumption and production-related industries and services. The manifest absence of these linkages put brakes on the concentration of commercial activities and services in towns.[12]

The studies of Goldfield and others might seem to suggest that the analysis of southern urbanization uniquely benefits from a regional perspective. But the principles that cities share a common history with their regions and that at the heart of such common history are cultural, political, and economic relations between city and country have wide applicability outside the South. These same principles, in fact, shine a bright light on urbanization in the northern United States, which followed a much different pattern.

City and country formed an early and enduring partnership in the culture and political economy of both New England and the Middle Atlantic regions, which subsequently spread across the northern United States. The linchpin in the city-and-country settlement system was the free family farming system of petty commodity producers who were thoroughly meshed in commercial relations with merchants, manufacturers, and various other creditors.[13] Virtually from the start, and despite an unquestionable commitment to producing their own subsistence, northern family farming was decidedly export oriented.[14] Central features in the history of the many subregions that comprise the North were ever-deepening and widening social divisions of labor. Family farmers became increasingly specialized around producing small grains and livestock for national and world markets. Without a readily expandable labor force, such as slaves were in the South, northern farmers maintained their competitive position by adopting an array of productivity enhancing technologies. These technologies themselves, in turn, became the province of specialized producers. The products of northern farms also required considerable processing, which stimulated another set of trade and industrial linkages. Furthermore, rising incomes, both on the farm and among the growing ranks of other specialized producers, generated consumer demand for goods and services—the province of yet another set of specialized goods and services producers.

This burgeoning agro-industrial complex in the northern United States supported a dense network of market towns and villages and, indeed, a full-fledged urban hierarchy. The social organization of farming permitted the provision of specialized goods and services to take place locally in towns and cities. As Richard Wade suggested in his aptly titled study *The Urban Frontier*, northern towns and cities were often founded at the same time as, if not in advance of, settlement in the surrounding countryside.[15] Merchants and artisans typically made their way west in the employ or with the sponsorship of an eastern business establishment. But eastern ties did not impede local business communities forming and developing their own momentum and attachments to the local region. In these ways towns and cities in the North were from the start integrated into both local and national political economies.

Because Appalachian Kentucky was settled by migrants carrying with them political traditions and cultural practices from established regions of the eastern seaboard, mountain settlement patterns should conform to historical antecedents. The further possibility exists that the settlement of Appalachia could be comprehended in terms of a wider regional framework, like that governing the North or the South. A mix of similarity and difference complicates any quick identity between Appalachia and these other regions, however, and thereby vitiates against such a direct point of departure in the study of settlement systems in Appalachian Kentucky.

Appalachia seemed to share the South's general pattern of urbanization throughout the antebellum era to the extent that towns were largely absent in both comparatively rural regions. But this shared physical settlement pattern arose under rather different conditions. Specifically, mountain agricultural production was neither dependent on plantation slavery, despite the scattered presence of slaves throughout Appalachian Kentucky, nor oriented around staple export crop production.[16] Appalachian Kentucky did share the North's agrarian structure of family farming around livestock and small grain agriculture. Yet here, too, the comparison falters. Unlike their northern counterparts, farmers in Appalachia were not specialized commodity producers, despite the fact that they were involved in commercial relations and marketed surplus goods.

These combinations of formal similarity and practical difference oblige a careful specification of Appalachian Kentucky's social and economic formations in order to shed light on its distinctive process and pattern of urbanization. The two axes of the region's settlement framework are (1) the political culture and geography of county governance and (2) the unspecialized family farming system.

The County Tradition

A useful beginning is during the late eighteenth and early nineteenth centuries, when settlers in southeastern Kentucky enjoyed wide latitude in locating themselves on the mountain landscape. No comprehensive public land survey had preceded them to parcel the land and direct their movements. Relatedly, there were no group settlement schemes as in central Kentucky. The common pattern was for settlers to arrive in small groups of related families and occupy land along streams promising fertile, if narrow, strips of bottomland and a continuous water supply.[17]

The fact that Kentucky land was not included in the national domain, and therefore was not subject to the township and range survey system, permitted settlers to continue the tradition of county subdivision and government forged in the Tidewater colonies of Virginia and Maryland. A town-based political economy, similar to that which eventually emerged in New England, had been envisioned for the Tidewater by the British colonial authorities.[18] Early town failures, local Tidewater geography, and the evolution of the colonial tobacco economy, however, encouraged instead a decentralized rural system of county governance centered on the courthouse. County courts became the central unit of local government administered by justices of the peace. Governors (colonial, and later, state) retained power to appoint justices, but this power rather quickly became a formality. In truth, county court justices were chosen locally, typically from among the largest landowners who usurped the offices for themselves. The power to create counties remained centralized in colonial and state legislative bodies, but here, too, the formality belied actual practice. During the colonial era when Tidewater colonies were expanding into the backcountry, the customary practice was for settlers to request separation of their locality into a new county when their numbers were sufficiently large to complain legitimately about distances to the existing courthouse.

This method of county subdivision, admirably suited to frontier rural settlement conditions, became permanently enshrined in state law, first in Virginia and later in its political and geographical offspring, Kentucky.[19] If the county was the heart of the Tidewater and Kentucky settlement system, the heart of the county was its court. County legislation designated a place where monthly and other periodic courts would meet, typically land sold or "donated" to the county by an early settler or landowner. But county seat designation did not automatically stimulate town growth. Courts met only periodically and did not require a continuous presence or, for that matter, local residence by any of their participants—save perhaps the county court clerk. County seats became highly animated on court days but often remained otherwise sleepy political outposts.

The continuing context for the perpetuation of the county tradition was that settlers came to the mountains to pursue rural livelihoods in farming. After the first wave of settlement at the turn of the nineteenth century, rural settlement in Appalachian Kentucky followed the paths of rivers, streams, and creeks as settlers sought arable mountain land. The dissected landscape offered a mixed bag of farming opportunities. Bottomland along wide streams was relatively scarce and was engrossed early by first family settlers. Owing to the topography, the search for arable land took later settlers as well as later generations increasingly farther afield onto ever smaller creek beds and branches. Rural settlement was thus a continuing process that pushed people farther and farther from initial nodes of settlement. The process also created conditions whereby creation of new counties could be justified again and again on the basis of population density and distance from existing county seats.

The settlement process in the mountains cannot be bracketed between tidy beginning and ending dates. So long as farming remained the center of Appalachian Kentucky's economy—that is, throughout most of the nineteenth century—the guiding settlement impulse was rural. The search for arable land provoked continuous new settlement within an area putatively considered "settled." Put simply, settlement was not a discrete, temporally limited process as it is commonly assumed to be in historical geography. Political traditions of county governance, initiated and perfected in the rural Tidewater, aided and abetted the continued rural movement of people within the mountains. The Tidewater tradition of county creation permitted the repeated political remapping of the regional geography. The net effects were population decentralization, attenuated lines of communication, and a rural settlement system that did not support or really require the growth of towns. The rural county tradition thus was doubly significant in Appalachian Kentucky, governing the form and driving the process of mountain settlement.

The Mountain Farming System

More than the simple fact of an agricultural economy drove the region's rural settlement momentum. The specific characteristics of the farming system also conspired in population decentralization and deconcentration. The nineteenth-century mountain farming system was a source of amazement to contemporaries and remains so today. With the aid of historical hindsight, some observers have questioned whether settlers took up land in Appalachian Kentucky as a way of escaping the nation's headlong rush into modernity.[20] It is impossible to know with certainty the aspirations of settlers who made their way to Kentucky. One can imagine they entertained a general wish for agrarian prosperity but still not know the extent to which that goal included, or indeed depended upon, expanding commodity production. In any case, the commercial ambitions mountain settlers might have had upon their arrival were rather thoroughly quashed by the Civil War.[21] Appalachian Kentucky's economy had become dominated by an unspecialized family farming system centering on domestic production for domestic use.

Broken topography, already seen as one cause of population decentralization, had further effects on the mountain farming system. Mountain geography permitted a rather limited set of agricultural practices, such as reliance on hand cultivation, which did not change greatly during antebellum era and, in fact, over the course of the nineteenth century. The continual settlement of Appalachian Kentucky thus meant replication of existing land-extensive practices on a increasingly smaller scale rather than innovation and intensification.

Surpluses of various goods were marketed locally and eventually found their way outside the region. Many goods produced elsewhere found their way into the mountains through the reciprocal process of long-distance trade. But evidence suggests that although farming was the economic base of Appalachian Kentucky's economy, agriculture did not become specialized and form an export base around a few commodity sectors. During the middle decades of the nineteenth century, the process of sectoral specialization in both agriculture and industry helped transform U.S. regional economies and, through them, the national economy as a whole.[22] The failure of Appalachian Kentucky to develop a specialized economic base during the era of regional economic specialization sharply differentiated the mountains from surrounding regions, not least of all from the rest of Kentucky.

These summary statements perforce mask the evident diversity of conditions within the population. Some families owned and farmed large acreages that yielded commercial surpluses. Many more families bartered or sold surplus goods and were no strangers to the world of commercial exchange.

Entries in the account book of Harlan County merchant Ewell V. Unthank between 1838 and 1840 indicate the nature of local trade and, by implication, the content of domestic production in and around Mt. Pleasant almost twenty years after the county was founded, and fully four decades after the area was first settled.[23] Unthank operated a retail store that was part of the larger mercantile partnership of Dickinson and Hamblen based across the state line in Virginia. The account book records items purchased, their price, and the purchasers' names. The account book also records the goods and services Unthank received and the amount of credit for each. Some transactions were in cash, but cash was the exception and not the rule. Because the account book extends over a two-year period, it is possible to detect an annual cycle of trade whereby furs and hides were traded largely during the winter and early spring, presumably when farm produce was in short supply. The account book also reveals Unthank consistently relied on a single person, Jacob Browning, for shipping: many entries credit Browning for "packing" one or several commodities over the mountain or back. Unthank also granted credit for a variety of labors. Table 10.1 lists the range of goods and labor services credited by Unthank between 1838 and 1840.

On the far other side of the Kentucky mountains exists supporting evidence about the nature of surplus production and exchange during the antebellum era. Original bills of lading from Catlettsburg flatboat and steamboat operator A. P. Borders provide a glimpse of commerce conducted along the Big Sandy River on the eve of the Civil War.[24] The bound volume contains bills dated between 20 September 1860 and 25 January 1861. Commodities imported to Pikeville, Prestonsburg, Paintsville, Louisa, and other Big Sandy ports included many boxes vaguely described as "merchandise," "hardware," "clothing," and "sundries." Specific items were also listed, however, ranging from apparent luxury items to household tools. Casks of

Table 10.1. Goods and Services Received by E. V. Unthank, Mt. Pleasant, Harlan County, 1838–1840

Tobacco	Wool	Cotton
Chickens	Killing hogs	Fur skins
Wax	Work packing	Muskrat skins
Lime	Making gun barrel	Beef
Cash	Working with hogs	Oats
Salt	Surveying land	Nails
Feathers	Making writing desk	Brandy
Sox	Feeding mare	Linen
Corn	Boarding	Pork
Kegs	Turnips	Bacon
Horse shoes	Beef hide	Tar
Cheese	Basket	Hauling fodder
Gloves	Sweet potatoes	Working month
Fodder	Honey	Work on store house
Table	Deer skins	General work
Seng	Coon skins	Making shovel
Vests	Irish potatoes	Making horseshoes and nails
Jeans (rough yardage)	Apples	Making bosoms
Tallow		

Source: Harlan County Circuit Court, Journal belonging to Dickenson & Hamblen Retail Store, 1838–1840, Kentucky Department for Library and Archives, Frankfort.

queensware, boxes of tumblers, and bundles of shirt collars were just some of the goods shipped to Paintsville and Pikeville. Commonly imported were several forms of bar iron, clearly to be fashioned locally into tools, but also tools themselves, such as shovels, plows, and buckets. Other imported goods found throughout the bills of lading were dyes and spices, coffee and tea, brooms, cotton yarn, and, perhaps because the shipments extended over the Christmas holidays, oysters, raisins, and brandy.

Of the almost 200 bills of lading, each a separate delivery contract with a Big Sandy Valley merchant, approximately 78 were for shipments of goods exported from the mountains to merchants as far away as Baltimore and Pittsburgh, but most commonly in Parkersburg, West Virginia, and Cincinnati, Ohio. While the Unthank account book indicated the content of local trade, these export bills of lading also indicated what commodities produced in the mountains entered into long-distance trade. Listed below is the complete range of mountain produce from the Big Sandy exported by A. P. Borders. The enumeration of these commodities, like those traded by E. V. Unthank in Harlan County, contains few surprises to the extent that or-

Table 10.2. Mountain Produce Shipped by A. P. Borders, 20 September 1860 to 24 January 1861

Merchandise	Brandy	Ginseng
Feathers	Furs	Wheat
Boots & Shoes	Tallow	Dried Peaches
Wool	Produce (not specified)	Beeswax
Flax Seed	Chestnuts	Angelica
Dried Apples	Beans	Tobacco
Rags	Yellow Root	S. Bark

Source: A. P. Borders & Co., Steamboat Bills of Lading Book, Original Historical Records, file KY Boyd C16, Boyd County Library, Ashland, Ky.

chard crops, roots, wax, and feathers have long been recognized as important trade goods in Appalachian Kentucky. Aside from the five shipments that each contained sacks of wheat and two containing tobacco, notably missing is evidence that agricultural staple crops were vital interregional trade links.

Although the bills of lading and account book are at best fragments of a historical record of mountain commerce, they lend support to the notion that mountain farm production was not dominated by specialized commodity production for export. Farm surpluses certainly existed and certainly entered into trade. But accumulated evidence suggests an export-oriented farm economy did not develop in Appalachian Kentucky by the time of the Civil War. The conclusion seems all the more apparent from the A. P. Borders bills of lading because the Big Sandy Valley was perhaps the most commercialized and economically integrated subregion of Appalachian Kentucky during the nineteenth century. If a specialized farm economy was to have emerged in the mountains, chances are it would have had its greatest efflorescence in the Big Sandy Valley.

Unspecialized farming and microlevel surplus exchange did not unleash a macrolevel momentum of deepening social and spatial divisions of labor.[25] In particular, the processing of household surpluses did not require specialized enterprises outside the household. As can be seen from the Unthank account book, processing took place within households before goods entered into trade: flax seed was separated; animal skins were cleaned; apples were dried; and pork was cured into bacon. Many country trade goods simply did not require processing: ginseng, chestnuts, and feathers merely had to be bagged and carried to the store. Unthank's account book bears witness to the fact that trade in country surpluses did not require specialized mercantile operations. The commodities he handled ran the gamut from live chickens and turnips to muskrat skins and horseshoes. The quantities of goods traded in each transaction were rather small: five pounds of wax, seven gallons of honey, two bushels of sweet potatoes—but in one instance forty-two pounds of tobacco and in another ninety-three pounds of pork. The unspecialized nature of commercial enterprises in the Kentucky mountains was one of the characteristics most often noted by agents of the R. G. Dun & Co. commercial credit rating firm as they traveled through the region.

Merchants in Appalachian Kentucky very likely survived precisely because they did not specialize in a particular line of trade. Merchants accepted surpluses that households chose or needed to trade, whatever their form or quantity, lending a decided unpredictability to their business. Seasonal vagaries of surplus production in farming, hunting, home manufacture, and root gathering offset the potential for mercantile specialization. Under these conditions of uncertainty, specialization would have exposed local merchants to much higher financial risk of failure. Commerce was fraught with uncertainties even in the best of times. Country merchants in Appalachian Kentucky wisely understood they could not improve their prospects by limiting their options.

In sum, an unspecialized farming system created its likeness in the structure of commercial enterprise throughout the mountains. With few merchants overall, and virtually all of them handling general merchandise and country trade, there was little economic impulse for merchants to cluster together in towns. This agrarian formation of general surplus production and exchange, coupled with the established political culture of county creation and governance, enforced a tendency toward population decentralization throughout the mountains that continually eroded the potential for urban development.

Despite this characterization of Appalachian Kentucky's regional settlement framework, it would be wrong to label the rural system "dispersed" and leave it at that. Nineteenth-century rural society was not inchoate. Creek beds sheltered rural neighborhoods that had their own integrity and provided a social identity to residents. Oral histories testify to the identification of mountain residents with the streams along which they lived; contemporary speech in the mountains continues to bear witness to this identification. Neighborhoods were far from autarkic, let alone self-sufficient, and cohered into a local social world.[26]

While the decentralized settlement system constrained town development, most of the services commonly associated with towns in agricultural

Table 10.3. Nonfarming Occupations

County	1850	1860	1870
Floyd	74	60	40
Harlan	30	35	29
Perry	16	22	6

Source: Population census manuscript schedules.

regions were available to mountain residents. Like most rural dwellers of the day, the mountain population was multiskilled in a range of activities including farming, basket making, food preservation, and clothing production. Many, if not most, households combined these skills under a single roof. But the services of other, more specialized skilled artisans were also available in the countryside. This is evident from close readings of the manuscript census schedules for Floyd, Harlan, and Perry Counties for the years 1850–80 tabulating nonfarmer occupations within each county's population.

Most generally, the tabulations adduce yet more evidence about the absence of deepening specialization within the economy during the middle decades of the nineteenth century, specifically before the 1880s. Table 10.3 lists the number of people in each county, virtually all men, who claimed an occupation other than farming in the three censuses.[27] Included among these skilled occupations were merchant, mechanic, blacksmith, cabinet maker, lawyer, stonemason, miller, and gunsmith.[28]

The tabulations revealed that these and other specialized occupations, such as shoemaker and carpenter, were sometimes listed jointly with farming. For example, a household head might be listed as "farmer and merchant" or "farmer and blacksmith." More commonly, individuals claiming a nonfarming occupation such as mechanic or shoemaker owned farms, further suggesting a combination of occupations. Census manuscripts further reveal that skilled artisans, along with preachers, merchants, and even doctors and lawyers, resided throughout each county and, particularly before 1880, did not significantly concentrate in county seat towns. For reasons to be described presently, the exception was Floyd County's Prestonsburg, which boasted a resident middle class from a very early date.

The point here is that mountain residents had access to "town functions" without the geographical presence of towns. This simple point rarely figured into contemporary representations of the mountain region. The growth of towns and cities is so thoroughly identified with modern society

Table 10.4. County Seat Populations, 1850–1880

County	1850	1860	1870	1880
Floyd (Prestonsburg)	145	239	226	275
Harlan (Mt. Pleasant)	31[a]	48	[b]	[b]
Perry (Hazard)	45[a]	[b]	[b]	76

Source: Population census manuscript schedules.
[a]Estimate based on undifferentiated manuscript evidence.
[b]Unable to differentiate.

that a general absence of urban places in a settled region such as Appalachia has been taken to mean the region existed outside modernity: the physical absence of towns in the mountains equaled the concomitant absence of organized social life.

A nonetheless inescapable conclusion is that towns were little needed before the onset of capitalist growth, in many cases including county seat towns. The dormancy of urban development during the mid-nineteenth century is supported by decennial census reports. In Floyd, Harlan, and Perry Counties, for example, county seat populations were not always enumerated separately from the rest of the county population. Careful line-by-line scrutiny of census manuscripts is necessary to discern the probable beginnings and endings of the county seat populations.[29] The numbers represented in Table 10.4 for the census years between 1850 and 1880, therefore, must be taken as close approximations.

In lieu of expanding county seats, commercial market towns, or some combination thereof throughout Appalachian Kentucky, the continuing process of rural neighborhood establishment gave rise to what I call "proto-urban" centers. These were sites of convenience for the internal movement of goods and information. These sites typically occupied the mouths of larger streams. Here would reside a merchant, more likely a merchant-farmer, who handled the local country trade and whose store perhaps would also serve as a post office for upstream neighborhoods. A case in point is the Mouth of Mud Creek in Floyd County (later the town of Laynesville), where resided James S. Layne, one of the largest landowners in the county at the time of his death in 1871. Layne's home was "the center of social life for miles around. He conducted one of the valley's largest stores, established the post office of Laynesville and operated one of the first flour mills."[30]

Mercantile reference books published in 1868 by R. G. Dun & Co. help

Table 10.5. Location and Number of Mercantile Establishments, 1868

Breathitt County	Laurel County
Crockettsville, 1	Bush's Store, 1
Middle Fork, 1	Laurel Bridges, 1
Clay County	*London, 12
*Manchester, 6	Lynn Camp, 1
Floyd County	Mershon's Cross Roads, 2
Mouth of Beaver, 3	Raccoon, 3
Mouth of Muddy, 1	Letcher County
*Prestonsburg, 6	*Whitesburg, 1
Harlan County	Perry County
*Mt. Pleasant, 5	*Hazard, 2
Mouth of Puckett's Creek, 1	Pike County
Poor Fork, 4	Enterprise, 1
Johnson County	Mouth of Pond's Creek, 2
Mouth of John's Creek, 2	*Piketon, 9
*Paintsville, 14	Whitley County
Knox County	Bark Camp Mills, 2
*Barboursville, 11	Marsh Creek, 3
Cumberland Ford, 2	Meadow Creek, 1
Cumberland Gap, 3	*Williamsburg, 13
Flatlick, 4	Woodbine, 2
Goose Creek, 1	
Lynn Camp, 1	
Poplar Creek, 1	
Yellow Creek, 2	

Source: R. G. Dun & Co., *The Mercantile Agency Reference Book* (New York: R. G. Dun & Co., 1868).
*Denotes county seat.

identify the locations of these sites of convenience cum proto-urban centers in the eleven-county area which then comprised Appalachian Kentucky.[31] The *Reference Book* listed merchants along with their locations throughout each county. Mercantile operations were clearly linked to the location of streams. This was true for merchants in county seat towns, which characteristically occupied sites along major streams, but also, if not especially, for country merchants. As Table 10.5 suggests, merchants occupied sites at the mouths of major streams outside county seats.

These mercantile locations help establish the internal coherence of Appalachian Kentucky's settlement system of stream-identified rural neighborhoods. These sites of convenience can be considered proto-urban centers because of their continuing significance in the economic geography of

Appalachian Kentucky. As the nineteenth turned into the twentieth century, stream confluences lost none of their convenience as points where the movements of people, goods, and information converged. Because of this, many of these sites went on to become small towns in their own right. An example is Mouth of Beaver in Floyd County, which became the town of Allen after the railroad was constructed in 1904 and "hotels and boarding-houses were built to care for the public traveling to and from the new Beaver Creek coal field."[32] In Harlan County the confluence of Looney's Creek with the Poor Fork of the Cumberland River was rechristened the town of Cumberland. As population increased at the turn of the century, many other such sites of convenience would become the location for small clusters of stores.

Perhaps typical for a region whose history is shot through with irony, dramatic transformations took place in Appalachian Kentucky's social and settlement systems at the turn of the century just as the region was gaining national notoriety as a rural backwater.[33] During the 1880s, capitalist investment in land, mineral, and timber resources began eroding the bases for the continued reproduction of the mountain region's unspecialized domestic economy.

During Appalachian Kentucky's capitalist transformation, local and absentee investors obtained resources, financed and built railroads into the region, and constructed camps and the occasional "model town" to house workers—all toward the ultimate goal of mining bituminous coal for export. The transition spanned three to four decades, a rather protracted era owing to a combination of micro- and macrolevel conditions. Locally, the system of land division, coupled with partible inheritance practices, had created a labyrinth of land titles and boundary lines. Obtaining clear title and consolidating tracts of land were time-consuming tasks requiring the labor of many lawyers and surveyors over sometimes many years.[34] In addition to these local obstacles to a rapid transformation, capitalist investment was also subject to national level economic perturbations. Most notable was the financial panic of 1893 and ensuing deep depression, which slowed capitalist expansion across the nation.

Because coal mining in Appalachian Kentucky represented a process of rural industrialization, the countryside would seem the logical place to look for immediate signs of profound transformation. To be sure, the capitalization of land, timber, and minerals undermined the unspecialized farm economy over the long term. Coal mining and its associated activities became competing land uses that economically and physically displaced farm production. But the established rural production system was able to coexist with capitalist investment at the turn of the century as it did with the early coal-mining industry. Many investors purchased only underground mineral rights, leaving farming intact on the surface; others permitted tenants to continue cultivating surface acreage. Under such conditions the number of farms in mountain Kentucky nearly doubled between 1880 and 1900.[35]

It is thus to the towns, and especially county seat towns, that we look for the early imprint of industrial capitalism. Capitalist investment in the Appalachian countryside provided a tremendous impetus to the growth of towns by generating new demands for new kinds of centralized, specialized economic activities. Most county seat towns had languished for lack of demand for such activities. Before relating the myriad changes in the size, structure, and function of county seat towns, however, we must first distinguish among different categories of their experience with capitalist development in Appalachian Kentucky.

Four different sorts of experience can be identified: (1) early expanding entrepôts, (2) early quiescent local centers, (3) late capitalist boomtowns, and (4) late quiescent local centers. The typology builds upon an early study by geographer Darrel Haug Davis that emphasized economic diversity within the Kentucky mountain region.[36] The two principles differentiating the categories were the relative age of the counties (and their county seat towns) and the timing and nature of capitalist development in the immediately surrounding county area. The county creation process typically related age to the locations of counties. Some of the oldest counties were along the edges of the mountains, which were settled earlier than the interior sections, whose counties were correspondingly younger. The more powerful principle distinguishing the county seat towns, however, was the nature and timing of capitalist development within county boundaries.

These two principles capture the extent to which, and how, a county seat was integrated into the emergent industrial economy. A few mountain counties boasted of towns from a rather early date preceding the full extension of capitalist production in the countryside. Still others remained without significant urban growth even after industrialization was well under way.

Two of the categories, early and late quiescent local centers, can be dispatched quickly. The first are county seat towns established during the first half of the nineteenth century whose growth remained in the shadows of neighboring towns and counties. In this category are Manchester (Clay County) and Whitesburg (Letcher County). The county court and local commerce guaranteed these towns a minimum steady level of social and economic activity. Limited industrial development, or industrial development orchestrated within a neighboring county, put brakes on their economic expansion, however, particularly at the turn of the century. The geography of timber and especially mineral resources was often the reason why these towns did not expand rapidly at the turn of the century. Despite their longevity, these county seat towns were upstaged by the growth of towns in neighboring counties. Growth in the town of Whitesburg, for example, was overshadowed by that in the neighboring boomtown of Hazard.

The second category to be reviewed quickly includes county seat towns located in counties created relatively late, during the second half of the nineteenth century, and that remained quiescent even during the era of capitalist transformation. Hindman, Hyden, and Inez, the seats of Knott, Leslie, and Martin Counties, respectively, epitomize this category. These remained crossroads towns with a courthouse and small retail and service sectors largely serving the local population. At the time of this writing, in fact, Knott County, including the town of Hindman, continues to boast the absence of stoplights. In no way did these towns and counties remain untouched by capitalist development, particularly the bituminous coal industry. In the case of Leslie County, for example, coal mining developed later in the twentieth century around truck transportation. Knott County's coal mines were extensions of operations based in its surrounding "parent" counties of Perry and Floyd; Martin County's mining development was similarly governed by neighboring counties. In other words, these late quiescent local centers remained somewhat peripheral to the main centers of capitalist development in the mountains at the turn of the century.

Early expanding entrepôts and capitalist boomtowns merit more extensive scrutiny for what they reveal about the capitalist transformation of Appalachian Kentucky over the long and short terms. Early entrepôts were county seats located on the boundaries of the Kentucky mountains that established an enduring role in long distance trade and communication. Barbourville in Knox County and Prestonsburg in Floyd County are the two towns that epitomize this category of historical experience. Knox and Floyd were the first two counties created in the mountains, both in 1800, as a result of localized population growth. Barbourville and Prestonsburg were named for the land speculators who "donated" the county courthouse site.

Their more significant shared experience, however, was rooted in the fact that both places straddled major interregional migration routes into the trans-Appalachian West. From their inception, both towns were way stations in the movements of people, goods, and information. Barbourville, in particular, benefited from its location along the Wilderness Road, which until the 1810s was considered the safer westward migration route than passage through the Ohio River country. Their peripheral locations at, respectively, the western and eastern edges of the mountains allowed Barbourville and Prestonsburg to become entrepôts for large parts of the region.

These early migration way stations continued to be important locations in the circulation of goods and information between the mountains, the rest of the Kentucky, and the nation as a whole. Locations along migration routes redounded to their continuing benefit by keeping the towns integrated into trade and transportation routes. An 1834 "tourist pocket map" of Kentucky illustrated the situation of both towns along the principal stage routes connecting at Lexington.[37] A twice-weekly stage line along the old Wilderness Road route connected Barbourville with Lexington to the north and with the Holston River valley to the south. Another stage line proceeded three times a week east from Lexington to Catlettsburg at the confluence of the Big Sandy and Ohio Rivers. From there a smaller road made its way up the Big Sandy to Prestonsburg and beyond.

During the first three-quarters of the nineteenth century, both Barbourville and Prestonsburg seemed to enjoy a quiet and continuous prosperity borne from their longevity and strategic locations. Their early lead in trade and services allowed them to become important local towns for their own and surrounding counties. For example, all of the counties along the Big Sandy Valley were once part of Floyd County. The town of Prestonsburg remained the center of Big Sandy Valley political and economic activity throughout the nineteenth century, even after the new counties had been formed. Between 1860 and 1880, Prestonsburg's 200+ population remained relatively steady (see Table 10.4). Settler families scattered kin members up and down the valley. Families in the nascent commercial and political elite took up residence in Prestonsburg while usually owning land in the nearby countryside. From at least the 1840s through the 1880s, members of elite families such as the Hatchers, the Harkins, the Derossetts, the Martins, the Mays, the Fitzpatricks, the Friends, the Strattons, the Harrises, and the Gearhearts had a continuous presence in Prestonsburg in commercial and professional occupations such as hotel keeper, lawyer, and merchant. Many Prestonsburg residents were also rural landowners who claimed the occupation of "farmer." At least some of these ostensible town-dwelling farmers were large landowners whose lands were worked by tenant farmers. The general point about Prestonsburg (and, similarly, Barbourville) is that the town's strategic location and longevity allowed a resident elite to coalesce there to an extent not possible in most other mountain county seat towns

Table 10.6. County Seat Populations, 1880–1920

County	1880	1900	1910	1920
Floyd (Prestonsburg)	275	409	1,120	1,667
Harlan (Mt. Pleasant/Harlan)		557	657	1,756
Perry (Hazard)	76	315	537	1,200[a]

Source: Population census manuscript schedules.
Note: Figures for 1890 are unavailable; census records were destroyed by fire.
[a]This is a low estimate based on reconstructing unusually disorganized census manuscript schedules that lump the town center together with various outlying areas under label of "Hazard City."

during the nineteenth century. The unspecialized domestic economy could support only two large towns, and those enjoying an early lead, such as Prestonsburg and Barbourville, suppressed the development of other commercial and service centers.

The growth of the early entrepôt towns accelerated at the turn of the century as the ranks of burgeoning county seats were joined by capitalist boomtowns. This final category of county seat town experience includes Mt. Pleasant/Harlan, Hazard, and Pikeville, all of which had languished for decades as sleepy courthouse towns of less that 100 souls. Even as late as 1880, Mt. Pleasant was not enumerated separately in the census; Hazard could boast a population of just 76. Although the county seats that became boomtowns all pre-dated capitalist development, the decades after 1880 mark their greatest period of expansion. These towns rightly can be considered "new towns" because, unlike Prestonsburg, their accelerated growth did not build upon an established social, economic, and political base.

The most obvious indices of dramatic growth in county seat towns are the population census figures presented in Table 10.6. Especially impressive were the population increases in Harlan and Hazard between 1910 and 1920, the decade of the World War I coal boom when the Kentucky field was opened, justifying their designation as capitalist boomtowns.

Common to towns in regions experiencing rapid economic transformation, the burgeoning populations of the county seats were a mix of newcomers and oldtimers.[38] The opening of the coalfields created a multitude of new profit-making opportunities in the mountains. Investors from around the country and abroad flocked to the mountains in what one observer called "a race for the prize."[39] County seat towns were the logical destination for newcomers. Typically these were the only towns in existence and thus at least represented an identifiable destination for one's migration to Appalachian Kentucky. More importantly, however, land, mineral, and timber investments involved property transactions that had to be recorded at the county court. County seats also housed the accumulated court records necessary to perfecting property titles. Migrants from outside the region jostled with members of long-established local families who also took up county seat residence in increasing numbers in their own search for new economic opportunities.

Besides sheer population growth, another principal index of capitalist expansion in county seats was the range of gainful occupations among town residents. The increasing occupational diversification mirrored the deepening social division of labor. Capitalist investors arriving from outside the area and investors and others arriving from the local area created new categories of work in the region. Furthermore, these new county seat residents generated new demands in county seat economies for specialized goods and services. Compare, for example, the distribution of occupations in Hazard during 1880, 1900, and 1910 (Table 10.7).

The changing structure and function of county seat towns underpin this changing occupation structure. Some of the same occupations, such as doctor, merchant, and political officer endured through all three censuses as their numbers increased. Other, new occupations can be related directly to the emerging resource base industries; included here are surveyor, real estate dealer, sawyer, and lumberman. No doubt much of the work of the many new lawyers was also linked directly to resource industries, as was the work of printers and typists. Many of the other occupations new to Hazard provided goods and services to the burgeoning town population itself. Rapidly expanding towns demanded construction workers (carpenters, bricklayers) and infrastructure personnel (telephone company managers). The entire realm of personal service occupations in mountain county seats was created de novo in the early twentieth century. The need for barbers, cooks, washerwomen, and hotel keepers reflected the presence of new migrants, many of whom were single men, whose daily maintenance depended on purchasing in commodity form goods and services typically produced within families by women. Other kinds of service workers, such as dressmakers, milliners, and in-house cooks and laundresses, illustrated the vitality of resident middle-class families enjoying luxuries similar to those of their counterparts in other regions.

One of the best investment opportunities was the very construction of the county seat towns. Population growth was manifested in the physical expansion of the towns. The deepening social division of labor within the population was further manifested in social and spatial differentiation

Table 10.7. Occupational Structure of Hazard, Kentucky, 1880, 1900, 1910

1880		1900		1910	
Doctor	1	Doctor	1	Doctor	4
Farmer	2	Farmer	23	Farmer	23
Huckster	3	Merchant	8	Merchant	7
Keeping House	11	Keeping House		Keeping House	
Laborer	9	Farm Laborer	11	Farm Laborer	7
Lawyer	2	Lawyer	9	Lawyer	16
Political Officer	2	Political Officer	4	Political Officer	7
Servant	3	Servant	7	Servant	12
Store Clerk	2	Store Clerk	3	Store Clerk	
		Sawyer	1	Sawyer	1
		Preacher	2	Preacher	2
		Druggist	1	Druggist	1
		Carpenter	2	Carpenter	4
		Hotel Keeper	1	Hotel Keeper	2
		Teacher	6	Teacher	10
		Teamster	1	Teamster	
		Soldier	1	Washerwoman	2
				Bricklayer	1
				Surveyor	3
				Laborer	51
				Dressmaker[a]	2
				Typist	1
				Telephone Co. Manager	1
				Cashier	1
				Real Estate Dealer	2
				Blacksmith	1
				Lumberman	1
				Barber	3
				Cook	8
				Printer	2
				Salesman	1
				Dentist	1

Source: Population census manuscript schedules.
[a]Includes one milliner.

within towns. Early in the twentieth century, mountain county seats assumed most of the internal geography that remains intact today. The towns developed distinct business districts typically, but not always, with the courthouse square at their center. Law offices and other professional services were situated around the courthouse along with retail establishments.

Residential areas took up clearly distinguished sites away from the business district, and these became increasingly differentiated by social class. All of this was a far cry from the early years of most mountain county seats, when court was held in a tavern or, lacking that, in the home of the court clerk.

The heart of county seat town building was not the aggregation of houses, offices, hotels, drugstores, or railroad stations, however. These physical forms signaled wider social changes, namely the full emergence and consolidation of a resident elite in Appalachian Kentucky.[40] Comprising the elite was a mix of newcomers to the region and descendants of first settler families. Some of the elite were parvenus, and others had long played key roles in political and economic affairs. The county seat town in the coalfields was a shared social space in which longtime residents and newly established families could merge their interests and define an identity as local boosters for capitalist development. Investors from outside the region brought capital to the mountains and helped members of the local elite accomplish what they were unable to do themselves, namely the capitalist transformation of the countryside.

Newly established county seat newspapers such as the Hazard *Herald* and the Harlan *Enterprise* championed the economic changes as they gave voice to the emergent elite. Distinctions between long-settled families and newcomers became blurred amid the pervasive booster rhetoric. For example, a May 1912 Hazard *Herald* article described Virginia investor C. B. Slemp as "almost a native Eastern Kentuckian from his long personal association and unusually wide acquaintance in this section."[41] In a later article the *Herald* went on to explain: "Mr. Slemp's desire is to focus as much attention as possible on our section here to the end of drawing all investment and development in this territory as he can. He bids fair to be the greatest factor in making Perry County the wealthy industrial center which everyone here has long hoped for."[42]

Appalachian Kentucky had little need for many towns so long as its economy was dominated by unspecialized family farming and home manufacturing. The few early towns that served as entrepôts for the mountains, along with the merchants and mechanics located throughout the mountains at numerous sites of convenience, fulfilled extant demand for the economic functions associated with towns and cities. Not until capital investment began transforming the mountains' natural resource base to support industrial development at the turn of the century did town development receive any significant stimulus. The refashioning of the countryside into a site of industrial production required the presence of new people in the region's county seats performing new kinds of work. The towns grew up to clothe, feed, house, and amuse the newcomers ushering in the new economic regime. The growth of county seat towns in Appalachian Kentucky was wholly dependent on the coal industry. By the 1930s the extent of growth and economic diversification in any county seat town bespoke the nature and extent of that county's integration into the coal economy.

Notes

1. The term *settlement ideal* is used here to denote settlement forms that have become iconic of Appalachian regional identity and whose representation often owes as much to "invented tradition" as it does to lived history. An insightful application of the concept is Joseph S. Wood, "Build, Therefore, Your Own World: The New England Village as Settlement Ideal," *Annals of the Association of American Geographers* 81, no. 1 (1991): 32–50.

2. Reference to "still photographs" is intentional and arises from the author's dawning understanding of the images that typically grace the dust jackets and photograph spreads of books about Appalachia. Compare covers of books as different as the Appalachian Land Ownership Task Force, *Who Owns Appalachia?: Landownership and Its Impact* (Lexington: University Press of Kentucky, 1983); Durwood Dunn, *Cades Cove: The Life and Death of a Southern Appalachian Community, 1818–1937* (Knoxville: University of Tennessee Press, 1988); and Ronald D. Eller, *Miners, Millhands, and Mountaineers: Industrialization of the Appalachian South, 1880–1930* (Knoxville: University of Tennessee Press, 1982).

3. Crandall A. Shifflett's recent study of company towns in southern Appalachia is a welcome palliative to the paucity of studies of urban growth in the region: *Coal Towns: Life, Work, and Culture in Company Towns of Southern Appalachia, 1880–1960* (Knoxville: University of Tennessee Press, 1991).

4. The touchstone here is the late Raymond Williams's masterful *The Country and the City* (New York: Oxford University Press, 1973). The tradition of linked rural and urban historical studies is well developed in Europe, as can be seen in Philip Abrams and E. A. Wrigley, *Towns in Societies: Essays in Economic History and Historical Sociology* (Cambridge: Cambridge University Press, 1978). A recent exploration of city and countryside interdependencies in the U.S. context is William Cronon's *Nature's Metropolis* (New York: Norton, 1991).

5. Philip Abrams, "Towns and Economic Growth: Some Theories and Problems," in Abrams and Wrigley, *Towns in Societies*, p. 9.

6. Ibid., p. 3.

7. Ibid.

8. David R. Goldfield, "The Urban South: A Regional Framework," *American Historical Review* 86 (1981): 1009–34, and *Cotton Fields and Skyscrapers: Southern City and Region, 1607–1980* (Baton Rouge: Louisiana State University Press, 1982). For a wider survey of southern city growth, see also David R. Goldfield and Blaine A. Brownell, eds., *The City in Southern History* (Port Washington, N.Y.: Kennikat Press, 1977).

9. Goldfield, *Cotton Fields and Skyscrapers*, p. 3.

10. Carville Earle and Ronald Hoffman, "Staple Crops and Urban Development in the Eighteenth-Century South," *Perspectives in American History* 10 (1976): 64.

11. Charles J. Farmer, *In the Absence of Towns: Settlement and Country Trade in Southside Virginia, 1730–1800* (Latham, Md.: Rowman and Littlefield, 1993).

12. Fred Bateman and Thomas Weiss, *A Deplorable Scarcity* (Chapel Hill: University of North Carolina Press, 1991); Charles Post, "The American Road to Capitalism," *New Left Review*, no. 133 (1982): 30–51; Eugene Genovese, *The Political Economy of Slavery: Studies in the Economy and Society of the Slave South* (New York: Vintage, 1967); Gavin Wright, *The Political Economy of the Cotton South: Households, Markets, and Wealth in the Nineteenth Century* (New York: Norton, 1978).

13. On the development of the urban system in the northern United States, see Diane Lindstrom, *Economic Development of the Philadelphia Region* (New York: Columbia University Press, 1978).

14. The debate over the predominant orientation of farming in colonial New England rages on. One of the latest salvos in the war between *mentalite* and market points of view by one of the chief combatants is Winifred Rothenberg, *From Market Places to a Market Economy: The Transformation of Rural Massachusetts, 1750–1850* (Chicago: University of Chicago Press, 1992). The rather immediate market orientation of Midwest farming has been little doubted: Harriet Friedman, "World Market, State, and Family Farm: Social Bases of Household Production in an Era of Wage Labour," *Comparative Studies in Society and History* 20 (1978): 545–96, and "Household Production and the National Economy: Concepts for the Analysis of Agrarian Formations," *Journal of Peasant Studies* 7, no. 2 (1980): 158–84.

15. Richard Wade, *The Urban Frontier* (Chicago: University of Chicago Press, 1959).

16. Sally Ward Maggard, "From Farmers to Miners: The Decline of Agriculture in Eastern Kentucky," in *Science and Agricultural Development*, ed. Larry Busch (Totowa, N.J.: Allanheld, Osmun, 1981), pp. 25–66.

17. For a vivid description of the settlement process, see John Egerton, *Generations* (Lexington: University Press of Kentucky, 1983).

18. A fuller discussion of differences between New England and Tidewater political traditions can be found in Richard Lingeman, *Small Town America: A Narrative History 1620–the Present* (New York: Putnam, 1980), chap. 1.

19. Kentucky's system of county governance during the nineteenth century is analyzed in two studies by historian Robert M. Ireland: *The County in Kentucky History* (Lexington: University Press of Kentucky, 1976), and *Little Kingdoms: The Counties of Kentucky, 1850–1891* (Lexington: University Press of Kentucky, 1977).

20. Statements to the effect that settlers in Appalachian Kentucky dropped out of early modern society exist across the range of historical writing about the region, including ostensibly "sympathetic" accounts: "They had stopped because a wagon broke down, some member of the family had got sick and was not able to go on, or the forest had lured them aside because of good hunting. . . . Here they scratched out a living on thin soil, hunted a great deal, got out timber and floated it downstream to big sawmills, and were content with their lot." This passage is taken from a locally written "amateur" account, Mrs. Kelly Morgan, *History of Clay County, Kentucky* (Manchester, Ky.: Morgan Book Co., 1976), p. 91.

21. For a corroborating discussion of this point, see Paul Salstrom, *Appalachia's Path to Dependency: Rethinking a Region's Economic History, 1730–1940* (Lexington: University Press of Kentucky, 1994).

22. David R. Meyer, "The Emergence of the American Manufacturing Belt: An Interpretation," *Journal of Historical Geography* 9 (1983): 145–74.

23. Harlan County Circuit Court, Journal belonging to Dickinson & Hamblen Retail Store, 1838–1840, Kentucky Department for Library and Archives, Frankfort.

24. A. P. Borders & Co., Steamboat Bills of Lading Book, Original Historical Records, file KY Boyd C16, Boyd County Library, Ashland, Ky.

25. V. I. Lenin, *The Development of Capitalism in Russia* (Moscow: Progress, 1956).

26. Laurel Shackelford and Bill Weinberg, *Our Appalachia* (New York: Hill and Wang, 1977).

27. These figures do not include farm laborers.

28. A fuller discussion is contained in the author's forthcoming book *An American History of Appalachia.*

29. Each of the four censuses between 1850 and 1880 holds somewhat different potential for revealing county seat populations. For example, the 1860 Harlan County census clearly distinguishes the population of Mt. Pleasant, although it fails to do so in either 1870 or 1880.

30. Information taken from an "Our Historic Heritage" advertisement (no. 37 in a series) for the First National Bank of Prestonsburg, Ky., Prestonsburg Community College Special Collections.

31. R. G. Dun & Co., *The Mercantile Agency Reference Book* (New York: R. G. Dun & Co., 1868). The reference book was a compilation of information gathered by field agents listing basic information about the name, location, and credit ranking of merchants in each county; reference books in later years also listed the type of business and banking town for each locality.

32. Information taken from an "Our Historic Heritage" advertisement (no. 30 in a series) for the First National Bank of Prestonsburg, Ky., Prestonsburg Community College Special Collections.

33. This ironic disjuncture is well treated in Henry Shapiro, *Appalachia on Our Mind: The Southern Mountains and Mountaineers in the American Consciousness, 1870–1920* (Chapel Hill: University of North Carolina Press, 1978), and David Whisnant, *All That Is Native and Fine: The Politics of Culture in an American Region* (Chapel Hill: University of North Carolina Press, 1983).

34. The protracted process of capitalist investment in Appalachian Kentucky resources is discussed in Mary Beth Pudup, "Land before Coal: Class and Regional Development in Southeast Kentucky" (Ph.D. diss., University of California, Berkeley, 1987), chap. 5.

35. Mary Beth Pudup, "The Limits of Subsistence: Agriculture and Industry in Central Appalachia," *Agricultural History* 64 (1990): 81.

36. Darrel Haug Davis, *The Geography of the Mountains of Eastern Kentucky* (Frankfort, Ky.: Kentucky Geological Society, 1924).

37. J. H. Young, *The Tourist's Pocket Map of the State of Kentucky Exhibiting Its Internal Improvements* (Philadelphia: S. Augustus Mitchell, 1834), Library of Congress.

38. Paul E. Johnson, *A Shopkeeper's Millennium* (New York: Hill and Wang, 1978).

39. Charles Dudley Warner, "Comments on Kentucky," *Harper's New Monthly Magazine*, January 1889, pp. 255–71.

40. Mary Beth Pudup, "The Boundaries of Class in Preindustrial Appalachia," *Journal of Historical Geography* 15 (1989): 139–62.

41. "Distinguished Men Greeted," Hazard *Herald*, 23 May 1912, p. 1.

42. Hazard *Herald*, 21 May 1914, p. 1.

Railroads, Deforestation, and the Transformation of Agriculture in the West Virginia Back Counties, 1880–1920

For the first century after settlers planted frontier society in what became West Virginia, change came slowly. The pace quickened with the penetration of industrial capitalism during the decades bracketing the Civil War, but then reached a crescendo between 1880 and 1920 with the industrial conquest of the vast ancient growth forest locked in the state's mountainous interior. During this period the world underwent a profound transformation for the scattered farm population occupying West Virginia's "back woods." The forest was indeed enormous, for as late as 1880 when timber extraction began in earnest, two-thirds of the state remained under a canopy of virgin forest. Nevertheless, by the 1920s West Virginia had been nearly denuded. The enormity of the timberman's calculations are difficult to comprehend, but it is estimated that over 30 billion board feet of lumber was stripped from the West Virginia landscape during this period.[1]

As with coal, the state's other major natural resource, the development of the timber industry was possible only after railroads were constructed to haul the timber to market. Every facet of life in West Virginia was affected by railroad and timber development; but no section of the state was so dramatically altered as the undeveloped back counties, and no sector of the back-county economy was so fundamentally transformed as agriculture. The primary purpose of this essay is to sketch the process precipitated by railroad development and the timber boom that transformed the subsistence agricultural system of the nineteenth century into the commercial system of the twentieth century. In southern West Virginia the transforming influences of the timber industry are difficult to separate from the impact of the more powerful coal industry because timber was cut and processed for consumption by local industry. In order to isolate the consequences of the extraction of timber for distant markets, therefore, the interior mountain counties where timber was the most important (and sometimes the only) industry are the primary focus of this study.

Economic development was neither a new concept for West Virginians nor was it imposed on them by "outsiders." Indeed, from the state's founding in 1863 well into the twentieth century, public officials promoted development of West Virginia's natural resource extraction industries.[2] In 1906 the *Manufacturers' Record* reported that in West Virginia "the entire machinery of State government" was utilized "to attract capital to the State to develop its railroads, its coal, and its timber interests." Governors, congressmen, and senators were all recognized promoters in eastern financial circles, and in this respect, the business periodical noted, "West Virginia holds a unique position not duplicated by the governmental machinery of any other State in the South."[3] Reinforcing the booster spirit among industrial developers was the aspiration of most West Virginians for material improvement in their economic condition. The assumption that the state's abundant timber and coal resources would provide the basis for industrial development grew into a conviction that was seldom successfully challenged, and neither was its corollary, that only the railroads to transport those resources to market were lacking.[4]

Boosters in West Virginia, as across the United States, were captivated by the popular conception of the railroad as the great modernizing agent that would rustle civilization out of the wilderness. Since the arrival of the first English colonists, Americans had equated the forest with primitivism, the lack of "civilized" society and high culture. Hence, its elimination connoted the triumph of civilization over "raw nature," the ascent to a European cultural standard. In this worldview, elimination of the wilderness became a metaphor for the rise of America as a civilized society.[5] West Virginia developers concurred with this view. "What wonder that the heart of West Virginia is set on railroads," proclaimed the *Wheeling Register* in 1881, "they are the life giving currents of modern civilization without which prosperity and progress are solecisms." The article captured the prevailing economic faith of the era in its proper metaphoric context when it declared, "We must have railroads. . . . We must help our people out of the woods."[6]

Two of the major railroad lines that traversed West Virginia on the eve of the transformation originally were constructed to link the East with the agricultural Midwest. The Baltimore & Ohio Railroad (B&O) entered the northern tip of the state and then followed the most direct route available to Ohio, completing its line through West Virginia to Wheeling in 1853. Twenty years later, in 1873, the Chesapeake & Ohio Railroad (C&O) completed a trunk line that dissected the southern part of the state, passing through the New and Kanawha river valleys to Huntington.[7] A third major railroad, the Norfolk & Western (N&W), penetrated the southern part of the state in 1888 and completed its main line between Norfolk, Virginia, and Huntington, West Virginia, in 1892. Unlike the B&O and the C&O, the N&W was organized for the purpose of tapping the rich coal reserves of southern West Virginia, and this line became the dominant force in the development of the southern coalfields. A better example of how large landholdings were concentrated in the hands of a few corporations, the characteristic pattern of the Appalachian coal industry, would be difficult to identify. The N&W essentially was a landholding company divided into land, coal, timber, and railroad divisions that controlled hundreds of thousands of acres.[8]

Between the B&O and the C&O lay a vast virgin forest. Neither of the two railroads initially intended to risk investment in state development, however, leaving a large field of opportunity for West Virginia capitalists, most notably the industrialist-senators Johnson Newlon Camden, Henry G. Davis, and Stephen B. Elkins, the first entrepreneurs to successfully build railroads into the state's interior forests. Their fledgling systems penetrated the central interior counties from the north and laid the foundation for exploitation of the timbershed on the western slopes of the Allegheny Mountains. The C&O completed the strategic encirclement of the mountains by constructing the Greenbrier Division northward up the Greenbrier Valley along the state's southeastern border to connect with the railroads penetrating the forest from the north.[9]

Numerous small, independent railroads sprouted from the main lines. These and more than 600 logging railroads completed an elaborate web of rails linking the processing mills along the main lines with the cutting face deep in the forest. Although railroad mileage is difficult to evaluate precisely because the tracks were constantly being pulled up and rebuilt, at least forty of the fifty-five counties in West Virginia had one or more logging railroads,

Map 11.1. Railroads and Back Counties in West Virginia

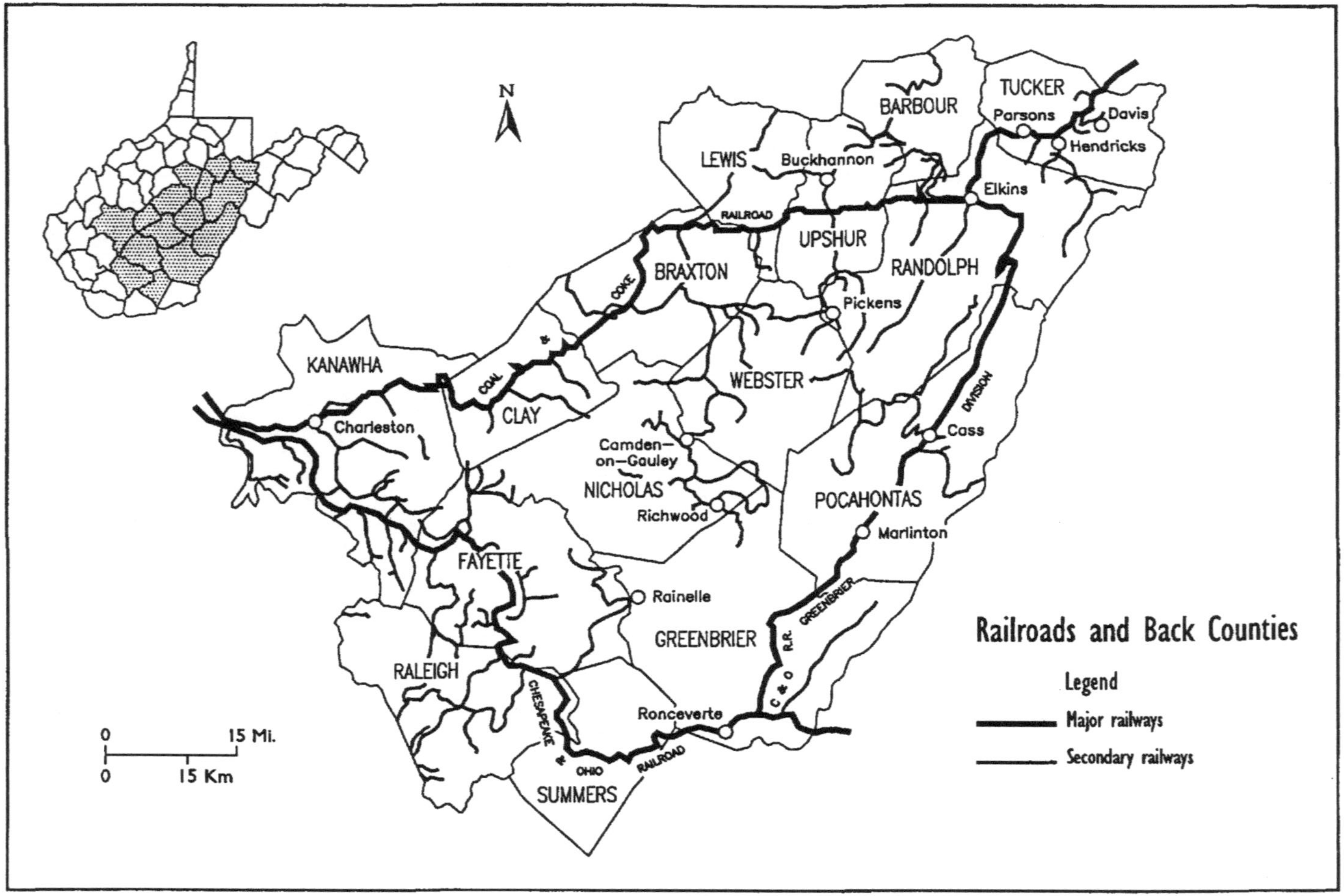

Railroads and Back Counties

Legend

— Major railways

-- Secondary railways

N

TUCKER
Davis
Hendricks
Parsons
Elkins
BARBOUR
Buckhannon
LEWIS
UPSHUR
Pickens
RANDOLPH
DIVISION
Cass
Marlinton
POCAHONTAS
WEBSTER
RAILROAD
BRAXTON
COKE
Camden-
on-Gauley
NICHOLAS
Richwood
GREENBRIER RY.
C & O
Rainelle
GREENBRIER
Ronceverte
RAILROAD
OHIO
SUMMERS
CHESAPEAKE
FAYETTE
RALEIGH
CLAY
COAL
KANAWHA
Charleston

15 Mi.

15 Km

0

0

the number varying from one in Taylor County to more than sixty in Pocahontas. Most of these lines were located in the interior mountain counties of Randolph, Tucker, Pocahontas, and Nicholas.[10]

Even if the small logging and tram roads are excluded, however, track mileage in the state doubled in the 1880s, doubled again in the 1890s, and covered 3,705 miles in 1917.[11] The coming of the railroads saw small towns spring up along the lines like wildflowers where previously there had been only a thin sprinkling of farmers. According to James Morton Callahan, a prominent state historian writing in 1913 at the peak of the timber boom, the railroads "carried into the silence of the primeval woods the hum of modern industry," which brought forth "gigantic lumber plants" and bustling new towns.[12]

Pro-industry newspapers seldom lost an opportunity to beat the development drum. In 1884, for example, a reporter for the *Wheeling Register* wrote from Buckhannon, Upshur County, that prior to the arrival of the short B&O connecting line the previous year, Buckhannon had been "a quiet, pleasant, but apathetic little country town." Now, he observed, the "noise of pounding hammers" was heard from every direction, drays moved constantly through the streets, and new churches, stores, and schools were built. Also, a large woolen mill, a handle factory, a large planing mill, two wagon and carriage factories, sawmills, lumberyards, a log boom, and two large flouring mills had been constructed in the village. Given the economic development stimulated by railroads, the reporter declared, "it is not surprising that the people further on in the interior are longing for the time to come when capital and enterprise shall reach their borders and unlock their doors."[13]

Capital and enterprise followed Senator Davis's Coal and Coke Railroad from Elkins to Durbin in the northern section of the mountains where forty-nine sawmills cut their way through the virgin timber along the main line alone. Capital also reached the Greenbrier Valley in 1903 with the completion of the Greenbrier Division of the C&O. The economic stimulus given to the mountain economy is illustrated in the observation of a visitor who reported in late 1903 that "the Greenbrier Valley has become a hive of industry" and that the newly opened territory in northern Pocahontas and along the Coal and Iron Railroad experienced "the influx of men and capital akin to an Oklahoma rush." The extent of development along the Greenbrier "astonishes the imagination," he continued, and "the fanciful dreams of a recent past are outstripped in the realization of today."[14] The Greenbrier Division hauled out almost exclusively products of forest and farm from along its 100 miles of main line and spawned the growth of lumber operations and mill towns that literally sprang up out of the wilderness. At least forty-four mills were in operation along the Greenbrier Railroad in 1902, and the railroad prompted the development of other wood product industries, such as a kindling wood plant, a stave mill, and two tanneries.[15]

The level of capital investment during the timber boom is indicated by U.S. census data on value of products in Tucker, Randolph, and Pocahontas Counties, three of the major lumber-producing mountain counties opened by the railroads. Between 1880 and 1920 production values exploded from $5,608 to $4,395,531 in Tucker County, an increase of 78,280 percent; from $49,487 to $7,583,106 in Randolph, an increase of 15,223 percent; and from $45,544 to $10,937,955 in Pocahontas, an increase of 23,916 percent.[16] As suggested by the investment data, the railroads signaled a new era in the exploitation of the virgin forest. Timber operators were able to haul in steam skidders, which were absolutely necessary for dragging logs out of canyons or across swampy areas, and steam loaders, which replaced men with machine power sufficient to load big timber onto flatcars.[17] Without the steam-powered heavy equipment required to cut, transport, and process the big timber, vast segments of the countryside could not have been deforested.

An economic interdependency existed between the railroads and the large mills. The railroads required a high volume of business to justify their investment; the mills required efficient transportation to urban markets.[18] An impressive number of band-saw mills, the most technologically sophisticated operations, were established in West Virginia between 1890 and 1910. In 1909, the all-time peak production year, 83 band mills and 1,441 other lumber establishments produced 1.5 billion board feet of lumber in West Virginia. The total number of band mills operating in the state during this period is estimated to have been 200.[19] The two largest mills were triple band mills, operated by the Blackwater Boom and Lumber Company at Davis, Tucker County, and the Meadow River Lumber Company at Rainelle, Greenbrier County. Their capacity was enormous. The Meadow River mill, for example, was capable of producing over 200,000 board feet of lumber in a single day. The largest hardwood lumber mill in the world for a time, it consumed 3,000 acres of virgin timber per year.[20]

Development of the timber industry attracted large numbers of workers seeking employment in the logging camps, lumber mills, or other forest-related industries (See Table 11.1). Not only did the population grow exponentially, it also became ethnically diversified through an infusion of workers from northern states, Pennsylvania in particular, where the timber supply was becoming depleted, and by foreign immigrants.[21]

Table 11.1. Population in Three Major Timber Counties

County	1880	1890	1900	1910	1920
Tucker	3,151	6,459	13,433	18,675	16,791
Randolph	8,102	11,633	17,670	26,028	26,804
Pocahontas	5,591	6,814	8,572	14,740	15,002

Source: *U.S. Census of Population.*

Trains carried away forest products, but they also returned with manufactured goods such as food, dry goods, household furnishings, farm supplies, and whatever else people ordered from the mail order catalogs that supplied the needs of town dwellers and improvement-oriented farmers. The railroad connected local communities to the national markets and, as elsewhere in rural America, exerted a profound influence on the way people lived.[22] With the circulation of cash and the rise of a significant population of wage earners, who either lived in town or came into town for the social life and/or supplies, merchants were increasingly attracted by the possibilities of trade with the surrounding countryside.[23]

Its economic vitality notwithstanding, the railroad and timber boom encountered some local opposition. The most wrenching changes spawned by deforestation were visited on agriculture, and these changes were not always enthusiastically received. Whereas the promoters of development looked to the world of the twentieth century and saw economic opportunity and material progress in big business, those who resisted chose to hold onto the world of the nineteenth century dominated by independent freeholders whose lives were ennobled by self-sufficiency and independence from those same large institutions. Instead of economic opportunity they often saw moral corruption. The developers attacked these conservative agrarians relentlessly in their newspapers.[24] As one promoter observed in the *Wheeling Register*, it was unfortunate for "the development of our rich young state [that] there is a good deal of the musty elements of old fogyism among our people," which served as a retardant to "progress and prosperity." Those who resisted development were a "powerful element" composed of "the old leaders who moulded [sic] public sentiment in former days when their antiquated ideas were adapted to the conditions which then existed." The paper rejected these "musty elements" because society had "passed into a new era, and stands on another stage where different principles apply and other methods are necessary to carry us forward with the onward tide of progression."[25]

Some farmers did ground their opposition in a conservative moral and social worldview. A. B. Brooks, the state's best-known conservationist, voiced their objections in 1910 when he wrote of "a great change in the character of the people." Within a comparatively few years nearly "the whole population," which previously had earned its living from the land, was "pushed out from places of seclusion into the whirl of modern industry." The railroads and timber operations attracted "a different class of people whose manners and language were readily adopted by the younger people." Thousands of young men were induced to work on the railroad, or in the logging camps and lumber towns where they were "thrown into intimate association with a rough, drifting, foreign element." Consequently, farmers frequently complained that their sons left the homesteads to take industrial jobs, and so the farms had fallen into neglect and were "grown up in briers." The young men became dissatisfied with farmwork, Brooks lamented, and "a spirit of selfishness and coolheaded business" took the place of the "hospitality that once prevailed."[26]

Many farmers opposed the railroads, including the logging lines, because they feared economic losses from the destruction of their livestock and property by the locomotives. For example, in the southern part of the state the *Greenbrier Independent* ran articles in 1872 opposing construction of the C&O because "it carried whiskey, killed chickens and cows, scared the horses, and threw teamsters out of employment."[27] Residents of Tyler County rejected a right-of-way for the B&O because "the trains would scare the game out of the country."[28] Similarly, farmers held public meetings to oppose the B&O running a line through Monongalia County to Pennsylvania, declaring, "We don't want our hogs and cows run over and killed."[29]

These concerns, seemingly quaint to modern readers, represented real problems to farmers of the nineteenth century. Because the industrialists ultimately prevailed, opponents of the railroads seem to have been out of touch with the times, their worries backward and archaic. But that is to misunderstand the dynamics within which they made their social and economic choices. West Virginia farmers had sound reasons for their fears. While they had legal tradition on their side, the world that had created that tradition was being deconstructed, isolating them, rendering them vulnerable in a way they were powerless to stop.

The Virginia legal tradition, which had been evolving since the early years of the republic, protected the agrarian status quo, including the interests of agricultural landowners against the encroachment of industrialists. As heirs to this judicial legacy, West Virginia jurists and lawmakers were compelled to modify the law and its interpretation if railroads were to lay the rails of economic development.

Since the 1970s a controversy over the role of the courts in America's industrialization has been waged among historians of the law and industrialization. The most prominent interpretation for the past two decades is that the courts "subsidized" industrial enterprise by depriving the victims, mainly farmers and workers, of just compensation for injuries imposed on them by industrialization. Scholars who take exception to this interpretation generally either dismiss it as a "conspiracy theory" of history or delve into case histories to demonstrate empirically that the courts were indeed protective of victims' rights.[30] The legal dimensions of this controversy for industrial development in West Virginia raise issues of such magnitude that to address them here would refocus the purpose of this essay. There can be no controversy, however, over the fact that the Virginia legal tradition took a new, decidedly pro-industry course in West Virginia much to the detriment of the agricultural interests.

Until the Civil War, American courts staunchly supported the legal rule of *sic utere tuo ut alienum non laedas*, "so use your own as not to injure that of another," in cases involving conflicts of property rights and nuisances emanating from the use of that property. At the beginning of the nineteenth century, jurists generally viewed property as a "natural right," and therefore, owners possessed the right against interference by others in the use of their property. This reasoning, of course, protected the status quo dominated by the agricultural interests. Industrial development, however, refocused natural property rights because of the nuisances created by industrialists in the use of their property.[31]

Throughout the nineteenth century the Virginia Supreme Court adhered to what has been called a "static" theory of property rights that focused on the rights of agricultural plaintiffs who generally prevailed against industrial defendants.[32] Early West Virginia nuisance decisions conformed with Virginia legal tradition by upholding the plaintiffs' right to be free of interference in the enjoyment of their property. In 1889 and 1890, however, the supreme court of appeals underwent a complete transition as an entirely new slate of justices took office. The new judges abandoned the static view of their Virginia-trained forebears and adopted a "dynamic" theory that recognized the economic use of property for commercial and industrial enterprise as well as for agriculture, reflecting the long-standing development wishes of business and government leaders.[33] The significance of this transformation of nuisance law readily became apparent to farmers in how jurists applied the law in fencing cases, in assessing damage liability for livestock killed by locomotives, and in cases involving fires ignited by locomotive sparks.

In Virginia, agriculture continued to enjoy legislative and judicial preference, but in West Virginia the court increasingly gave priority to industrial developers. The Virginia Code required railroads to protect livestock by fencing in the right-of-way.[34] In 1903, in *Sanger v. Chesapeake & Ohio Ry. Co.*, the state court went even further to declare that "a railroad company is liable to the owner of stock killed or injured on its track by one of its trains, although he owned no land either at the point where the stock was killed or injured, or at the point where the stock came upon the track, though the only negligence alleged was the failure of the company to fence its track as required."[35]

This was a far more sweeping protection of the farmers' property than in West Virginia, where aggrieved farmers were forced to prove that the railroad was negligent in operating its equipment in order to secure damages. Moreover, the West Virginia Supreme Court of Appeals consistently placed the burden of proof squarely on the shoulders of the plaintiff.[36] In 1916 the court ruled that "in order to charge a railway company with damages for killing stock straying upon its tracks, negligence on the part of the company must appear, and the burden of showing it rests upon the plaintiff."[37]

Neither was it necessary in West Virginia for the railroads to fence their right-of-way to prevent livestock from straying onto the tracks, unless required to do so by the terms of charters or by statutory enactment.[38] While the railroads were bound to take "ordinary" precautions to avoid injury to trespassing animals, they were not required to maintain such a "rigid observation" as to "discover" livestock on the track.[39] The logical progression of this reasoning culminated in 1919 when the state enacted legislation "making it unlawful for horses, cattle, etc., to run at large on a railroad right of way, and fixing a penalty on the owner if injury to property results therefrom."[40]

Steam-powered locomotives were notorious for showering the countryside with sparks from their boilers, and hot coals often fell out of their cinderboxes, setting fire to field and forest. Ambiguities in the Virginia law were settled in the favor of farmers by the Featherstone Act of 1908, which was held to be constitutional in 1917 and interpreted to mean that a railroad was liable for damages from fires occasioned by sparks or coals beyond the railroad's right-of-way onto the plaintiff's property. The constitutionality of the act was reaffirmed in 1932 when the Virginia court ruled that a railroad was liable for damages resulting from "fire caused by sparks from locomotives, regardless of whether it was negligent."[41]

In dramatic contrast, on the question of fire liability West Virginia law evolved in precisely the opposite direction, toward protecting the railroads from suits brought by farmers. The West Virginia Supreme Court of Appeals ruled in 1911, for example, that "in absence of its negligence, a railroad company is not liable for injury to property contiguous to its line from fire starting from sparks from its locomotive." The railroad was, however, required to take ordinary precautions to prevent property damage, such as equipping locomotives with spark arresters.[42]

Case law that evolved during the industrial transformation, therefore, rendered it increasingly difficult for West Virginia's agrarians to protect themselves against railroad abuses. The legal preeminence secured by the railroads in West Virginia gave a green light to large-scale investment in natural resource extraction but flashed a danger signal to the farmers, who recognized that they were confronted with a direct assault upon their traditional legal protection.

Another important reason farmers resisted railroad development was the attempt by railroads to shift the financial burden for their construction from themselves to farmers. In order to capitalize railroad construction, companies often expected counties to impose taxes on themselves by acquiring stock in the company. Such was the case in 1885 and 1886 when promoters of the Chicago, Parkersburg, and Norfolk Railway urged the leaders of Pocahontas County to schedule a public vote on the question of purchasing $50,000 of the company's stock to help finance the road's extension through the county. The proposal created considerable controversy over assuming such a debt, and the court decided not to hold a referendum when it became clear that a majority of the citizens opposed the proposal.[43]

The comments of Wheeling businessman Henry B. Hubbard, who was in the Pocahontas County seat of Huntersville on business at the time, reveal the nature of the opposition to the proposed railroad. Hubbard wrote that a "more hopeless outlook" for the village could hardly be imagined, therefore "it would be natural to suppose that every man, woman and child in the county would be in favor of a railroad." But such was not the case, "as most of the solid men are reported as unfavorable to it, and to be using their influence to prevent it being built." To Hubbard and his associates, such opposition was "almost incredible." A better understanding of "the habits of this class of people, however, did much toward removing our incredulity" and caused Hubbard to wonder if, after all, "they were not wise in their opposition so far as they are individually concerned being as they are a preeminently pastoral people with no desire for the rush, strife and turmoil of trade, but perfectly satisfied with their thousand acres covered with flocks and herds, and the comforts and influences derived from them. A tripling or quadrupling of the value of their lands would not add to their happiness nor change their occupation, but would add to the amount of their taxes without producing an extra blade of grass."[44]

Many farmers also worried that the railroads would undermine their individual economic well-being. Not only were they concerned about the destruction of fields and livestock, but with the viability of legal recourse increasingly questionable, they also worried that the railroads would depress the price of livestock and feed in the local markets. Farmers understood that when the railroads came to haul away timber, they would also bring in cheaper products that could undersell their own in the local markets. When the B&O surveyed a route through Monongalia County, West Virginia, into Greene County, Pennsylvania, for example, many local citizens opposed the route. At public meetings they declared that railroad construction should be halted at Cumberland, "and then all the goods will be wagoned through our country, all the hogs will be fed with our corn, and all the horses with our oats."[45]

Whether resistance stemmed from changes in traditional legal protection, higher taxes, or the threat to their dominance in local markets, West Virginia farmers responded to the same forces of economic change that ignited agrarian protests such as the Granger, Greenback, and Populist movements.[46] Agricultural unrest in West Virginia took its regional political shading from the early period of railroad extension through the state when the railroad companies employed heavy-handed tactics to engineer the election of friendly politicians, and used sharp business practices such as charging higher rates for short hauls to eastern markets than for long hauls from the Midwest. Such practices made farmers in the older established farm districts of the eastern panhandle and the northern counties hostile to the railroads, particularly the B&O.[47]

The political atmosphere had already been poisoned by acrimonious relations between farmers and the railroads, therefore, when the railroads penetrated the interior counties to transport the big timber to market. Back-county farmers were much less likely to participate in organized railroad opposition than were their counterparts in the more developed counties. Back-county farmers were too thinly settled, and their economy was still founded on household production and consumption.[48] The timber industry changed that. Removal of the forest eliminated the food supply on which farmers traditionally ranged unfenced livestock, and farmers were forced to abandon subsistence farming for commercial agriculture. The older developed counties, where the forests had been cleared for farming earlier in the nineteenth century, had evolved gradually into the commercial system independently of the railroad until the mid-century mark. Berkeley and Jefferson Counties, for example, were 90 percent cleared in 1894, and the northern counties of Hancock, Brooke, Ohio, Monongalia, and Harrison were 80 to 90 percent cleared for crops and pasture.[49] Conversely, the rural mountain counties remained covered with dense forests at the beginning of the transformation. The same State Board of Agriculture data shows that 55 percent of Tucker County, one of the first interior counties to be targeted for timber development, was still covered by ancient growth in 1894. Other mountain counties remained primarily wilderness in 1894. That same year, for example, Hardy County was only 32 percent cleared; Randolph, 30 percent; Pocahontas, 33 percent; Pendleton, 25 percent; and only 15 percent of Webster County had been cleared. Even in Greenbrier County, one of the earliest settled mountain counties with long-established commercial ties to Virginia, 50 percent of the primeval forest remained uncut in 1894.[50]

Prior to large-scale timbering in the back counties, subsistence farmers generally raised food for their own household consumption, and livestock were driven to market to generate cash for necessities the household could not produce for itself. Organized for household consumption, the back-county agricultural economy was unable to supply the railroad and lumber camps with sufficient food for the workmen. Local newspaper editor John E. Campbell of Huntersville, Pocahontas County, outlined the nature of the back-county agricultural system when he testily responded to complaints from "the railroad people" that they were forced "to import nearly everything they need in the way of supplies," and the "half contemptuous remark by a stranger that the county was hardly self-supporting." This assertion was unwarranted, Campbell snapped, "for while we may not be able to sell the contractors all the farm products they need, still a great many of our people have a surplus in the bank at the end of a year's work. On the farm the market ruled, and for most of the products the only market was the home market, the long haul in wagons precluding any competition with or from the markets of the world. . . . Farm products have invariably commanded a higher price here than at the depot."[51] A local sage summed up the difference between the commercial system found in the lowlands of eastern

Virginia and the subsistence system practiced in the mountains of West Virginia: "There they eat what they can't sell, and here they sell what they can't eat."[52]

Although farm commodities were produced for local consumption in the mountains, livestock was the backbone of West Virginia's agricultural economy. Prior to the arrival of railroads, once or twice a year mountain farmers drove their stock to regional gathering points, where large herds were purchased and driven to distant markets by professional drovers.[53] Railroads changed this regional pattern and precipitated a shift to modern commercial stock farming. Stockmen of Pocahontas County who formerly had driven their cattle over the mountain to White Sulphur Springs or to Covington, Virginia, began instead to ship their cattle, sheep, and hogs to market from local depots along the Greenbrier Division. In 1910 the railroad hauled 1,200 carloads of sheep and cattle out of the Greenbrier Valley.[54] But along with direct connections to urban markets came competition with cattle shipped from other regions to those same markets, and the competition dictated that mountain stockmen adopt more efficient methods. The rugged, open-range cattle capable of withstanding the rigors of foraging for themselves under the old open-range system, therefore, were soon replaced with improved breeds that brought a higher price on the hoof. The investment in better-quality herds and the removal of the forest lands where mountain livestock traditionally grazed precipitated the replacement of open-range grazing with the enclosed pasture. Fenced pastures allowed for controlled feeding and, most significantly under the commercial system, enhanced the potential financial return on the farmers' investment.

Throughout the mountains the timber industry first generated an industrial economy. As the forests were removed, agriculture shifted from the subsistence to the modern commercial system.[55] Data from the U.S. Census of Agriculture comparing the pre-timber boom year 1870 with peak-timber boom year 1910 clearly demonstrates the correlation between the demise of the forest and the ascent of the system of commercial stock raising (see Table 11.2). For example, in Tucker County the number of cattle and sheep nearly tripled, and the number of swine doubled between 1870 and 1910. Similarly, in Randolph County during these same years, the number of cattle and swine more than doubled, and the number of sheep just about tripled. Expansion in Pocahontas County livestock during this period was almost identical; the number of cattle and swine doubled, while sheep nearly quadrupled.[56] Even though agricultural prices declined during the long depression that engulfed American agriculture in the late nineteenth century, the value of all domestic animals (cattle, horses, mules, asses and burros, swine, sheep, and goats)

Table 11.2. Livestock on Farms in Three Timbered Counties

Year	Cattle	Sheep	Swine	Total Valuation of All Domestic Livestock
		Tucker County		
1870	1,646	2,608	1,045	$112,583
1880	2,391	3,545	3,655	112,917
1890	3,549	3,287	2,305	141,870
1900	5,062	6,112	2,983	—
1910	4,144	7,602	2,462	317,427
1920	4,226	5,278	2,248	477,598
		Randolph County		
1870	8,228	8,523	2,834	$369,158
1880	14,657	12,403	9,458	474,241
1890	11,894	17,992	2,347	533,310
1900	18,191	23,570	7,023	769,775
1910	17,200	24,662	5,487	984,134
1920	14,684	18,214	5,128	1,502,266
		Pocahontas County		
1870	7,916	10,824	2,789	$358,239
1880	9,043	14,707	5,313	294,718
1890	11,894	25,146	4,684	444,860
1900	12,063	33,062	6,324	598,992
1910	13,208	41,517	5,408	859,923
1920	13,272	35,110	8,437	1,474,026

Source: West Virginia Department of Agriculture Biennial Reports, respective years.

raised in these timbered mountain counties also expanded dramatically between 1870 and 1910: more than 200 percent in Tucker, nearly 300 percent in Randolph, and close to 250 percent in Pocahontas.[57]

Another clear indication of the shift from subsistence to commercial agriculture is evidenced by the increasing reliance on fertilizers. Without transportation, remote rural farmers were unable to utilize bulky commercial fertilizers even if they could afford them. However, the trains that hauled out the timber returned with commercial grade fertilizer, resulting in a dramatic increase in the total value of fertilizers purchased by farmers in the mountain counties. Farmers used very little commercial fertilizer of any kind in 1879, but by 1919 the value of fertilizers utilized in Tucker County had increased more than thirty-two times, in Randolph more than fifty-six times, and in Pocahontas forty-six times.[58]

Another consequence of deforestation was an increase in the number of farms in the interior mountain counties (see Table 11.3). Some of this increase is accounted for by the continuous subdivision of farms under the practice of partible inheritance so common in Appalachia. The explanation is much more complex than that, however. Population growth that accompanied the timber boom partially explains the growth in the number of farms during this period. Woodsmen typically were from a farming background, and when the boom was over, many who had saved enough money purchased their own land. Moreover, under the old system of open-range grazing and forest fallowing, fields declining in fertility were revitalized by allowing them to revert to forest cover. Farmers required much greater acreage under this system because two-thirds of the land was always either under or reverting to forest cover and therefore was unavailable for agricultural use. Many farmers reduced their total acreage by selling their woodlands and then using the money to shift to the fenced-pasture commercial system.[59]

The explanation for the decrease in farm size is also much more complex than simply the other side of a Malthusian trap in which population growth put pressure on a fixed quantity of land. While partible inheritance subdivided the land into smaller plots, large blocks of land were also subdivided into small units for sale by the timber companies. Lumber operators usually purchased their properties for the timber and, once the forest was removed, preferred to sell the denuded land. The State Department of Agriculture actually established a program to assist lumbermen in the subdivision of their cutover lands for sale as small farms.[60]

Most companies sold their properties and moved on, but others consolidated cutover lands into huge holdings that were withheld from agricultural production. The West Virginia commissioner of agriculture reported in 1920 that "several million acres" of cutover land was suitable for agriculture, particularly for raising livestock and poultry or for gardening. Much of this land, however, was held by timber companies in large tracts ranging from 2,000 to 60,000 acres. The commissioner reported that "no organized or systematic use" was being made of these lands for any purpose, except summer ranging of livestock. West Virginia Pulp and Paper Company (WESTVACO), for example, accumulated hundreds of thousands of acres to insure a steady supply of pulpwood for its large paper mill in Covington, Virginia. The federal government also purchased hundreds of thousands of acres of barren land for the Monongahela National Forest, and the State of West Virginia acquired additional tens of thousands of acres for its extensive system of parks and forests. These, too, were lands withdrawn from the

Table 11.3. Number and Size of Farms and Use of Commercial Fertilizers

Year	Number of County Farms	Average Farm Acreage		Commercial Fertilizers
		County	State	
		Tucker County		
1870	223	—	—	—
1880	385	223	—	$456
1890	659	129	142	393
1900	768	122	114.7	1,130
1910	828	112.7	103.7	3,559
1920	724	124.5	109.6	14,726
		Randolph County		
1870	575	—	—	—
1880	1,186	360	—	$910
1890	1,358	332	142	3,460
1900	1,787	202.8	114.7	9,670
1910	1,856	155.8	103.7	18,068
1920	1,774	170.4	109.6	51,558
		Pocahontas County		
1870	604	—	—	—
1880	682	451	—	$679
1890	908	351	142	1,513
1900	1,051	241.5	114.7	5,070
1910	1,198	195.2	103.7	9,507
1920	1,283	207.6	109.6	31,292

Source: U.S. Census of Agriculture.
Note: Valuation of commercial fertilizers was reported in the decennial census, but for the years 1879, 1889, 1899, 1909, 1919.

agricultural land market. Constricting the availability of good farmland even further, especially the all-important bottomland, was the takeover of more and more prime acreage by railroads, mines, factories, and towns as the industrialization of West Virginia progressed.[61]

The population-to-farm ratio was further extenuated by the environmental disaster inflicted by deforestation. This disaster was well understood by conservationists even as it evolved, but their alarm was drowned out by the clamor for industrial development. The old forest was mature with a fully developed canopy, and when the tops of the giant trees were cut away, the dry slashing, which was left on the floor to rot, became a virtual tinderbox awaiting the careless spark. With all the heavy steam equipment in the forest, such as locomotives, steam skidders, and steam loaders, sparks were ever present to ignite the inevitable conflagration. Fire followed fire until many areas of the state were forever altered from what nature had created.[62]

The extent of the damage caused by these fires is staggering. In 1908, for example, the number of fires reached 710, burning an area of 1,703,850 acres, more than one-tenth of the entire surface of the state, one-fifth of its forested area, and 3 percent of the state's standing timber. Seventy-one percent of the fires were caused by locomotives, and 20 percent were started by sawmills and campers, dramatically underscoring the destructive role of steam locomotives in the process of deforestation.[63] The vast majority of forest fires originated with the production process. In July 1930, for example, fire broke out in a big slashing of the Cherry River Lumber Company in the Tea Creek district of the Williams River, and within a week it burned over an area seven miles long and three miles wide. "So intense was the heat that . . . everything above ground [was] consumed and in places the loamy soil itself burned down to the rock," a local newspaper reported.[64] Destruction of the deep humus that had built up on the forest floor for thousands of years reduced countless acres of land to bare rock in the higher elevations of the interior counties.

People who lived downstream from where the forests had been removed, particularly farmers, also were seriously affected by deforestation. When the higher elevations of the interior counties were denuded, erosion further disfigured the land. Rain washed away the already thin layer of topsoil, gullies formed in sandy soils, and clay surfaces washed away in sheets and leached fertility out of the soil.[65] What washed off the hillsides went into the streams, and farmers' organizations publicly lamented the serious pollution of the state's waters.[66] The trouble began at the tops of the mountains, A. B. Brooks wrote, "where the cutting of the timber has bared the ground, caused the drying up of springs once pure and perennial, and substituted surface drainage over the hard and packed soil." Lower down, the water picked up drainage from tanneries, pulp mills, sawmills, factories, coal mines, and towns, rendering it intolerably polluted.[67]

Governor William M. O. Dawson established the West Virginia Natural Resource Commission in October 1908 to investigate the condition of the state's natural resources. The commission's report was alarming. Cattle, it claimed, died from drinking the waters of the Cheat River, once synonymous with purity. Nearby Decker's Creek contained not a living thing and was cited as another "example of what deforestation and pollution have done." Brooks confirmed these findings in 1911, reporting that steamboats on the Monongahela River "could not use the water from some of the pools without ruining their boilers." Water in the Cheat River was even worse, for "it put locomotives out of commission" and "took the hair off the legs of cattle that stood in it in fly time, and was fatal when they drank it." According to Brooks, "scarcely a living fish remains in Cheat River between its forks and its mouth." These conditions were more or less replicated throughout the state.[68]

From the highest to the lowest elevations, therefore, cutting the virgin forest was not simply a process of chopping down large trees. It involved the virtual elimination of entire ecological systems, the consequences of which were profound for the social as well as the natural world.

By 1920 even the most strident promoters of West Virginia's industrialization had ample reason to contemplate the consequences of the transition to capitalism. Railroads had laid the iron rails of progress into the most isolated interior reaches of the state; the courts had revolutionized the law to sanction industrialization and mowed down the judicial status quo that had protected farmers; and a great flock of wage earners who had settled in the multitude of new mill towns sawed their way through a mountain wilderness the scale of which few Americans of 1920 could even imagine. Most importantly for indigenous farmers, subsistence agriculture was pushed aside by a modern commercial system that tied the fortunes of the West Virginia back counties to the national markets. Initially, this seemed cause for optimism among interior farmers, but those hopes soon dimmed as they were forced into competition with midwestern producers who confronted fewer geographic disadvantages than mountain farmers.

West Virginia farmers who could not compete in the national markets but remained on the land saw the size of their farms steadily decline as West Virginia was transformed into an industrial economy and its people into wage earners. Nevertheless, West Virginians remained overwhelmingly rural, and many of those who continued to live in the countryside acquired small farms where they supplemented their wages by raising a few head of livestock, tilling fodder crops, and cultivating extensive gardens. Whether they attempted to compete in the commercial markets or became supplemental farmers, however, the results were the same: agriculture increasingly became marginalized, and rural folk were forced to fall back on traditional survival strategies characterized by scholars as the "subsistence-barter-and-borrow" system, or the "informal economy."[69] To the people it was simply "making do."

In the 1920s the question of whether West Virginia farmers would benefit from linkage with the national markets that resulted from industrialization had been answered for those who understood the signs; the dream of early industrial promoters that railroads would "help our people out of the woods" was fulfilled. Railroad and timber development did not stimulate the growth of a vibrant agricultural sector but, rather, forced farmers to either abandon the countryside for a new life in the industrial towns or face a life of rural marginality at the periphery of the American, and now global, economy.

Notes

1. Roy B. Clarkson, *Tumult on the Mountains: Lumbering in West Virginia, 1770–1920* (Parsons, W.Va.: McClain, 1964), p. 39.

2. The literature on this subject is extensive. A minor classic is Charles Henry Ambler, *Sectionalism in Virginia from 1776 to 1861* (Chicago: University of Chicago Press, 1910). For a recent chapter-length study, see Van Beck Hall, "The Politics of Appalachian Virginia, 1790–1830," in *Appalachian Frontiers: Settlement, Society and Development in the Preindustrial Era*, ed. Robert D. Mitchell (Lexington: University Press of Kentucky, 1990), pp. 166–86. For the views of a statemaker, see Waitman T. Willey, *An Inside View of the Formation of West Virginia* (Wheeling, W.Va.: News Publishing Co., 1901). See also, M. F. Maury and William M. Fontaine, *Resources of West Virginia* (Wheeling, W.Va.: Register Co., 1876), pp. 336–37.

3. *The Manufacturer's Record* 50 (October 1906): 338; Ronald D. Eller, *Miners, Millhands, and Mountaineers: Industrialization of the Appalachian South, 1880–1930* (Knoxville: University of Tennessee Press, 1982), p. 47.

4. John Alexander Williams, *West Virginia and the Captains of Industry* (Morgantown: West Virginia University Library, 1976), pp. 168, 170.

5. There are several excellent studies that treat this subject extensively. See, for example, Richard G. Lillard, *The Great Forest* (New York: Knopf, 1947); Thomas R. Cox, Robert S. Maxwell, Phillip Drennon Thomas, and Joseph J. Malone, *This Well-Wooded Land: Americans and Their Forests from Colonial Times to the Present* (Lincoln: University of Nebraska Press, 1985); Michael Williams, *Americans and Their Forests: A Historical Geography* (New York: Cambridge University Press, 1989).

6. *Wheeling Register*, 10 November 1881.

7. John F. Stover, *History of the Baltimore and Ohio Railroad* (West Lafayette, Ind.: Purdue University Press, 1987), pp. 65–78; Eller, *Miners, Millhands, and Mountaineers*, pp. 66–69; Charles Vernon Bias, "A History of the Chesapeake and Ohio Railway Company and Its Predecessors, 1784–1977" (Ph.D. diss., West Virginia University, 1979), pp. 101–25.

8. Joseph T. Lambie, *From Mine to Market: The History of Coal Transportation on the Norfolk and Western Railway* (New York: New York University Press, 1959), pp. 26–46, 128–33.

9. George A. Fizer, "The West Virginia and Pittsburgh Railroad," *The Log Train: Journal of the Mountain State Railroad & Logging Historical Association* 7 (1989): 3–7 (hereafter *Log Train*); E. Lawrence Marquess, "The West Virginia Venture: Empire out of Wilderness," *West Virginia History* 14 (1952): 5–27; Donald L. Rice, *Bicenten-*

nial History of Randolph County (Elkins, W.Va.: Randolph County Historical Society, 1987), pp. 66–72.

10. Benjamin F. G. Kline, "The Nature of the Logging Railroads of West Virginia," *Log Train* 2 (1984): 12. See, for examples, Michael J. Dunn III, "The Beech Mountain Railroad Company," *West Virginia History* 23 (1962): 79–85; Wayne Lincoln, "Porter's Creek & Gauley Railroad," *West Virginia Hillbilly*, pt. 1, 12 January 1989, pp. 5, 9, and pt. 2, 19 January 1989, p. 15.

11. Williams, *Captains of Industry*, p. 168; James Morton Callahan, *Semi-Centennial History of West Virginia* (Charleston, W.Va.: Semi-Centennial Commission of West Virginia, 1913), pp. 306–7; "Map of West Virginia Showing Railroads," West Virginia Geological and Economic Survey, 1917, MC 1, DWR 5, West Virginia and Regional History Collection, West Virginia University, Morgantown. This map is oversized and relatively inaccessible, but a readily available adaptation may be found in Clarkson, *Tumult on the Mountains*, insert.

12. Callahan, *Semi-Centennial History*, pp. 212–13.

13. *Wheeling Register*, 17 August 1884.

14. Quoted in William P. McNeel, "Lumber Industry in Pocahontas County," in *History of Pocahontas County, West Virginia* (Marlinton, W.Va.: Pocahontas County Historical Society, 1981), p. 179.

15. William P. McNeel, *The Durbin Route: The Greenbrier Division of the Chesapeake & Ohio Railway* (Charleston, W.Va.: Pictorial Histories, 1985), pp. 35–37; Otis K. Rice, *A History of Greenbrier County* (Lewisburg, W.Va.: Greenbrier Historical Society, 1986), p. 348.

16. U.S. Bureau of the Census, *Report on the Manufactures of the United States, 1880* (Washington, D.C.: Government Printing Office, 1883), and *Census of Manufactures, 1919* (Washington, D.C.: Government Printing Office, 1923).

17. Clarkson, *Tumult on the Mountains*, pp. 73–75.

18. McNeel, *Durbin Route*, pp. 13–14; Roy B. Clarkson, *On Beyond Leatherbark: The Cass Saga* (Parsons, W.Va.: McClain, 1990), pp. 18–29.

19. Clarkson, *Tumult on the Mountains*, p. 31.

20. Ibid., p. 30; Rice, *Greenbrier County*, p. 355.

21. In 1910 the foreign immigrant population was 16.1 percent in Tucker County, 7.9 percent in Randolph County, and 5.5 percent in Pocahontas County (U.S. Bureau of the Census, *Thirteenth Census of the United States, Population, 1910* [Washington, D.C.: Government Printing Office, 1913]).

22. McNeel, *Durbin Route*, pp. 35–37; Rice, *Greenbrier County*, p. 348.

23. Callahan, *Semi-Centennial History*, p. 212. The dramatic increase in the variety and volume of manufactured goods that became available in areas previously isolated from the national marketplace is graphically revealed in advertisements placed in local newspapers of the region.

24. There were many newspaper editors in West Virginia who followed a "booster" editorial policy toward industry in addition to the Wheeling newspapers cited in this study. For example, the role of the *Logan Banner* is assessed in Altina L. Waller, *Feud: Hatfields, McCoys, and Social Change in Appalachia, 1860–1900* (Chapel Hill: University of North Carolina Press, 1988), pp. 144–46; the position of

the *Pocahontas Times* is discussed in John Hennen, "Benign Betrayal: Capitalist Intervention in Pocahontas County, West Virginia, 1890–1910," *West Virginia History* 50 (1991): 54–60.

25. *Wheeling Register*, 17 August 1884.

26. A. B. Brooks, *Forestry and Wood Industries* (Morgantown, W.Va.: West Virginia Geological Survey, 1911), 5:44–46.

27. Callahan, *Semi-Centennial History*, p. 192.

28. Ibid., p. 121 n.

29. Quoted in ibid., p. 111 n.

30. The most influential legal historian who expounds the subsidy thesis is Morton J. Horwitz, *The Transformation of American Law, 1780–1860* (Cambridge, Mass.: Harvard University Press, 1977). Those who reject this thesis have not yet found their equal of Horwitz, but an excellent refutation can be found in Gary T. Schwartz, "Tort Law and the Economy in Nineteenth-Century America: A Reinterpretation," *Yale Law Journal* 90 (1981): 1717–75.

31. Horwitz, *Transformation of American Law*, pp. 74–80, 98–99; Jeff L. Lewin, "The Silent Revolution in West Virginia's Law of Nuisance," *West Virginia Law Review* 92 (1989–90): 244–46, 251.

32. Lewin, "Silent Revolution," pp. 252–53.

33. Ibid., pp. 253–54, 270–72.

34. *Virginia Code* 1887, p. 1259, as amended by *Acts*, 1897–98, cc. 250, 283.

35. *Sanger v. Chesapeake & O. Ry. Co.* (1903), 45 S.E. 750, 102 Va. 86. Quoted in *Virginia and West Virginia Digest* 16 (1970): 358 (hereafter cited as *Digest*).

36. *Johnson v. Baltimore & O. Ry. Co.* (1885), 25 W.Va. 570; *Maynard v. Norfolk & W. Ry. Co.* (1885), 21 S.E. 733, 40 W.Va. 331; *Talbott v. West Virginia, C. & P. Ry. Co.* (1896), 26 S.E. 311, 42 W.Va. 560; *Christian v. Chesapeake & O. Ry. Co.* (1916), 89 S.E. 17, 78 W.Va. 378; *Daniels v. Chesapeake & O. Ry. Co.* (1923), 117 S.E. 695, 94 W.Va. 56, in *Digest* 16:363.

37. *Christian v. Chesapeake & O. Ry. Co.* (1916), 89 S.E. 17, 78 W.Va. 378.

38. *Blaine v. Chesapeake & O. Ry. Co.* (1876), 9 W.Va. 252, and *Baylor v. Baltimore & O. Ry. Co.* (1876), 9 W.Va. 270; *Starks v. Baltimore & O. Ry. Co.* (1915), 87 S.E. 88, 77 W.Va. 93.

39. *Ellison v. Norfolk & W. Ry. Co.* (1919), 98 S.E. 257, 83 W.Va. 316.

40. *Acts* 1919, sec. 3, c. 59; *Warden v. Hines* (1919), 106 S.E. 130, 87 West Virginia 756, in *Digest* 16:360.

41. *Acts*, 1908, p. 388; *Chesapeake & O. Ry. Co. v. May* (1917), 92 S.E. 801, 120, Va. 790; *Norfolk & W. Ry. Co. v. Spates* (1917), 94 S.E. 195, 122; *Virginia Code* 1910, 3992; *Southern Ry. v. American Peanut Corporation* (1932), 164 S.E. 261, 158 Va. 359, in *Digest* 16:369.

42. *West Virginia Code*, 1913, sec. 3518, c. 62, 54; *Jacobs v. Baltimore & O. Ry. Co.* (1911), 70 S.E. 369, 68 W.Va. 618, quoted in *Digest* 16:369–70; *McLaughlin v. Baltimore & O. Ry. Co.* (1911), 83 S.E. 999, 75 W.Va. 287.

43. McNeel, *Durbin Route*, pp. 2–3.

44. Quoted in ibid.

45. Callahan, *Semi-Centennial History*, p. 111 n.

46. The most important studies of the agricultural reform movements are John D. Hicks, *The Populist Revolt* (Minneapolis: University of Minnesota Press, 1931); Richard Hofstadter, *The Age of Reform: From Bryan to FDR* (New York: Knopf, 1955); Lawrence Goodwyn, *Democratic Promise: The Populist Movement in America* (New York: Oxford University Press, 1976).

47. William D. Barns, *The West Virginia State Grange: The First Century, 1873–1973* (Morgantown, W.Va.: William D. Barns, 1973), pp. 35–64; William D. Barns, "The Grange and Populist Movement in West Virginia, 1873–1914" (Ph.D. diss., West Virginia University, 1946), pp. 241–64.

48. Barns, *West Virginia State Grange*, p. 36; Barns, "Grange and Populist Movement," p. 922.

49. *Second Biennial Report of the West Virginia State Board of Agriculture, for the Years 1893 and 1894* (Charleston, W.Va.: Moses W. Donnally, 1894), p. 45.

50. Ibid.

51. *Pocahontas Times*, 19 August 1899. Subsistence agriculture and production for household or local market consumption, a system found throughout America in the eighteenth and nineteenth centuries, often is misunderstood as the product of presumably "backward" or "maladaptive" people who settled in Appalachia. For an excellent corrective, see Mary Beth Pudup, "The Limits of Subsistence: Agriculture and Industry in Central Appalachia," *Agricultural History* 64 (1990): 61–89.

52. *Pocahontas Times*, 28 September 1894.

53. Paul C. Henlein, *Cattle Kingdom in the Ohio Valley, 1783–1860* (Lexington: University of Kentucky Press, 1959), pp. 1–20; John Edmund Stealey III, "Notes on the Ante-Bellum Cattle Industry from the McNeill Family Papers," *Ohio History* 75 (Winter 1966): 38–47, 70–72.

54. McNeel, *Durbin Route*, pp. 35–37; Rice, *Greenbrier County*, p. 348.

55. For examples of this transition at the local level, see Jo Ann Sereno Teets, *From This Green Glade: A History of Terra Alta, West Virginia* (Terra Alta, W.Va.: Jo Ann Sereno Teets, 1978), pp. 69–70; Rice, *Greenbrier County*, pp. 389–90. For a contemporary novel depicting professional cattle drivers in West Virginia, see Melville Davisson Post, *Dwellers in the Hills* (New York: Putnam, 1901).

56. *U.S. Census of Agriculture*, respective years.

57. Ibid.; West Virginia Department of Agriculture Biennial Reports. For the agricultural depression confronting West Virginia farmers (as elsewhere in the United States), see Barns, *West Virginia State Grange*, pp. 21–23.

58. *U.S. Census of Agriculture*, respective years.

59. John Fraser Hart, "Land Rotation in Appalachia," *Geographical Review* 67 (1977): 150–54. John Solomon Otto has published extensively on forest farming in the southern highlands. See, for example, J. S. Otto, "The Migration of the Southern Plain Folk: An Interdisciplinary Synthesis," *Journal of Southern History* 51 (1985): 183–200; J. S. Otto and M. E. Anderson, "Slash-and-Burn Cultivation in the Highland South: A Problem in Comparative Agricultural History," *Comparative Studies in Society and History* 24 (1982): 131–47; J. S. Otto, "The Decline of Forest Farming in Southern Appalachia," *Journal of Forest History* 27 (1983): 18–27. For a contemporary confirmation of this widespread practice and some of the problems it inflicted

on the forest, see Charles S. Sargent, *Report on the Forests of North America*, Department of the Interior, Census Office (Washington, D.C.: Government Printing Office, 1884), pp. 492–93.

60. West Virginia Department of Agriculture, *Fourth Biennial Report of the West Virginia Department of Agriculture, 1919–1920* (Charleston, W.Va.: Tribune, 1920), pp. 11–12.

61. Ibid.; WESTVACO owns over 300,000 acres of land in West Virginia. Total acreage of public park and forest lands in the state are divided as follows: federally administered land totals 1,161,642 acres; state administered land totals 407,247 acres; locally administered land totals 21,327 acres. This amounts to 1,590,216 acres, approximately 10 percent of the land mass in West Virginia. (See Governor's Office of Community and Industrial Development, Community Development Division, *West Virginia State Comprehensive Outdoor Recreation Plan* [February 1989], pp. 1–2.)

62. Clarkson, *Tumult on the Mountains*, p. 43.

63. A. B. Brooks, *Report of the West Virginia Conservation Commission*, 1908, p. 23. By comparison, fifty-four forest fires were reported in West Virginia in 1888. (See Sargent, *Report on the Forests of North America*, p. 492.)

64. *Pocahontas Times*, 17 July 1930. West Virginia's poet laureate, Louise McNeill Pease, who grew up in Pocahontas County during these years, writes of the smoke from this fire in her autobiographical work *The Milk-Weed Ladies* (Pittsburgh: University of Pittsburgh Press, 1988), p. 99.

65. Brooks, *Forestry*, p. 35; Brooks, *Report of the Conservation Commission*, p. 42.

66. *Report of the Farmers' Institutes*, West Virginia State Board of Agriculture, no. 5, 1907, p. 8.

67. Brooks, *Forestry*, p. 32.

68. *Illustrated Monthly West Virginian* 2 (1908): 42–44, quotes from p. 43; Brooks, *Forestry*, p. 34.

69. Paul Salstrom, *Appalachia's Path to Dependency: Rethinking a Region's Economic History, 1730–1940* (Lexington: University Press of Kentucky, 1994), chap. 3.

Class Formation in the Southeastern Kentucky Coalfields, 1890–1920

T he transition to industrial capitalism presupposes three important developments. First, a situation emerges in which labor is
separated from control over the instruments of labor. The historical processes leading to this situation vary from place to place, but it
always involves the restriction of access to the means of production and its
monopolization by a dominant class consisting of landholding, industrial,
and/or financial interests. Second, the transition to modern capitalism presupposes that capital is free to be invested for its own self-expansion. Labor
must be free to be exchanged on a contractual basis. Capitalists are thereby
freed of any legal and/or moral obligation to maintain members of the
working class beyond brief contractual periods of time. Labor can then be
hired or fired to meet the requirements of modern industrialists. This is
significant in that precapitalist modes of production are frequently characterized by a condition in which labor is either bound to a particular estate
(plantation or hacienda) or has relatively free access to resources such as
land and can therefore avoid wage labor as a primary means of subsistence.

When investors are freed of long-term labor obligations and when workers' access to resources such as land is limited, the labor market can more readily expand to meet the requirements of capital. Similarly, geographical and political barriers to investors' freedoms must be overcome. Railroads, ports, and other infrastructural services must be created to assure that goods can get to market. Politicians with probusiness attitudes must be cultivated. Attitudes inconsistent with acquisitive, free-market behavior must be replaced with ideas that reinforce investors' moral rights to pursue their interests unhindered. In addition, especially in the case of peripheral industrialization, those components of premodern culture that interfere with the class privileges of modernizing elites must be modified or replaced with something more hospitable. A moral and intellectual climate that favors the free movement and accumulation of capital needs to be established. Finally, an infrastructural foundation for the maintenance and reproduction of new class relations is socially constructed. Laws reflecting the new order must be designed. Schools, housing, roads, sanitation, and other institutional supports for the new society need to be established.

The extension of these legal, economic, cultural, and ideological changes to precapitalist settings rarely occurs as a neat package. A plurality of historical decisions and actions combines to set the stage for the onset of industrialization. There exists, in other words, no iron law that industrial capitalism necessarily rises in one particular way. The social histories of specific communities depend upon numerous empirically variable circumstances that can best be understood through concrete historical study.

In southeastern Kentucky, capitalism emerged against a background that was predominantly characterized by simple, small, petty, or independent commodity production. Each producer worked at and had access to the means and products of labor. There were, to be sure, other modes of production in southeastern Kentucky. As other essays in this volume illustrate, significant slaveholding and wage labor can be found in specific localities. Also, a number of local individuals became successful entrepreneurs prior to the coming of international capital to the region. Timber, lumber, salt, and iron production by small locally owned firms was common in southeastern Kentucky during these years. Nonetheless, the independent mode of production predominated. The absence of a feudal (or plantation/hacienda) tradition meant that the bonds of personal dependence that complicated transition in various European and South American settings were not major obstacles to capitalist growth in southeastern Kentucky. Instead, the main obstacles to be overcome were (1) the shortage of wage labor for hire, (2) the absence of a suitable transportation system, (3) the lack of control over area resources, and (4) the absence of an adequate infrastructural foundation for the maintenance and reproduction of modern class relations. This paper will explore these developments in four southeastern Kentucky counties where coal production was established as the predominant means of subsistence for workers by World War I. These counties include Bell, Harlan, Letcher and Perry; they constitute a major portion of United Mine Workers of America (UMWA) District 19 and were served primarily by the Louisville & Nashville Railroad (L&N).

The Emergence of a Working Class
in Southeastern Kentucky

The pre-1860 period was characterized by a condition in which producers were neither employees of capital nor employers of labor to a significant extent. There was certainly a growing level of entrepreneurial activity, mainly in resource extraction and manufacturing areas. Nonetheless, one writer described early mining in southeastern Kentucky this way: "The mining as well as the shipment of coal was in the hands of the farmer who owned the land and operated at such times as he was not engaged in lumbering or tilling the soil."[1] As if to corroborate this view, the U.S. Bureau of the Census data on mining regularly placed early coal production figures for these counties under a column titled "Farmers' Diggings" rather than under the commercial coal production column. Farmers, working with their neighbors and kin in their spare time to satisfy very limited markets, were the major producers of coal during these years. In manufacturing, a similar condition existed. Small, family-owned sawmills and timber cutting operations can be found throughout the area. Salt production was also an important mountain manufacturing activity in several southeastern Kentucky counties.[2] In nearby Clay County, for instance, salt production reached 7,000 bushels annually as early as 1810 and by 1845 increased to 250,000 bushels. Nonetheless, these firms were small in terms of capital investment and workforce. One of the largest salt producers was a Perry County firm that boasted a capital investment of $18,000 and a workforce of only eleven.[3] A similar situation existed in the area of iron production. *The Iron Manufacturers' Guide* lists several iron furnaces in southeastern and northeastern Kentucky by 1850. Some of these iron operations were quite extensive. In northeastern Carter County, company (log) houses were provided to furnace workers along with commissaries, stables, and schools. "Practically every necessity of life was provided for by the furnace company."[4] Significant entrepreneurial activities were obviously present. Yet the pre-1870 period was one in which most producers fell outside the system of industrial capitalism.

By 1930, southeastern Kentucky had become a transformed society of wage laborers linked with some of the industrial giants of the day. Names such as International Harvester, U.S. Steel, Peabody Coal, Bethlehem Steel, Consolidated Coal, and The American Association became commonplace. People increasingly came to live in company towns apart from the family farms and businesses that had previously provided a means of subsistence. Immigration and natural increase added to the local population. The four county (Bell, Harlan, Letcher and Perry) population totals increased from 15,384 in 1870 to well over 141,000 in 1930, with most of this increase taking place between 1915 and 1925. Coal mine employment figures increased from 0 in 1890 to 26,168 in 1930.[5] Put differently, within a few years nearly 20 percent of the population worked directly for the mining industry. These dramatic changes raise many questions for social scientists. What induced, cajoled, or forced workers into the capitalistic labor market? What prevented them from flowing out again? What forces led to the decline of precapitalist forms of production and the ascendance of industrial capitalism?

The Politics of Transition

As early as 1828 some Kentucky politicians displayed dissatisfaction with the policy of granting land to small settlers at nominal prices. Land, they argued, should be granted to "monopolizing capitalists" for the "purpose of speculation."[6] Such a restrictive land policy was designed to drive people into the labor market and thereby create a favorable political climate for industrial improvement. Kentucky politicians explored these approaches toward economic development through the middle years of the nineteenth century, but it was the Civil War that finally forced them to give more systematic attention to their application.

The growth of concern over labor policy after the war was a result of the dramatic impact of abolition on the economy of the economically dominant, Bluegrass portion of Kentucky. The whole agricultural and industrial system of a large portion of the state was brought to a halt due to lack of what was perceived as a "suitable" labor supply. One document, dated 1871, lists the evils inflicted by the war as follows: "Kentucky had an efficient and reliable system of labor. During the war . . . , portions of her territory were ravaged and property of her citizens destroyed or consumed; the tranquil pursuit of agriculture was violently disrupted; living in the country remote from cities and military stations became perilous; the citizen and his family were subject to perpetual alarms; cattle and other livestock were slaughtered; horses were pressed into service; slaves were insubordinate and after several years of such demoralization the colored people were freed." The sudden emancipation of 205,781 slaves valued at over $100 million "struck our industrial system down."[7] The bitterness of slaveholding politicians was exacerbated even further by the fact that the "General Government, notwithstanding the formal obligation to pay for them [the slaves], was guilty of repudiation, and slaveholders received nothing for their property." At the very least, these slaveholders felt, the "General Government" should slowly phase in the freedom of the black people. This would allow former slaves to become "somewhat habituated to their new privileges and responsibilities." The government, they complained, failed to see that "their interests [slaves and slaveholders] were identical, not antagonistic."[8] Despite such pleas, abolition was to become a reality, and efforts to rebuild a labor system in the Bluegrass would produce profound effects for eastern Kentucky. Policymakers increasingly would look to scarcely populated, resource rich mountain counties as a lure to entice industrial capital and a new working class to Kentucky.

The tone of the new flurry of political discussions that followed the war was set in the governor's message to the legislature on 6 January 1868. "A change in the domestic policy of Kentucky," the governor wrote, "has become forced upon her people by a fundamental alteration of her domestic institutions." Governor Stevenson warned that policy changes were inevitable and permanent and that lawmakers had to meet the challenge with reasoned and enlightened temperaments. The best solution to the economic crisis, he argued, relied upon an attempt to recruit a new class of laborers.[9] "The present need of the state is a sufficient supply of efficient labor. It can only be obtained by largely increased foreign emigration." Kentucky, which Stevenson described as the "Garden of the American Union," should have little difficulty in attracting its share of prospective laborers, provided that sufficient information was made available to them. Immigration to Kentucky "is now an essential requisite to our prosperity. It lies at the root of all social and material wealth. It is a question which towers in importance at this time over any, except revenue."[10]

Throughout the next year, various approaches to labor policy were explored. In early 1869, at the Commercial Convention in Louisville, businessmen proposed creating a general immigration agency for the whole South as the best method to encourage increased immigration. The agency, to be jointly financed by the southern states, would be authorized to prepare, distribute, and translate propaganda favoring the South as a place to settle.

White European immigrants were considered the most suitable targets of these schemes. Accordingly, the members of the convention suggested preparing advertisements in French, English, German, Italian, Dutch, Danish, Swedish, and Norwegian. Kentucky politicians appraised the merits of such a plan but did not seem overly enthusiastic about its prospects and therefore continued to forge their own separate policies.[11]

By December 1869 Governor Stevenson was stressing the importance of broadening their focus to combine strategies to attract labor with plans to entice capital to the state. "For a sufficient supply [of labor]," he wrote, "we must look to foreign immigration. But our need does not stop there. We must look to Europe also for capital . . . if we desire to increase our population and develop our industrial and mineral wealth. How then, is the tide of European immigration [and capital] to be induced to flow into Kentucky?" In answer to his question, the governor proposed a program devoted to the systematic promulgation of information favoring the commonwealth of Kentucky as a place for laborers to settle and as an area for capitalists to invest. For labor, propaganda should aim to remove prejudice from the minds of emigrants before they left Europe and should instruct them about the resources available in Kentucky and the advantages of permanent settlement. For capital, several propaganda vehicles were proposed. Messages to specific interests would be one means to familiarize outsiders with conditions and opportunities in Kentucky. "The iron-masters of Europe," for instance, "must become acquainted with our industrial and mineral wealth." The distribution of geological surveys showing that "Kentucky possesses a greater area of coal of good quality than is contained within the limits of any other State in the world" would help impress a favorable image on the minds of European capitalists. Another approach suggested was the distribution of information at the industrial expositions of England, France, Germany, and Russia. Specimens of Kentucky coal, iron, and timber, accompanied by exact geological survey statements, could demonstrate the superiority of Kentucky resources. Stevenson's goal was to set out a general position on the best ways to encourage internal economic development and formulate specific strategies for dealing with foreign capital and labor. Kentucky's economic policy should "inform them of the rich and boundless deposits of iron ore which accompany the coal; the accessibility of both to commercial transit by rivers and railroads now completed or in the course of construction; the high elevation of our coal and iron bearing lands . . . [to] impress upon foreign miners, furnace men and machinists the inducements to emigration, as developed by the liberal compensation of the American workingman over the wages of Europe."[12]

For the governor and his supporters, it was imperative that the legislature act as soon as possible to establish some sort of agency designed to accomplish these goals. But the summer of 1870 had arrived and no legislative action had been finalized. In an effort to emphasize the urgency of the matter, Stevenson presented a letter that he received from Colonel Blanton Duncan. While in Europe, Duncan had made the observation that the conditions for inducing labor to leave Europe for Kentucky were favorable and that immediate action was required or the opportunity would be lost. The colonel advised setting up a state agency authorized to coordinate immigration policy and activity. With the state in control of such authority, he wrote, "influential men will be induced to take the lead, and the supply and demand of labor will go hand in hand." To speed up the process, he recommended that the state finance workers' journeys (to be repaid with interest, of course) and that workers be guaranteed employment upon arrival in Kentucky. Again, Duncan urged policymakers to act quickly since the favorable conditions to attract labor would soon evaporate. "The war now raging [in Europe] affords an additional argument. We have no powerful neighbors, no possibilities of entanglements, no danger of conscription to take off the laboring classes." There was little time to waste. Speaking of Germany, Duncan wrote, "There will be no surplus population . . . for the next ten years. The dead, the maimed, and the useless population . . . will not reach less than 500,000 adult males before the close of the war. . . . The labor market will be so depleted that there will be ample occupation for every remaining laborer . . . and their government would feel bound to throw obstacles in the way of continued emigration."[13]

Duncan's letter appears to have had the desired impact as legislative action finally took shape in early 1871. Alfred T. Pope, chairman of the Committee on Immigration and Labor, presented a bill to establish a bureau of immigration for the state. The bill won swift acceptance. The bill was important. It provided a formal, comprehensive statement of the government's position on labor. It thereby offered a glimpse of the attitudes taken toward land and capital, particularly outside capital, and preferred paths to economic improvement.

In the opening pages the bill recognized the crucial importance of systematic immigration as "not inferior . . . to any question that may come before the Senate." Committee members remarked that "the development of this country is not due to the labors of the gentle classes of England . . . but rather to the sturdy frames and strong arms of the humble and needy who have been hardened by a life of toil and privation." They recognized the "immense capital value of immigration [labor]." To corroborate this view, drafters of the bill presented a statistical analysis to demonstrate that the increase in the wealth of the nation proceeded in exact ratio to the increase of labor that, they pointed out, resulted largely from increased immigration.

Besides recognizing labor as the source of wealth, the authors also emphasized the crisis that made large-scale immigration into Kentucky imperative. After the war, they wrote, "the colored people flocked to the cities, herded in tenements and ate the rations of idleness and indolence. . . . The result was the general derangement and paralysis of our system of labor." The problem, as they saw it, was that "Kentucky possessed every essential component of production, save labor and capital."[14] Moreover, the best possible substitute for the old labor system could be found in Europe, where an "exhaustless supply" of labor existed, "where land is scarce . . . where people are crowded, wages low and living difficult." Put simply, immigration was perceived as the surest remedy to the disintegration of the old labor relations, and it also offered the promise to furnish "men of our race" for the laboring classes.[15]

The Bureau of Immigration was designed to achieve three central objectives. First, it was designed to entice European labor to this country and then to Kentucky. Besides a commissioner, appointed by the governor, one agent was to operate out of New York, and two would be stationed in Europe. Their functions included keeping in touch with the chambers of commerce of major European cities as well as the organization and distribution of information in relative surplus population areas. Second, the bureau was designed to make maximum utilization of the rail system. The offices were located in Louisville, the railroad center of the state, in order to more easily distribute immigrants to areas with labor shortages and to maximize labor mobility in general. Finally, the bureau was designed to serve employers, especially large employers. To best serve these interests, the bill proclaimed that the intention was to work as junior partners with industry. Agents of the bureau were instructed to gear their efforts toward securing the "cooperation" of the captains of industry and never to assume "exclusive control." The labor commissioner was charged with the major responsibility of registering all applications for laborers and then distributing them "equally" over the state.

These efforts to formulate a statewide labor-industrial policy were clearly designed to create a favorable political climate for the development of international capitalism. Images of labor as well as the role of the state in internal improvement were substantially established by 1875. This view contained the following basic assumptions:

First, labor was recognized as a crucial commodity for the development of capitalist production. In the governor's message of 1876 we find the statement that "labor makes capital and labor and capital together give life and impetus and strength to a State or nation."[16] Without reasonably priced labor, it was supposed that all interests in society were endangered, as the production of social wealth would be discontinued. The role of government, therefore, was to protect all the interests of the state by encouraging the growth of a labor pool large enough to guarantee the proper balance between the forces of supply and demand in the capitalistic labor market.

Second, Kentucky's economy needed more than labor. It needed an adequate capital base and a correct balance between capital and labor. To achieve this balance, Kentucky politicians followed two general policies. First, they sought to entice outside capital and labor through generous tax laws and information peddling outside the state. Such was the purpose of the Bureau of Immigration, the staging of commercial conventions, and other efforts to attract the attention of specific industrial interests. Second, to assure the development of a capitalistic labor market, politicians resolved to prevent immigrants from flowing into noncapitalist modes of subsistence. They sought immigrants who had few resources to set up as independent commodity producers and had little intention of granting them free or inexpensive land.[17] Even in this so-called age of laissez-faire, Kentucky politicians believed that some government intervention was advantageous, namely, to assure favorable conditions on the labor market for capitalists.

Third, Kentucky state politicians generally took a favorable stand on the question of outside capital. They realized that, weakened by the war and by the loss of their labor supply, there was a need to rebuild a reliable labor-industrial system. In this effort, state officials actively solicited outside capital as the preferred avenue to economic development. Preference for outside capital, as opposed to indigenous capitalist growth or noncapitalist growth, encouraged patterns of absentee ownership and political power that would influence the eastern Kentucky economy throughout the twentieth century.

Finally, politicians felt it their duty to provide essential services for those whom they planned to own the means of production by functioning as a sort of clearinghouse for the distribution of labor and as a propaganda machine to entice industrial capital into the state. From the standpoint of many Kentucky politicians, these policies were presumed to be good for all the interests of the state. For the absentee owners of large mineral and landholdings, this assumption was proved valid. For those who worked for many of the corporations and for those independent commodity producers and small farmers of the state, the presumptions seem dubious at best.

The Coming of Industrial Capital

For decades prior to the onset of industrialization, land speculation in eastern Kentucky had been a sort of sport for high society in the Bluegrass and elsewhere. Land was cheap, surveys indicated future potential, and much land was not even registered. In addition, the land warrant system, which awarded soldiers property in return for wartime service, allowed many to obtain large tracts of land. Thus, prior to 1880, there was already considerable concentration of land in the hands of a few owners. In Bell County in 1850, for instance, 45 percent of the assessed acreage was held by taxpayers who owned more than 1,000 acres each. Landownership was similarly concentrated in the hands of these "large taxpayers" (50 percent of Harlan County, 29 percent of Letcher County, and 30 percent of nearby Leslie County). Some industries did develop out of this early land speculation. One notable example is the Asher Lumber Company. The Asher Brothers bought vast holdings in at least ten eastern Kentucky counties, land they had built up through years of speculation. They also owned substantial sawmills in both Bell and Clark Counties. But these early investors were not typically the ones that contributed most to widespread industrialization of the region. Even the Asher Brothers, among the most important of the early investors, were squeezed out of the lumber business by 1896 as it was taken over by Michigan interests and renamed the Burt and Brabb Lumber Company.[18]

The casual speculation of the pre-1880 period was soon replaced with a qualitatively different form of investment. The "new" investors typically operated on a much grander scale. Where once only a few hundred souls lived, usually at the county seat, complete cities were built. Some were designed to include such extravagant features as parks, luxury hotels, hot springs, theaters, and health resorts. The pace and volume of these investments varied from place to place; they did not all occur at the same time. In some places, investment was booming as early as 1890. In others, the boom did not come until after 1910. Whatever their form and timing, these investments contributed in a major way to, first, the establishment of capital-labor relations as the primary means of subsistence for the community and, second, the transformation of land into capital.

By 1892 these new investors had made considerable headway into the region and were clearly identifiable. In the tax lists the names of large landholders were increasingly those of a new breed of investor, usually land, coal, development, timber, and/or mining companies. Names of individuals were increasingly replaced by those of large, widely recognized corporations. What this represented was more than a mere acquisition of land by a corporation in a "free market"; it represented a *new form* of property that grew and developed out of the old form of land use and ownership.

The penetration of outside capital into southeastern Kentucky can be demonstrated with a cursory examination of these tax lists. In 1892, the last year in which the tax lists for all eastern Kentucky counties are available, the amount of land concentration in the hands of the top twenty to thirty taxpayers of each county was quite impressive. It would be twenty years before the railroads and coal operations would appear overtly in Harlan, Lecher, and Perry Counties. Large-scale industrial developments had only started in Bell County during the previous two years. Yet a virtual land monopoly had already been established. As Table 12.1 indicates, over 80 percent of Bell County was owned by a few large landowners, and with twenty years left before the onset of industrialization, approximately 60 percent of Harlan, Letcher, and Perry Counties were in the hands of large taxpayers. While the numbers in Table 12.1 appear rather exaggerated, there are two good reasons to believe that they are more likely to be conservative estimates of the true level of land concentration. First, there are indications that a number of large taxpayers understated their true landownership for tax purposes. In Bell County there are at least two important examples of this practice. For tax purposes, the Log Mountain Coal, Coke and Timber Company claimed title to 20,400 acres of Bell County land in 1892. In the company's own correspondence and letters to potential investors, however, the company claimed ownership of at least 26,000 acres, and it probably owned more. That is at least 6,000 acres left out of the tax books and out of the calculations of land concentration. Another example of this practice can be found with the American Association Ltd., a British-owned firm and the largest landholder in the county in 1892. For tax purposes, the association claimed ownership to only 19,000 acres of Bell County land, but in their own public statements they claimed ownership of 80,000 acres and an addition 5,398 acres owned through the Middlesborough Town Company. That leaves an additional 66,398 acres that were never entered into the calculations in Table 12.1. Second, there is good reason to believe that the "nonresident" category is understated. According to tax procedures of the time, a company was considered a resident landholder by the tax assessor if it had an office in the county. The English investors behind the American Association Ltd. were, therefore, not considered out-of-county taxpayers/landholders. As a result of this practice, the true degree of nonresident landownership in Table 12.1 is likely very understated. Still other considerations are important. Chief among these is that these figures reveal patterns

Table 12.1. Land Concentration in Selected Eastern Kentucky Counties, 1892

County	A: Number of Large Taxpayers	B: Total Assessed Acreage	C: Acres Held by Large Taxpayers	D: Acres Held by Large Nonresidents	C as % of D	D as % of B
Bell	29	375,404	303,343	197,374	80.5	52.6
Harlan	38	315,564	194,728	a	61.7	—
Letcher	31	287,067	119,774	a	42.0	—
Perry	40	410,803	263,480	194,367	64.1	47.3

Source: Tax assessor's book, respective counties, 1892, State Archives, Frankfort, Ky.
Note: A large taxpayer owns more than 1,000 acres.
aIn these counties in 1892 the tax assessor did not distinguish between resident and nonresident taxpayers.

of landownership; they do not take account of mineral and timber rights that were also purchased with great zeal during these early years. With these reservations in mind, it is reasonable to believe that Table 12.1 offers a very conservative estimate of the true level of land (resource) monopoly in 1892.

The conquest of the region's productive resources was a profound development that may have been little comprehended by the local population. The monopolization of land and resource ownership by new industrial and financial interests was weakening the material basis upon which farmers and other independent commodity producers operated and was simultaneously strengthening the inflow of outside capital. It generated irrepressible tendencies for the gradual decay of the older way of life. In addition, with the coming of the railroads, workers for the new industries could be drawn, with the aid of government, from surplus populations around the world. Other laborers could be recruited from those mountaineers displaced by the dramatic changes at work in resource-rich counties. To be sure, many independent commodity producers continued their regular activities. Some undoubtedly prospered with access to new markets in the new industrial communities. But the coming of the railroads and capital meant the increased flow of workers into the capitalistic labor market and the transformation of the social relations that governed daily living in these mountain counties.

The formation of new class relations varied from place to place, but some general points are noteworthy. The creation of a land monopoly prior to the "industrialization" of these counties destroyed the conditions under which it was possible to carry on an independent mode of production and, in turn, led to its gradual decay. Moreover, the boosterism of town builders coupled with the building of new retail enterprises must have been intoxicating for many. The development of a labor market that offered income, from wages, to purchase a startling array of new products from capital further weakened the independent mode of production. New production strategies bring forth new consumption (subsistence) strategies, and the dominance of capital over the productive resources of the area was coupled with an almost exclusive control over the towns, stores, and recreational facilities—the means of consumption.

Bell County provides an example of how quickly and thoroughly these changes came to eastern Kentucky. In 1885 or 1886, Alexander A. Arthur, a representative of Scotch and English capitalists who owned and lumbered a large tract of land in North Carolina, entered Bell County through the Cumberland Gap to examine firsthand the famous tracts of timber there, as well as coal and iron deposits. Within a year Arthur was in London, England, giving glowing accounts of what he had seen to the directors of the Barring Brothers banking house, the stockholders of the Watts Iron and Steel Company of Middlesborough, and other prominent English capitalists. After receiving reports from other qualified experts, the American Association Ltd. was capitalized with a stock valued at $2 million. In the 1887 *Mine Inspector's Report* (for Kentucky), the name of the American Association appeared for the first time as a Bell County coal operator. A branch line of the L&N was completed in 1888 from Corbin, Kentucky, to Pineville. Local historians point to this coming of the railroad as the beginning of the new industrial period in Bell County. What it more accurately marked was a significant moment in the reshaping of class relations and everyday life in the area. Soon the predominantly rural society of independent commodity producers would be replaced by an urban society of wage laborers. Middlesboro would grow from a town of fifty souls in the spring of 1889 to an industrial city of over 10,000 by 1892.

The emergence of new class relations in Bell County was, as elsewhere, accomplished through the systematic development of a number of closely related business organizations. These businesses came to play an ever-increasing role in the productive and consumptive lives of local people. The centerpiece of this business network was the American Association Ltd., a land company that owned in excess of 80,000 acres of Bell County. Control over land would prove to be a crucial factor in the ability of the new investors to shape change and development well into the future. The second piece of the puzzle was the Middlesborough Town Company, later named the Middlesborough Town Land Company, which owned the 5,398 acres that would become the city of Middlesboro. Another company, the Cumberland Gap Park Corporation, was formed in 1890 to begin construction of a luxury hotel, a sanitarium, and a casino.

The control exerted by these new investors extended to ownership of some of the most important infrastructural services for industrial operations. The Middlesborough Belt Railroad, for example, which circled the town with branch lines leading to mine sites, was completely controlled by the association. Two other railroads were partially controlled by the new interests—the Knoxville, Cumberland Gap, and Louisville Railroad, and the Knoxville Southern Railroad. The first of these lines operated 73 miles of track leading to Knoxville, Tennessee. The latter operated 110 miles of track between Knoxville, Tennessee, and Atlanta, Georgia. Still other companies could be added to the list of firms that constituted this network. The Watts Iron & Steel Syndicated, for example, controlled large tracts of land containing iron ore and coal deposits only five miles south of Middlesboro near Arthur, Tennessee. The point, however, is that capitalist development was not merely the product of technological superiority. It emerged from fundamental social changes wherein new power and influence were exerted through exclusive, interlocking control over key business organizations, including railroads, development firms, and consumption-oriented enterprises.

Figure 12.1 illustrates how interconnected these firms were. Note that the names of the English investors behind the network appear only in information directly dealing with the American Association proper. In most cases, American representatives served as both directors and executive officers on this side of the Atlantic.

The plan of development embraced by those in this network was based on the idea that the American Association Ltd. assume the position of landlord—building a few initial industrial facilities but mostly restricting activities to leasing of property rights. According to an 1890 brochure, the plan was to "lease, on royalties . . . coal, iron, clay, timber and quarry privileges . . . rent cleared farms on reasonable terms . . . [and] sell or lease lands suitable for manufacturing industries of all kinds." Town lots, of course, were to be leased or auctioned off through the Middlesborough Town Company. This strategy to promote development was not unique in Bell County. Another important landholder, the Log Mountain Coal, Coke, and Timber Company, followed a similar plan for growth. With its 26,000+ acres, plans were to "strictly maintain the position of landlords . . . leasing coal mines, stone quarries, clay beds, and farms, selling specified timber stumpage for tanneries, charcoal for iron furnaces, saw-mills, carriage and

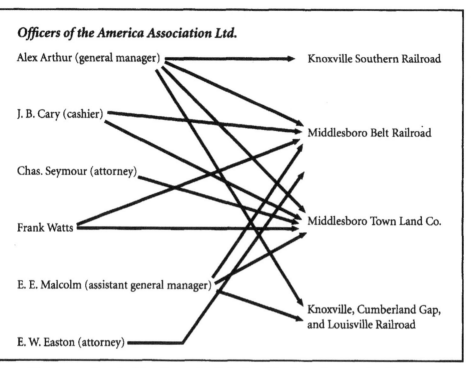

Figure 12.1. Interlocking Executive Relationships in and around Middlesboro, 1890

wagon material, furniture and other woodworking factories, selling village and town lots, controlling all water supplies for both domestic and manufacturing uses, and generally to extract from the property the actual intrinsic value of its resources."

Similar patterns of investment and business organization came to Harlan, Letcher, and Perry Counties but were delayed for several years. When the L&N completed its branch line to Pineville in 1888, a decision was made, partly influenced by the American Association, to develop the rail connections south to Knoxville and Atlanta rather than to enter other eastern Kentucky counties where known coal reserves were located. Accordingly, while the L&N had a branch line going to Big Stone Gap and Norton on the Virginia side of the mountain, none entered Harlan, Letcher, or Perry Counties. Some L&N executives protested the decision to bypass these counties, but it would take pressures of a wholly different kind to move H. Walters, chairman of the railroad, and others to order this line built.

Between 1900 and 1910 two important developments helped spark a movement to built an L&N branch into these other counties. First, several coal land deals were negotiated and were given much publicity. In the

Manufacturers Record, an important magazine covering southern financial and industrial developments, the editors noted that heavy investments were being placed in "Harlan and other mountain counties . . . in Kentucky by Eastern and Northern capitalists." These investments were regarded as "the forerunner of a railroad extension into one of the richest regions of the state." The Kentenia Corporation, probably the largest coal landowner in Harlan County at the time, already claimed title to over 100,000 acres, although for tax purposes only 39,000 were recognized. The Wisconsin Steel Company, a subsidiary of the Morgan-McCormick International Harvester Corporation, purchased another 20,000 acres on which it was busy equipping its mines with "electrical machinery . . . for a daily output of 2,000 tons of coal and constructing 300 coke ovens." In nearby Leslie County the Fordson Coal Company (owned by Henry Ford) was allegedly in the process of acquiring approximately one-half of that county's acreage. In short, what was taking place was the creation of a land monopoly prior to any rail penetration. For the new investors, the reasons for making land deals quickly were clear. Speedy land transactions provided an opportunity to acquire resources before the local inhabitants realized "the true intrinsic value of their property." They also helped the new investors secure a hegemonic position in the new society for years to come. By securing control of local resources, investors were better positioned to shape new developments along lines consistent with their goals—that is, in the interest of greater capital accumulation.

The second development that helped give the L&N reason to build a rail extension into these eastern counties came from activities carried out by the rival Southern Railroad corporation, which started buying trackage rights for a line between Middlesboro and the Harlan County coalfields. The Southern line was started but never completed. In a 1904 letter marked confidential, H. Walters described, to Morgan Jones a large landowner in Harlan County and a railway builder, the threat posed by the Southern activities and the L&N's means to combat that threat.

> I think I told you while you were here that I had information that the Southern Railroad had made a survey up the Cumberland River to Harlan Court House . . . at the solicitation of the Harvester people of Chicago who purchased coal land in that valley. I would be very glad to see a line built up the Cumberland River by someone who was independent, so that the Louisville & Nashville could make some kind of contract with them by which it would enjoy the business. We do not propose to let Southern get into that territory. . . . Under a trackage right, they now use

our [mile-long] tunnel [under Cumberland Gap] down to Middlesborough, but they have no right to go beyond Middlesborough, according to our lawyers.

What would be your plans for building this road? How would you
provide money and how would you expect to operate it?

By 1914 the L&N had built its own branch line into Harlan and several
other counties; it entered Harlan in 1911. At that time, over 70 percent of the
total assessed acreage of Harlan County was concentrated in the hands of
twenty-six large taxpayers. The eight largest of these, including the Kentenia
Corporation, Wisconsin Steel, and the Black Mountain Corporation, controlled 45 percent of the assessed land in Harlan County.

The dominance of these new investors is also reflected in coal production
statistics. In Harlan County, Wisconsin Steel produced about 43 percent of
the total coal output between 1911 and the onset of World War I. When this
production is combined with that of the Wallins Creek Coal Company,
another Morgan-McCormick controlled firm, the percentage changes to 76.
In Letcher County the Consolidated Coal Company produced 1,273,248 of
the total 1,539,070 tons of coal for 1914, 82 percent of the county total. Only
Perry County had a different pattern; in 1914 seven major companies, each
producing less than 60,000 tons of coal, operated.

While the emergence of capitalist relations of production in these four
southeastern Kentucky counties was limited, in some respects, by conditions on the world market, few restrictions posed much of a problem at the
local level. The whole pattern of development rested upon the absolute
domination of the means of production and consumption. Resistance
against such a combination of resource monopoly and modern business
organization would prove difficult. The new investors were clearly in a
position to shape the general character of social change and development
for years to come.

Coal Camps: The Infrastructural
Foundation for New Class Realities

Along with an increase in investment and political interest came a dramatic
increase in the size of the working class in these southeastern counties.[19]
The new class of miners typically found themselves living in company
towns, apart from preindustrial modes of subsistence. These company-
controlled communities provided the infrastructural foundation for the
maintenance and reproduction of new class realities in the mountains. Laws

reflecting and reinforcing the new order were designed. Schools, housing, roads, sanitation, recreation, and other amenities were also established.

Some of the new coal operators viewed their creations with pride. They believed that their company towns were superior to anything found in the surrounding countryside. In the midst of what they perceived as barren wilderness, entire cities were built, sometimes complete with spacious homes, electricity, bath houses, parks, and hotels. For coal operators, however, the real value of company towns was not so much in the lavish accommodations provided for workers but in the fact that the social organization of the company town solved real problems.

At first, company towns provided operators with a means to deal with the important problem of labor scarcity. Production was expanding so fast that operators increasingly resorted to raiding one another's labor supply. Higher wages and better accommodations were often used to win new recruits. The general quality of town life and housing thus became an important factor in attracting new workers. Later, after the problem of labor scarcity was under control, company towns served another purpose: to weaken labor organization and promote labor stability. For operators, a stable and peaceful workforce was one that recognized the value of individual, as opposed to collective, bargaining arrangements. Operators wanted a workforce that did not readily resort to collective action to achieve their goals. Unionism was perceived as undemocratic. Organizers were variously described as instigators, rattlesnakes, bolshevists, and enemies of freedom. Unionization activities of any type were actively opposed.[20]

The use of company towns to stifle labor militancy and to stabilize industrial relations led to some of the bitterest episodes in U.S. labor history. Accounts of these struggles can be found in newspapers, magazines, and journals, but one report stands out for its ability to shed light on the issues troubling the industry. The 1925 *Report of the United States Coal Commission* (USCC) provides a detailed sketch of company town life in the early years of the twentieth century. With unusual clarity, the authors of this report document how coal operators socially constructed an infrastructural foundation to maintain an open shop and stifle oppositional culture.

Denial of Civil Rights

Among the most important practices designed to restrict unionization in the coalfields was the use of repressive measures against miners and their families. Through their disproportionate control over police, housing, and jobs, operators frequently denied miners their basic civil rights to free speech and free association. Researchers for the USCC wrote that "a few operators attempted to compete with the Union for the loyalty of their employees, but most of them have resorted to methods of force which fall into two groups—those that affect the rights of workers as citizens and those that are more purely industrial practices."[21] Concern about the widespread character of these practices is found throughout the 1925 report.

> Abundant evidence has been received that in the campaign against the union the mine workers in many non-union fields have been denied their rights of free speech and free assembly, of intercourse with persons objectionable to the company, and of free movement from place to place. The operating companies have been able to abridge these fundamental rights through ownership and control of communities in which workers live, an ownership often including not only houses and stores, but roads, and public buildings and, at times, the Post Office.[22]

Furthermore, law officials were frequently paid directly from corporate coffers. This gave additional incentive for local law officers to pay careful heed to the wishes and likes of company officials. When asked by one researcher what his major responsibility was, one local town sheriff frankly stated, "It is my job to keep the union out of —— County."[23]

Work Contracts

Working in a coal camp in southeastern Kentucky often meant living in company-owned housing. Work contracts were thus doubly important, potentially defining conditions at work and at home. Evidence from the report of the USCC indicates that these work contracts were worded in such a way as to preclude the opportunity for workers to organize in their own self interests. Known as yellow-dog contracts, these agreements were widespread throughout the coalfields until they were outlawed in the 1930s.[24] These contracts prohibited employees from being members of or "in sympathy with" any labor organization. The list of outlawed labor organizations included both openly revolutionary organizations, such as the International Workers of the World, and more conservative unions, including the UMWA or "any other mine labor organization." The problem, for miners, was simple. What constituted a violation of this contract was largely left to the discretion of the mine foreman, operator, or company-paid law enforcement official. Word from the mining office that a worker had pro-union sympathies was sufficient justification for firing or, if the miner resisted, incarceration on the grounds of breech of contract, threat to private property, and/or sedition.[25] The contract included "molesting" or "annoying" either customers, employers, or employees as grounds for dismissal. Miners were thus hindered from exercising their civil rights; legal acts of resistance, including strikes, pickets, public speeches, and boycotts were prohibited. Even less open acts such as expressing bad feelings or ill will toward the company were not tolerated.

Housing Leases

Another crucial practice designed to control the labor force involved the construction of carefully worded housing leases. A typical lease would allow the miner and his family to occupy a company house under the following conditions: (1) the miner's right to occupy the house terminated whenever he ceased to work for the company; (2) rent would be deducted from the miner's paycheck along with miscellaneous deductions for the costs of damages incurred in repairing the house; (3) only five days notice, on average, was necessary for eviction; and (4) the miner's family was prohibited from harboring or entertaining persons objectionable to the company. Housing leases functioned to ensure more effective control over the workforce. This legally secured mechanism ensured the insecurity of housing tenure for miners' families. It placed marked limitations on workers' control over community affairs.

Scrip and Wage Deductions

Two other practices that were designed to preserve and reproduce the new class realities were scrip and arbitrary wage deductions. Scrip involved a system of granting company tokens to workers in place of cash. Company commissaries would exchange the scrip for goods sold through the store. This practice ensured the company store of a ready market, even though the prices were frequently not competitive. It also provided a lucrative prospect for coal companies in that it helped them recapture some of their wage expenditures.[26] For miners, payment in scrip decreased their financial independence and employment security. Merchants from independent stores would redeem scrip but only after a substantial discount, frequently as high as 20 percent. Also, company officials kept track of miners' expenditures in the commissary and rewarded those who showed loyalty to the corporation. Faced with heavy discounts and operator hostility toward buying from independent merchants, miners were obliged to purchase goods through the company store network. Such a practice served to funnel expenditures on wages back into corporate coffers and to increase the dependency of the miner's family upon the operator.

The practice of making deductions from miners' paychecks also worked to cement the new class realities in favor of operators. It was customary in many coal camps to deduct special occupational and personal charges from miners' earnings. The problem was that such deductions were frequently exorbitant. Given the operators' almost total control over accounting procedures—most did not even provide employees with a detailed account of deductions—claims that operators were profiteering at miners' expense were inevitable. According to the USCC, there was significant evidence to give credence to miners' claims that "operators make an undue profit off some of the supplies furnished and that charges for such services was exorbitant."[27] The significance of these deductions is hard to overestimate. The services provided by the company touched virtually every aspect of the lives of miners and their families. In addition to occupational charges for items such as smithing tools, powder, and fuses, there was a long list of personal charges for household coal, rent, bills at the commissary, visits to doctors or hospitals, schools, and bath houses. The benefits of coal town living were not provided "free of charge" to mining families. Instead, the social costs of production were deducted from miners' wages with little negotiation over the quantity, quality, and price of services provided. Add to this the practice of docking workers' pay for disciplinary infractions. Insubordination, poor attendance, and UMWA sympathies were routinely given as justifications for wage deductions.[28] This discretionary authority to reduce miners' purchasing power was yet another way to support and reinforce labor discipline.

Together these social practices combined to produce an infrastructural foundation for the coal towns of Appalachia. Miners, distributed among dozens of mining camps located in hard-to-reach valleys, found themselves in a tightly controlled and repressive social environment where the company appeared to have a clear hand at dictating the direction of social change and development. Housing leases, work contracts, arbitrary foremen's authority, local law enforcement officials, and work rules all seemed designed to guarantee operators' hegemony.

In real life, however, plans frequently go astray. Despite the best efforts of operators and their allies, the very design of these coal camps encouraged miners to develop new, innovative strategies to undercut employers' authority and increase employees' job and health security. From their remote communities, miners became some of the most militant and class-conscious workers in the United States, building a strong oppositional culture in the mountains and providing leadership for industrial unionism in the CIO.[29]

Conclusions

Known largely for its breathtaking natural beauty and its cultural traditions, southeastern Kentucky quickly became a center of industry in the United States. Miners and their families, distributed among dozens of industrial towns in remote valleys, came to populate one of the most industrialized rural regions of the nation. The path leading to this new class society in the mountains is a complex web of complicity and coercion, of power and resistance. This chapter has focused upon three important elements in this transition.

First, after the Civil War, Kentucky politicians struggled to promote a new industrial and labor policy for the state. They sought to entice immigrants from Europe, "men of our own race," to make up the new laboring classes following the abolition of slavery. Kentucky's political leaders rejected blacks as an appropriate labor supply during the difficult period of postwar reconstruction. Through the Bureau of Immigration, Kentucky politicians sought to act as a sort of employment agency to serve the needs of expanding capitalist enterprises. Kentucky politicians also took a very favorable approach to the use of outside capital as a means to provide the economic stimulus to promote general social progress. Various strategies, including information peddling outside the state and the promotion of Kentucky as a resource-rich area ripe for exploitation, were designed to attract capital to the state. Politicians, in a word, worked to attract foreign industry through the creation of a favorable political climate.

Second, a situation in which labor was separated from control over the instruments of labor was achieved through a combination of resource [land] monopoly and tightly networked business organizations. Prior to the onset of industrial production, and before local inhabitants understood the "real intrinsic value" of their land, investors from all over the world came into southeastern Kentucky with the express goal of obtaining as much land as possible. By the time of rail penetration, a small collection of large, mostly nonresident, landowners had purchased over 80 percent of the surface acreage in Bell County. In Harlan and Letcher Counties similar levels of land concentration can be found by 1911. To support and reinforce this control over land, industrialists built transportation and town infrastructure. They owned, either in whole or in significant measure, railroads, stores, theaters, groceries, residential homes (for rent to miners), and resort hotels. They exerted significant influence in the local courthouse and in the sheriff's office. Virtually every aspect of daily life required dealing, on some level, with the company.

Finally, an infrastructural foundation for the maintenance and reproduction of the new class realities was constructed in the social/physical relations of the company-controlled community. Work leases tied continued employment with a workers' pledge to resist with heart, mind, and will any tendency to join, or show sympathy with, any labor organization such as the UMWA. Housing leases were written in such a way that having dinner with someone objectionable to the company could get one evicted and fired. Sedition laws were carefully used to remove organizers from labor struggles and provide an example to other would-be champions of their class. Scrip and arbitrary wage deductions were used to bind the miners to the company in relations of dependence and create a sense of felt obligation on the part of the miner's family for the coal company and its owner(s).

Notes

1. Mary Verhoeff, *Kentucky River Navigation* (Louisville, Ky.: Filson Club Publication no. 28, 1914), p. 177.

2. Other important manufacturing activities included the marketing of forest products and iron production. Timber was usually cut up at locally owned sawmills or floated downstream, where it was purchased by timber dealers such as the Burt & Brabb Lumber Company in Ford, Ky. Iron was typically produced on a small scale in local charcoal furnaces. An exception to this was the coming of the American Association Ltd., a British investment firm, which tried to develop large-scale iron production in the Middlesboro area during the 1890s. For more about the Middlesboro story, see John Gaventa's excellent book, *Power and Powerlessness* (Urbana: University of Illinois Press, 1980). The Papers of the Burt & Brabb Lumber company can be found in Special Collections, University of Kentucky library, Lexington.

3. Verhoeff, *Kentucky River Navigation*, pp. 151, 154. While modest from a national standpoint, these firms were often very important locally. In an important study of the Tug River Valley, which borders Kentucky and West Virginia, Altina L. Waller showed the importance of early entrepreneurs as agents for change both prior to and during the industrial transition. See Waller, *Feud: Hatfields, McCoys, and Social Change in Appalachia, 1860–1900* (Chapel Hill: University of North Carolina Press, 1988).

4. See *The Iron Manufacturers' Guide* (New York: Wiley, 1859); Donald E. Rist, *Iron Furnaces of the Hanging Rock District* (Ashland, Ky.: Hanging Rock Press, 1974); "The Rise and Growth of the Iron Industry in and about Ashland, Kentucky," n.d., Special Collections, Berea College library, Berea, Ky.

5. Much of this increase in coal employment occurred over a relatively short period of time rather than over a long and gradual period. The dramatic increase in coal employment and population was concentrated in the 1910 to 1930 period.

6. "Governor's Message," *Kentucky Senate Journal*, 1828.

7. *Kentucky Senate Journal*, 1871, p. 208.

8. Ibid.

9. Slaveholding interests were very reluctant to hire freed slaves as wage laborers. There was a tacit consensus that the new working class needed to be comprised of "men of our own race." As a result, many blacks were deprived of an opportunity to participate fully during the Reconstruction period and beyond.

10. The quotes from Governor Stevenson were taken from "Governor's Message," *Kentucky House Journal*, 1868, pp. 21–24.

11. Indeed, interest in a southern regional immigration-labor agency declined for the next five years as politicians in a number of states worked on their own plans to satisfy labor requirements.

12. "Governor's Message," *Kentucky House Journal*, 1869–70, pp. 20–24.

13. "Letter from Colonel Blanton Duncan to Governor Stevenson, August 28, 1870," *Kentucky House Journal*, 1871.

14. Again, it is worth noting that it was not the lack of labor resources that plagued Kentucky industrial boosters but, rather, their reluctance to extend the rights of wage labor to recently freed slaves. Here we find the post–Civil War origins of the legacy of exclusion that would influence the lives of black American families for generations.

15. "Bill to Establish a Bureau of Immigration," *Kentucky Senate Journal*, 1871, pp. 207, 215, 211.

16. "Governor's Message," *Kentucky Senate Journal*, 1875–76, p. 17.

17. These intentions were clearly spelled out in "Bill to Establish a Bureau of Immigration," *Kentucky Senate Journal*, 1871. Also, note that Kentucky politicians were generally more interested in offering inducements to labor that did not involve land grants. In 1871 Governor Stevenson wrote that "in new countries the grand feature is their ability to endow the immigrant with a free homestead, which overcomes the reluctance to encounter hardship and to give up the comforts and protection afforded by more civilized settlements. To meet this difficulty, Kentucky, *having no land to give*, might substitute other inducements [to labor]" (*Kentucky Senate Journal*, 1871–72, p. 211 [italics added]).

18. Two points: First, the term "large taxpayer" is admittedly awkward. It refers to taxpayers with landholdings in excess of 1,000 acres in any given county, not to big persons who pay taxes. Second, the estimates of the percentage of land held by large taxpayers in each county are based on data contained in the tax assessor's book of the respective counties. These can be found in the State Archives, Frankfort, Ky.

19. One measure of the importance of coal employment can be found in a cursory look at the proportion of workers directly hired by coal firms. Nearly one of five in the general population worked directly in the coal mining industry. If male mine employees are calculated as a percentage of all gainfully employed male workers, the dependence of community residents on jobs in the coal industry becomes even more apparent. By 1930 Bell County miners formed roughly 44 percent of the gainfully employed male workforce. Perry County miners constituted 65 percent of all gainfully employed men, and in Harlan County, coal operators employed 75 percent of the male workforce. Each county's dependence on the coal industry for jobs suggests that the resource sector in general and mining in particular were dominant factors shaping economic and social life. Anyone or anything that threat-

ened the land monopoly, operators' profits, and/or employers' interests represented a potential threat to the livelihood of the working population.

20. Opposition to unionization declined temporarily during World War I. Increased prices for coal and government regulation of coal production and distribution under the United States Fuel Administration made excessive open shop activism unprofitable.

21. United States Coal Commission, *Report of the United States Coal Commission*, 5 vols. (Washington D.C.: Government Printing Office, 1925), p. 1331.

22. Ibid.

23. Ibid.

24. To get a better sense of the wording of a typical work contract, see ibid., p. 1389.

25. Due to perceived threats from radical labor organizations, the Kentucky legislature passed an antisedition bill in 1920. The bill was passed over the objections of Governor Morrow, who questioned its constitutionality. For miners the danger of the bill was in the vagueness of its definitions. Sedition was defined as "the advocacy or suggestion by word, act, deed or writing of public disorder or resistance to the Government of the United States or the Commonwealth of Kentucky." In the bill it is clearly stated that anyone who defied a strike injunction or espoused "un-American" ideas was guilty of sedition. At one point the lawmakers wrote that it was seditious to "print, publish, utter, circulate, picture, or have in his possession, any book circular, picture or other thing which advocates, suggests, counsels, or advises forcible resistance to constituted authority." The list of proscribed items included revolutionary banners, flags, placards, tags, circulars, or bumper stickers. The law also contained the provision that it was unlawful to "incite or fix enmity, discord, or strike or ill feeling between classes of persons for the purpose of inducing public tumult."

For law officials in company-controlled towns in 1922 this law was a dream come true. Definitions of illegal activities were so vague that they provided no clear limits on what or who could be deemed unlawful. Anything or anyone who resisted, caused bad feelings, or joined a picket line could be found guilty of sedition. For coal miners and their families this law could easily become a nightmare. Being found guilty of sedition carried a penalty of $10,000 and/or ten years at hard labor. See *Acts of the General Assembly of the Commonwealth of Kentucky*, 1920, p. 520. Morrow's objections to the bill are discussed in "Governor's Message," *Kentucky House Journal*, 1922, 1:23.

26. For more on this, see Keith Dix, *What's a Coal Miner to Do?: The Mechanization of Coal Mining* (Pittsburgh: University of Pittsburgh Press, 1988), pp. 16–26.

27. *Report of the U.S. Coal Commission*, p. 1319.

28. Ibid., p. 1325.

29. For example, see Dwight Billings, "Religion as Opposition: A Gramscian Analysis," *American Sociological Review* 96 (1990): 1–31; David Corbin, *Life, Work, and Rebellion in the Coal Fields: The Southern West Virginia Miners, 1880–1922* (Urbana: University of Illinois Press, 1981); Ronald D. Eller, *Miners, Millhands, and Mountaineers: Industrialization of the Appalachian South, 1880–1930* (Knoxville:

University of Tennessee Press, 1982); John Hevener, *Which Side Are You On? The Harlan Coal Miners, 1931–1939* (Urbana: University of Illinois Press, 1980); Ronald Lewis, *Black Coal Miners in America: Race, Class, and Community Conflict, 1780–1980* (Lexington: University Press of Kentucky, 1987); Dix, *What's a Coal Miner to Do?*; Curtis Seltzer, *Fire in the Hole* (Lexington: University Press of Kentucky, 1985).

Feuding in
Appalachia

Evolution of a
Cultural Stereotype

I n American popular culture, feuds are specifically associated with
"hillbillies," uneducated rural people who live in the southern Appalachians or Ozarks. The very term *feud* immediately evokes images of
the Hatfields and the McCoys brandishing Winchesters and, for no apparent reason, attempting to exterminate one another. These images and stereotypes are so deeply ingrained that they have become the standard by
which all other cases of interfamily violence are measured. But they also
dominate and define our perceptions of the southern mountains and the
people who live there as fundamentally different from ourselves.[1] The assumption that Appalachians have a genetic or cultural propensity to family-
based, extralegal violence has been pervasive in popular culture since the
last decade of the nineteenth century when a dozen family feuds in the
mountains of Kentucky claimed the attention of the national press. The
Hatfield-McCoy feud became the most notorious, but at the time the names
of Martin-Tolliver in Rowan County, Hoskins-Johnson in Bell County,
Howard-Turner in Harlan County, French-Eversole in Perry County, and
Hargis-Cockerill in Breathitt County were just as well known.[2] Most of the

Table 13.1. Appalachian Feuds Reported in the *New York Times*, 1851–1910

Feud	County/State	First Report
Rogers-Johnstone	Carter/Tenn.	1867
Ward-Tardy	Virginia	1872
Strong-Little	Breathitt/Ky.	1874
Underwood-Holbrook[a]	Carter/Ky.	1877
Martin-Tolliver[a]	Rowan/Ky.	1884
French-Eversole	Perry/Ky.	1885
Hoskins-Johnson	Bell/Ky.	1885
Howard-Turner	Harlan/Ky.	1885
Turner-Parton-Sawyer	Bell/Ky.	1887
Lee-Taylor	Letcher/Ky.	1887
Hatfield-McCoy	Pike/Ky.-Logan/W.Va.	1888
Rose-Fustian	Whitely/Ky.	1888
Smith-Messer-Slusher	Knox/Ky.	1890
Deskins-Patrick	Magoffin/Ky.	1893
Baker-White-Howard	Clay/Ky.	1899
Hargis-Cockerill	Breathitt/Ky.	1902

Note: These are all conflicts reported as feuds that have more than two citations in the *Times*.

[a]Although the Underwood-Holbrook and Martin-Tolliver feuds are not really in the mountains—as James Klotter argues, they are in the "foothills"—I have included them because they are close to the mountains and have always been associated with Appalachian feuding. In addition, these two together probably received more news coverage than any of the Appalachian feuds (including Hatfield-McCoy).

violence accompanying these feuds occurred between 1885 and 1895, a time when personal and collective violence was at a high point in the rest of the country as well. (See Table 13.1.) Labor conflict and strikes, lynchings, and homicides were common newspaper fare of the day. Feuding, however, gripped the popular imagination and fastened on the people of southern Appalachia a cultural stereotype of violent irrationality that is still potent today.

Indeed, this cultural stereotype has recently been infused with new blood by the publication of David Hackett Fischer's widely read and controversial *Albion's Seed: Four British Folkways in America*.[3] Fischer argues that the original white settlers of the "backcountry"—defined much more broadly than just the mountain region—came from the borderland areas of northern England, the Scottish lowlands, and northeastern Ireland where warlike conditions continually exacerbated an already violent culture. When people from these areas emigrated to the southern backcountry, they simply transplanted a violent culture that was then reinforced by conditions of poverty, inequality, and isolation from social and political institutions. Feuds, along with high levels of other kinds of violence, were simply a way of life, according to this argument.

Yet the historical reality of such assumptions about a culture uniquely characterized by feuding has rarely been scrutinized. Although much scholarly attention has been devoted to arguments over the causes of apparently high levels of *southern* violence, serious consideration of mountain feuds as a separate category of analysis has been almost nonexistent. This is all the more surprising since anthropologists and some historians have developed theoretical frameworks to deal with feuding in medieval and early modern as well as present-day tribal cultures.[4] But until recently, with the publication of my own work on the Hatfield-McCoy feud and David Hackett Fischer's analysis of borderland culture, most American scholars have either ignored feuding or accepted the popular stereotype.[5]

This willingness to accept the stereotypes and ignore the historical context of feud conflicts is a curious phenomenon in its own right—one explored by Henry Shapiro in his pathbreaking book, *Appalachia on Our Mind*. Shapiro examines the ways in which, beginning in the 1870s and 1880s, Americans perceived Appalachia as a strange place inhabited by "peculiar" people. This perception, he argues, came not from the reality of Appalachian peculiarity but from the needs of middle-class Americans in industrializing America to project their own nostalgia for the past and fears about the future onto a people perceived as different. Appalachia became the "other," a place and a people to be admired, patronized, converted, taught, uplifted, disciplined, and sometimes even emulated. The importance of such a place, where the people were assumed to be everything most Americans were not, but were still clearly of similar heritage and culture, offers hints as to why myths about Appalachia were, until recently, so deeply ingrained as to make them impervious to scholarly inquiry.

Shapiro argues that American perceptions of Appalachia—and he makes no attempt to define any Appalachian reality—are not and have never been based on evidence. I argue that feuding is an excellent example of this point. Unlike other types of violence such as lynching, vigilantism, or riots, there are no scholarly studies that quantify feuds or feud violence in Appalachia or anywhere else in the United States.[6] Popular histories of feuds identify a dozen or so southern mountain feuds in the late nineteenth and early twentieth centuries and proceed to make generalizations about a pervasive culture of feuding.[7] But how widespread was feuding? Where did it take place? Was it confined to the southern mountains, or did it exist in other areas as well? Was feuding institutionalized in the same way that it was in sixteenth-century Scotland or nineteenth-century Corsica? How and by whom were conflicts defined as feuding? Perhaps it is true that feuds arose from a peculiar propensity to exaggerated family loyalty and cultural traditions of ignoring legally constituted authority, but if so, very little evidence exists; the history of feuding in America has remained a joke rather than a theoretical problem for scholars to investigate.[8]

Thus there are two distinct problems. The first is the metamorphosis of the feud stereotype, an intellectual exercise that requires examining popular images of feuding and how they changed over time. The second is a search for the historical reality of feuding; we need to describe and analyze the conflicts that came to be identified as feuds. Finally, what is the relation of the popular images to social realities in the southern Appalachians? My own work on the Hatfield-McCoy feud told me a great deal about the social and economic patterns of community conflict and local versus state/national authority that lay behind that infamous feud; yet it also raised ever more persistent questions about how this feud became part of national folklore. This essay is an attempt to make some connections between actual conflicts in mountain communities and their portrayal in the press and literature.

Modern American images of feuding are defined by the Hatfields and the McCoys; that is, we assume feudists to come from a specific class—the uneducated, rural poor—and to inhabit a specific place—the mountains of southern Appalachia. There are, however, other images that come to mind as well—Romeo and Juliet, Corsica, Mexico, and the Scottish highlands. These are images of Europeans—aristocratic Europeans engaged in family conflict that is also political and economic. These are two different, almost diametrically opposed images—the poor mountaineer versus aristocratic Europeans—and the former is unique to American culture in the twentieth century. How and when, then, did this pervasive image of the drunken, hillbilly feudist emerge in American popular culture? The first important point to note is that the feud as a distinct category of violence was not sharply defined during most of the nineteenth century, nor was it used as frequently as it is today. Examination of the *New York Times* and indexes to popular periodical literature before the 1890s show that the term *feud*, although used commonly and imprecisely in many news articles and fictional stories, was rarely perceived as a category important enough to index. In fact, *feud* did not appear as a separate category until after 1910.[9] Before that time, feuds, when included in such indexes at all, were listed under *vendetta* and even then were usually subsumed under a state or a geographical region.[10]

Preference for the term *vendetta* rather than *feud* in the pre-1910 era is in itself revealing. Since the eighteenth century the banditti and feuds of the Mediterranean island of Corsica had been popularized by tourist guidebooks and romantic literature.[11] Apparently journalists assumed that American readers would automatically connect vendettas and feuds with Corsica. In 1869, for example, the *New York Times*, in reporting a feud story, concluded that "the Vendetta, driven from the glens and mountains of far off Corsica, is revived in our own day in the Valley of the Mississippi."[12] A rash of Kentucky feuds in the 1870s prompted the *Times* to label that state the "Corsica of America."[13] In 1889 *New York World* reporter T. C. Crawford wrote the first book-length sensationalized account of an Appalachian feud, titling it *An American Vendetta*.[14] The term *vendetta*, however, has been largely superseded in our century by *feud*, with its corollary assumption of a direct descent from the Scottish highlands. According to Henry Shapiro, this attempt to link Appalachian family feuding and the clan feuds of the Scottish highlands occurred only when writers and scholars became interested in tracing the cultural legacy of feuding to the geographic origins of the Appalachian mountaineers. But despite the present tendency to associate feuding in Appalachia with the bloodfeud of the Scottish highlands, in the nineteenth century, Mediterranean vendettas were the prototypic feuds.[15]

Nineteenth-century journalistic comparisons of American feuds to Corsican vendettas demonstrate that popular conceptions about the class structure and geography of feuds have changed dramatically. Corsican feuds (along with Scottish bloodfeuds and Shakespeare's *Romeo and Juliet*, for that matter) were instigated and fought by elite families, sometimes with the help of outlaws and bandits, but always under the control of an aristocratic class. As Stephen Wilson tells us about Corsica and Keith Brown reveals about Scotland, these images are not without foundation; feuding was widely recognized and institutionalized in these societies.[16] In the nineteenth century the American press utilized that model. Conflicts identified as feuds or vendettas were conflicts between gentlemen of property and standing and not without a significant romantic aura. An early Kentucky (although not Appalachian) feud illustrates the point. In the 1854 feud between the Hill and the Evans families in Kentucky, both leaders were physicians, town officials, and property owners whose dispute had its origins in conflict over the ownership of a slave.[17] This led to a series of conflicts over land, lawsuits, and finally gunfights in the street between their less socially prominent followers—a pattern closely following popular accounts of Corsican vendettas but hardly consonant with twentieth-century images of drunken and usually brutal hillbillies ambushing each other in mountain passes.

A similar pattern of upper-class conflict appears in the Darnell-Watson feud, a conflict important to our understanding of feuds because it was the basis for Mark Twain's feud stories. Both protagonists were socially prominent landholders.[18] Their dispute, too, began with an argument over a slave, expanded to property disputes and court cases, and ended in a shooting. When Mark Twain transformed this feud into the Grangerford-Shepherdson feud, using it both in *Huckleberry Finn* and *Life on the Mississippi*, he preserved the respectable, middle-class status of the participants but exaggerated the long-term nature of the conflict and its violent consequences.[19] These examples suggest that the social status of the contestants was essential in distinguishing between feuding and the backcountry rough and tumble fighting so well described by Elliot Gorn in " 'Gouge and Bite, Pull Hair and Scratch': Fighting in the Southern Backcountry."[20] Before the Hatfields and McCoys seized the imagination of middle-class America, poor backwoodsmen may have been frequently described as brutal and violent, but only upper- and respectable middle-class men and women engaged in vendettas and feuds—the same people, in fact, who were identified with dueling.

Both the Hill-Evans feud and the Darnell-Watson feud challenge another recent stereotype as well, the association of feuding with the southern mountains. Although Doctors Hill and Evans faced off in Kentucky, their homes in Garrard County, south of Lexington, cannot be classified as Appalachia. These foothills were most frequently regarded as part of the genteel Bluegrass, not the rugged mountain backcountry that came to be associated with feuding. Neither was the Darnell-Watson feud located in Appalachia. Far from it, this much-publicized feud occurred along the Mississippi River near the border between Tennessee and Kentucky. Mark Twain learned about it in the 1860s when he was working on a riverboat.[21] Another feud involving William Faulkner's family indicates that feuds and duels were common in the flat delta lands of Mississippi.[22] However, even when a feud actually took place in Appalachia, it was not described in the context of geography. In a story about one of the earliest Appalachian feuds to appear in the *New York Times* (1872), the article was headed "A Virginia Vendetta." The protagonists were two Virginia "gentlemen" with a history of quarreling that ended in one shooting the other. The killer was arrested and tried but acquitted, and the *Times* predicted that the hostility "will shortly blossom into a good, old-fashioned Southern feud."[23] Nothing in the article revealed that the events described occurred in *Appalachian* Virginia. What was emphasized instead was the "southernness" of the feud; until the mid-1880s, feuds were more likely to be southern than Appalachian.

Although it is clear that descriptions of feuds nearly always followed the Corsican model, it is also abundantly obvious that feuding as a type of violence was rarely emphasized or set apart from other forms of violence. In the post–Civil War era the problems of racial conflict and lawlessness plagued communities in the mountain and plantation South equally and were usually conflated. Terms such as *grudge, feud,* and *vendetta* were included in stories about lynching, mobs, Ku Klux Klan activity, riot, and murder. Although many such instances were blamed on personal or family conflict, whiskey, or the carrying of concealed weapons, most were attributed to the racial and political problems of Reconstruction.[24] This ambiguity about feuds and their relationship to other types of violence is most apparent in press reports of the 1870s. As Table 13.2—a list of feuds reported in the *Louisville Courier-Journal* from all sections of Kentucky—shows, the mid- to late 1870s form a clear first phase of such conflicts after which reporting of feuds declines dramatically until its sudden revival in 1885. What is significant about this early group of feuds is their lack of focus on feuding as the central issue. The Kennedy-Sellars feud in Garrard County, the Jett-Little shootings in Breathitt, the Walker-Smoot feud in Owen, and the Henry County conspiracy were all intertwined with political and racial violence. In each case one or the other faction were Republicans who were blamed for supporting black voting. Even in Carter County, where the primary issue was supposed to have been horse thievery, the accused horse thieves, the Underwoods, had been Union loyalists and Republicans.[25] Thus, the high levels of violence seemed unusual, but the causes were not; those were judged to be endemic to the South.

Early signs of change in the perception of feud violence, however, did appear with the rash of feuds occurring between 1874 and 1879. What perplexed the editors of the *Times* was their geography; most occurred in Kentucky. Headlines such as "Kentucky Outlaws," "The Law Defied in Kentucky," "Riotous Mobs in Kentucky," "Kentucky's Bloody Feuds," and "The Recent Lawlessness in Kentucky," abounded, making it clear that the focus had shifted from *southern* violence to *Kentucky* violence.[26] Groping for some explanation of this rash of violent outbreaks, the *Times* theorized that the causes must have something to do with Kentucky's political structure.[27] The Republican *New York Times* blamed the Democratic state government for dividing the state into too many "pauper" counties, which fragmented authority and put uneducated poor men (Democrats) into positions of

Table 13.2. Kentucky Feuds Reported in the *Louisville Courier-Journal,*
1874– 1895

Feud	County	Region	First Report
Walker-Smoot	Owen	Central	1874
Davies-Thompson	Mercer	Central	1874
Kennedy-Sellars	Garrard	Central	1874
Korb-Shantz	Jefferson	Central	1874
Chambers-Withers	Anderson	Central	1874
Little-Strong	Breathitt	Mountains	1874
Armstrong-Omohundro	Mason	Central	1876
Blair-Gillen	Fayette	Central	1876
Harrod-Riley	Franklin	Central	1876
Holbrook-Underwood	Carter	Foothills	1877
Hatfield-McCoy	Pike	Mountains	1882
Barnet-Helton	Menifee	Mountains	1883
Martin-Tolliver	Rowan	Foothills	1884
Maynard-Waller	Lawrence	Mountains	1884
Collins-Lee	Bell	Mountains	1884
Harris-Lankesly	Laurel	Mountains	1884
Burkhart-Gross	Knott	Mountains	1884
French-Eversole	Perry	Mountains	1885
Hoskins-Johnson	Bell	Mountains	1885
Taylor	Union	Western	1885
Fow-Linnerman	Jefferson	Central	1885
Baker-Early	Webster	Western	1885
Howard-Turner	Harlan	Mountains	1885
Banks-Frazier	Letcher	Mountains	1885
Stepstone	Floyd	Mountains	1885
Edward-Rogers	Green	Central	1885
Tuggle	Knox	Mountains	1885
Lisle-Wallace	Green	Central	1885
Jones-Wright	Letcher	Mountains	1885
Dugan-Arnold	Washington	Central	1886
Arnold-Little	Fayette	Central	1886
Unnamed	Boyd	Foothills	1887
Holcrum-Oller	Grayson	Western	1887
Dowell-Edwards	Green	Central	1887
Sawyer-Turner	Bell	Mountains	1887
Hatfield-McCoy	Pike	Mountains	1888
Rose-Fustian	Whitely	Mountains	1888
Sizemore-Garrison	Clay	Mountains	1889
Smith-Slusher	Knox	Mountains	1890
Turner-Parton	Bell	Mountains	1892
Deskins-Patrick	Magoffin	Mountains	1893

leadership.[28] Even when discussing Breathitt County, the only truly Appalachian county, the *Times*, while mentioning its isolated location and rugged terrain, opined that the problems were rooted in "too much attention to politics and not enough to corn."[29]

This political interpretation of Kentucky violence—whether it was in the mountains or not—was actually taken from the reports and editorials appearing in the *Louisville Courier-Journal*, which the *Times* called "the chief interpreter of Kentuckian ideas to the world outside."[30] Despite the difference in political orientation of the two papers—the *Courier-Journal* was Democratic while the *New York Times* was Republican—both supported economic development and modernization called for by proponents of the "New South"; Henry Watterson, the editor of the *Courier-Journal*, was a leading proponent of racial peace and economic modernization, key components of New South ideology.[31] Disturbed by this unusual rash of violent outbreaks in Kentucky, the *Louisville Courier-Journal* devoted much editorial space to an assessment of the problem, concluding that this early group of Kentucky feuds was rooted in racial and political issues. Watterson identified the Jett-Little imbroglio in Breathitt County as a legacy of the Civil War. "The White and Negro Rioters of Breathitt," read a headline relating to that violent eruption.[32] In Carter County the *Courier-Journal* attributed the "war" to a "transient" population that frequently caused "disturbances" originating from the depredations of "horse thieves and family feuds."[33] The same article suggested, however, that the underlying problem was not the local people but, rather, the transients brought in by the railroad that ran through the county. In none of these cases did the *Courier-Journal* accuse mountaineers of being inherently more violent than Kentuckians or southerners, or of addiction to a peculiar form of interfamily violence. Watterson argued that more stringent laws against carrying concealed weapons and increased centralization of state government would encourage the industrial development that would end the violence. Thus, before 1885, the editor of the *Courier-Journal* insisted that economic, social, and political circumstances created the conditions for violence wherever it occurred. He frequently defended this position by references to the Molly Maguire violence in the coalfields of Pennsylvania, chastising northerners for being so self-righteous in their condemnation of Kentucky or southern violence.[34] Significantly, however, nowhere did the *Courier-Journal* single out the mountains as a locus of violence or a particular kind of violence called feuding.

In 1885, however, the reporting of feud violence changed dramatically as the mountains and impoverished mountaineers began to be singled out as the unique locus of family feuding. It was the Rowan County "war" known as the Martin-Tolliver feud that proved to be the watershed. This deadly conflict grew out of the 1877–79 feud known as the Underwood-Holbrook war in Carter County. Rowan is adjacent to Carter and, like it, is close to but not really in Appalachia; both are located in the foothills and along major transportation routes. At first the Rowan County feud was treated the same as the earlier outbreaks in Carter, Breathitt, Garrard, Owen, and Henry Counties. In early reports of the feud, the *Times* stressed the political origins of the "bad blood" in its headline: "Many Lives Sacrificed in a Political Quarrel."[35] Both the regional and the national press were almost obsessed with this feud; it received far more coverage that any previous feud (or any subsequent feud). In the summer of 1885 when attention was focused on Rowan County, however, two murders occurred in the Appalachian counties of Bell and Harlan that prompted the *New York Times* to shift its focus from Kentucky as a whole to a particular section of Kentucky, its mountain region. Not only did the *Times* single out Appalachian Kentucky, but it shifted its analysis of the causes of violent conflict. Abandoning a political explanation, the *Times* argued that the origin of the violence was personal, cultural, or even genetic. For the first time the mountain region of eastern Kentucky was judged guilty of producing individuals who possessed defective character traits; they were, according to the *Times*, "savages."[36]

It is a poor, weak-spirited county in Eastern Kentucky now that has not its feud and its band of thugs protected by the courts. . . . The savages who inhabit this region are not manly enough to fight fairly, face to face. They lie in wait and shoot their enemies in the back. . . . One can hardly believe that any part of the United States is cursed with people so lawless and degraded. The *Courier-Journal* asserts that in these counties "the increase of idiocy is so rapid that in a short time the idiots will outnumber the murderers and then exceed the number of voters. Eastern Kentucky can be redeemed, but it is clear that its redemption must come with the extension of railroads in this benighted region whose natural resources invite development."

In this editorial the *Times* brings out three elements that henceforward will be crucial to the development of present-day images of feuding. The first element is the characterization of Appalachians as more savage, degraded, and lawless than other Americans or even other southerners. The second is the placement of feuding in the mountains; from this point on, the reader will have no difficulty determining where feuds are taking place— the mountain environment will always be described in great detail. The third element is the admonition that economic development (especially railroads) is the only cure, since it will also bring schools, churches, and other "civilizing" forces. The modern myth of mountain feuds was beginning to take shape.

In quoting the *Louisville Courier-Journal* the *Times* claimed the Kentucky paper to be the source of its new insights. Indeed, in another editorial published in the same month, the *Times* explicitly acknowledged its debt to the *Louisville Courier-Journal.* For a long time, says the *Times,* the *Courier-Journal* seemed to defend "promiscuous homicide" as "manly" but now has come to the conclusion that this "prolonged massacre" will "eventually disgrace the Commonwealth."[37] The *Times's* attribution to the *Courier-Journal* of these ideas, however, was mistaken. When the New York paper, in July 1885, quoted the *Courier-Journal* as saying, "The increase of idiocy is so rapid that in a short time the idiots will outnumber the murderers and then exceed the number of voters," it misrepresented the views of Watterson's paper. In a *Courier-Journal* editorial printed on 30 June 1885 from which the *Times* had taken its quote, Watterson had deplored the violence and crime in Bell and Harlan Counties but had continued to blame the structural problems of state versus local government. County officials, argued Watterson, resented new taxes being imposed from the state level and sought to recoup their loses by making financial claims on the state. Criminal prosecutions and support for paupers were both paid for from state rather than local funds, so local governments claimed frequent reimbursement for both. Therefore, argued Watterson, "there is no local restraint on such expenditures, and these two items have swollen to such proportions that they actually threaten to impair the State's credit." The state was being billed, argued Watterson for criminals and idiots that did not exist. Mountaineers may have been shrewd at milking the government, but this is far different from the meaning attached to this editorial by the *New York Times.* It was true, Watterson conceded, that this lack of respect for the state frequently led to violence and lawlessness in these counties; but his remedy was an improved legal system under a new constitution and more centralized power. He had most definitely not, as the *Times* argued, come to the conclusion that mountaineers were all criminals, idiots, and savages, more prone to feuds and violence than people in other parts of Kentucky.

Ironically, although Watterson reacted to the *Times* distortion of his editorial on Kentucky violence with an indignant denial, in less than six months the *Courier-Journal* had, indeed, changed its attitude toward the Appalachian region of the state.[38] During the summer and fall of 1885 the *Courier-Journal* reported feuds and violence in the mountain counties of

Letcher, Harlan, Bell, Perry, Floyd, Breathitt, and Knox, but it also continued to focus on feuding in counties far removed from the mountains such as Webster, Green, Rowan, and Jefferson, showing that Watterson had not yet been convinced that mountain dwellers possessed a peculiar tendency to feuding.[39] The most troublesome feud for Watterson and his *Courier-Journal*, ironically, occurred not in Appalachia but in the foothill county of Rowan. Nevertheless, examination of Watterson's changing editorial response to this feud allows glimpses of the process by which mountain stereotypes were constructed. The feud began with an election-day shooting in the summer of 1884 but escalated dramatically in the summer of 1885 when all the news reports indicated that political party loyalty was at the root of the feud. Republicans and Democrats were killing each other over the control of their county, and although family groups were closely identified with political parties, the *Courier-Journal* was explicit and emphatic regarding its political origins.[40] By October 1885, however, Henry Watterson began to lead a crusade for the *religious* redemption of Rowan. In a series of editorials, Watterson urged people to contribute to the Reverend Guerrant's appeal for funds to build a church in Morehead, the county seat of Rowan; the newspaper even contributed the first $50.[41] Even more peculiar was Watterson's identification of Rowan as a mountain county when he wrote, "The mountain counties where lawlessness prevails must be redeemed. [The Church] must regenerate them . . . from their evil ways."[42] Not only had Watterson moved Rowan to the mountains, but he had recast his claims about the causes of violence. This was a virtual revolution in the *Courier-Journal's* attitude toward Appalachia, the first time that Watterson had suggested there might be something wrong with mountain character or culture. Political or economic reforms were no longer sufficient to "save" the mountaineers. But why this change in attitude?

Perhaps part of the explanation is to be found in the same editorial when Watterson concluded by expressing "regret" that the *Courier-Journal's* "criticism" of the Rowan County war—consisting of over 100 articles that were reprinted widely across the country—had "given the whole state a bad reputation." There was much more to Watterson's change of heart than Kentucky's honor as a civilized state, however. The *Courier-Journal's* editor had come to see the economic development of the mountains as the salvation of Kentucky and, indeed, the entire South. As early as 1871 Henry Watterson had proclaimed his support for the New South with a program he called the "New Departure."[43] As a basis for political reunion and economic development he urged Kentuckians and all southerners to embrace the new constitutional amendments, to accept the political equality of freedmen, and to work on making the South attractive to northern investors. In the 1870s, however, his focus was not primarily on the mountain region. Only an occasional editorial appeared in the *Courier-Journal* advocating development of timber and coal resources in eastern Kentucky.[44] In fact, in the 1870s any kind of coverage of the mountain counties was rare; even riots, feuds, and a severe famine in 1874–75 did not garner much attention from Kentucky's premier newspaper. One gets the impression that the mountains were peripheral to the political, economic, and social issues of the day. They may have been wild, rugged, isolated, and sometimes picturesque but were hardly crucial to the political functioning and economic health of the state. When the mountains did receive attention, it was most often because of battles between moonshiners and the Internal Revenue Service; in these cases the *Courier-Journal* defended the moonshiners. In 1877, for example, Watterson's paper criticized the unnecessary killings of moonshiners by Internal Revenue agents. "It is bad enough, in all conscience," argued Watterson, "to carry them . . . hundreds of miles from their homes and friends to be tried, but it is far worse to provoke them into a conflict and shoot them down."[45] In this scenario, the mountaineers were "provoked" to conflict; they were not its cause. Thus, in the 1870s Watterson's view and that of most Americans was a kind of amused sympathy with mountaineers that saw them as more innocent and pastoral than dangerous and violent.

By the mid-1880s, however, the situation had changed. The repeated calls for industrial development in the New South had not resulted in significant economic progress. The depression of the mid-1870s had left the whole country reeling and the South stagnated; New South proponents saw their hopes and expectations dashed. When the economy began to pick up again in the early 1880s, local boosters, the *Courier-Journal,* and many other newspapers and government officials of states with coal-rich mountain regions began promoting development of the mountains as an antidote to their economic ills.[46] In the mid-1880s those appeals escalated.[47] In one typical long editorial in 1884, Watterson, after describing the wealth of timber, iron, and coal in the mountains, argued, "It is the most inviting field for the speculator, the investor, the manufacturer, the railroad builder, that the whole country offers."[48] The *Courier-Journal* portrayed the resources of the mountain region as the economic salvation of the South. More than simply modernizing the mountain region, however, economic development would bring prosperity to the whole state. For example, the *Courier-Journal* endorsed a speech given by a Kentucky politician who hoped to persuade the legislature to appropriate money for advertising the riches of eastern Kentucky. Once we attract northern railroad investors, he argued, and get access to the resources of eastern Kentucky, the mountain counties will no longer be a disgrace to the state. More importantly, all Kentuckians would benefit.[49] Gleefully the *Courier-Journal* reported the visits of investors to many mountain counties, urging local citizens to cooperate by offering public financial support of railroad, coal, and timber companies.

In the light of this concentrated development effort, the Rowan County war presented a problem for Henry Watterson and the *Courier-Journal.* Rowan County troubles were clearly rooted in political conflict and took place in a town that already had a railroad and significant commercial development. In fact, the violence in Rowan had grown out of an earlier conflict in neighboring Carter County. Both these counties were on rail lines, and in fact Watterson had earlier attributed the violent outbreaks not to local people but to the "transients" brought in by economic development. Given another framework, one might just as easily have concluded that economic development had caused the violence. In fact, it is easy to find articles in many local papers as well as the *Courier-Journal* that link railroad and mining towns with higher levels of violence than rural areas.[50] Indeed, Watterson himself had repeatedly cited the violence in the coalfields of Pennsylvania in his defense of rural Kentuckians. But in the mid-1880s this was not the preferred frame of mind for Henry Watterson or other advocates of the New South. They were genuinely convinced that economic development must inevitably bring peace, prosperity, and profits. Seeming to forget that he had earlier characterized the county seat of Rowan as "a thriving little town on the C&O Railroad" in which a "political" feud had driven almost everyone to take sides, Watterson now, in his own mental geography, associated Rowan with the mountains.[51] What it meant to be "in the mountains" after 1885 was to be cast as primitive, even "savage" in character, culture, and social institutions. Thus, the economic development of the mountains was no longer simply an important contribution to the economic health of the region or the state; it also could be justified as imperative to the "redemption" of the primitives who inhabited the region. Linking economic modernization with religion became an oft-repeated clarion cry in the urban press. "Redemption," argued the *New York Times,* would only come with the "extension of railroads." In an 1887 editorial, "Railroads as Civilizers," the *Times* proclaimed that "the new [rail]roads will serve as missionaries to transform gradually the character of the secluded villages, and put an end to the feuds and vendettas in which the energies of an isolated people have been expended."[52] This time Henry Watterson did not object. Although he continued to defend Kentuckians and southerners against charges of excessive violence rooted in inheritance or culture, he no longer did so for Appalachians. *They*, it seems, had been sacrificed to the politics of economic modernization.

If the political economy of the New South led to the sacrifice of mountain whites to the feuding stereotype, there was another process at work involving racial relations and the political reconciliation between North and South. In the northern press, southern violence was an endemic problem. Watterson himself had fed that stereotype by lamenting, again and again, in editorial after editorial, the practice of carrying concealed weapons, the ineffectiveness of the judicial system, and the weakness of the state government in enforcing the law. Lynching, riots, and homicide were all clearly identified as southern activities.[53] The *Times* was quite direct in many of its editorials accusing the South of barbarity and "unregulated passions" that characterized an uncivilized population.[54] When, in the mid-1880s, the focus of news reporting on violence was shifted from the South to the mountains, northerners could be distracted from the daily racial and political violence that continued to increase in the last two decades of the century. In the 1880s, in a climate of reunion—as Nina Silber puts it, the "romance" of reunion—northerners were encouraged to ignore, if not condone, the racial violence that accompanied political "redemption."[55] While Shapiro and Silber have argued that the mountaineers became a more acceptable focus of missionary efforts than freedmen had been, it is also true that mountain whites earned the distinctly unromantic reputation of being more irrationally violent that other southerners, or at least more attention was focused on them than other southerners. In the light of reunion politics, this must have seemed a plausible recasting of southern violence. It also seemed to work; for while southern whites in the black belt engaged in an orgy of lynching in the 1890s, it was mountain feuding that elicited sensationalistic reporting.[56] For Henry Watterson and his readers in Bluegrass Kentucky, it was undoubtedly a relief to focus on the suppression of violence in mountaineer culture that industrialization would soon bring about rather than confront the uncomfortable reality of increasing racial violence in their own backyard. For all these reasons, then, it was with alacrity that Henry Watterson adopted the *Times*'s image of the mountaineers' innate savagery.[57]

Once the "real" problem had been identified, mountain feuds seemed to proliferate in a startling manner. As both Tables 13.1 and 13.2 show, the ten-year period between 1885 and 1895 was the classic era of Appalachian feuds, with ten reported in the *New York Times*. Despite the fact that most were directly related to political party conflict and featured participants who were frequently wealthy merchants and prominent community leaders, the press described them as irrational and barbaric. Typical was a *Times* headline for a story about the Howard-Turner feud in Harlan County: "All the Result of A Drunken Quarrel."[58] This title also indicates that not only had feuding become region specific, it was now also class specific, originating in drunken fights with no real cause. Although most of these feuds took place in eastern Kentucky, journalists had stopped asking, Why Kentucky? and had begun to ask, Why the mountains? The answers were varied—from women to whiskey to unregulated passions to a cultural addiction to hatred and violence. But all pointed to something mysterious, incomprehensible, and intractable about mountain character and culture. In 1888 and 1889 the Hatfield-McCoy feud in southern West Virginia and northeastern Kentucky prompted the publication of T. C. Crawford's *An American Vendetta: A Story of Barbarism in the United States*. In this book, Appalachians were no longer simply violent southerners; they were specifically identified with an isolated mountain "culture" of feuding, inhabiting a place Crawford called "Murderland."[59] Mountaineers, wherever they lived, were rapidly being removed from the real world of political and economic conflict and located in a mythological universe of instinctual passions and legendary hatreds.

Still, this new explanation was not accepted as received truth by most Americans until after 1900. The key to its eventual entrenchment is to be found in its wholesale and unquestioning adoption by writers of popular fiction. Surprisingly, this happened rather suddenly. Of approximately 350 articles and fictional stories written before 1900 about southern mountaineers, only a tiny fraction mentioned feuding.[60] Local-color writers had tramped Appalachia avidly searching for the different, the quaint, and the frightening, but had failed to notice any feuding.[61] When they encountered moonshining, it was more often than not treated sympathetically, with the moonshiner portrayed as a principled resistor of unfair federal regulations.[62] Even John Fox, Jr., who later became the most influential purveyor of the brutal feudist image, did not at first seem to be aware of this peculiarity of the mountains. His first mountain story, "A Mountain Europa," published in *Century* magazine in 1892, was a formulaic concoction concerning a simple but beautiful mountain girl and an educated engineer struggling with his own inner conflict between the intuitive and the rational. However, two years later, Fox "discovered" feuding and published "A Cumberland Vendetta."[63]

In this story John Fox brought together all the elements that would make up popular myths about Appalachian feuds. Putting together aspects of newspaper stories about the Hatfield-McCoy feud, French-Eversole in

Perry, and Howard-Turner in Harlan, Fox forged the feud image. In the first paragraph of his tale Fox had "primitive" mountaineers hiding out in a cave, toting "Winchesters" and speaking an ignorant dialect. Even Fox's hero, Rome Stetson, shared in the degradation of mountaineers, as shown when "an evil shadow" came over his face. Entirely irrational, Fox's mountaineers had no idea of the origins of their hatred. "When the feud began no one knew," wrote Fox, "Even the original cause was forgotten." Although the feuding families had been on opposite sides in the Civil War, Fox contended that the war was not the cause; it had only armed them and "brought back an ancestral contempt for human life." Rome Stetson had decent impulses and several times sought escape from revenge and killing, but driven by his family (especially his bloodthirsty old mother) and his own ancient vengeful instincts, he carried out the final battles. Here in dramatic form Fox fleshed out the outline provided earlier by the newspapers for mountain feuding. Gone were the earlier journalistic preoccupations with race and political conflict, with election-day animosities and the poverty of county government. Mountaineer character and culture were at fault, and they could only be redeemed by economic modernization. Fox ended his story with the coming of the railroad.[64]

Popular response to this story was so enthusiastic that Fox began to write primarily about feuding, especially emphasizing the stark contrasts between the "civilized" Bluegrass and the "primitive" mountain regions of Kentucky. It was a formula that made his fortune, especially with two books published after 1900, *The Trail of the Lonesome Pine* (1908) and *The Little Shepherd of Kingdom Come* (1903).[65]

Fox, more than anyone else, shaped middle-class perceptions about southern Appalachians.[66] In 1898 academic sociologist George E. Vincent traveled through Appalachia and wrote an article about mountain society and customs for the *Journal of American Sociology*. It is a measure of Fox's influence that Vincent, finding little evidence of feuding, turned to Fox for information and cited him extensively as an authority on the subject.[67] Fox's *A Cumberland Vendetta*, wrote the sociologist, "seems to be typical of mountain wars."[68] From the 1890s onward, in a fascinating dialectic, journalists and scholars followed suit, echoing John Fox's feud construction until the hillbilly feudist became a stock character in popular culture and literature.

But what of the historical reality of feuding? Despite the distortions in the press and literature, *something*, one intuitively believes, must have been going on. Naturally one wants to ask, as James Klotter has done, why such a rash of family feuds broke out in Appalachia at this particular time.[69] In an attempt to answer that question, I undertook an in-depth study of the most famous feud, the one between the Hatfields and the McCoys.[70] My research demonstrated that the violence associated with this feud was related more to the economic and political modernization of the region than to family animosities of ancient or unknown cause. The two sides were contesting who would control the process of capitalist development, the local elite or distant corporations.[71] The McCoys were allied with outside capitalists, while the Hatfields attempted to preserve their own local control over railroad and timber lands. Because family played such an important role in the mountains, as it does in most "traditional" societies, family relationships were highly visible in the conflict. Yet these family animosities did not turn violent until the political and military power of the state, backing capitalist development, threatened the functioning of the local justice system. Neither did the mountaineers themselves use the term *feud* to describe their troubles or wars. That construction of events was fastened on them by the press, led by the *Courier-Journal*, which insisted that the irrational family loyalty and a propensity to extralegal violence were at the root of the violence.[72] In fact, the Hatfield-McCoy feud proved extremely useful to the *Courier-Journal* and other Kentucky newspapers in their attempt to demonstrate that feuds were not just Kentucky's problem, but that they cropped up everywhere in the southern Appalachians. The Kentucky press was delighted to portray the Hatfields of West Virginia as the villains, attacking the innocent McCoys of Kentucky.

Examination of local records and newspaper stories, however, reveals a refutation of the claim of the *Courier-Journal*; most conflicts reported as feuds did take place in Kentucky. More importantly, Appalachian conflicts were firmly rooted in political and economic contests over the course of economic development. The example of Breathitt County is especially illustrative, for it has one of the longest histories of feud violence of any county. Violence broke out there in 1874, 1878, 1885, and 1902. In each case the violence was much more overtly political than the Hatfield-McCoy feud had been. Murders and assaults were invariably connected with elections, a judge was killed, and mobs besieged the courthouse. Reporting of these outbreaks in the *Courier-Journal* confirms the pattern already described of changing attitudes toward Appalachian Kentucky. The earliest instance of violence, in the fall of 1874, involved racial tensions and seemed to parallel the "kukluxing" so common everywhere in the postbellum South.[73] In 1878, when the county judge was shot and killed and troops, once again, were sent in, the *Courier-Journal* argued that the roots of the conflict were political, Republicans versus Democrats, and primarily based on old Civil War loyalties. In 1884–88 violence broke out again in connection with the French-

Eversole feud in neighboring Perry County, but this time family feuds and ancient grudges were blamed. Missing in the newspaper reports were the severe economic threats faced by Breathitt County farmers.

In the 1870s Breathitt County faced the same postwar crisis caused by a population explosion and a declining supply of farmland as other mountain counties. By 1874, just before the first violence erupted, cash-poor farmers were confronted with rising taxes due to the state's efforts to "equalize" taxation.[74] In addition, the state's legislature authorized the county to levy taxes to help support the building of a railroad, a measure that would aid Louisville railroad entrepreneurs but was opposed by local residents. The Breathitt County court judges struggled with these requirements, coming up with a variety of methods to avoid what they saw as "unfair" taxation. For example, in 1874 the county court disbursed $4,027.20 to forty-nine individuals, ostensibly for teaching school; this was obviously a method of refunding such unjustified taxation. More direct methods were also tried; the judges simply "exonerated" numerous residents from paying taxes at all, arguing that they had been "improperly charged under the equalization law." The court also brought a lawsuit against wealthy absentee landholders who had never paid their assessments to the county; unfortunately, in what could only have seemed a kind of conspiracy against them, the county lost the case in a higher court.[75] Adding to these frustrating economic wrangles with the state was the severe famine/drought in the winter and spring of 1875.[76] Crops failed and farmers lacked the cash to purchase food for their families; in the light of these hardships, increased taxation mandated from Frankfort must have seemed even more onerous.

The spark for the 1878 outbreak of violence came in the fall of the previous year when J. W. Burnett, a lawyer and newcomer to Breathitt County, ran for and won—by a very small margin—the position of president of the county court. He was supported by the Union-Republican faction in the county, reputed to be vicious bushwhackers during and since the Civil War. More threatening, however, was Burnett's support for public funding for railroads and equalization of the tax laws. Still there was no overt opposition until a year after Burnett became the county judge, when it came time to elect the county school commissioner—an important post since the school commissioner controlled the disbursement of funds to teachers as a way to obtain tax "refunds." The election was a tie that Burnett broke by voting; he then refused to consider any requests for "reconsideration." The magistrates proceeded to remove Burnett temporarily while they conducted another election for school commissioner. After this was successfully done, Burnett was allowed to return to his position as head of the county court.[77]

Although these intricate legal maneuverings were peacefully conducted, a highly charged atmosphere of bitterness and resentment simmered just beneath the surface. A few days later Judge Burnett was shot and killed on the street outside the courthouse, and for the second time in four years the governor sent troops to keep the peace in Breathitt.[78]

This struggle was far more than local animosities or ancient hatreds. Burnett was new to the county and clearly in collaboration with outside interests, such as the Kentucky Union Railroad, which as the *Courier-Journal* reported, owned almost half the land in Breathitt County.[79] Repeated attempts by community residents to oppose such policies created a bitter, emotionally charged atmosphere and de facto abandonment of county governance. In such a context the conflict appears remarkably similar to that of the later Hatfield-McCoy feud in which outsiders and their collaborators attempted to take control of the local economy, county government, and judicial system.

The pattern of conflict evinced in Breathitt County in the 1870s proved to be a precursor of the violence that would emerge in many of its neighboring mountain counties in the mid-1880s. Although Breathitt did not have its own "feud" in the 1880s, the *Courier-Journal* linked Breathitt violence to feuds in Bell, Harlan, and especially Perry Counties. Close examination of all these classic Appalachian feuds—French-Eversole in Perry County, Howard-Turner in Harlan County, Turner-Parton-Sawyer in Bell County, and Martin-Tolliver in Rowan County—reveal similar economic patterns. Local merchants and lawyers sought to boost economic development by bringing railroads and "modern" government and taxation systems to their regions and were bitterly opposed by rural farmers. This time, however, the stakes were higher because of geological survey reports that confirmed the presence of extensive high-quality coal deposits and the readiness of railroad companies to begin surveying and building. With agricultural opportunities declining rapidly and another severe famine in 1884, mountain farmers and local businessmen were more prepared than ever to fight—outsiders and each other, if necessary—for their share of the profits of economic development. Ironically the modernizers resorted to violence as frequently as their opponents. In Perry County, "Bad Tom" Smith was sponsored by the French faction in the French-Eversole conflict, to terrorize its opponents. The Frenches were merchants and representatives of an outside timber company trying to buy up county lands. In this case, Smith, one of the worst desperadoes identified with mountain feuds, was the agent of economic modernization.[80] These struggles were also similar to the conflict in rural Missouri described by David Thelen. Conceptualized by Thelen as a contest for "ownership of the law," this struggle between traditions of local autonomy and state-level attempts to force economic development fits, far better than a family feud model, the political and economic nature of Appalachian conflict.[81]

My research reveals that there was indeed an outbreak of unusual violence in Appalachia in the mid-1880s. However, it was not caused by a Civil War legacy, ancient hatreds, or family vengeance but, rather, by the advent of economic and political modernization, whether fostered by local elites or by outsiders. But it should be clear that I am not attempting to argue about whether Appalachian culture is or was more violent than the rest of the country; there is as yet no quantitative evidence to ascertain this.[82] I am arguing that whatever violence existed in that period did not emerge from an ancient culture of feuding; it was not genetic, cultural, or irrational but, rather, a politically motivated struggle over economic development. As social and economic historians turn their skills to investigating the mountain preindustrial past, the reasons for a high level of frustration, anxiety, and violence, especially on the part of young men, becomes apparent. If there were local elites accumulating capital and attempting to bring about economic development, as Mary Beth Pudup has shown, there was also, as Paul Salstrom tells us in a recent book, a significant decline in the agricultural production and availability of land for the young men of the region.[83] In such a context it is not surprising to find an increase in "dangerous" young men and "desperadoes" willing to prove their manhood with whiskey and guns. When these local social and economic tensions were juxtaposed on the efforts of state officials and outside capitalists to engross huge tracts of land and create a system of wage labor, some kind of violence became almost inevitable.[84]

Still, the *Courier-Journal*, or even John Fox, Jr., could not have accomplished this transformation of the feud image single-handedly. The middle-class readers of the *New York Times* were ready to accept, with both fascination and horror, the brutality, tragedy, and irrationality of passionate family loyalty. It was a time when middle-class families, feeling threatened by family breakdown, were obsessed with the dark side of family life. Reading about feuds allowed them both to express and to distance themselves from the potential for family violence. Only within this cultural environment could John Fox, Jr., and other writers of fiction take advantage of the new feud stereotype offered by Watterson's *Courier-Journal*. Fox was particularly suited to embellish the stereotype. He came from a well-to-do Bluegrass family, attended Harvard, and then went into the family business, which involved both coal mining and real estate development in the Appalachian region of Virginia.[85] In Big Stone Gap, Virginia, Fox joined a vigilante group to enforce law and order in the mountains, and many of his later feud tales were based on these experiences. He did not turn to the literary exploitation of the mountains, however, until after the family business failed.[86] It hardly seems surprising that when Fox did begin to write, he found it easy to perceive the local mountaineers who had resisted his law-and-order vigilante group as irrationally brutal feudists.[87]

What made Fox interesting as well as the most prolific popularizer of mountain feuds, however, was his obvious empathy with the mountaineers as they confronted the wrenching reality of industrialization.[88] He himself as well as many middle-class Americans agonized over family relationships and the problems of social and cultural identity created by corporate capitalism. He tailored these issues so they resonated remarkably well with the middle-class readers of his stories and books. Anguishing over the inner turmoil caused by conflict between the impersonal competitiveness of industrial capitalism and older, communal, cooperative values, Fox explored common middle-class social and psychological dilemmas by projecting them onto the mountaineers.

The life experiences of Fox himself as he struggled to earn a living and gain status in the literary world shaped his portrayal of mountain life and conflict. After John Fox graduated from Harvard, he went to New York with the goal of becoming a newspaper reporter and a novelist. Fox's efforts, however, to secure a salaried position with the *New York Times* came to naught, and the young writer was embarrassed by having to rely on his family for an income. Acute anxiety concerning his lack of standing in upper-class New York society and his desperation to acquire the financial underpinning to enter that society pervade his personal letters in the 1880s. Finally, Fox was forced to return to Kentucky, eventually joining in the family business enterprises first in East Tennessee, then in Big Stone Gap. When the depression of the early 1890s destroyed the business, Fox turned once again to writing, exploring his own internal struggles in the context of mountain culture.

His *The Trail of the Lonesome Pine*, perhaps his most famous novel, illustrates his method. This novel reveals much about Fox. The hero is a young engineer, John Hale, who comes to the mountains of southwestern Virginia to work in the family business just as John Fox had done. The boomtown in which he locates his story is Big Stone Gap, in Wise County. At the beginning of the novel, Hale meets a young girl—more a child, really—June Tolliver, who belongs to a large mountaineer family. The members of the family are ignorant, innocent, tough, brutal, and gentle all at the same time. The primary story, that of the relationship between Hale and young June, winds in an out of a long, complicated tale of conflict over land prices and titles and an ancient feud between the Tollivers and another family. Hale is charmed by the innocent, uncorrupted beauty of June and takes on the task of educating and "civilizing" her, seemingly unaware of the sexual tension that is obviously between them despite her tender age. When June nears mature young womanhood, Hale sends her to the city to his sisters so that she can learn the social graces that will make her worthy of him. She is an apt pupil who learns quickly, and when she returns to the mountains, dressed like a lady and clearly enjoying her newfound sophistication, Hale is appalled. He is now confronted with a serious dilemma. He wants June's mountain innocence back, for it is what had attracted him all along, but sweet innocence alone is fraught with danger because it is inevitably accompanied by the out-of-control passions exhibited by her father and brothers in their feuds. Fortunately June solves the dilemma for him by realizing that even with her newly acquired sophistication she not only must, but still desires to, preserve the intuitive innocence that comes from her mountain home and family. She and Hale decide to live in the city, where he will work, but return to the mountain cabin every summer where they can, together, return to "nature," refreshing purer values of a simpler time. Hale has what he needs to succeed in a competitive world as June rejects career and sophisticated "surface things" to serve her "lord" and wear homespun clothes.[89] John Hale, like John Fox, Jr., and many other middle-class men, was able to preserve values of love, cooperation, and compassion—clearly liabilities in the world of business—by investing them in wife, hearth, and summer vacations.

As one literary historian has suggested, Fox's novels belong more to a genre of "home and hearth" than to local color.[90] Although he sets his story in the mountains and constructs his plots around mountaineers and their feuds, Fox is really pursuing issues of personal identity, family relationships, and the role of women and the home in middle-class life. As readers identified with his struggles, however, they were absorbing images of Appalachians that would endure for generations.

Another even more ironic example of this pattern of Appalachian stereotypes being defined by the agents of economic modernization is to be found in the widely circulated feud tales of Harold Wilson Coates. In the 1920s Coates wrote a series of short, soft-cover pamphlets titled *Stories of Kentucky Feuds* that were bought, published, and circulated, without cost, by an Appalachian-based coal company.[91] These proved immensely popular and were reprinted several times, finally being brought together into one book in 1942. Ironically, of the twelve feuds discussed in the book, only seven, or a little more than half, actually take place in the Appalachian region of Kentucky. Nevertheless, this book has become one of the standard references used by authors and journalists to prove that feuds, if not unique to Appalachia, were characteristic of that region. It seems understandable that coal company executives and managers would want to see Appalachian violence not as a reaction created by their own business ventures but, rather, as irrationality on the part of the uneducated and ignorant. It is also understandable that most people (like John Fox, Jr.) actually believed the images they portrayed. It is also not difficult to comprehend why middle-class readers of these tales would be so fascinated with the romance as well as the frightening aspects of family passions and loyalties. What is surprising is that historians have done so little to deconstruct these images by investigating the actual conflicts and the communities from which they emerged. Such an endeavor might reveal patterns of historical change regarding the integration of nonindustrialized communities into the world capitalist order—a process that is more active than ever today. Like Edward Said's analysis of "orientalism" and the new field of "subaltern studies," Appalachian history can reveal something of the complex dialectic that operates between subordinate and dominant societies to create cultural hierarchies and stereotypes.[92] In Appalachia that process has for 100 years obscured the struggle for control of Appalachia's economic riches by trivializing and mythologizing its people's struggle to accommodate, adapt, or resist. The pejorative term *feud* was used by the dominant culture as a politically useful category to explain the violence of mountain dwellers as well as excuse the violence incurred in their subjection. Uncovering a more accurate version of such conflicts and the political uses of their distortion is one way to prevent the construction of such stereotypes in the future.

Notes

1. The process by which southern Appalachia came to be defined by Americans as different is brilliantly explored by Henry Shapiro in *Appalachia on Our Mind: The Southern Mountains and Mountaineers in the American Consciousness, 1870–1920* (Chapel Hill: University of North Carolina Press, 1978). See also Alan Batteau, *The Invention of Appalachia* (Phoenix: University of Arizona Press, 1993).

2. For an excellent overview of Kentucky feuds with detailed references to newspaper stories on each, see James Klotter, "Feuds in Appalachia: An Overview," *Filson Club History Quarterly* 56 (July 1982): 290–317. For a recent popular account of the famous Kentucky feuds, see John Ed Pearce, *Days of Darkness: The Feuds of Eastern Kentucky* (Lexington: University Press of Kentucky, 1994).

3. David Hackett Fischer, *Albion's Seed: Four British Folkways in America* (New York: Oxford University Press, 1989), pp. 605–782.

4. Examples include Jesse Byock, *Feud in the Icelandic Saga* (Berkeley: University of California Press, 1982); William Miller, *Bloodtaking and Peacemaking in Saga Ireland* (Chicago: University of Chicago Press, 1990); Christopher Boehm, *Blood Revenge: The Enactment and Management of Conflict in Montenegro and Other Tribal Societies* (Lawrence: University Press of Kansas, 1984); Stephen Wilson, *Feuding, Conflict, and Banditry in Nineteenth-Century Corsica* (New York: Cambridge University Press, 1988); James B. Greenberg, *Blood Ties: Life and Violence in Rural Mexico* (Tucson: University of Arizona Press, 1989); Philip Adams Dennis, *Inter-village Conflict in Oaxaca* (New Brunswick: Rutgers University Press, 1987): Keith Brown, *Bloodfeud in Scotland, 1573–1625: Violence, Justice, and Politics in an Early Modern Society* (Atlantic Highlands, N.J.: Humanities Press, 1986); Jacob Black-Michaud, *Cohesive Force: Feud in the Mediterranean and the Middle East* (Oxford: Blackwell, 1975).

5. Altina L. Waller, *Feud: Hatfields, McCoys, and Social Change in Appalachia, 1860–1900* (Chapel Hill: University of North Carolina Press, 1988).

6. Phillip Shaw Paludan makes this point in *Victims: A True Story of the Civil War* (Knoxville: University of Tennessee Press, 1981), which explores violence in Shelton Laurel, North Carolina.

7. See Harold Wilson Coates, *Stories of Kentucky Feuds* (Cincinnati, Ohio: Holmes Darst Coal Corp., 1923); Charles G. Mutzenburgh, *Kentucky's Famous Feuds and Tragedies* (Hyden, Ky.: Hyden, 1899); L. F. Johnson, *Famous Kentucky Tragedies and Trials* (Cleveland: Baldwin Law Book Co., 1916); John F. Day, *Bloody Ground* (Garden City, N.Y.: Doubleday, 1941); Pearce, *Days of Darkness*.

8. Exceptions, of course, are Klotter, "Feuds in Appalachia," and Waller, *Feud*.

9. Indexes consulted include *New York Times*, *Poole's*, and the *Reader's Guide to Periodical Literature*.

10. In the *New York Times*, for example, until well after 1900 there is no way to locate feuds except by looking under the particular state for instances of homicide, riot, lynching, or activity by the Ku Klux Klan. One then has to read the stories to determine whether the term *feud* or *vendetta* is actually used and then, more often than not, check the town or county on a map to find out whether the incident took place in the mountains.

11. Wilson, *Feuding, Conflict, and Banditry*, p. 14; Dorothy Carrington, *Corsica: Portrait of a Granite Island* (New York: John Day, 1971); Moray McLaren, *Corsica Boswell: Paoli, Johnson, and Freedom* (London: Seeker and Warburg, 1966), pp. 16, 21.

12. "The Awful Tragedy at Island No. 10—Three Men Shot Dead," *New York Times*, 24 March 1869, reprinting the St. Louis *Missouri Republican*, 19 March 1869. Both quoted in Edgar Marquess Branch and Robert Hirst, *The Grangerford-Shepherdson Feud by Mark Twain* (Berkeley: Friends of the Bancroft Library, University of California, 1985), p. 66.

13. *New York Times*, 26 December 1878. Quoted in Klotter, "Feuds in Appalachia," p. 294.

14. T. C. Crawford, *An American Vendetta: A Story of Barbarism in the United States* (New York: Bedford Clarke, 1889); "A Kentucky Vendetta," *New York Times*, 12 June 1899.

15. Shapiro, *Appalachia on Our Mind*, pp. 105–7. According to Shapiro, only when feuding became associated with Appalachia did writers and scholars begin to suggest cultural origins for feud violence. For a recent example of an analysis based on this Scotch-Irish cultural legacy, see Fischer, *Albion's Seed*, p. 623. An occasional exception to this can be found in the press. For example, in an editorial about the Walker-Smoot feud in Owen County, Ky., the *Louisville Courier-Journal* (August 1874) compared the conflict to "the clans of the Scottish Highlanders." Ironically, Owen County is in central Kentucky, not Appalachia, and the *Courier-Journal* was not trying to make a link between two mountain cultures.

16. Brown, *Bloodfeud in Scotland*; Wilson, *Feuding, Conflict, and Banditry*.

17. J. J. Thompson, *A Kentucky Tragedy: A History of the Feud between the Hill and Evans Parties of Garrard County, Kentucky* (Cincinnati, Ohio: James, 1854), pp. ix–xi.

18. Branch and Hirst, *Grangerford-Shepherdson Feud*.

19. Ibid., pp. 15–25, 29–32.

20. Elliot Gorn, " 'Gouge and Bite, Pull Hair and Scratch': Fighting in the Southern Backcountry," *American Historical Review* 90 (1985): 18–43.

21. Branch and Hirst, *Grangerford-Shepherdson Feud*, pp. 42–50.

22. Bertram Wyatt-Brown, *Southern Honor: Ethics and Behavior in the Old South* (New York: Oxford University Press, 1982), pp. 351–53.

23. "A Virginia Vendetta," *New York Times*, 14 October 1872. This pattern is also true of the Rogers-Johnstone feud in Elizabethtown, Carter County, Tenn., in 1867. See "A Feud of 20 Years Ended," *New York Times*, 19 January 1867. The Underwood-Stamper feud in Carter County, Ky., was blamed on Civil War animosities and horse theft. Although Carter County is not really in Appalachia, this feud was later identified as an Appalachian feud, and most writers have considered it so ever since. See articles in the *New York Times*, 9, 10, 12, 16, 18 July 1877, 13 September 1879; *Louisville Courier-Journal*, 8, 13, 18 July 1877.

24. See, for example, stories of such violence in the nonmountain counties of Kentucky in the *Louisville Courier-Journal*: Mercer County, 4, 5 January 1874; Owen County, 2 February 1874; Anderson County, 2, 3, 9 July 1874; Garrard County, 23, 24, 27 August, 5 September 1874.

25. "Kentucky Horse Thieves," *New York Times*, 16 July 1877.

26. *New York Times*, 10, 18 July 1877; 30 November, 30 December 1878.

27. "Lawlessness in Kentucky," *New York Times*, 16 December 1874.

28. "Kentucky Politics," *New York Times*, 26 September 1874.

29. Ibid. For references to the Strong-Little feud in Breathitt County in 1874, see *Louisville Courier-Journal*, 19, 14, 28, 29 September, 6, 17 October 1874.

30. "The Vendetta in Kentucky," *New York Times*, 9 July 1885.

31. Joseph Frazier Wall, *Henry Watterson: Unreconstructed Rebel* (New York: Oxford University Press, 1956), pp. 96–98.

32. "The White and Negro Rioters of Breathitt," *Louisville Courier-Journal*, 28 September 1874.

33. *Louisville Courier-Journal*, 11 July 1877.

34. "Crime on the Rampage," *Louisville Courier-Journal*, 3 July 1877; "The 'Law Abiding North,' " *Louisville Courier-Journal*, 16 July 1877.

35. "The Rowan County War," *New York Times*, 6 July 1885; "Feudalism in Kentucky—Many Lives Sacrificed in a Political Quarrel," *New York Times*, 8 July 1885.

36. *New York Times*, 26 July 1885.

37. "The Vendetta in Kentucky," *New York Times*, 9 July 1885.

38. *Louisville Courier-Journal*, 10 July 1885.

39. *Louisville Courier-Journal*: Letcher County, 3 December 1884, 26 February, 1, 26 June, 10, 15, 25, 27, 29, 30 July, 2, 3 August, 23 September 1885; Harlan County, 22 February, 15 March, 15 July 1885; Bell County, 19 December 1884, 9 January, 13, 15, 16, 19, 28, 30 May, 1 June, 16, 17, 18 July 1885; Knox County, 21 March, 26 July 1885; Green County, 21 July, 28 July, 3 August 1885; Rowan County, 28 November, 3, 11, 13, 14 December 1884, 8, 30 March, 2, 3, 4, 5, 6, 7, 12, 15 April, 23 May, 29, 30 June, 11, 12, 15, 16, 17, 20, 21, 22, 23, 27, 29, 30 July, 5, 6, 7, 8, 12, 13, 18, 22, 25 August 1885.

40. Ibid., 5 August, 13 December 1884, 30 March 1885.

41. "Bibles for Rowan," *Louisville Courier-Journal*, 22, 23 October 1885.

42. "Dr. Guerrant's Appeal," *Louisville Courier-Journal*, 23 October 1885.

43. Wall, *Henry Watterson*, pp. 96–97.

44. Between 1874 and 1880 only about six stories or editorials in the *Louisville Courier-Journal* dealt with development of mountain resources. See "Our Mountain Counties," 29 February 1874; "The Geological Survey," 4 January 1876; "State and City," 12 February 1876; "Our Mountain Country," 4 September 1876; "Internal Improvements," 8 October 1877; "The Kentucky River," 9 December 1878.

45. "Muskets and Moonshine," *Louisville Courier-Journal*, 3 July 1877. See other similar stories on 13 and 22 October 1877.

46. For an excellent overview of this process, see Ronald D. Eller, *Miners, Millhands, and Mountaineers: Industrialization of the Appalachian South, 1880–1930* (Knoxville: University of Tennessee Press, 1982).

47. Examples from the *Louisville Courier-Journal* include "A Few Words for Kentucky," 10 January 1884; "Through Eastern Kentucky," 11 January 1884; "Kentucky River," 18 January 1884; "From Frankfort," 19 March 1884; "Kentucky's Resources," 8 December 1884; "A Strange Region," 10 December 1884; "Out Prospecting," 24 December 1885; "Buried Breathitt," 25 December 1884; "Eastern Kentucky," 2 February 1885; "East Tennessee," 7 May 1885; "The Kentucky Union [Railroad]," 15 June 1885; editorial, 25 September 1885.

48. "Through Eastern Kentucky," *Louisville Courier-Journal*, 11 January 1884.

49. "A Strong Speech," *Louisville Courier-Journal*, 30 April 1884.

50. Waller, *Feud*, p. 201.

51. "On War's Brink," *Louisville Courier-Journal*, 30 March 1885.

52. *New York Times*, 26 July 1885; "Railroads as Civilizers," *New York Times*, 20 September 1887.

53. *Louisville Courier-Journal*, 19 June 1884, 30 May 1885.

54. *New York Times*, 8 July, 26 October 1880, 2 February, 16 August 1883, 20 May 1884.

55. Nina Silber, *The Romance of Reunion: Northerners and the South, 1865–1900* (Chapel Hill: University of North Carolina Press, 1993).

56. Edward Ayers, *The Promise of the New South: Life after Reconstruction* (New

York: Oxford University Press, 1992), pp. 156; W. Fitzhugh Brundage, *Lynching in the New South: Georgia and Virginia, 1880–1930* (Urbana: University of Illinois Press, 1993), pp. 7–8; George C. Wright, *Racial Violence in Kentucky, 1865–1940: Lynchings, Mob Rule, and "Legal Lynchings"* (Baton Rouge: Louisiana State University Press, 1990). Wright argues, however, that just as many lynchings occurred in the Reconstruction era as in the 1880s and 1890s. In that era, however, there were very few lynchings in Appalachia.

57. *Louisville Courier-Journal,* 22, 23, 31 October 1885.

58. "The Harlan County Feud," *New York Times,* 28 October 1889.

59. Crawford, *Vendetta,* p. 9.

60. Carvel Collins, "The Literary Tradition of the Southern Mountaineer, 1824–1900" (Ph.D. diss., University of Chicago, 1944), pp. 54–57. Shapiro, in *Appalachia on Our Mind,* also notes that feuding changed fundamental perceptions about Appalachia but not until after 1900 (see p. 102).

61. Shapiro, *Appalachia on Our Mind,* pp. 3–31; Collins, "Literary Tradition," pp. 26–28.

62. Collins, "Literary Tradition," pp. 46–47; [John Esten Cooke], "Moonshiners," *Harper's New Monthly Magazine,* February 1879, pp. 380–90, is a good example of the sympathetic portrayal of moonshiners.

63. John Fox, Jr., "A Cumberland Vendetta," *Century Magazine,* June, August 1894, pp. 163–78, 366–73, 496–505, later reprinted in *A Cumberland Vendetta and Other Stories* (New York: Harper Brothers, 1895).

64. Ibid., pp. 164–65.

65. For a publishing history of these and other Fox works, see Warren I. Titus, *John Fox, Jr.* (New York: Twayne, 1971).

66. Silber, *Romance of Reunion,* pp. 147–49.

67. George E. Vincent, "A Retarded Frontier," *American Journal of Sociology* 4 (1898): 1–20.

68. Ibid., p. 19.

69. Klotter, "Feuds in Appalachia," p. 294.

70. Waller, *Feud.*

71. This kind of analysis is rare among scholars, journalists, and writers who write about feuding. A rare economic analysis is provided by A. L. Lloyd, "Background to Feuding," *History Today* 2 (July 1952): 451–57.

72. Waller, *Feud;* see chap. 8, "On Trial," pp. 207–34.

73. *Louisville Courier-Journal,* 28 September, 17 October 1874. Both these stories stress the racial difficulties in Breathitt, blaming the problems on the Freemans, a "family of four negroes who have been, ever since the war, the terror of this county."

74. Paul Salstrom, *Appalachia's Path to Dependency: Rethinking a Region's Economic History, 1730–1940* (Lexington: University Press of Kentucky, 1994), pp. 9–40; Waller, *Feud,* pp. 94–101. For a discussion of "equalization" elsewhere in the South, see Wayne Durrill, "Producing Poverty: Local Government and Economic Development in a New South County, 1874–1884," *Journal of American History* 71 (March 1985): 764–81.

75. Breathitt County Court Minutes, 18 May 1874, 19 April 1875, 18 January, 2 March 1876, 3 October 1878, Kentucky State Archives, Frankfort, Ky.

76. *Louisville Courier-Journal*, 2, 11 June 1875.

77. Breathitt County Court Minutes, 16 September 1878, p. 510; 2 October 1878, p. 515; 19 November 1878, p. 548. See also Pearce, *Days of Darkness*, pp. 32–40; *Louisville Courier-Journal*, 30 November, 9 December 1878.

78. Ibid., 12 December 1878, p. 576. See *New York Times*, 30 November, 1, 2, 7, 9, 15, 21, 30, 31 December 1878.

79. "Central Kentucky," *Louisville Courier-Journal*, 26 November 1875, and "Buried Breathitt," 25 December 1884. The Kentucky Union Railroad owned 600,000 acres of land.

80. Charles Hayes, *The Hanging of "Bad Tom" Smith and the Events Leading to His Hanging* (Jackson, Ky.: Breathitt County Historical Society, 1969). See also "The Hanging of Bad Tom Smith," *Harper's Weekly* 10 August 1895, p. 748. For the business elite context of the French-Eversole feud, see Mary Beth Pudup, "Land before Coal: Class and Regional Development in Southeast Kentucky" (Ph.D. diss., University of California, Berkeley, 1987), pp. 224–26.

81. David Thelen, *Paths of Resistance: Tradition and Dignity in Industrializing Missouri* (New York: Oxford University Press, 1986), pp. 59–85.

82. Despite David Hackett Fischer's attempt to quantify violence in the backcountry, he does not segregate feuding from other kinds of violence, and he defines the backcountry as a much larger region. See Fischer, *Albion's Seed*, pp. 765–71.

83. Mary Beth Pudup, "Land before Coal: Class and Regional Development in Southeast Kentucky" (Ph.D. diss., University of California, Berkeley, 1987); Salstrom, *Appalachia's Path to Dependency*.

84. This is the argument made by Gordon McKinney in "Industrialization and Violence in Appalachia in the 1890s," in *An Appalachian Symposium: Essays in Honor of Cratis D. Williams*, ed. J. W. Williamson (Boone, N.C.: Appalachian State University Press, 1977), pp. 131–44.

85. Titus, *John Fox, Jr.*, pp. 23–25. See also Darlene Wilson, "Fresh Tracks Encountered: On the Trail of a Silver-Tongue Fox," course paper for English 393, Clinch Valley College, Wise, Va., April 1993.

86. Titus, *John Fox, Jr.*, pp. 57–58; "Our Police," *Big Stone Post*, 12 September 1890.

87. This is an early version of what David Whisnant has described as "the politics of culture." His focus, however, is on the founders of mountain settlement schools in the early twentieth century; he argues that they constructed Appalachian culture in a benign way and with the best of intentions but nevertheless aided eastern capitalists in exploiting mountain people. See Whisnant, *All That Is Native and Fine: The Politics of Culture in an American Region* (Chapel Hill: University of North Carolina Press, 1983). Newspaper editors and writers such as John Fox, Jr., were much less benign in the political uses of their cultural construction in their earlier treatment of Appalachian culture.

88. Ayers, *Promise of the New South*, pp. 364–65.

89. John Fox, Jr., *The Trail of the Lonesome Pine* (New York: Charles Scribner, 1908), p. 412–13.

90. Frank Luther Mott, *Golden Multitudes: The Story of Best Sellers in the United States* (New York: Macmillan, 1903), pp. 214–15.

91. Harold Wilson Coates, *Stories of Kentucky Feuds* (Cincinnati, Ohio: Holmes-Darst Coal Co., 1923), p. v. Republished in 1924 and 1942.

92. Edward Said, *Orientalism* (New York: Pantheon, 1978); Edward Said, *Culture and Imperialism* (New York: Knopf, 1993). For a recent assessment of subaltern history, see "AHR Forum," *American Historical Review* 99 (1994): 1475–1545.

Mary K. Anglin is assistant professor of anthropology at the University of Kentucky. She has been writing about the southern mountains since the late 1970s.

Alan Banks is professor of sociology at Eastern Kentucky University. He teaches courses in Appalachian studies and has written several essays about social change in Appalachia for regional journals and books. Alan lives near the Kentucky River in a house that he built with his wife, Pat.

Dwight B. Billings is professor of sociology at the University of Kentucky. He has written widely on the historical sociology of Appalachia and the American South, including a book entitled *Planters and the Making of the "New South"* (1979). He is currently completing a longitudinal study of the "Beech Creek" communities of Appalachian Kentucky with Kathleen M. Blee.

Kathleen M. Blee is professor of sociology at the University of Kentucky. She is the author of *Women of the Klan* (1991) and is currently completing a book with Dwight Billings about the roots of violence and chronic poverty in Appalachia.

Wilma A. Dunaway is assistant professor of sociology at Colorado State University. She has been an Appalachian activist for nearly twenty years, including a decade of service with the Knoxville Area Urban League, and has served on the boards of several state and regional organizations, including the Council of the Southern Mountains. She is the author of several articles about land tenure, antebellum tenancy, slavery, and Native Americans in southern Appalachia. Her book, *The First American Frontier: Transition to Capitalism in Southern Appalachia, 1700–1860* (1996) is the first regional history for the antebellum period.

John R. Finger is professor of history at the University of Tennessee, Knoxville. He is the author of numerous articles and two books about the Cherokees: *The Eastern Band of Cherokees, 1819–1900* (1984) and *Cherokee Americans: The Eastern Band of Cherokees in the Twentieth Century* (1991). He is currently writing a history of the Tennessee frontier.

John C. Inscoe is associate professor of history at the University of Georgia and editor of the *Georgia Historical Quarterly*. He is the author of *Moun-*

tain Masters: Slavery and the Sectional Crisis in Western North Carolina (1989), coeditor of *Ulrich Bonnell Phillips: A Southern Historian and His Critics* (1990), and editor of *Georgia in Black and White: Explorations in the Race Relations of a Southern State* (1994). He and Gordon McKinney are currently coauthoring a study of the Civil War in western North Carolina.

Ronald L. Lewis is Eberly Professor of History at West Virginia University. He is the author of *Black Coal Miners in America: Race, Class, and Community Conflict, 1780–1980* (1987) and *Coal, Iron, and Slaves: Industrial Slavery in Maryland and Virginia* (1979) and, with Philip Foner, is coeditor of the nine-volume *The Black Worker: A Documentary History from Colonial Times to the Present* (1979–89). He is currently completing a book entitled "Transformation of the Appalachian Countryside: Railroads and Deforestation in West Virginia, 1880–1930."

Gordon B. McKinney is professor of Appalachian Studies and director of the Appalachian Center at Berea College. He is the author of *Southern Mountain Republicans, 1865–1900: Politics and the Appalachian Community* (1978) and coeditor of *The Papers of Zebulon Baird Vance* (1987). He is presently working on a history of the Civil War in western North Carolina with John Inscoe.

Ralph Mann teaches U.S. social history at the University of Colorado, Boulder. He is the author of *After the Gold Rush* (1982) and is currently engaged in research about several Virginia mountain communities under the stress of the Civil War and the coming of the coal industry.

Mary Beth Pudup is assistant professor of community studies at the University of California, Santa Cruz. She has published several articles about the historical geography of Appalachian Kentucky and is currently completing a book entitled "An American History of Appalachia."

Paul Salstrom is the author of *Appalachia's Path to Dependency: Rethinking a Region's Economic History, 1730–1940* (1994). He holds a doctorate in comparative history from Brandeis University and is currently assistant professor of history at Saint Mary-of-the-Woods College in Saint Mary-of-the-Woods, Indiana. In the 1970s he homesteaded in Lincoln County, West Virginia, and managed the Appalachian Movement Press in Huntington, West Virginia.

Altina L. Waller is professor and head of the history department at the University of Connecticut at Storrs. She is the author of *Reverend Beecher* *and Mrs. Tilton: Sex and Class in Victorian America* (1982) and *Feud: Hatfields, McCoys, and Social Change in Appalachia, 1860–1900* (1988).

John Alexander Williams is professor of history and director of the Center for Appalachian Studies at Appalachian State University. He is the author of three books about West Virginia and, with Mark Samuels, of the script for *West Virginia: A Film History*, a three-part documentary (1995).

Appalachian Historiography: Appalachian history as absence, 6; commercial versus subsistence debate, 15–17; second-level Appalachian history, 15–18
Appalachian Journal, 7
Appalachian Land Ownership Task Force, 233
Appalachian Plateau, 77, 86, 211
Appalachian Regional Commission (ARC), 77
Appalachian studies: and class analysis, 8; and culture-of-poverty theory, 5–6; and dependency theory, 6; and ethnography, 3–5; as field, 2–10; and modernization theory, 4–6; and political economy, 14–18
Appalachian Studies Association, 7
Appalachian Volunteers, 6
Ayers, E., 119, 120, 361, 368

Baltimore and Ohio Railroad (B&O), 213, 214, 299, 304
Banks, Allen, 14
Baptist Valley, Virginia, 133; effects of transportation revolution on, 149; farm size and distribution, 142; increased wealth in land, 149; land availability in, 137; rising absentee ownership, 149–50; tenancy in, 142
Barbour, Mary, 119
Barbourville, 287, 288
Barter, 82, 278
Basketry: among Cherokees, 28, 37
Bateman, Fred, and Weiss, Thomas, 273
Batteau, Allen, 4, 110
Beaver, Patricia, 4
Beech Creek, Kentucky, 235–63; absentee ownership in, 260; changing balance of land and population, 256–57; changing landownership patterns, 257–58; comparisons with Midwest and Northeast, 247, 254; decline of agriculture in, 247–63; declining farm productivity, 252–63; declining

size of households, 252; forest clearance, 261; forest farming in, 237, 260–61; impact of Civil War on, 256; income, 235; population growth in, 260; social origins of farming patterns, 235; soil erosion in, 235; tenancy, 255. *See also* Clay County, Kentucky
Berea College, 111–12
Berwanger, Eugene H., 115
Bethlehem Steel, 324
Bickley, George, 146
Billings, Dwight, and Blee, Kathleen, 86, 157, 239, 240, 258
Blalock, Keith, 177
Blauner, Robert, 6
Blethen, Tyler H., 85, 86
Blethen, Tyler H., and Wood, Curtis W., 84, 166
Blue Ridge Country, 77
Bode Frederick A., and Ginter, Donald E., 156, 165, 239
Boomtowns, 287, 289
Boone, Daniel, 57
Bowen, Rees, 135
Boyer, Paul, 11
British Proclamation Line (of 1763), 50, 51
Brown, James, 4, 235, 236, 243, 257, 259
Brown, John, 109
Brown, Joseph E., 118
Brown, Keith, 351
Brown, Uria, 57, 59, 61
Brownlow, William G., 116
Brundage, Fitzhugh, 120
Bryant, Carlene, 4
Bureau of Indian Affairs, 39
Burkes Garden, Virginia, 133; farming in, 143; increase in local landownership, 152; land availability, 144; population diversity, 144; slaveholding in, 144; social stratification, 153; speculation and absentee ownership, 137, 143; tenancy in, 138, 143–45, 153
Bushyhead, George, 39

Cabbel, Edward, 106
Calk, William, 58
Campbell, David, 114
Campbell, John C., 2, 3, 108
Cash, W. J., 107, 108
Caudill, Harry M., 6, 7, 9, 110
Cheoh, 31–32, 34, 36, 39, 41
Cherokee Indians: accommodation to white culture, 25; agricultural practices, 26, 35, 42, 44; and alcohol, 31, 38, 41, 42; ballplay/stickball and dispute resolution, 37; basketry, 28, 37; changing gender roles, 26; citizenship, 32, 35, 39, 41; and "civilization" program, 25–26; Confederate service, 37; corruption, 65; cultural conservatism among, 36; cultural persistence, 25, 34, 44; cultural syncretism, 27, 33; Eastern Band of, 30, 39, 41, 43, 44; education of, 41–42; effects of land speculation on, 63–64; establishment of reservation, 39; expulsion, 63; government recognition, 39; hunting and fishing, 26, 35; impact of the Civil War on, 37–39, 42; intermarriage with blacks and whites, 25, 43; as Jeffersonian yeomen, 32–33; as labor source, 31, 34; land disputes with white settlers, 51; landownership, 32, 63; literacy among, 27, 33; and missionaries, 26, 27, 33; move toward a patrilineal society, 26; and nationhood, 27; as obstacle to state expansion, 28–29; poverty among, 41; relations with federal government, 29–31, 34, 39, 41, 42, 43; removal bill of 1830, 29; removal, 29–30, 51; slavery among, 26, 32; and southern race relations, 35; and syllabary, 27; and timber industry, 43–44; Trail of Tears, 29; Treaty of New Echota, 29; tribal politics, 27–28, 36, 38–39; Union sympathies, 38; wage labor among, 44; written constitution, 27
Cherokee Phoenix, 27

Chesapeake and Ohio Railroad (C&O), 212, 214, 299, 304, 360
Civil War: and development of market economy, 170–72; and dissolution of nuclear family, 169; divisions over Confederate conscription policy, 176; effects on Cherokee Indians, 37–39, 42; and establishment of national banking system, 95; Mountain secessionists, 118; Union sentiments in Appalachia, 110–11, 116–17; and violence, 177–78; and western North Carolina, 163, 167–78
Class: class consciousness, 341; class resentment and antislavery views in Appalachia, 114–15, 123; effects of market economy on, 173; formation of working class in Kentucky coalfields, 321–43; structure and differentiation, 80, 166, 187
Clay County, Kentucky: African American presence in, 239; agricultural productivity, 242; antebellum agriculture in, 239–46; early settlement and development, 236–39; home manufacturing, 243–45; isolation of, 239; local elites, 239; off-farm employment, 242; salt industry in, 237, 238, 246, 253; social stratification, 238; tenancy in, 239–41. *See also* Beech Creek, Kentucky
Coal industry: African American presence in, 107; and cheap labor, 91; class consciousness in, 341; coal towns, 91; company towns in Kentucky, 337–41; and growth of towns in Appalachian Kentucky, 285, 287, 289, 293; mining, 285; mining fatalities, 91; subsistence agriculture as subsidy to coal operators, 91–92; UMWA, 91; wage labor in, 323–24; wages in West Virginia, 90–91
Coates, Harold Wilson, 369
Coffee, John, 65
Commercial enterprise: in Appalachian

Kentucky, 281; growth of entrepôts, 287, 289; relation to unspecialized family farming, 281

Community studies, as field: and Appalachia, 12–14; and New England, 11–14

Company towns: dependency of miners on, 340–41; functions of, 338–41; in Kentucky coalfields, 337–41; labor control, 339–40; and labor militancy, 341; manipulation of contracts, 339–40; repression in, 338–39; yellow-dog contracts, 339

Confederacy, 169; and Cherokees, 37; divisions over conscription policy, 176; postbellum purge in West Virginia, 222

Connelley, William E., and Coulter, E. M., 4

Consolidated Coal Company, 324

Conti, Eugene, 17

Corbin, David Alan, 91, 92

County courts, 220, 286; as central unit of local government, 275–76

County seat towns: and divisions of labor, 271; effects of coal industry on, 285, 287, 289, 293; growth of business districts in, 293; importance of in Appalachian Kentucky, 271; and social differentiation, 271; social and spatial differentiation, 290–91; typology of, 286

Cove, Virginia, 132, 135; changing labor system, 149, 156; changing social structure, 147, 149; as elite community, 142; family strategies in, 136; increased speculation, 147; increase in improved land, 147; landownership patterns, 136; slaveholding in, 142, 149; tenancy, 149

Coxe, Tench, 81

Crawford, Martin, 157, 167, 176, 187

Crawford, T. C., 351, 362

Credit, 94

Cunningham, Rodger, 116

Danhof, Clarence H., 164, 165

Davidson and Moore, 55, 38

Davis, Darrel Haug, 220, 286

Deaderick, David, 109

Debt, 93–94

Deforestation, 261, 312, 313, 314; effects on agriculture, 309–10; environmental degradation, 313–15; extent of in West Virginia, 309

Degler, Carl N., 115

Deyton, John Basil, 187

Douglas, Frederick, 109

Dowd, Gregory, 30

Dublin, Thomas, 197

Ducktown Basin (East Tennessee), 38

Dunaway, Wilma, 14, 17

Dunn, Durwood, 12, 88, 166, 194

Earle, Carville, and Hoffman, Ronald, 273

Eaton, John, 108, 121

Education: of Cherokee, 26–27, 33, 36, 41–42; interracial, and Berea College, 111–12

Elites: development of, 166–67; emergence in Appalachian Kentucky, 292; flexibility of, 222; local elites and family persistence, 156; occupational structure and, 290; political and economic advantages of, 218; social origins of, 17, 22; and West Virginia politics, 210, 217–23

Eller, Ronald D., 9, 83, 156, 233, 298, 299

Emancipation: acceptance in East Tennessee, 121

Entrepôts, 286–89, 292

Environmental degradation, 235, 313–15. *See also* Deforestation

Family and kinship: dissolution of nuclear family during Civil War, 169; nuclear family as basic unit of production and consumption, 169; and preindustrial political system in West Virginia, 211; and social structure, 173–74, 177

Inscoe, John, 14, 84, 167, 188, 192, 195, 234

Intermediate Appalachia, 84–86

Internal colonialism thesis, 6–8, 233

International Harvester, 324

International Workers of the World (IWW), 339

Iron industry, 81–2, 234

Jackson, Andrew, 29

Jackson, Thomas Jonathan "Stonewall," 219

Jefferson, Thomas, 59, 216

Johnson, Andrew, 38, 117

Johnson, Lyndon B., 5

Jones, Alexander, 116

Jones, Loyal, 108

Kennedy, John F., 5, 10

Kentucky: absentee ownership in, 329–331, 334; capitalist industrialization of, 285; coal industry in, 285, 287, 289, 293; company towns in, 324, 337–41; concentration of land, 330, 332; county system of governance in, 275–77; decline of independent production, 332; decline of unspecialized domestic economy in, 285; development of labor market, 332; elites, 334; emergence of resident elite in, 292; European immigration to, 326–28; immigration policies of, 325, 327; increase in working class, 337; industrial recruitment strategies, 326; labor policies of, 324–28; lack of economic specialization in Appalachian Kentucky, 278; land policies of, 61, 324; land speculation in, 330; myth of Two Kentuckies, 237; occupational differentiation and growth, 290–91; patterns of investment and business organization in coal industry, 335; population growth in coalfields, 324; railroad control in, 334; rejection of black labor, 342; and rural neighborhoods,

284; settlement patterns in Appalachian Kentucky, 270–93; slaveholding in, 325; tax policies of, 329; violence in, 353–55

Kentucky Agricultural Society, 245

Kephart, Horace, 3, 233

Kinship. See Family and kinship

Klotter, James C., 106, 177, 351, 363

Kousser, J. Morgan, 121

Ku Klux Klan (KKK), 119, 353

Kulikoff, Allan, 13, 14

Labor: control of, 340, 342; development of labor market in Kentucky coalfields, 322; policies in Kentucky, 324, 325, 327, 328, 342; scarcity, 338; as source of wealth, 328; women's labor, 189–90, 192–94, 197–98. See also Agriculture; Coal industry; Timber industry; Wage labor

Land alienation system, 216, 220

Land and landownership: categorization of deeds, 55–56; disputes, 51; expropriation in the Valley of Virginia, 52; illegal acquisitions, 51; inequitable distribution, 62–63, 64, 67–68; monopolization of, 53–53, 62, 332; myth of free land, 62; policies regarding Cherokee landownership, 63; policies in West Virginia, 215–17, 220, 222; redistribution, 64; role of land jobbers, 57, 60; sales in Southern Appalachia, 52–53; and squatters, 62, 64–66; taxation of, 308; techniques of appropriation (of southern mountains), 54–55. See also Absentee ownership; Landlessness; Property; Speculation

Landlessness, 63, 66–68

Lanman, Charles, 33, 37, 120

Lemon, James T., 81, 93, 164

Lewis, Helen, 6

Lincoln, Abraham, 110, 117

Lockridge, Kenneth, 11, 164, 262, 263

Logan, George W., 175

Prestonburg, 287, 288
Property: changing conceptions of, 305; fencing cases, 306; and transformation of nuisance law, 305
Prosser, Gabriel, 121
Proto-urban centers, 283, 284
Public lands: and class struggle, 65; expropriation of squatters from, 65; speculation on, 64–66
Pudup, Mary Beth, 16, 18, 156, 166, 190, 214, 218, 235, 282, 285, 286, 292, 367

Quakers, and Indian education, 42
Qualla Boundary, 39, 42, 43
Quallatown, 30, 33, 34, 35, 36, 39

Race and race relations in Appalachia, 103–23; class resentment and anti-slavery views, 114–15; compared to other U.S. regions, 115, 119, 123; complexity of racial attitudes among whites, 122–23; contradictory views, 113; disfranchisement, 121–22; emancipation, 121; leniency of racial views among mountain legislators, 121; lynchings as a consequence of economic transformation, 120; myth of ethnic homogeneity (whiteness), 105, 106; myth of racial liberty, 109, 112; racial violence in postbellum mountain South, 119–20; representations in fiction, 104–5; similarity of views with other southerners, 113–14, 123; Union sympathies and support for slavery, 116–17. *See also* African Americans; Slavery; Violence
Railroads: as civilizers, 360; and commercialization, 135, 155; development in West Virginia, 212–15; effect on agricultural economy, 90, 146–57; effect on community, 146–57; effect on labor system, 156; exploitation of forests, 302, 309; fire hazard of, 314; independent, 299; industrialization, 315–16; and legal development, 305–7; modern commercial stock

farming and, 310; as modernizing agent, 298–99, 301; opposition to, 303–4, 307–8; promotion of land market, 155; and social stratification, 155; and timber industry in West Virginia, 297–16; and town development, 301
Raine, James Watt, 3
Redfield, Robert, 3
Religion, affiliations, 33
Republican Party: defeat in West Virginia, 228; in Southern Appalachia, 121
Reservation schools: establishment of, 42
Ross, John, 27, 29
Rothenberg, Winifred B., 13, 164, 173
Ruffner, Henry, 111
Rutman, Darrett, 167

Said, Edward, 370
Salstrom, Paul, 13, 14, 166, 367
Salt industry, 81, 237, 238, 246, 253, 323
Sand Mountain country, 83
Scott, Shaunna, 4
Scott, Winfield, 29, 31
Scrip, 340
Secession, 116–17
Semple, Ellen Churchill, 1, 105, 112
Senedos, 50, 67
Sequoya, 27
Settlement patterns, 26, 31, 46, 61 92–93, 138–39, 212; in Appalachian Kentucky, 270–93; Appalachian settlement ideals, 270; and commercial enterprise, 281; dormancy of urban development in Appalachia and South, 274, 283; effects of coal industry on, 285, 287, 289, 293; effects of county governance on, 275–77; effects of mountain farming system on, 277–85; effects of mountain geography on, 277; free family farming system and, in New England and Middle Atlantic states, 273–74; importance of county seat towns,

271; plantation agriculture and, in South, 272–73; rural neighborhood establishment in Appalachian Kentucky, 283–85; typology of county seat towns, 286; in West Virginia, 214

Shaler, Nathaniel S., 105
Shanks, Henry, 117
Shapiro, Henry D., 2, 9, 38, 285, 349, 351
Sharkey, Robert P., 95
Sharp, Cecil, 3
Shawnees, 50, 67, 135
Shenandoah Valley, 79, 83
Shepherd, Muriel Earley, 3, 108
Silber, Nina, 106
Silvers, Alfred, 185–86
Silvers, Charles, 185–86, 189
Silvers, Francis Steward, 185–89, 198
Simon, Richard, 8
Slavery in Appalachia, 106–7, 117–19, 122, 139, 166–68, 246, 253; agricultural production and, 89, 90, 195, 140, 116, 149; attitudes toward, 114, 115; and class resentment and antislavery views, 113–15, 123; and domestic service, 195; gender of slaves, 194; and household manufactures, 195; and labor, 109, 116, 168, 253; living conditions of slaves, 119; owners, 168, 238, 239, 240, 246; schedule on, 190, 194, 198; slave markets, 118; as source of wealth, 328; and testimony of former slaves, 119; Union sympathies and support for, 116–17; value of in manufacturing and mercantilism, 195, 237
Smith, Lillian, 114
Social relations, 145
Social structure, 142–45, 147
Sophie, Aunt, 119
South: compared to North, 273; urban growth and plantation agriculture in, 272–73
Southern Mountain Research Collective, 8
Speculation: and absentee planters, 52–55, 60, 66–67; on Cherokee land,

63–64; and delay of resettlement, 61–62; land, 52–67, 80–82, 133, 216–21, 285, 287, 290; and land jobbers, 57; and landlessness, 63, 66–68; and land monopolization, 53–54, 62, 65–67; and local elites, 57–61, 66–67; and merchant capitalists, 56–60; mineral, 53–54, 66, 285, 286, 290; and polarization of Appalachian society, 65–68; and public corruption, 59, 65; on public lands in northern Alabama, 64–66; and tenants, 60; and timber, 285, 290; and wage laborers, 60. *See also* Absentee ownership; Land and landownership
Squatting, 156
Stephenson, John, 4
Styron, William, 108
Subaltern studies, 370
Summers, George W., 223
Swimmer, 44

Tazewell County, Virginia: distinct agricultural communities in, 132–57; family networks in, 145; influx of wealthy farmers, 146; rising absentee ownership in, 147; Tecumseh, 30; transport revolution in, 146
Temple, Oliver P. 116
Tenancy, 138, 139, 142–43, 156, 168, 239, 241, 255, 286
Tennessee: early land policies in, 64
Thelen, David, 366
Third North Carolina Mounted Infantry Volunteers, 38
Thomas, William H. 32, 34, 35, 37, 38, 39, 171
Timber industry: boom, 261; and Cherokees, 43–44; conflict with forest farming, 260–61; and deforestation, 309–10, 313, 315; development of, 87, 297, 302; effects on agriculture, 298, 309–13; effects on migration, 302–3; farmer opposition to, 303–4, 307–8; and railroads, 297–16; and transition to market economy,

297–316; relations with Tidewater oligarchy, 210, 219, 222; Republican defeat in, 228; role of lawyers in politics of, 217–18; settlement patterns in, 214; timber industry in, 297–316; transition to wage labor in, 315; United Mine Workers in, 91; Unionism in, 224, 227

West Virginia Pulp and Paper Company (WESTVACO), 312

Whisnant, David, 15, 103

Who Owns Appalachia, 8

Wilkinson, Richard, 91

Williams, Cratis, 156

Williams, John Alexander, 18, 298, 301

Williams, Leon F., 109

Wilson, Samuel Tyndale, 3, 106

Wilson, Stephen, 351

Wise, Henry A., 223

Wolfe, Thomas, 106

Women: as conservators of tribal tradition, 37; as farm operators, 192–94; as free traders, 190; household production among, 194–97; and labor, 190–91, 197, 198; laws in North Carolina regarding, 189–90; as portrayed in census, 189–90; and property ownership, 189; silence surrounding women's role in Appalachia, 186–87; slaves, 194–95. *See also* Gender

Wood, Curtis, 85, 86

Woodfin, Nicholas W., 172

Woods, Samuel, 225

Woodson, Carter, 112

Work contracts, 339

Wright, Gavin, 165, 273,

Wright, George C., 120

Yans-McLaughlin, Virginia, 188, 190

Yellow-dog contracts, 339

Yonaguska (Drowning Bear), 30, 32, 33

Zuckerman, Michael, 11

CPSIA information can be obtained
at www.ICGtesting.com
Printed in the USA
LVHW032035221221
706957LV00001B/72